# INSIGHT GUIDES

# Sardinia

## APA PUBLICATIONS
### Part of the Langenscheidt Publishing Group

## INSIGHT GUIDE
# Sardinia

### Editorial

**Editor**
**Clare Griffiths**
**Editorial Director**
**Brian Bell**

### Distribution

*UK & Ireland*
**GeoCenter International Ltd**
The Viables Centre, Harrow Way
Basingstoke, Hants RG22 4BJ
Fax: (44) 1256 817988

*United States*
**Langenscheidt Publishers, Inc.**
36–36 33rd Street 4th Floor
Long Island City, NY 11106
Fax: 1 (718) 784 0640

*Australia*
**Universal Publishers**
1 Waterloo Road
Macquarie Park, NSW 2113
Fax: (61) 2 9888 9074

*New Zealand*
**Hema Maps New Zealand Ltd (HNZ)**
Unit D, 24 Ra ORA Drive
East Tamaki, Auckland
Fax: (64) 9 273 6479

*Worldwide*
**Apa Publications GmbH & Co.**
**Verlag KG (Singapore branch)**
38 Joo Koon Road, Singapore 628990
Tel: (65) 6865 1600. Fax: (65) 6861 6438

### Printing

**Insight Print Services (Pte) Ltd**
38 Joo Koon Road, Singapore 628990
Tel: (65) 6865 1600. Fax: (65) 6861 6438

©2006  Apa Publications GmbH & Co.
Verlag KG (Singapore branch)
*All Rights Reserved*
*First Edition 1991*
*Third Edition 2001*
*Updated 2006*

**CONTACTING THE EDITORS**
We would appreciate it if readers
would alert us to errors or out-
dated information by writing to:
**Insight Guides, P.O. Box 7910,
London SE1 1WE, England.**
**Fax: (44) 20 7403-0290.**
**insight@apaguide.co.uk**

**www.insightguides.com**
*In North America:*
**www.insighttravelguides.com**

# ABOUT THIS BOOK

**T**he first Insight Guide pioneered
the use of creative full-colour photography in travel guides in 1970.
Since then, we have expanded our
range to cater for our readers' need
not only for reliable information about
where to go and what to do in their
chosen destination but also for a real
understanding of the culture and
workings of that destination.

Now, when the internet can
supply inexhaustible (but not
always reliable) facts, our
books marry text and pictures
to provide those much
more elusive qualities:
knowledge and dis-
cernment. To achieve
this, they rely heavily
on the authority and
experience of locally
based writers and
photographers.

### How to use this book

This fully updated edition of *Insight
Guide: Sardinia* is carefully struc-
tured to convey an understanding of
the island and its culture as well as
to guide readers through its sights
and activities:

◆ The **Features** section, indicated
by a yellow bar at the top of each
page, covers the history and culture
of the island in a series of informative essays.

◆ The main **Places** section, indicated by a blue
bar, is a complete
guide to all the sights
and areas worth visit-
ing. Places of special
interest are coor-
dinated by number
with the maps.

◆ The **Travel Tips**
listings, with an

orange bar, provide a point of reference for information on travel, hotels, shops, restaurants, and more. The section is conveniently indexed on the back flap.

## The contributors

This edition of *Insight Guide: Sardinia* was commissioned and edited by **Clare Griffiths** from Insight's London office.

**Alison Ellis**, who lives in Cagliari, updated the Places section of this edition of the book. Ellis was born in Italy to British parents and moved to Sardinia in 1990. She works as a local tour guide and specialises in the ancient history, archaeology and ecology of the island.

The Features section of the book was updated by **Ernestina Meloni**, who was born in Cagliari and moved to London in 1985. She has an MA in Applied Linguistics and teaches Italian in Oxford. Meloni wrote new essays on *Geography and Wildlife* and *Art and Craft*.

The History section of the book was updated by **Jonathan Keates**, an Italian specialist living in London while the *Insight On...* picture stories on wildlife, costume and jewellery and murals were written by Clare Griffiths.

This edition of the book builds on the work of **Joachim Chwaszcza**, the project editor of the original edition. **Dr Rainer Pauli** contributed the original chapters on the island's history and language, and stories on the shepherd's knife and the cork oak. **Wofftraud de Concini** contributed to the history section of the book, and wrote the original chapters on Sassari and the area from Alghero to Oristano. Among the Sardinian contributors was **Mario Massaiu** who wrote the story on banditry and Grazia Deledda and the chapters on Cagliari, Cagliari to Olbia, and the Barbagia. His wife **Clotilde Merlin-Massaiu,** wrote the story on caves and cavers. **Antonio Bassu** wrote the chapter on food and drink while **Cora Fischer** wrote about the Costa Smeralda. The original chapter about Sardinian folklore was written by **Leandro Muoni**.

The top-rate photographs were provided by **Franco Stephano Ruiu**, **Jörg Reuther**, **Nevio Doz**, **Joachim Chwaszcza**, **Paul Pauli**, **Jerry Dennis** and **Gregory Wrona**. Picture research was by **Monica Allende**.

Thanks are also due to **Alessandra Smith** of the Italian Tourist Board in London and to **Meridiana** airlines. The book was expertly proofread by **Helen Partington** and indexed by **Elizabeth Cook**.

## Map Legend

| | |
|---|---|
| — ·· — | International Boundary |
| — — — | Province Boundary |
| —·—·— | National Park/Reserve |
| — — — | Ferry Route |
| ✈ ✦ | Airport: International/Regional |
| 🚌 | Bus Station |
| ❶ | Tourist Information |
| ✉ | Post Office |
| ⛪ † ⊤ | Church/Ruins |
| † | Monastery |
| ☾ | Mosque |
| ✡ | Synagogue |
| 🏰 ⛫ | Castle/Ruins |
| ∴ | Archaeological Site |
| ∩ | Cave |
| ⓘ | Statue/Monument |
| ★ | Place of Interest |

The main places of interest in the Places section are coordinated by number with a full-colour map (e.g. ❶), and a symbol at the top of every right-hand page tells you where to find the map.

# Insight Guide
# Sardinia

# CONTENTS

## Maps

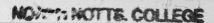

Leaping the rocks on the shoreline

## Travel Tips

## Insight on ...

## Information panels

## Places

# THE ISLAND BELONGING TO NOWHERE

*Sardinia sits equidistant from Italy and the coast of Tunisia and is the second-largest island in the Mediterranean*

Sardinia's geographic position prompted D. H. Lawrence to write that the island was "lost between Europe and Africa and belonging to nowhere". Its isolation has worked both for and against the island, producing the unique character of its people and flora and fauna but also attracting a succession of foreign rulers eager to exploit its strategic position and fertile land.

Phoenicians and Romans, Arabs and Spaniards, Savoyards and Italians have all left their mark on the cultural, artistic and architectural life of the island. Historically mingling these influences with their own has produced a rich and varied Sardinian identity, but it has also led to islanders maintaining a detached and somewhat cynical attitude towards foreigners. Indeed, this has given rise to the island's most famous maxims: "*Furat chi de su mare venit*" (Whoever comes by sea comes to rob us). Although Sardinia has been part of Italy since 1861, even today many islanders wish it were not.

D. H. Lawrence produced *Sea and Sardinia* during a brief visit in 1921. "Sardinia is not up-and-down at all, but running away into the distance…", he wrote, "this gives a sense of space, which is so lacking in Italy… It is like liberty itself, after the peaky confinement of Sicily". Modern travellers who are familiar with Italy will also find striking differences between the island and the mainland, but they will also discover many similarities. Little has changed since Lawrence's visit – at least, as regards the island's fundamental character. Sardinia's individual regions are completely different from one another, and villages which may lie only a few kilometres from each other will often seem worlds apart, so much so that the island can appear to be a miniature continent.

Sardinia's beautiful beaches have attracted many visitors but the most popular sun spots along the coast are now over-developed. The expansion of the tourism industry has seen the growth of watersports facilities, and dive centres have been set up to explore the island's thriving marine life. Sardinia's rocky coastline also provides an ideal habitat for gulls, while birds of prey can be found swooping over the mountains of the interior and flamingos rest during their winter migration in the coastal marshes and lagoons. The Barbagia region in the interior offers opportunities for walking, hiking, rock climbing and speleology. Horse trekking has also become very popular in recent years with the development of *agriturismo* (farm holidays) in the provinces of Oristano and Sassari. ❑

**PRECEDING PAGES:** lobster fisherman in Porto Vecchio; windsurfers assess the surf; shepherd of the Gennargentu massif; shepherd and kid.
**LEFT:** the pace of life is gentle in Sardinia.

STAGNO DI CAGLIARI.

Saline

L'Annunziata

Fortini

Ciarella

Saline di

Ponte della Scassa

Vascello incagliato, e brucciato da Francesi

Cialuppa parlamenti

GOLFO DI CA

STAGNO

S. Lorenzo
...uccini

La Polveriera

da P. di B...

dei P. del Carmine

S. Lucifero

Monticello

Monte Orpino

S. Bardilio

V. di Buonaria

Eredi di Filippo Pinna

Stagno

Stagno

Cavalleria

Gppe Umana

L I A R I

Saline

Gppe Passio

Quartiere fanteria

V. di Luc...

Fortini

Fanteria

Fortini

Avanguardia Guastat...

C.

Paolico Pinna

Lazzaretto e Porto

di S. Ignazio

di S. Steffano

Pietra Aliada

di Calamoscas, o dei Segnali

fanteria

Torre di C.

C A

A N C E S I

# Decisive Dates

## BEGINNINGS TO 1100 BC

**350,000 BP** First traces of human presence (flint tools) dating back to Early Paleolithic age are found.
**13,000 BC** First human bones dating back to end of Late Paleolithic age are discovered.
**6000 BC** Sardinia's inhabitants trade in obsidian with Corsica and the South of France.
**4000–2700 BC** Archeological finds at Bonu Ighinu and Ozieri date the island's earliest cultures from this period.
**1800–500 BC** Period of the Nuraghe, squat, cone-

shaped stone buildings used as forts and citadels and for communal purposes during peacetime.

## PHOENICIANS, CARTHAGINIANS, ROMANS

**1000 BC** The earliest Phoenician traders arrive in Sardinia from today's Lebanon.
**9th–8th centuries BC** Phoenician colonies established around major ports, including Cagliari, Oristano and Sant'Antioco.
**500 BC** Carthage controls the Sardinian economy.
**264–238 BC** The First Punic War between Rome and Carthage. Rome annexes Sardinia but unrest continues in the island.
**218–201 BC** Second Punic War. General Caecilius Metellus is rewarded for his Sardinian victories.

**1st century BC–5th century AD** Period of Roman rule in Sardinia.

## THE ARABS

**5th–8th centuries AD** The Roman empire collapses as barbarian tribes invade Western Europe. In the late 7th century, Arab invaders seize control of North Africa and begin raids on coastal cities across the Mediterranean.
**711 AD** Earliest Arab raids on Sardinia.
**815–827** Sardinians beg for help from Emperor Louis the Pious against Arab raiders. Arab conquest of Sicily cuts off Sardinia's links with Christian powers such as Byzantium and drastically affects the island's economy.

## PISANS VERSUS GENOESE

**1015–16** Victory by combined Genoese and Pisan navies over an Arab fleet from Mallorca. Rivalry between Genoa and Pisa for control of Sardinia. Island is divided into four *giudicati*.
**1130** Fiercely opposed by the other *giudicati*, Comita d'Arborea, *giudice* of Oristano, tries to seize control of the island with Genoese backing.
**1146** War between the *giudicati* ends with a peace treaty arranged by Archbishop Villario of Pisa.
**1164** Supported by Emperor Frederick Barbarossa, Barisone d'Arborea is crowned King of Sardinia in the north Italian city of Pavia.
**Late 12th century** The monastic orders begin a religious revival and improve Sardinia's agriculture.
**1190–1200** A prolonged struggle with the Genoese leaves Pisa in firm control of Sardinia.
**13th century** The island's great families wrestle for power with the Pisans.
**1284** After defeating Pisa at the battle of Meloria, Genoa becomes the dominant power in the northwestern Mediterranean.
**1297** Pope Boniface VIII names James II of Aragon as regent of Sardinia, in an effort to end the Pisan-Genoese rivalry within the island.
**1323** Defeated at Santa Gilla, Pisa renounces its claims to Sardinia, which becomes part of the Kingdom of Aragon.

## THE CENTURIES OF SPANISH RULE

**14th century** Sardinia is subdivided into 376 fiefs, many awarded to Spanish noblemen, under an Aragonese viceroy. Power-struggles between the old *giudice* families; the island economy declines.
**1383** Eleonora Doria, daughter of the *giudice* Mariano, becomes Regent of the island.
**1392** Eleonora publishes the *Carta de Logu*, a con-

stitution of common law written in the Sardinian language.

**1417** With the death of William of Narbonne, *giudice* of Arborea, the *giudicato* system ends, and Sardinia is directly ruled by Aragon.

**15th century** Plague and famine reduce Sardinia's population from 340,000 to 150,000. Aragon attempts resettlement with Catalan immigrants, especially in the port of Alghero. Jewish settlers arrive as traders and doctors.

**1469** King Ferdinand of Aragon marries Isabella, Queen of Castille. The union of the crowns creates the Kingdom of Spain.

**16th century** The Spaniards partially increase the island's defenses against pirate raids. Meanwhile the islanders are steadily stripped of their basic rights.

**1610–12** The bandit Manuzio Flore rouses the poor against oppressive taxes and corrupt officials.

**1708** During the War of the Spanish Succession English and Austrian forces seize Sardinia from King Philip V of Spain.

**1714** Sardinia awarded to Austria by the Treaty of Rastadt.

**1718** Briefly reassigned to Spain, Sardinia is then given to the Dukes of Savoy by the terms of the Treaty of London.

## SARDINIA UNDER THE HOUSE OF SAVOY

**1720** The Duke of Savoy is officially acknowledged a monarch, as King of Piedmont and Sardinia.

**1735–38** The Viceroy De Rivarolo ferociously tries – but fails – to eradicate banditry.

**1793** French troops attempt to invade Sardinia but fail. In 1797, the army of the French Republic invades Italy.

**1799** Driven from his capital Turin by the French, King Charles Emmanuel III of Piedmont seeks refuge in Sardinia.

**1806** The "Olive Tree Enactment" allows peasants who plant olive trees to enclose their land.

**1820** The Enclosures Act, defining agricultural and pasture land, creates tensions between shepherds, peasants and wealthy landowners .

**1839** Abolition of the Sardinian feudal system and preparation of the island's first land register.

**1847** Growing economic problems encourage requests for complete incorporation with Piedmont, proclaimed on 30 November.

LEFT: the extravagant viceroy, Carlo Emanuele III (1730–73). RIGHT: Giuseppe Garibaldi (1807–82), a tireless fighter for Italian freedom.

## SARDINIA IN THE KINGDOM OF ITALY

**1861** Victor Emmanuel II of Piedmont proclaims himself King of Italy. Sardinia ceases to be a kingdom in its own right.

**1870–1900** Banditry increases as nomadic sheep-farming revives. Growth of mining industry sees a wave of miners' strikes reaching a tragic climax at Buggerru in 1904.

**1915** Italy enters World War I. 13,000 Sardinians die on the battlefield.

**1921** Sardinian Action Party formed to politicise young people and peasants.

**1924** So-called "Law of the Milliard", promulgated by the Fascists, aims to reduce Sardinian unrest.

**1925** Inspectorate of Public Works begins rural regeneration programme.

**1926** Grazia Deledda (1871–1936) wins the Nobel Prize for Literature.

**1940** Italy enters World War II.

**1946** Italy becomes a republic.

**1948** Sardinia established as autonomous region.

**1962** Heavy industry and business sectors are stimulated. The Aga Khan creates the Costa Smeralda syndicate and the tourism industry opens up.

**1985** Francesco Cossiga from Sassari is elected President of the Italian Republic.

**1995** Mining industry in crisis.

**2001** An ancient fleet of Roman cargo ships is unearthed in the Bay of Olbia. ❏

# BEGINNINGS

*Beautiful artefacts suggest that the mysterious origins of civilisation
on Sardinia could predate even the wonders of ancient Greece*

The single most important factor that has determined Sardinia's fate down the centuries is its status as an island. Whatever the nature of earth-shattering events that have occurred in mainland Italy or further abroad, the natural boundary afforded by the sea has provided insulation, and a considerable degree of cultural autonomy. Conversely, fundamental social and cultural changes have come about in Sardinia primarily as the result of outside influences. Thus the *istranzu* (the Sardinian word for "stranger", from the Latin *estraneus*), as harbinger of news and developments *kie venit dae su mare* ("from across the sea") has always played a pivotal role in island life.

## The first Sardinians

There seems little doubt that the island's first inhabitants themselves came from across the sea. But who they were and when the island was first settled is less certain. Until recently the accepted authoritative opinion was that the first colonists arrived here at the beginning of the Neolithic era, that is, approximately 6,000 years ago. However, the recent discovery of stone tools near Perfugas in the north of the island, and corroborative geological evidence, suggests that the first human inhabitants arrived during the warm inter-glacial period between the Riss and the Würm Ice Ages some 120,000 to 200,000 years ago.

Latest finds place the advent of a Sardinian people still further back, in the Palaeolithic era. But archaeological finds that hint at signs of life from the early Clactonian period (some 700,000 years ago) have yet to be confirmed. Either way, fairly precise dating has attributed human and animal bones found in the Grotta Corbeddu – a cave near Oliena – to the late Palaeolithic era (13,000 years ago).

It seems likely that the first Sardinians came from the European mainland. During glacial periods large quantities of water were frozen

as ice sheets, thereby lowering the sea level by more than 100 metres (330 ft). Thus Sardinia and Corsica formed one large island, separated from the coast of Tuscany – which then jutted much further into the sea than it does now – only by a relatively narrow strip of water. This channel proved to be quite traversible by man

and deer (and indeed any animal that was a strong swimmer) alike.

The evidence seems to indicate that, after this, Sardinia remained cut off from the continent for many thousands of years. It was not until the beginning of the Neolithic era that a completely different race of men appeared on the island.

They had already learned to make clay pots, for example, and had clearly reached a more advanced stage of civilisation than their predecessors. It could well be that the original Sardinians suffered the same fate as the Indians of North America and the Amazon basin. For the new arrivals, Sardinia must have been like

---

**LEFT:** the main tower of the Nuraghe Losa.
**RIGHT:** well-temple of Predio Canopoli.

the proverbial happy land: here they found everything they needed for a peaceful existence: dense forests filled with game, broad lagoons with an inexhaustible supply of fish and shellfish, fertile plains and rolling hills for arable farming, excellent conditions for cattle raising, and – above all – obsidian, their "black gold". Lumps of this black volcanic glass as big as a fist or even a head can be found in large quantities on Monte Arci, an extinct volcano east of Oristano. Razor-sharp splinters of obsidian were ideal for the manufacture of tools and weapons of all kinds, to the extent that the substance became the most prized raw material of

life corresponded to a fairly uniform conception. The customs and conventions of that time have been further developed and refined over the centuries. Archaeologists have named the two principle periods of this development after the sites at which signs of life from those times were first discovered: the Bonu Ighinu culture (circa 4000–3500 BC) and the Ozieri culture (3500–2700 BC).

## Artistic artefacts

Some of the artefacts from these cultures are genuine works of art. The discoveries include relatively sophisticated pottery of remarkable

the New Stone Age, and was often traded across distances of more than 1,000 kilometres (600 miles). As long ago as 6000 BC, the obsidian trade routes, radiating out from Monte Arci, passed through Corsica on their way to destinations such as the south of France. These commercial contacts must have played a significant role in establishing the high level of civilisation attained in Sardinia during the Neolithic era.

By the 4th millennium BC, the island's farmers, shepherds and fishermen had achieved a considerable degree of cultural independence, with a pronounced degree of originality. Tools, pottery, burial gifts, funeral rites and way of

quality, frequently artistically decorated with pictorial and geometric forms, engraved or scratched before firing and sometimes filled out in colour. Limestone was used for the creation of perfectly formed stone vessels and female cult statues. Of these idols, the older ones tend to be round and naturalistic, the younger ones slim, heavily stylised and bearing a strong resemblance to religious icons from the eastern Mediterranean (particularly from Cyclades and Anatolia). Their true significance is unclear; whether or not they were symbols of a mother goddess, as is the usual assumption, they were obviously of religious importance. Like the ceramic *objets d'art* – which are elaborately adorned with magic symbols – the idols were mostly found in graves, but also at places of worship: Monte d'Accoddi, not far from Sassari, is a tiered mound whose similarity to the ziggurats of Mesapotamia is as striking as it is inexplicable.

The most noteworthy relics left by the evidently deeply religious ancient inhabitants are the burial chambers. Well over 1,000 of them, hewn from solid rock with primitive stone chisels, have been found. The simplest of the tombs, dating to the Bonu Ighinu

the wooden houses of the period, with ridge pole, roof spars, supporting columns, fireplace, sleeping area, doors and windows.

## LIFE AFTER DEATH

In 4000 BC it was believed that life continued after death on a different plane. The dead were brought to their resting place, together with household items and food.

## Tomb fairies

The Sardinians called the tombs *domus de janas*. According to local superstition, the powerful but not always benevolent *janas* (fairies) are tiny female creatures who live in these houses *(domus)*. The walls of the tombs were very often adorned with bas-reliefs of magic symbols such as more or less stylised bulls'

period around the 4th millennium BC, consist of a hidden vertical entrance shaft and a small chamber usually large enough for only one body. These were known as *forredus* ("ovens") because of their spherical shape. In later years several such chambers were linked together to form underground burial apartments with a common antechamber – often high enough to allow a man to stand – and an entry corridor. Some of the burial vaults consist of more than 20 chambers; many imitated, on a smaller scale,

**LEFT:** horn reliefs in a burial niche on Montessu.
**ABOVE:** the interior of a *domus de janas* (fairy house) on Montessu.

heads, and motifs featuring horns, spirals and a range of geometric patterns. The remains of murals (mostly reddish ochre in colour) can also be seen. Particularly impressive are the necropolises of Sant'Andrea Priu near Bonorva, and Montessu near Santadi, where several dozen linked tombs form a town of the dead.

With the end of the Neolithic era and the start of the Bronze Age there began a transitional period of approximately 1,000 years, often known as the Copper Stone Age. It was a time of violent change, about which archaeology has uncovered very little. The ramparts which were built around previously peaceful villages were typical of this restless epoch, as was the relatively rapid pace at which the various cultural periods succeeded each other: These eras can be defined as: the Abealzu-Filigosa (*circa* 2700 –2500 BC); the Monte Claro (*circa* 2500–2000 BC); and the Bell-beaker (*circa* 2000–1800 BC).

New influences and arrivals brought the whole inventory of Western megalithic culture to the island: dolmens, standing graves, obelisks, stone circles, rows of menhirs and even well-developed menhir statues hitherto only found in some regions of northern Italy and southern

> **NUMEROUS NURAGHE**
>
> On the high plateau surrounding Macomer and Abbasanta, in the hills of the Trexenta and Marmilla, or on the Sinis peninsula near Oristano *nuraghe* towers can be found a few hundred metres apart.

France. This cultural heritage gave birth to Sardinia's great Bronze Age civilisation, the earliest phase of which was known as the Bonnanaro Culture (*circa* 1800–1600 BC).

## The Nuragic civilisation

The Nuragic civilisation lasted from around 1800 BC to 500 BC. Sometime during the first half of the 2nd millennium BC the first *nuraghe* appeared, dotted across the Sardinian countryside like upturned giant buckets. These circular towers were constructed without the use of mortar from massive blocks of stone. Even today some of these structures, which could reach heights of up to 27 metres (89 ft), are still

standing. The largest and technically most perfect megalithic buildings in Europe, they are found only in Sardinia, in awe-inspiring profusion. Today some 7,000 are registered as historic monuments. There can be few other places where visitors find themselves so frequently confronted with prehistory. On average you can expect to come across a *nuraghe* once every 2,000 metres (6,600 ft) on this 24,000 sq. kilometre (9,250 sq. mile) island.

So who were the builders? The Nuragic civilisation had no written language and thus little means of leaving records for us to decipher. It's therefore unlikely that the mysteries of their culture will ever be solved, even though in the last 4–5 years so much new information has been gathered through new archaeological research. As far as we can judge today, the Nuragic appear to have reached the highest standards of all Bronze Age peoples in the western Mediterranean, especially in the fields of architecture, metallurgy and sculpture.

It's difficult to ascertain exactly what purpose was served by these thousands of towers. There is no comparable example of such frenzied building activity exercised by a prehistoric people across several centuries. It is tempting to draw comparisons with the gigantic statues of Easter Island. The *nuraghe*, however, are not the grotesque invention of an island race completely cut off from the rest of the world. The people traded with other Mediterranean countries and their civilisation came up with a number of quite remarkable achievements, such as exquisite spa temples and the enchanting bronze statuettes placed in them as votive gifts.

The basic form of a *nuraghe* is a blunt-topped cone – a round tower that becomes narrower towards the top, and that ends in a platform. An entrance corridor at ground level leads to the interior, a more or less concentric circular room with a domed vaulted roof. This classic design is thus known as a Domed *nuraghe* or Tholos *nuraghe*. The *tholoi*, such as the famous "Treasury of Atreus", were beehive-shaped Mycenean tombs built of rings of stones; the diameter of each layer was smaller than the previous one, resulting in a dome in the shape of a pointed arch or an oval. The largest, and perhaps the finest, dome is that surmounting the Nuraghe Is Paras near Isili. Both the Myceneans and the Nuragic built these domed structures from about the 16th century BC. Is there any connection? Recent investigations have shown that the basic principles on which the Myceneans built their underground vaulted tombs were quite different from those upon which the Nuragic constructed their domes. The larger *nuraghe* towers consist of up to three storeys of rooms, each smaller than the one beneath. A staircase was then hollowed out of the walls – which were in any case constructed without the use of mortar. It led around the vaulted ceilings to the upper rooms and finally to the roof platform.

placed until they decomposed into skeletons), "sleeping towers" (in which the living could escape from marauding mosquito by sleeping at higher altitudes), sun temples, kilns or primitive astronomical observatories. As indicated by the common suffix *kastru* (from the Latin *castrum*), the Romans regarded the *nuraghe* as *kastelle* (forts). Some would say that it's typical of the Romans to apply a military interpretation.

In addition to the solitary *nuraghe* towers, there are also hundreds of *nuraghe* settlements of all sizes, ranging from a pair of neighbouring towers linked by two walls enclosing a courtyard to full-size fortresses consisting of a dozen

## The Roman interpretation

The original meaning of the word "nuraghe" has been lost down the millennia. Over the course of the centuries, travellers and scholars have produced a whole range of fanciful explanations for the word. Sometimes these have been elaborated into complex theories, often passionately defended by their adherents. According to the assorted myths, *nuraghe* could imply any of the following: tombs, mausoleums, "towers of silence" (where corpses were

**LEFT:** Nuragic bronze figure in the Museo Archeologico in Cagliari. **ABOVE:** Su Nuraxi, dating from 1500 BC, during the Middle Bronze Age.

*nuraghe* forming a turretted citadel and surrounded by a protective wall enclosing several courtyards, wells and storage rooms intended to keep enough provisions to enable the people to survive any potential siege.

The largest and most interesting *nuraghe* complexes are the Nuraghe Santu Antine near Torralba, the Nuraghe Losa near Paulilatino, the Nuraghe Su Nuraxi near Barumini and the Nuraghe Arrubiu near Orroli. The function of these strongholds was probably similar to that of medieval castles: in peacetime they may have served as the official residences of tribal chiefs, but they were, in addition, likely to have been the centres of a wide range of communal activities (lookout posts, general stores, venues for the performance of religious rites and so forth). In times of war they provided a refuge for the inhabitants of the surrounding villages.

The military role of these *nuraghe* fortresses is evident from their numerous defensive strategic features, such as the embrasures and the overhanging balustrades that once surmounted the towers and walls. It is unfortunate that no examples of the latter have survived. However, you can find in the island's museums quite a number of stone or bronze models of *nuraghe* that were originally used for ritual purposes. These models give a fairly good idea of both

proved beyond doubt that all *nuraghe* – even the largest complexes – were built during the 2nd millennium BC. Recent excavations in Barumini unearthed the remains of a balustrade that dated from the 13th–14th century BC.

## The Greek claim

The geographers and historians of ancient Greece were among the first to attempt to answer the question: who built the *nuraghe*? They believed Sardinia to be the largest island in the Mediterranean (it's actually the second-largest, after Sicily), describing it as a wondrous place of freedom and happiness. They

the powerful impact of the originals and the methods used in their construction.

The superstructures rested on huge stone bases and overhung the main tower by about a metre (3 ft). On some *nuraghe* – for example, on the parapet of the well in the courtyard of the Nuraghe Su Nuraxi near Barumini – one can still see the stones employed, each of which weighs more than a ton. Strategic refinements of this nature seem to be unique in the entire western Mediterranean, and apparently also in the Aegean. Thus for many years it was assumed that these perfectly designed and highly complex *nuraghe* citadels must be of a much more recent vintage. Today it has been

found that civilisation and agriculture flourished. They refer to the "numerous and magnificent buildings" as *daidaleia* – thus attributing them to Daedalus, the Athenian architect and inventor who, according to the legend, built the famous labyrinth for King Minos of Crete before fashioning wings for himself and his son, Icarus, by which they could escape their imprisonment. Daedalus fled to Sicily, whence he travelled on to Sardinia with a group of Greek settlers.

The Greek writers were apparently so impressed by Sardinia that they were happy to deceive posterity into thinking that the Nuraghi accomplishments were actually the product of

Greek intellectual and practical ingenuity. Although in recent years archaeologists have found evidence of trading links between the Myceneans and the Nuragic from at least the 14th century BC, it has nevertheless become clear that the golden age of the Nuraghian civilisation was the cause, and not merely the effect, of this contact. Comparatively insignificant cultures, such as that on Corsica, offered no attractions as trading partners.

## Graves of the giants

The uniqueness of *nuraghe* to Sardinia suggests that their culture, too, must be indigenous, *zigantes* (in Italian, *tombe di giganti*). Like the *nuraghi*, the graves of the giants have no obvious parallel on the mainland. The base of one such grave is formed by a burial chamber measuring between 5 and 15 metres (16 and 50 ft) long and 1 to 2 metres (3 to 6 ft) high. It is built from well-matched stones and is usually covered by a more carelessly constructed burial mound that, from the outside, resembles the hull of an upturned boat. Thus far, the method of construction bears a marked resemblance to the megalithic standing graves commonly found in locations between France and southern Italy.

At the beginning of the 2nd millennium BC,

based on the existing cultural traditions of the western Mediterranean. Irrefutable evidence for this assertion can be found in the so-called graves of the giants, a type of burial place whose origins go back to the beginning of the 2nd millennium BC and which the Nuragic developed and maintained for over 1,000 years.

The tombs of the men who built the *nuraghe* are as monumental as the towers themselves. Sardinians call these burial places – that range in length from 27 metres (89 ft) – *tumbas de sos*

**LEFT:** archaeological site at the giants' grave at San Cosimo near Arbus. **ABOVE:** grave of the giants at Lu Coddu Vecchiu near Arzachena.

however, during the early years of the Nuragic civilisation, the tombs on Sardinia took on their characteristic form. On each side of the entrance, at right angles to the main chamber of the grave, a pair of walls was added. They demarcate a semicircular forecourt 10 metres to 20 metres (32 ft–65 ft) wide. The imposing facade thus formed gave the graves an appropriately monumental and possibly mournful and private ambience.

In the case of the older graves (*circa* 1800–1400 BC) this impression is underlined by a finely chiselled stone stela (in this case an upright slab or column decorated with figures or inscriptions that was common in prehistoric times) some 3 or 4 metres (10–13 ft) tall. The stela resembled an imposing doorway, with a tiny opening at ground level that could be closed by a stone and served as an entrance to the grave. In the vicinity of the grave there are often vertical stone obelisks which may have been used to represent those gods, or possibly ancestors, who watched over the dead.

These menhirs are known as *baityloi* (or, in Italian, *betili*). The word is derived from the Hebrew *beth-el* ("Home of the Deity").

### THE GIANTS' GRAVES

The unique giants' graves at Madau, not far from Fonni, contain five graves clustered together, all dating from different periods.

portal stelae are the giants' graves of Li Lolghi and Coddu Vecchiu ("Capichera") near Arzachena. You can also see imposing menhirs next to the graves at Tamuli near Macomer.

## Water temples

A few hundred giants' graves are not the only remains that bear witness to the religious nature of the Nuraghi. The most elaborate and remarkable structures from this era to be encountered in the Sardinian countryside reflect not only Nuragic architecture but also the

The forecourt contains a fireplace and often an encircling stone platform used as a seat or table for sacrificial offerings. This was the setting for both funeral rites and commemorative ceremonies in honour of the dead. The members of a tribal group, clan or village met to pay their respects to the dead, who were buried by the community with no consideration for rank or privilege, and without funeral gifts of any value. The graves of the giants constructed by the Nuragic should be seen rather as charnel houses, in which the bones of the dead were piled up after skeletonisation was complete. Some graves contain as many as 100 to 200 skeletons. Particularly worth visiting for their

chronic water shortage that has hampered the island throughout its history.

The water temples built on the site of natural springs acted as focal points for ritual tribal gatherings or as places of pilgrimage. So far, approximately 50 of these unusual complexes have been identified, with their design almost always following the same basic plan. The heart of a water temple (or spa temple; *tempio a pozzo* in Italian) is the Nuragic domed vault, sometimes situated underground, in which the sacred spring water was collected. A staircase linked this pump room with the temple antechamber at ground level. The antechamber was ringed by small stone benches upon which votive gifts or cult objects were placed. There was also often a sacrificial stone with a small gully; this seems to point to blood sacrifices or possibly specific rites involving the use of what was believed to be holy water.

Some water temples, presumably those of an earlier date, were built, like the *nuraghe*, from roughly hewn blocks of stone. Conversely there are some particularly fine complexes such as the Temple of Predio Canopoli in Perfugas, Su Tempiesu near Orune, Santa Cristina near Paulilatino and Santa Vittoria near Serri. Such is the remarkable perfection and precision of the limestone and lava blocks from which they were constructed that, for many years, these temples were thought to have originated at some point during the 8th to 6th centuries BC, thus inviting comparison with Etruscan burial architecture. More recent finds, however, have led archaeologists to believe increasingly that the temples are several centuries older than this, and that they thus reach back into the time during which there was close contact with the late Mycenean kingdom in Greece and Cyprus.

The perfection of some water temples was clearly meant to serve as a representation of their religious significance: it is surely no accident that the spiritual attraction of the most beautiful temples continued unbroken into the Christian era. In Perfugas, for example, the Nuragic pagan temple was discovered directly beneath the church square; and Santa Cristina (Paulilatino) and Santa Vittoria (Serri) are places of pilgrimage even today. Indeed festivals are marked by the arrival of believers who have travelled long distances from the surrounding countryside in order to attend the Christian church rituals. Even the celebrations take place more or less as they did 3,000 years ago – with wine and food, song and dance.

## Little bronze statues

Of the countless votive presents that the pious visitors to the water temples would leave behind, a number of little bronze statues have survived. These statues represent the most beautiful examples of Nuragic culture. If you are interested in seeing them, allow plenty of time to visit at least one of the two most impor-

tant archaeological museums in Sassari or Cagliari. Most of the bronzes are only an inch or two (a few centimetres) tall, so to fully appreciate their splendour, a careful scrutiny is essential. Like the votive plaques in the pilgrimage churches, these votive statues provide the observer with an insight into everyday life. One can admire not only miniature copies of household items, farming implements, tools, weapons and magnificently decorated boats, but also exquisitely naturalistic representations of wild and domestic animals and, above all, people. With a little imagination we can glimpse their different activities and recognise

**LEFT:** Santa Sabina near Macomer, linking the Nuraghi with Christendom. **RIGHT:** Nuraghi bronze figure in the Museo Archeologico in Cagliari.

the social strata: shepherds, farmers, musicians, worshippers, the sick, mourners, priests, aristocrats, and soldiers, some of whom, armed with assorted weapons, bear the terrifying countenance of demons.

Each bronze statuette is a unique specimen of incalculable worth, and each falls into one of three Bronze-Age Nuraghi art categories: the Baroque, the Geometric and the Popular. It is uncertain whether these styles existed more or less simultaneously, or whether they represent a long period of technical and artistic development. Nor has it proved possible to date the figures with any degree of precision. A lot of

Nuragic bronzes were found on the Italian mainland in Etruscan graves that date back to the 8th to 6th centuries BC.

Recently, however, considerable support has been won for the theory that some Nuragic bronze art is in fact much older than any comparable artefacts found in the western Mediterranean. But these assumptions do not fit into the generally accepted picture of the Nuraghi civilisation as one of the relatively unimportant fringe cultures of the Mediterranean region. According to the latest research, the island's rich ore deposits, especially its lead and copper mines, played a key role. Indeed the Nuragic golden age coincided with an upsurge in the importance of metalworking. It seems likely that the bronze boom and the resulting trade with the eastern Mediterranean gave the island a cultural impetus that, for unknown reasons, was not shared by anyone else.

## The mysterious Sardana

Recent theories seem to lend credence to the notion – which was particularly prevalent in the 19th century – that the Nuragic of Sardinia may have been the mysterious people known as the Sardana. In the 14th century BC these Sardana are mentioned in some Egyptian texts as being enemies, and in others as mercenaries in the service of the pharaoh. Archaeological evidence has proved that the Nuraghi had made contact with eastern lands by this time. It is not clear to what extent they relied on the Myceneans for these contacts, and to what extent they navigated the trading routes themselves. What is remarkable is the increased frequency of communications with eastern Mediterranean societies, especially with the island of Cyprus – even after the 12th century BC when, following the Trojan Wars and the eclipse of the royal house of Mycenae, Greece entered a dark age which was to last many centuries.

It was due to its trading links that Sardinia continued to flourish culturally – which fact is confirmed by the high standard of its bronze artefacts. Remarkable examples of the skill of the craftsmen are the statues of warriors found in 1974 on Monte Prama. They are exact copies of the little bronze statuettes, but are almost 3 metres (10 ft) tall and carved in stone. You can see fragments of these statues in the Archaeological Museum in Cagliari.

If, as has been suggested by archaeologists, the first large Nuragic sculptures were created in the 8th century BC, they predated even the oldest Greek sculptures. Examples of this kind of sculpture are the result of radical changes in the tribal-based society of the Nuragic people. Indeed, there are a number of signs that, in some places, Nuraghi life was demonstrating characteristics more typical of a city-based social structure. Archaeologists have no doubt that the reason for this development was the arrival of the first Phoenician settlements on the Sardinian coast. ❑

**LEFT:** giants' grave at Li Lolghi.
**RIGHT:** part of a lucky charm from a Punic necropolis.

# PHOENICIANS, CARTHAGINIANS AND ROMANS

*The dawn of Sardinian history was marked by a succession of invasions by the powers that dominated the ancient Mediterranean arena*

The first Phoenician traders to do business on the island probably arrived in about 10,000 BC. Excavations of Nuragic sites have unearthed a number of bronze statuettes of Phoenician deities that were presumably imported from Syria or Palestine at around this time, and which doubtless influenced the Nuraghi in the development of their metal-working skills. Indeed, it was the Orient's demand for raw materials, above all metals, that drove the Phoenicians so far westwards.

During the 9th and 8th centuries BC, at about the time when the city of Carthage was being founded on the coast of what is now Tunisia, the Phoenicians built their first urban colonies around the principle harbours on the Sardinian coast: Karali (Cagliari), Nora and Bithia (both near Pula), Sulki (Sant'Antioco), Tharros (near Oristano), possibly Bosa and others. It is quite possible that, in some places at least, these settlements were built with the approval of the resident Nuragic tribes. While our knowledge of the Phoenicians remains somewhat sketchy, the results of recent excavations on Sardinia, at the town of Sulki for example, suggest that the traditional image of the Phoenicians as industrious artisans, skilful traders and courageous seafarers is misleading.

Scarcely 100 years after they founded the city of Sulki, the colonists had succeeded in conquering the entire fertile hinterland and the access routes to the lucrative mining areas. They secured their conquests with smaller outposts and well-fortified towns. The dominant position of the garrison town on the plateau of Monte Sirai near Carbonia reveals much about the Phoenicians' intentions: they were determined to establish a new homeland here, almost 3,000 kilometres (1,900 miles) west of their native ports on the Lebanese coast. Maybe they were attracted by the island's

**LEFT:** the ruins of Tharros on the Sinis peninsula.
**RIGHT:** Phoenician gryphon head.

isolation, or its distance from their neighbours and enemies, the Assyrians and Babylonians. In the 6th century BC the Greeks began to take an interest in Sardinia. The ancient world's writers cite Olbia, for example, as a town

founded by the Greeks, but no archaeological evidence has been found to support this claim.

## Truth dawns on the Nuraghi

The Phoenicians, for their part, tried to strengthen their hold on the island. It seems likely that the Nuragic, finally realising that their island had been invaded by hostile forces, banded together to mount a counterattack and fight for their survival. The events that followed mark the island's entry into the annals of history: classical literature gives us a precise record of what happened on Sardinia. In 540 BC Carthage sent an army of reinforcements to its Phoenician sister cities; the same troops had successfully fought under General Malchos against the Greeks on Sicily. But the expedition ended in disaster, and the army was routed. The island fortresses played no part in the Nuraghi's military success; they had lost their importance in about the 9th and 8th centuries BC, and had been largely left to decay. Excavations on Monte Sirai confirm that the Phoenician garrison was reduced to ashes at about the time of Malchos's campaign.

In Carthage, the shock of this defeat gave rise to a reform of political and military institutions. The military formed the basis for the Carthaginians' empire-building aspirations and

## Punic Sardinia

The Carthaginians quickly secured their new territories with a frontier to repel the mountain-dwellers. By the 5th century BC the interlopers occupied two-thirds of the island – not only the coastal regions, but also the entire southwest (Iglesiente) with its mining areas, and the fertile lowlands and hill slopes. They also controlled the volcanic plateaux in the interior, which was good sheep-farming country.

They founded towns such as Macopsisa (Macomer), built numerous forts, including those on the northern boundary of the Campidano high plains near Bonorva, on the Catena

before long it despatched well-organised armies of mercenaries to Sardinia. The island was soon so firmly under Carthaginian rule that, in 509 BC, the Romans were compelled to sign a contract recognising that all trading with Sardinia was subject to Carthaginian control.

The Nuragic, now virtually prisoners on their own island, could choose between a life of bondage as serfs and mercenaries, or an impoverished but free existence as shepherds in the mountains, which, not being of any agricultural value, was of no interest to the occupiers. The eclipse of the Nuragic marked the start of a period of almost uninterrupted occupation and a history linked with that of its colonial masters.

del Margine above Macomer, and in the northern Giara region of Gesturi, near Genoni. Hand in hand with a vigorous policy of deforestation, farming land was criss-crossed by an amazingly dense network of paths and farmsteads: the island was being transformed into the granary of Carthage. According to classical sources, the Carthaginians utilised the services of immigrant Libyan farm labourers as Sardinia became an overseas extension of Carthaginian territory. The island had closer military, administrative, ethnic and cultural links with North Africa than did any other part of the Punic empire.

Sardinian museums allot considerable space to the role played by Sardinia and Carthage as the oldest and most important Phoenician centres in the West. One of the most fascinating aspects of Phoenician art is the often daring manner in which the artists borrowed styles and forms from trading partners before blending them with their own aesthetic traditions to create highly individual works. Although the museums reveal the dominant influence of Egypt in sculpture, a close study of the miniature works of art shows that the proverbial wealth of the Phoenician empire was due not only to its seafaring traders, but also to the skills of its craftsmen. Most of the items are burial gifts: jewellery, amulets, talismans, incense burners, perfume flacons and unguent jars, but also frightening masks designed to keep evil spirits away from the dead. The most remarkable element of Phoenician architecture is its use of very large building blocks.

Outside the museums, traces of this period are not so accessible. The Romans destroyed virtually everything, and what little has remained is often of interest only to specialists. But Monte Sirai and Tharros are definitely worth a visit. Monte Sirai is a fine example of a self-sufficient garrison town complete with necropolis and its own sacrificial altar for burnt offerings. It is situated on a high plateau and is interesting for its dominant strategic position and the clear-cut military plan of its acropolis.

Tharros is situated on a narrow promontory about 2 kilometres (1 mile) long, with two hills: one for the town, one for the necropolis. It is a classic example of a Phoenician coastal town: it has a safe harbour, an easily defended single narrow land approach, shallow lakes with copious stocks of fish nearby and an extensive, fertile hinterland.

## Child sacrifices

A little-understood Phoenician custom was the sacrifice of young children by fire to the deity Baal, or later to the Carthaginian goddess Tanit. The Phoenicians called this ritual *molk*. (In the Old Testament, Moloch was a Semitic deity to whom parents sacrificed their children). The sacrificial altars, referred to as *tephatim* in the

**MYSTERIOUS DEPARTURE**

It has never been discovered why the Romans abandoned the site of Monte Sirai in the 2nd century AD.

Bible, were specially erected outside the towns. The first such *tophet* was only discovered in 1889, significantly not in the Middle East but near Nora in Sardinia. Here, and on half a dozen other *tephatim* discovered on the island, archaeologists have found thousands of clay urns filled with charcoal and human remains, as well as hundreds of stone votive stelae recalling the sacrifice (to prolong its efficacy). Of these sites, only the *tophet* at Sulki on the island of Sant'Antioco has been left virtually untouched following excavations.

Here visitors can get an impression of the complex's original layout and the positioning of the urns and stelae.

Archaeologists suggest that the stories behind these hundreds of child-sized urns are not quite as repulsive as they have seemed to historians since ancient times. Some urns contain remains of substitute animal sacrifices, mostly lambs or kids – the Bible recounts how Abraham sacrificed a lamb instead of his son, Isaac – and it is also evident that young children who died of natural causes were subsequently cremated in the *tophet*. This can be deduced from the evidence that no babies were buried in Phoenician or Carthaginian necropolises. Thus the 5,000

**LEFT:** an *ex voto* lamp with bronze deer figurines dating from the 7th–8th century BC.
**RIGHT:** children's urns in the Tophet of Sulcis.

urns found in the *tophet* at Tharros lose some of their nightmare quality. It is possible that the Phoenicians, faced by high rates of infant mortality, regarded children as the deity's property.

Rome and Carthage first crossed swords in the First Punic War (264–241 BC). The Romans, who had been forced to recognise the importance of Sardinia to the Carthaginians, both as a naval base and as a troop and grain store, did not hesitate to take advantage of the situation when a mutiny by Sardinian mercenaries put pressure on the Carthaginians. Reneging on the peace treaty, Roman troops annexed Sardinia in 238 BC without encountering much resistance.

In the following years, the Carthaginians put up more of a fight; the island played reluctant host to a series of battles fought out by the great powers between 236 and 226 BC.

## Allies against Rome

In the course of the Second Punic War (218–201 BC), there were several attempts by the Carthaginians on Sardinia to overthrow the Romans. All failed, although – as the Roman chronicler Livy reported – they were supported by the local mountain dwellers. This alliance between erstwhile enemies enmeshed the Romans ever deeper in what today would be termed guerrilla warfare. General Caecilius

Metellus, who had fought with distinction and commanded two legions in Sardinia, was the eighth and last officer to be awarded the honour of a triumph by the Roman senate in recognition of his victories over the Sardinians. As the foreign war dragged on, the citizens of Rome started to view the island as an unnecessary burden that was not worth carrying. Historians record the people's hatred of the island.

In 54 BC, when Cicero took on the defence of a certain Scaurus, a man who had acquired more than the usual degree of wealth during his time as governor of Sardinia, the lawyer's polemical plea for his client precisely echoed the popular mood: Sardinia was a Roman province but not a single town was friendly towards Rome; and the Sardinians as a race were the descendants of the nefarious Carthaginians.

In fact, as the Roman republic approached its last days, Sardinia was the only one of more than 30 Roman provinces without a single city whose inhabitants were entitled to Roman citizenship. This shortcoming was not remedied until 27 BC, with the foundation of the Roman colony of *Turris Libisonis*.

And Cicero was basically right, too, in his depiction of Sardinians' provenance. The year of Sardinia's annexation was of purely political significance; in cultural terms, the Carthaginian influence on Sardinia remained evident for many centuries after Carthage had been destroyed by Rome. An inscription dating from the year AD 200 mentions a Sardinian *Sufete* (as the Carthaginian mayors were called) with the very un-Roman name of "Bodbaal".

The general situation on the island improved during the reign of the emperor Augustus. The residents of many towns were awarded the right of Roman citizenship and a dramatic upsurge in the amount of building testifies to increasing prosperity. By now even the mountain folk had accepted Roman rule and the occupiers could restrict their supervisory activities to mediating in the feuds between the sheep-farming tribes of the *barbaria* (known as the Barbagia today) and the Sardinian peasants on Roman estates. But to the Romans the island was doomed to remain a much-hated imperial doormat, not least because the dreaded malaria was found to be prevalent there.  ❑

**LEFT:** the Ponte Romano in Porto Torres.
**RIGHT:** part of a Roman mosaic floor in Nora.

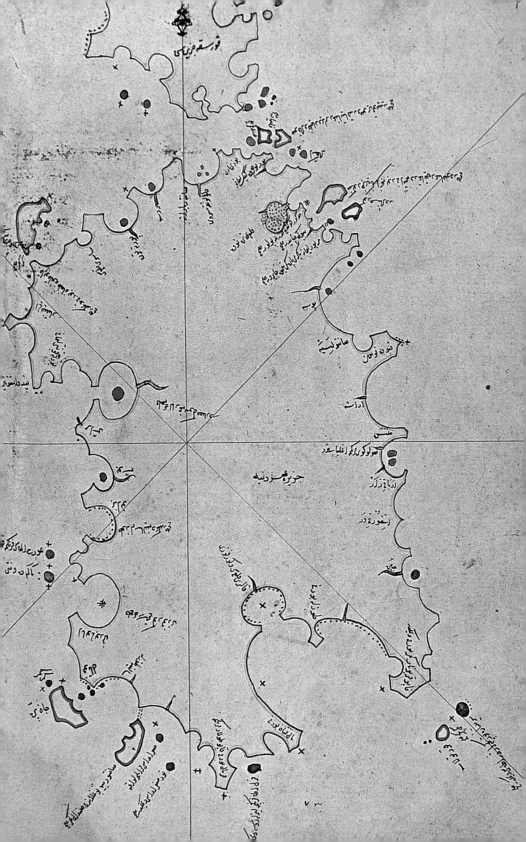

# THE ARABS

*After Arab invaders cut off Sardinia's links with the Christian powers,
the Pisans and the Genoese entered into a battle for control*

Arabs first ventured ashore on Sardinia in AD 711. In that year the soldiers of Mussa-Ibn-Nucair captured the town of Cagliari and occupied various regions along the coast. Though this Saracen visit was short-lived, when they set out to sea again it was with some substantial booty. It appears that the Saracens ran into a storm during the journey home, and that they and their plundered gains ended up in a watery grave. This mishap did little to discourage the intrepid and warlike Arabs from their dreams of a vast empire.

From outposts in Spain, North Africa and Sicily they resumed their raids, terrorising the Sardinian coast, stealing food and kidnapping the natives. Those poor souls for whom no ransom was forthcoming ended up in the slave markets of north Africa. For 300 years, until 1015, not even frequent sea storms deterred the Saracens. The initial, ill-fated raid on Sardinia was followed by others in 722 and 735–736. After yet another campaign in 752–753, Abd-ar-Rahman decreed that a number of Sardinian towns which had already been sacked and laid waste should buy back their freedom.

In about 807 a Saracen fleet was ambushed and destroyed off the west coast of Sardinia near Sulcis. Only six years later the same fate befell the Arab general Abbu-el-Abbas and the armada of 100 ships under his command. And yet, despite the boost of their unexpected naval victories, by 815 the Sardinians were in desperate need of liberation. They sent a message to the Emperor Louis the Pious, begging him for assistance in their struggle against the Arabs' increasingly bold attacks.

Their pleas fell on deaf ears. After only a short interval of peace, in 816 and again the following year, Cagliari was destroyed once more. And then again several years later. Only in 1015–16 did the Sardinians eventually end this reign of terror. In alliance with the maritime republics of Genoa and Pisa they finally succeeded in routing the forces of the Prince of Mogeid-al-Amiri.

## Museto the conqueror

The prince, known as "Museto" in Italian records of the time, had already conquered the

Balearic Islands and Denia in Spain when he set sail from Mallorca with a fleet of 120 ships. Museto had recognised the strategic importance of Sardinia and was now toying with the idea of subjugating the island once and for all. The states bordering the Tyrrhenian Sea were roused from their lethargy by the fact that en route the Saracens had raided some of the Tuscan coastal towns, including Luni. What was more, the Italians feared that the invaders – forced to abandon temporarily their dreams of empire following defeat at Poitiers in 732 at the hand of Charles Martel – might revive their former ambitions and use Sardinia as a base from which they could set out to conquer Italy and the rest of Europe.

**LEFT:** an Arabian sea-chart that includes the island of Sardinia.
**RIGHT:** Castello Las Plassas in the Marmilla.

Pope Benedict VIII felt particularly threatened and used his influence over Pisa and Genoa to persuade them to unite in the common cause against the Arabs on Sardinia. The two republics would have had reason enough to go to war even without the Pope's intercession, for their aspirations to dominate the trading routes across the Tyrrhenian Sea were at stake. A Sardinia in Arab hands would represent an unacceptable threat. And so the fleets of Genoa and Pisa put to sea and routed

> ### EARLY ARAB RAIDS
>
> A Saracen chronicler commented tersely on the Arab raid on Sardinia of 821–822: "They gave some beatings and received some in their turn; and then they departed from that place."

the island's interior radically changed the social structure. The abandoned towns were no longer focal points of trade and commerce as they had been during the time of the Vandals and the Byzantine era. In rural regions a land-based curtilage economy (farming based around a small courtyard attached to a house) sprang up which was only able to supply the needs of a few villages. A fluctuating population led to the establishment of new farming communities in all areas. Even Cagliari was moved to Santa

the Saracens, together with the armies of the Sardinian *giudici* – the rulers of the four medieval *giudicati*, the defensive alliances of Cagliari, Arborea, Gallura and Torres – with whom they then proceeded to establish lively trading links.

### In Arab hands

The occupation of Sicily by the Arabs in 827 marked a much darker chapter in the island's history, for it cut off the links with Byzantium and forced the island to rely on its own resources. The historian Alberto Boscolo has pointed out that the Arab supremacy at sea and the associated mass exodus from the coast to

Igia, not far away but better protected, with marshes on one side and the ocean on the other.

The results of countless raids by a succession of new invaders were dramatic: many of the seaside towns and villages were destroyed or left to decay. Since the Sardinians believed even then that danger invariably came from across the sea, many of them left the fertile coastal regions in order to make new homes in the rougher and less economically viable interior. They paid dearly for the security thus acquired: whilst life in the new settlements was marked by hardship and became progressively more depressing, large stretches of the previously fertile coastal margin regressed into malarial swampland. It was not only the pride and fear of the Sardinians which prevented the establishment of contact with the Arab invaders; the latter were also cruel and greedy, so that no true cultural exchange was possible.

Worst hit by the Saracens' plundering raids were the regions surrounding Cagliari, Porto Torres and Olbia. The Sardinians fled and built new settlements not far from their devastated or burned-out cities. Sulcis and Bithia were founded in the hinterland of Cagliari on the site of what is now San Giovanni Suergiu; Tharros and Neapolis (the present-day Oristano and Terralba) lie in the hinterland of the Gulf of Oristano; Cornus (Cuglieri) and Bosa lie between Oristano and Alghero; Turris lies in the north-west; Coclearia (S. Teodoro) and Feronia (Posada) lie in the north-east.

By contrast, it is maintained that Dorgali, in the hinterland of the Bay of Orosei, was founded in about 900 by the Saracen pirate Drugal. The population in this area certainly displays a number of ethnic and linguistic characteristics which distinguish them from the other inhabitants of the island. Significantly, Islamic motifs can be found in the decoration of the Church of San Paolo di Dolianova in Cagliari, which dates from 1160–1289. They are ascribed to the Saracen stonemasons who helped build it.

## The Genoese and the Pisans

The victory won in 1015–16 over the 120 ships of Sultan Museto's fleet established the naval supremacy of Genoa and Pisa over the Tyrrhenian Sea, vital for developing their extensive trading interests. The mainland republics quickly recognised the strategic value of Sardinia. The island could play a crucial role in helping to fulfil their future military, economic and political plans.

At this time, Sardinia was divided into four *giudicati*: Torres, Gallura, Oristano and Cagliari. Each of these provinces, originally formed as a defensive alliance, had its own jurisdiction and its own social order. The ruler of the *giudicato* was known as the *giudice*; he lived with his family and an armed bodyguard in a castle. He was responsible for the administration of justice and the government of affairs

LEFT: roof of San Gavino church in Porto Torres.
RIGHT: the church of Santissima Trinità di Saccargia near Sassari.

of state. He was aided by the clergy and a secular civil service, as well as by the *curatores,* each of which governed in his name a *curatoria,* a region consisting of a number of villages and estates. The individual communities were run by the *majori,* men who enjoyed the trust of the *curatores.*

The *giudicati* were made up of state property *(rennu)* and the private property of the *giudice (depegugiare).* The status quo comprised a number of social classes. The hierarchy was divided into estates into which one was born: freemen – ranging from wealthy and powerful owners of large estates to the poor –

and peasants and serfs. The latter estate was further subdivided into three groups, depending on how many days per week they were required to work for one or more masters.

The *integri* had to work the whole day for their master, the *laterati* owed him half a day's work and the *pedati* worked for him for a quarter of the day. On their time off the *laterati* and *pedati* could work on their own plot of land – if they possessed one – or could undertake other work.

The serfs' position was considerably better than it had been during the latter years of the Roman Empire. The villages, with their clearly defined administrative order, formed the kernel of the *giudicati*, together with the surrounding region consisting of private land, *latifundia* and village estates.

The arrival of the Genoese and Pisan forces on Sardinia marked their first encounter with this politico-administrative and economic system. And before long they, too, were delighted to discover that the island was rich in natural resources, with extensive salt works as well as a flourishing agricultural economy, and above all plenty of scope for cattle farming.

> **A NEW KING**
>
> The Emperor Frederick Barbarossa was proclaimed Barisone d'Arborea King of Sardinia, on 10 August 1164 in the church of San Siro in Pavia.

the entire island under the aegis of the d'Arborea family. There was vigorous opposition to this plan from the other three *giudici* of Torres, Gallura and Cagliari; not until 1146 did the Archbishop of Pisa, Villario, manage to persuade the three of them to meet in Oristano to conclude a provisional peace treaty. A few years after this, Barisone d'Arborea took up the family struggle for power on the island once more. The troops of the *giudicato* of Torres supported the Pisans; together, they besieged

## Caught in the middle

The fierce rivalry between the two maritime republics also affected Sardinia. At the beginning, especially after the victory over the Saracens off the Balearic Islands (1113–15) Pisa had the upper hand. The city's superiority lay not only in military success but also in its archbishop: as the metropolitan of two Sardinian dioceses he was in a position to step in as arbiter in the frequent disputes between the powerful families within a *giudicato* and mediate between two warring *giudicati*.

After AD 1130 Genoa decided to bestow its especial favour on one single *giudice*: it supported Comita d'Arborea in his attempt to unite

Barisone in his castle in Cabras. With Genoese help the latter finally succeeded in breaking the siege; he then appealed to the Emperor Frederick Barbarossa to proclaim him King of Sardinia. This was duly done and the coronation took place on 10 August 1164 in the Church of San Siro in Pavia.

Even this success was not enough to satisfy Genoa, which continued undaunted to cling to its dreams of hegemony. As a first step it took the precaution of ensuring the benevolence of the Papal States and then persuaded all four *giudici* to sign a number of treaties which declared them to be virtually the vassals of Genoa. This strengthening of the position of the Ligurian republic was a severe blow for Pisa, which thereupon resumed the fight against its archrival. Once more, Emperor Frederick I intervened and divided the island into two separate dependent territories; Lugudoro and Campidano were subject to Genoa, and Gallura to Pisa. This event was a turning point in the history of the island.

> ### CLASSIC CHURCHES
>
> The church of Santa Maria di Betlem in Sassari was built by Benedictine monks and consecrated in 1106.

From this time onwards, wealthy Ligurian and Tuscan families with a long tradition of seafaring and trading brought increased prosperity to the island's economy. Both Genoa and

of worship. The monasteries soon began to attract unemployed labourers and local farmers anxious to learn the new agricultural methods which the monks had brought with them from Italy or other more advanced regions of Europe. They began to till fields which until now had never been cultivated, and land which had long ago been fertile but now lay desolate. Yields were improved by the introduction of new strains.

The effort and the changes wrought proved worthwhile, for before long the sight of fields

Pisa sent monks from a number of orders to convert the islanders to Catholicism: Benedictines Camaldolese, Vallombrosians, Cistercians, followers of St Victor of Marseilles and Benedictines from Monte Cassino. They built abbeys and churches the length and breadth of the island.

The presence of so many priests led to a rapid spread of the Catholic faith and to a blossoming of culture. Craftsmen and painters from the mainland were summoned to adorn the places

**LEFT:** the Torre dell'Elefante in Cagliari.
**ABOVE:** Santissima Trinità di Saccargia, decorated in a style reminiscent of Tuscany.

full of flowers attracted people's attention, reawakening interest in the arts throughout the land. The churches built were hardly sophisticated Byzantine edifices, but they satisfied the needs of an agriculturally based society.

## Foreign feuds

The feud between Genoa and Pisa, waged on Sardinian soil through the Sardinian *giudici*, was not forgotten. At the end of 1190, following a complicated dispute over the succession between Ugone Ponzio di Bas and Pietro d'Arborea, Barisone's son, the governor's throne in Cuglieri (Cagliari) was occupied for the first time by a man from the mainland,

Oberto di Massa, who adopted a policy favouring Pisa. His successor, Guglielmo di Massa, declared war on Constantino di Torres. He forced him to surrender after laying prolonged siege to his stronghold, the Castello del Goceano. The *giudicato* fell victim to a campaign by the Genoese, who besieged and plundered Sant' Igia in 1194 before pressing on to Oristano. Ugone Ponzo di Bas was forced to flee, and the cathedral chapter had no option but to appoint Guglielmo as *giudice*. The two rivals were later to be brought closer to one another, not least through new family ties. At the end of the 12th century Sardinia was under the control of Pisa.

declaration of loyalty and allegiance. When Visconti died, the Pope secured his position by proposing that Visconti's young widow, Adelasia, should marry Guelfo Porcari, a man who enjoyed his trust. Adelasia's choice, however, fell on Enzo, the illegitimate son of Frederick II of Swabia. Enzo's father had his son proclaimed King of Sardinia, whereupon the Pope avenged himself by excommunicating the couple.

By the middle of the 13th century, a complicated policy of arranged marriages, planned over a long period, brought virtually the entire island under Pisa's sway. Giovanni Visconti

In 1215 the death of Guglielmo di Massa revived the power struggle between the two seafaring republics, but this time the first families of Sardinia were also involved. They tried to gain an advantage by forming new alliances with one of the warring parties or with other Sardinian families. In 1219 the Visconti routed the army of the *giudice* of Torres, subsequently hastening to secure their new position by means of a succession of marriages. The perpetual strife between the feuding families and rival power groups reached a climax in 1235, when a popular uprising led to the establishment of Sassari as a city state. In 1238 Pope Gregory IX extracted from Ubaldo Visconti a formal

took up residence in Gallura, Guglielmo di Capraia in Arborea and the Dukes of Pisa themselves in the Castle of Cagliari. Supported by various Ligurian families – the Malaspinas, the Dorias and the Spinolas – the *giudicato* Logudoro attempted to organise resistance to the Pisans. And so a political wrangle slowly drew to a close, a scenario in which the principal actors – apart from the maritime republics striving for supremacy – were the most powerful families in the land. The majority of Sardinians, most of them involved with the everyday problems of town life, took no part in the affair. Thus came the end of a highly promising Golden Age in which culture, religion, the arts and the economy had flourished, without giving rise to a local political or economic power which would have been in a position to take control of the country's future.

## Pisa struggles for control

The Pisans were forced to face a humiliating defeat between 1250 and 1260. The *giudice* Ghiano di Massa drove the Tuscans from Cagliari, settling into the town's castle and concluding a treaty with the Genoese, who sent an expeditionary force to reinforce his position.

Pisa transferred the representation of its interests to two *giudici*, Giovanni Visconti and Guglielmo di Capraia. Accompanied by a wild horde of soldiers, Gherardo di Donoreti was sent to Sardinia to support them. The decisive battle took place near Santa Igia. The Pisans won and moved back into the castle, taking Ghiano prisoner and eventually putting him to death. He was succeeded by his cousin, Guglielmo III Cepolla, who in 1257 was forced to sign a treaty of capitulation which guaranteed him a safe passage to Genoa or Sassari.

Towards the end of the 13th century the position of the factions in Pisa itself deteriorated; it was not long before the effects spread to Sardinia too. As a result of the bitter feud between the Guelphs and the Ghibellines, Anselmo di Capraia, Ugolino Donoratico and Giovanni Visconti were faced with banishment and the expropriation of their estates on the island.

After the Battle of Meloria in 1284, the enmity between the Podestà of Pisa, Ugolino Donoratico, and his nephew Ugolino Visconti, who commanded the army, spread as far as Sardinia. The Pisans, however, were able to turn the feud to their own advantage by bringing under their direct control some regions and sections of the economy, especially mining. Further to the north, the Genoese had not been idle. They occupied the town of Sassari and the area of the Logudoro which was previously in the possession of Mariano d'Arborea.

In 1297 the Papal States intervened again in the dispute. On 4 April, during a formal ceremony in St Peter's, Pope Boniface IV named James II of Aragon as seigneur in perpetuity over the islands of Sardinia and Corsica. At first this change of regency had little effect on the

island, but during the early years of the 14th century James II saw his opportunity to take an active part in the affairs of the land. The population was still waiting and hoping for someone to put an end to the machinations of the representatives of the rulers of Pisa, which by this time had become intolerable.

Thus it was that, on 28 February 1323, the armed forces of Aragon and Pisa, both sailing across the sea towards Sardinia, actually met at the Santa Gilla Lagoon, just outside Cagliari. Pisa suffered defeat; later that year, on 19 June, a peace treaty was signed in which the vanquished state abandoned its claim to nearly all

its rights associated with towns and estates on the island. Only a section of the fortress at Cagliari and the harbour remained in their possession, and that only for one more year.

This marked the beginning of the suzerainty of the Kingdom of Aragon, which was followed over four centuries by the kings of Spain in an institution which – as if by some irony of fate – came to be known as the *Regnum Sardiniae*. In spite of the disadvantages of the Genoa and Pisa occupation, many aspects of life on the island were enriched. Sardinians gained access to the mainland and a wide range of better quality goods – including fabrics from Tuscany and Flanders – were imported as a result. ❏

**LEFT:** the church of San Saturno in Cagliari.
**RIGHT:** the facade of Santa Maria di Betlem in Sassari.

# SARDINIA UNDER THE SPANISH

*The impact of Spanish rule on Sardinia was slight, but clear traces of their influence can still be found in urban architecture*

I n 1297, Pope Boniface VIII gave the *Regnum Sardiniae et Corsicae* in fief to the King of Aragon, James II. The two men knew each other personally, having previously both been in Sicily – James as King, and Boniface (still known at that stage as Cardinal Benedetto Caetani) as Papal Legate. They shared an antipathy to France and Anjou.

Boniface claimed the right to dispose of Sardinia as he thought fit on the basis of a deed of gift of Louis the Pious, although the document was almost 500 years old and the subject of controversy. Dante Alighieri was not altogether wrong in his Divine Comedy when he accused Pope Boniface of selling high offices and depicted him in hell.

It could hardly be claimed that Sardinia was a no man's land at the time. It was subdivided into four independent administrative regions: the *giudicati* Logudoro and Gallura in the north, Arborea in the west, and Cagliari in the south. At the head of each region was a *giudice*, a judge, whose position – depending on the writer's historical perspective – has been variously described as almost that of an independent monarch or as a mere puppet of the mighty Pisan and Genoese republics. Sardinia was at this period under the control of the rival maritime city states. Both exploited the island and its people alike, valuing it for its rich salt, silver mines and its fields of wheat.

King James II's first task was to take the reins of government from these mainland traders, who had a considerable vested interest in their Sardinian estates. Unfortunately, the Kingdom of Aragon, in spite of having just been awarded the island in fief, had no large fortune at its disposal. It was 26 years later that sufficient funds were raised for a campaign; half of the cost of the army was actually paid for by the Pope. Were it not for the fact that the ruler of Arborea appealed to Aragon for assis-

tance against Pisa and Genoa, it might have been longer still before the King embarked on the military conquest of Sardinia.

As it was, in 1323 the Aragonese set foot on what was for them an unknown island. The Infante Don Alfonso set sail with 10,000 men and landed at the Bay of Palmas in the south-

west of Sardinia. He captured Iglesias immediately and Cagliari during the following year, gradually advancing across the entire island. Here and there he encountered resistance from the Pisans and the Genoese, who were not prepared to relinquish without a struggle the influence and economic advantages they had enjoyed here.

## Division of the spoils

Once Sardinia had been appeased it was placed under the regency of a Viceroy from the Kingdom of Aragon. The land was subdivided into 376 fiefs. Half of them were awarded to Spanish noblemen whose one aim was to

**LEFT:** map of Sardinia in the 16th-century *Cosmographia Universalis*.
**RIGHT:** detail from a *retablo*, a Spanish altar painting.

increase their fortunes at the expense of their Sardinian estates. The underpopulated, impoverished, malarial island was entirely at the mercy of foreign interests; its fate was decided in faraway Saragossa, over the heads of the local citizens.

Of Sardinia's former masters, only the rulers of Arborea had been able to maintain their previous position: Hugo II had acted as advisor to the Aragonese during their occupation of the island. However, this compact dynasty whose roots went back to Sardinia's earliest history was a thorn in the flesh of the Spanish, who wanted to fill positions with their own

preserve the independence of his *giudicato*, he had no option but to change sides: instead of fighting with the Spanish against the Genoese Doria clan, he now decided to fight with the Doria against the Spanish. He received valuable assistance from one of the Dorias with the descriptive name Brancaleone, "The Lion-Catcher". In order to confirm the latter's allegiance, and knowing he was an ambitious man, Mariano agreed in 1367 that Brancaleone should marry his daughter Eleonora. Subsequently known as the *Giudicessa* Eleonora is still remembered by Sardinians today as a symbol of the island's independence.

incumbents who were loyal to the throne. In order to destroy the Arboreas' power they encouraged discord between the two sons of the *giudice* Hugo II by favouring the younger son, Giovanni, rather than his elder brother Mariano.

The situation, however, did not develop as the Spanish had expected: Mariano was the one who came to power, despite the Aragonese preference for his brother. He summarily laid siege to Giovanni's castle and held him prisoner for the rest of his life. Disillusioned at the greed of the new colonial rulers, the *giudice* Mariano IV declared: "The Sardinians were expecting a new king, but now found themselves faced with a new tyrant in each village." In an attempt to

After Mariano died of the plague he was initially succeeded not by Eleonora but by her sickly but strong-minded brother, Hugo III. He ruled harshly and strictly, imposing a high tax burden and rigid military conscription, for he was obsessed with the aim of freeing his country from the hated Aragonese. He, the little ruler of Arborea, swore to wage "perpetual war" against the Spanish, challenging alone the expanding Aragonese-Catalan empire. He described himself as the "*signore de'Sardigna*", declaring that he intended to transform his state into one where rich and poor would enjoy the same rights. His approach, however, was too dictatorial; his exaggerated sense of justice made him unpopular with many people. On 6 March 1383 he and his daughter were assassinated during an uprising in Oristano. Three days later his brother-in-law, Brancaleone Doria, appeared at the court of the King of Aragon in Saragossa and proposed that his son Frederick should succeed Hugo, with his wife Eleonora as Regent.

## Judicious ruler

By means of a judicious mixture of concessions and tax relief, Eleonora brought the country

### ELEONORA D'ARBOREA

Eleonora d'Arborea (1340–1404) is remembered for the enlightened *Carta de Logu*, which called for equal legal status and rights for all Sardinians.

Spanish, who spread both Catalan and Castilian, and during the rule of the Kings of Savoy, who introduced Italian as the official language.

The *Giudicessa* Eleonora died in 1404, followed by her son in 1407. It was rumoured that the latter was murdered on the orders of his megalomaniac father; Brancaleone Doria himself was to die in prison soon afterwards. Margrave William III of Narbonne took over the post of ruler in the *giudicato* of Arborea. He was a distant cousin of Eleonora who found himself having

under control within a few months. Her popularity increased when, in 1392, she published the *Carta de Logu*, a written constitution of common law on which her predecessors and their legal advisors had worked for half a century, and which was to remain in operation until the beginning of the 19th century. The glorification of this legal code, which basically contained no innovations, was due to the fact that it was written in the Sardinian language. It thus became one of the cornerstones of Sardinian national consciousness, both under the

**LEFT:** a Spanish fort (no longer standing) in Sassari.
**ABOVE:** the Piazza Eleonora d'Arborea in Oristano.

to face Aragon in battle shortly after arriving on the island. He and an army of 20,000 men confronted a much smaller force under the leadership of the King of Sicily, Martin of Aragon.

Despite their patriotic goodwill, the Sardinian soldiers under William III were no match for the better strategy and more modern weapons of the enemy. William conceded defeat and fled from Sardinia. King Martin died shortly afterwards, a victim of the malaria which was to plague the island into the 20th century. Legend, however, had it that he succumbed to the "Beauty of Sanluri", who had demanded of the Spanish ruler excessive feats of love. William III thereupon returned to Sardinia, leaving the island for the last time in 1417 and abdicating his rights in return for adequate compensation some three years later. One hundred years after their first military invasion, the Kingdom of Aragon finally had the entire island under its control. For the Sardinians, however, this offered no prospect of a rosy, peaceful future.

Sardinia was ravaged by devastating epidemics of plague in 1404, 1477, 1529, 1582, 1652 and 1655. Failed harvests and famine claimed thousands of victims, so that in the middle of the 16th century Parliament lamented that the country was suffering from *estrema pobreza*, "utter poverty". The misery was compounded

by the frequent uprisings which flared up across the land. The most violent was led by Leonardo Alagon, the Margrave of Arborea, who in 1478 suffered a crushing defeat on the plains near Macomer at the hands of an overwhelming joint army of Spanish and Sicilian troops.

## Immigration

This meant that the population declined drastically; at the beginning of the 14th century, at the time of the Aragon conquest, there were 340,000 inhabitants; by 1483 this figure was reduced to 150,000 – representing only six inhabitants per square kilometre. In order to provide partial compensation for this decline

and at the same time to increase the Spanish element on the island, settlers from the Iberian peninsula were transported to Sardinia. During the 14th century the town of Alghero was resettled with Catalan immigrants loyal to the throne, after the native population had been driven away in retaliation for an attempted coup against the Aragon rulers. (Even today, Catalan is spoken, written and sung by folk groups in this lively port.)

Jewish immigrants had also reached Sardinia at about the same time as the Catalan settlers. They established themselves in Alghero and Cagliari as money-changers and traders and controlled the island's important trade links with Marseilles and Sicily. They also had a reputation as doctors; in the middle of the 15th century, a certain Ibrahim produced a scientific treatise on herbal remedies and the island's climate.

However, in spite of their contribution to the otherwise stagnant local cultural life the Jews were driven out towards the end of the 15th century. The few who preferred conversion to Christianity in order to remain were forced to face the Spanish Inquisition, which arrived at this time. Suspect people were expropriated and sentenced to large fines – if they escaped being burned at the stake like Sigismondo Arquer.

Arquer was born on Sardinia in 1525, and studied law in Pisa and theology in Siena. During his travels across Europe he met Sebastian Münster in Basle. The latter, a Franciscan monk and geographer converted to Protestantism, was in the process of compiling his six-volume *Cosmographia Universalis*. Arquer himself wrote a *Compendio de las Historias de la Tenebrosa Serdenya*, a "Brief History of the Bleak Island of Sardinia", which was included in the second volume of Münster's world history. In correspondence with Protestants from the circle surrounding Erasmus of Rotterdam, Arquer not only supported Luther's theories, but also voiced energetic criticism of the deplorable behaviour of the Sardinian clergy – reason enough for the Church to have him tortured and condemned to death. In June 1571 he was burned at the stake in Toledo.

This case is just one example of the lamentable activities of the Spanish Inquisition. Events of the time help to explain how a clerical institution came to enjoy such enormous political influence. In 1469, with the marriage of King Ferdinand of Aragon and Isabella of

Castile, the linking of the two crowns created a unified Spanish kingdom. In order to be able to deal "appropriately" with the large numbers of Arabs and Jews in their land, the two monarchs – who were highly praised for their Christian virtues – asked the Pope to reintroduce the Inquisition, requesting the right to appoint the Inquisitors themselves.

The long arm of the Inquisition reached as far as Sardinia. Here, however, influential people were able to avoid its grasp thanks to their powerful protectors; those who landed in its net were mostly small fry – blasphemers, bigamists and women accused of witchcraft.

Sardinia slipped still further into oblivion. Nor could the Sardinians expect a greater share of the attention of Charles V, the grandson of Ferdinand and Isabella of Spain on his mother's side and heir of the Habsburg Emperor Maximilian and Duchess Mary of Burgundy on his father's; he had inherited a difficult legacy with far-reaching consequences. Furthermore, he was fully occupied by his wars against King François I of France, his struggles against Luther and problems caused by the spread of the Reformation; he had no time to devote himself to his Mediterranean island. Sardinia was no more than a pebble on the beach of his world

## Forgotten island

The Spanish crown exploited the Sardinian population wherever it could, without undertaking any measures which might have led to an improvement in the standard of living on the island. Ferdinand and Isabella now ruled over an expanded united kingdom. In 1492, following the discovery of America, their interest was diverted from the Mediterranean towards the more promising territories in the New World, and the mountainous, uneconomic island of

**LEFT:** the Easter procession in Alghero.
**ABOVE:** the climax of the procession is the taking down of the cross.

empire; since 1535 it had even lost its significance as a supplier of silver, for Hernando Cortez had discovered far more profitable deposits in Mexico.

Nonetheless, Charles V relieved the Sardinian populace of the humiliation of not being masters in their own country. They had been allowed to enter Alghero, a Catalan settlement, only by daylight on their way to work. This restriction also applied to Castello, the fortified quarter of Cagliari, which all Sardinians had to leave by sunset. And anyone disobeying the cry *foras los Sards* – "Sardinians out!" – would be thrown unceremoniously over the castle wall. This prohibition – an example of the presumptuous arrogance of the foreign rulers – was lifted in 1535, when Charles V paid Sardinia one of his very occasional visits.

The monarch was, in fact, only passing through, for he was accompanying Andrea Doria, the Genoese mercenary leader. The latter set sail for Tunis with a 30,000-man army, eliminating Khair-El-Din, the notorious pirate Redbeard, plundering his fleet and freeing 20,000 Christian slaves. Six years later, Charles V and Andrea Doria set sail from the Sardinian port of Alghero once more on a joint expedition against the buccaneers of Algiers – this time without success. During his brief stay in troops, they supplied the Sardinians with weapons. Since the latter were required to pay for the arquebuses and lances they received, the cost to the Spanish crown of the defence of their dominions on Sardinia was actually nil. Philip II, who had succeeded Charles V, imposed a high export duty on Sardinian cattle farmers in order to raise funds to cover the costs of repairs and munition supplies for Cagliari and Alghero, the two key towns in the Sardinian defence – thereby ensuring once again that no expenditure was involved.

The royal financial advisors found an equally neat solution in the case of the coastal

Alghero, the Spanish-Habsburg emperor described the local inhabitants as *todos caballeros* – "all gentlemen" – in a speech thanking the citizens for, as was the common practice of the day, supplying food for the mercenary forces while their ships lay in the bay.

In the turbulent years of the 16th century, when attacks by pirates goaded on by the Turks were an everyday occurrence, Sardinia's totally inadequate system of defences lay in the hands of 86 men, who stood watch over the island from hilltops near the coast. Since the maintenance of a Spanish defence regiment would have been too expensive, the colonial rulers devised another method: instead of sending watchtowers, which Philip had constructed towards the end of the 16th century. A survey indicated that to provide real protection against enemy attack, Sardinia would have needed 132 "Saracen towers", standing at roughly 15-km (9-mile) intervals along the coast.

In fact, only 66 were built – in other words, just half the number required. The towers were financed by the barons or the town councils on whose property they stood.

A very detailed map of Sardinia entitled *Description de la Isla y Reyno de Sardena*, printed during the 17th century under Philip II and currently in the Bibliothèque Nationale in Paris, shows illustrations of these coastal towers. The map also depicts the coat of arms of the Kingdom of Sardinia: a shield with a red cross and four Moors' heads bearing a headband as a sign of their royal status (they may represent four dark skinned Moors defeated in different battles in the 11th century). Across the centuries, the band slipped down, representing their complete defeat. Since the 19th century the Moors' heads with the blindfolded eyes have remained symbols of the Sardinian claim to the self-determination denied them for so long.

### KNIGHTS OF THE STAR

The Sartiglia festival of Oristano is clearly of Spanish origin. Cervantes describes a *Sortija* of this kind in his novel, *Don Quixote.*

Baroque, which celebrated the triumph of the Counter-Reformation. But they banned the Italian Renaissance, through which man had discovered a new self-awareness.

## Social changes

In order to keep close tabs on the better-educated classes, in the middle of the 16th century the Jesuits – known for their devotion to the Spanish king's cause – were sent to the island. They founded two colleges – one in Cagliari and the other in Sassari; both attracted large numbers of students and were

During the 400 years of Spanish colonial rule, the Sardinians were systematically deprived of their rights. Even in the cultural sphere strict censorship was imposed. Only the Spanish crown, the Spanish viceroys and the Parliament of the island, to which no Sardinian belonged, were allowed to determine which aspects of art and culture could be imported, and which not. They permitted the Catalan Gothic style, which extended the art of the Middle Ages into the 16th century and the Spanish

**LEFT:** during the Sartiglia of Oristano, a metal star has to be picked up at full gallop.
**ABOVE:** a rider in the Sartiglia.

promoted to the status of universities early in the 17th century. To prevent their being corrupted by alien philosophies, Sardinians were banned from studying at foreign universities outside the Spanish empire. The Jesuits were also responsible for another far-reaching measure. They imposed the use of Castilian (i.e. Spanish) as the official language, thus bringing some order to the Babel of languages under which the island laboured. The medieval Carta de Logu was written in Sardinian, and until this time announcements in the main towns were made in Spanish, while the clergy conversed in Latin. In Cagliari and Alghero the upper classes spoke Catalan while the common people spoke Sardinian, and in Sassari the Catalan, Castilian, Italian, Corsican and Sardinian languages co-existed.

The country people spoke exclusively Sardinian, for the descendants of the early settlers had been unwilling to abandon their traditional tongue. In these times, in which they had been robbed of almost all they possessed, it represented their only wealth. The nomadic shepherds were impoverished and neglected; the peasants were equally poor, for they were exploited by everyone. The towns demanded their grain at cut-throat prices, the Church demanded its tithes, the nobles and merchants

would only lend them money at exorbitant rates of interest, and the Spanish monarchy commandeered soldiers, horses, grain and vegetables.

In the presumptuous arrogance and blatant injustice which characterised the attitude of the upper classes to the common people were sowed the seeds of Sardinian banditry. Totally lacking protection, but exposed to interference and corruption in every sphere of life, the poor had no option but to fall back on their own resources. They resorted to self-defence without recourse to – or sometimes directly against – the forces of law and order, since the latter were either unable or unwilling to fulfil their duties. The alarming increase in robberies and cattle

thefts first became a cause for serious concern to the authorities at the beginning of the 17th century. A particular problem was posed between 1610 and 1612 by the 20-strong band of robbers under Manuzio Flore from Bono. He incited the populace to refuse to pay its taxes, and, like a Sardinian counterpart to Robin Hood, directed his attacks especially against all officials who were "poor when they assumed office and rich when they retired".

During the 17th century, Spain went through a period of crisis: many of its colonies rebelled against the crown or declared independence, while the Thirty Years' War brought additional turmoil and losses. Once again, the rulers had more pressing problems than to tackle the plight of the exploited people of Sardinia.

Towards the end of the century, the attention of the major powers in Europe was directed towards the Iberian monarchy. Charles II, the last Spanish Habsburg king, had no male heir. And then, in a final desperate attempt to ignore the inevitability of death, the Spanish viceroy suddenly decided to try to revive his country's ailing Sardinian policy. Whilst, on the mainland, the prelude to the power struggles which would accompany the War of Spanish Succession began to make itself felt, on Sardinia a move was afoot to "repeal the old laws", to "encourage trade as the only true source of prosperity" and to "create a positive climate for agriculture in this patently fertile land", in order to "export its produce throughout Europe". Unfortunately time had run out for the Spanish rulers of Sardinia to translate their new theories into reality.

## New owners

In 1708 the Spanish were forced to surrender to the English and the Austrians on Sardinia. Finally, in 1714, the Treaty of Rastadt ceded the island to Austria. In 1717 Giulio Alberoni, an Italian gardener's son and militant cleric who had risen to the rank of Minister of State under the Spanish, succeeded in winning back Sardinia for Spain, now ruled by the Bourbon dynasty. But then, in 1718, as part of the Treaty of London, Sardinia was passed from the Austrians to the Dukes of Savoy in exchange for the more useful island of Sicily. ❑

**LEFT:** a portrait of Philip V of Spain (1683–1746).
**RIGHT:** detail from the *retablo* of Castelsardo.

# SARDINIA UNDER THE HOUSE OF SAVOY

*The rulers of Savoy placed great stress on reconstruction and reform,
yet the islanders ended up discontented and frustrated*

During their 1,000-year history, the rulers of Savoy had managed no more than to extend their domains in the Isère Valley of France across the Alps into the Piedmont, and to acquire for themselves the title of duke. The signing of the Treaty of London in 1718 ceded Sardinia to them, immediately doubling the area of land under their control and granting them the right to be called kings.

Sardinia, however, was not a country to which they had aspired (they tried repeatedly to exchange it for territory on the mainland). They could arouse neither interest nor understanding for the island; nor could they make themselves understood there. The natives spoke Sardinian and the educated classes Castilian and Catalan; the rulers of Savoy-Piedmont, however, spoke French. The regular reports sent from Sardinia to the capital, Turin, by the Baron de Saint-Rémy – the first Viceroy of the Piedmont – did not sound encouraging: "The nobles are poor, the country itself miserable and depopulated, its citizens idle and without any sort of trade – and the air is most unhealthy." Further on, he claimed: "The vices to which these people are most inclined are theft, murder and cheating." Nor do the 400 years of Spanish indifference seem to have been good for the clergy: the priests showed so little respect in their personal appearance "that they wear a peasant's cap and greatcoat in public, even at church during celebration of the Mass".

## Mismatch

These reports echo the consternation and helplessness of the Piedmontese in the face of the unfavourable situation. At the same time, they indicate their determination to search for a solution. However, in one of the clauses of the

Treaty of London the rulers of Savoy had had to agree to leave everything on Sardinia as it was: all laws, decrees, rights and privileges pertaining to the feudal lords were to remain. Furthermore, quite apart from this promise, during the

first years of their rule the Piedmontese wanted to avoid interfering in local matters on Sardinia, lest they should provoke the already suspicious populace. Instead they observed, registered and detailed weekly reports to Turin. Their aim was honourable: to get to know this new, unknown European country and to assist it towards more order and discipline by means of administrative reform. And so they measured reality, and the Sardinian mentality, against Piedmontese standards, and tried to make the Sardinians fit into a Piedmontese mould.

This lack of comprehension of the Sardinian psyche was a fundamental mistake, and one of which the order-loving Piedmontese were fre-

**LEFT:** Alberto La Marmora, who gave his name to the highest mountain on the island.
**RIGHT:** Piedmontese King Charles Emmanuel III founded the town of Carloforte on the island of San Pietro.

quently guilty during their 130-year regency. They simply could not understand that it was impossible to reconcile two such totally different worlds; that a Sardinian shepherd and a Piedmontese city-dweller could never be reduced to a common denominator.

## Bandit problems

Apart from their concern at the poverty and the desolate economic and cultural state of the island, the Piedmontese were troubled at the internal unrest and the increasing lawlessness. In some regions the bandits had formed regular armies. Particular notoriety was achieved by

one feud involving families and gangs, which raged in the village of Nulvi in northern Sardinia during the 1730s. One side was led by a woman of about 40 called Lucia Delitala, who "had a moustache like a grenadier's and who had not married because she claimed that she did not want to be dependent on a man".

Problems of this nature were described by the Piedmontese viceroys in their reports. The quotation is taken from one produced by Signore de Rivarolo, who served as Viceroy of Sardinia between 1735 and 1738. The fact that his previous post was as governor of the Savoy prisons may help to explain his uncompromising severity in the bandit question, which he

systematically tried to eradicate with military expeditions, accelerated trials and harsh punishments. In Oristano he left the corpses hanging on the gallows until they were consumed by flies. During the three years he was in office he had 432 people executed and more than 3,000 condemned to severe punishments. But his deterrents brought few results; the bandits fled to Corsica or into the impenetrable mountains of the island, returning to their native villages when things were quiet. The Piedmontese justified their lack of success with their attempt to bring Sardinia under control: the nomadic shepherds and the inaccessible mountainous terrain were the obstacles which doomed their project to failure.

The shepherds – who comprised more than half the entire population at the time – were portrayed as potential criminals. Decrees were issued restricting their freedom of movement: "All shepherds must erect their huts in easily accessible places, where they may easily be found." Some of the other official regulations were absurd: subjects were forbidden to wear a beard which was more than one month old, for a long beard of the type favoured by bandits and other outlaws altered the facial characteristics and made them unrecognisable. That a decree should limit the period of mourning, traditionally lengthy on the island, was seen as an insulting infringement of an ancient and revered custom. And there was another problem: as judges employed on Sardinia confirmed, the bandits were able to pay for the clemency of the local dignitaries, who tolerated or even encouraged this state of affairs.

In order to master the situation, the Piedmontese had an idea which rapidly became an obsession: they wanted to transform the nomadic shepherds – whom they saw as the root of all evil – into settled (and therefore more easily controllable) peasants, and replace them by Piedmontese peasants. A first step in this direction was the colonisation of extensive, sparsely populated regions of northern Sardinia by Piedmontese peasants. What awaited the farming families from the mainland was not the fertile paradise they had been promised by the officials in Turin, but a sun-baked, malaria-infested land in which they, as immigrants, were completely ostracised by the native populace. They eventually gave up and returned disillusioned to their homes in Piedmont.

The Piedmontese regents had more success in 1736 with the settlement of fishing families of Ligurian origin on the island of San Pietro, and 30 years later on the island of Sant' Antioco. The settlers were the descendants of Ligurians from the Riviera village of Pegli, who had been kidnapped by pirates in the 16th century and taken to the coral-fishing town of Tabarka on the northern coast of Tunisia. They continued to ply their trade here in their new homeland and transformed the towns of Carloforte and Calasetta into flourishing fishing ports. Thus, for the first time, a scheme introduced by the Piedmontese government

tive account of the true situation on the island, was the first member of the Piedmontese government to recognise that Sardinia's problems were not so much due to the character of its inhabitants, but rather to the neglectful treatment the island had received at the hands of its former rulers, whose only interest had been in securing their own advantage. And so he began to introduce a reform programme: he improved the administration of justice, but attempted primarily to encourage agriculture by the distribution of seed and loans for farmers.

Some progress was made thanks to Giuseppe Cossu, who travelled tirelessly throughout the

actually produced concrete results which were financially viable.

The reformist attitude which the rulers of Savoy had long cultivated in their mainland territories spread to Sardinia as well at the mid-18th century. Count Giovanni Battista Bogino, who was appointed Minister of State of the Piedmont in 1759, was known for his open-mindedness; as his advisor in Sardinian affairs he chose Giuseppe Cossu, a lawyer and a native of Cagliari. Count Bogino, receiving an objec-

**LEFT:** an 18th-century engraving of the Torre dell' Elefante in Cagliari.
**ABOVE:** Cagliari silhouetted against the morning sky.

island, pleading eloquently for modernisation of the hopelessly antiquated agricultural practices still employed. Not all reforms met with success: attempts to grow rice and tea failed because of the unsuitable climate, and the introduction of cotton and mulberry bushes for silkworm breeding were both abandoned due to violent opposition from the shepherds, who feared for the survival of their pastureland.

But generally the attitude of the Piedmontese continued unchanged, characterised by an inability or refusal to grasp the situation. In April 1780, only a few years later – after one of the failed harvests which were a regular occurrence on Sardinia – the starving peasants in Sassari rioted, plundering the granaries and storming the town hall. The revolt was quelled the very next day, however, not by force of arms, but by holding up a portrait of the King: a picture of the monarch and his ancestors was carried through the protesting mob, whereupon the latter reverently doffed their hats and fell down on their knees, calling out *Viva il re!* (Long live the King!).

During the last years of the 18th century the riots increased in frequency, and the prestige of the monarchy was no longer

### HIGH TIMES

Despite the stringency of the times, the extravagance of the household of Charles Emmanuel III led a senior Sardinian official to note that "everyone was better off when the Viceroy ruled the island".

his only place of sanctuary. To gain favour with the nobility and clergy, he and his successor, Victor Emmanuel I, bestowed honorary titles and decorations on all comers.

The ideas and aims of the French Revolution had only found resonance among the educated élite. Clubs with Jacobin tendencies sprang up, and the first French constitution was even printed and distributed in Sardinian. And so the French troops who invaded the island from the south-west in 1793 believed that they had

sufficient to calm the masses. This period of unrest coincided with the French Revolution, but the two phenomena are not strictly comparable. In Paris the revolt was against the monarchy, whilst on Sardinia the cause of the uprising was the presumptuousness of the feudal lords. Although they had never seen him in the flesh, the Sardinians remained loyal to a man to their sovereign in faraway Turin.

### Sanctuary

The island populace finally had the chance to see their king and his retinue in 1799, when Charles Emmanuel IV, driven from Turin by the French, realised his despised dominion was

discovered a "revolutionary" land. They met with no resistance at all in Carloforte, on the island of San Pietro. They were able to erect their Tree of Freedom, re-christening the island "Freedom Isle" and establishing a republic which, however, was to prove short-lived. In some other districts of the island the French military campaign was to end in failure, however: for example, on the island of La Maddalena, where a promising young artillery captain by the name of Napoleon Bonaparte took part in the fighting.

The victory over the French army was solely due to the prompt intervention of a 4,000-man Sardinian regiment, called together overnight by the nobility and clergy, who feared that they would lose their privileges under French rule. The Sardinians were of the opinion that their courageous defence of their native land was worthy of a reward, and they accordingly requested the king in Turin to appoint Sardinian natives to all public positions, and to grant them the right of direct involvement in all governmental affairs on the island. Their wishes and demands, however, were categorically denied. The Sardinians gave vent to their rage and disappointment at this ungrateful response: on 7 May 1794, 541 Piedmontese officials were arrested and shipped back to the mainland.

Now, for the first time in 500 years, Sardinia was under Sardinian rule – but without breaking trust with the king. The royal standard still fluttered from all public buildings, and protestations of loyalty to the monarchy could be heard from all quarters. The revolution was directed against the hated feudal regime. The most energetic representative of the new Sardinian national consciousness, and the one who enjoyed the highest esteem, was the *giudice* Giovanni Maria Angioy. At the head of an army of peasants he marched in triumph across the island, finding widespread support for his appeasement policy.

In May 1796, however, the Piedmontese signed a peace treaty with France. Since their possessions on the island were no longer under threat, they did not need the support of the Sardinians. Angioy and his followers were proclaimed rebels. Accompanied by a small entourage, he set sail from Porto Torres and fled via Corsica to France. He died in exile in Paris in 1808, impoverished and forgotten.

In spite of considerable efforts, the Piedmontese had still not succeeded in giving the necessary impetus to Sardinian agriculture. All their attempts in this direction failed due to a peculiarity of the land use system in operation: there was no private ownership. For centuries the village communities had decided the distribution and right of use of land under their jurisdiction in accordance with the *Carta de Logu*. One year a field would be available to the peasants for agricultural purposes, and the next to the shepherds as pasture. But the latent

hostility between the peasants and the nomadic shepherds could not be checked. And so, with their "Olive Tree Enactment" of 1806, the rulers of the Piedmont took a first cautious step along the road towards the privatisation of common land. A peasant who planted olive trees was granted the right to enclose his land; planting more than 4,000 trees gained him a title.

## Property problems

The measure of success enjoyed by this edict – which was no doubt more attributable to the incentive of the title than to any sudden change in the traditionally conservative attitude of the

Sardinian mentality – encouraged the Piedmontese, in 1829, to introduce an Enclosures Act, which turned out to have a sting in its tail. The *Editto delle Chiudende* was intended to put an end to the perpetual conflict between peasants and shepherds by providing a clear distinction between agricultural land and pasture, eliminating the traditional system of crop rotation and increasing yields by a more intensive use of the land. In addition, it was hoped that Sardinians would become accustomed to the concept of private property.

Within a very short period of the passing of the new act, however, the land was criss-crossed by the maze of dry-stone walls which

---

**LEFT:** ceremony in Turin celebrating national liberation.
**RIGHT:** the first great statesman of the new Italian state, Camillo Cavour.

are still a characteristic of the Sardinian countryside. And once again it was the wealthy who gained the upper hand: with more labour at their disposal and more skill at cutting a path through the bureaucratic jungle, they were able to lay claim to larger areas of land. A peasant who had erected a fence round his fields with unseemly haste subsequently had to lease it from the new proprietors at inflated prices.

With this well-intentioned decree, which once again failed to take into account Sardinian traditions and customs, the Turin government succeeded in making the rich even richer and the poor even poorer. Once again riots broke

out: whilst the women demonstrated in front of the municipal offices, the men were out in the countryside destroying the enclosures.

In the first instance the Piedmontese were ruthless in quashing the unrest; in 1833, however, they were forced to repeal the edict, forbidding the rebuilding of the walls which had been destroyed for the time being. Six years were to pass before the enclosure of land was permitted again, as part of the large-scale reorganisation of property laws and the preparation of a land register following the abolition of the feudal system. Sardinia thus took an important and irreversible step forward into the modern world. But the traditional equilibrium within

the island's society had been destroyed forever.

The gangs of bandits who came to the fore again represented true egalitarian ideals: during a visit by the archbishop of Sassari, the inhabitants of Orgosolo called upon divine justice and justified their cattle thefts by claiming that they led to a more equitable distribution of property: "How can it be that God in his mercy, who is master over all living creatures, is prepared to observe how the shepherds in Gallura own 500, 800 or even 1,000 sheep, whereas we have only a tiny flock of 100 sheep?" Whereupon the archbishop commented: "The people here could lecture at the universities of Europe on the subject of communism!" The attitude of the Piedmontese regents to the increase in lawless banditry can be seen from the fact that in 1838 they granted Nuoro a municipal charter so that they could use it as a base from which to lead the fight against the bandits, who were becoming increasingly concentrated in the Barbagia.

## "Fusion with the motherland"

The economic situation on the island was so catastrophic that the islanders could see only one way out of the dilemma: the incorporation of Sardinia into Piedmont, in order to guarantee the same treatment as the much wealthier mainland state. And so, in November 1847, a delegation of Sardinia's leading citizens made the journey to Turin, where they requested the island's "perfect fusion with the Motherland". Unification with Piedmont was proclaimed on 30 November.

Instead of the hoped-for improvements, the Sardinians found themselves faced with still more disadvantages: nomadic sheep farming was banned, entire forests were felled, and the mines were exploited by foreign companies. It became increasingly difficult for the Sardinians to identify with the newly created nation state. In 1848 the Sardinian theologian, Frederico Fenu, explained the problem in graphic terms: "The attempt to transfer mainland laws and regulations to Sardinia, which is fundamentally totally different, can be compared to an attempt to make adult clothes fit a child or to dress a man in a woman's skirt." ❑

**LEFT:** memorial tablet dedicated to Carlo Felice by Emmanuel I.
**RIGHT:** the face of traditional Sardinia.

# THE RISORGIMENTO

*The Kingdom of Sardinia ended with unification in 1861, bringing a degree of much-needed prosperity to the island*

Sardinia was now attached to the Piedmont, thus becoming part of the embryonic state of Italy. At this time the latter was being formed by a Piedmontese politician, Count Camillo Cavour (1810–61), fought for by the leader of a volunteer army, Giuseppe Garibaldi (1807–82), and ruled over by the House of Savoy. In 1848, however, when the deputies assembled in the Baroque Palazzo Carignano in Turin, there was no sign of the Sardinian coat of arms among the emblems of the Kingdom's other provinces.

Furthermore, Giovanni Siotto Pintor – the Sardinian senator who had been one of the most eloquent supporters of the "perfect fusion" between Sardinia and the Piedmont – was prevented from entering the Parliament building by a guard in gala uniform. He had arrived dressed – as was his wont on his native island – in a coarse woollen cloak and the *berretta*, the characteristic Sardinian headgear. Such was the contrast with the elegant tailored suits of his fellow deputies from the Piedmont, Liguria and Savoy, that he was assumed to be a peasant, a stranger with no right of access to the hallowed parliamentary sanctum.

These episodes are not as trivial as they might seem, for they were typical of the permanent condescension of the Piedmontese to the island which, 130 years previously, had entitled the Dukes of Savoy to the monarch's crown. And hardly anyone bore in mind the trusting enthusiasm with which Sardinia had surrendered its ancient right of autonomy upon unification with the Piedmont in 1848. The islanders had high hopes that the Italian Risorgimento would pave the way for a second resurgence in their own neglected homeland.

## A sorry state

Conditions on Sardinia were deplorable – a fact recognised by the entrepreneurs from the mainland who began to invest capital in the island.

**LEFT:** Garibaldi on Caprera.
**RIGHT:** monument to Victor Emmanuel I in Sassari.

Count Carlo Baudi di Vesme, a Piedmontese nobleman, displayed a profound sympathy for Sardinia; he revived the mining industry in Iglesias and attempted to establish model farms. "Sardinia is in a pitiful state," he wrote in 1848. "The fields lie fallow, the countryside abandoned, the cattle stocks largely destroyed.

Poverty and famine are rife in most villages." Despite the exorbitant taxes levied, communities received nothing in return. For this reason, explained Baudi di Vesme in his study, "the inhabitants are often forced to live on an unhealthy diet of herbs which they have gathered in the countryside... Theft is a frequent occurrence, not because the people are wicked by nature, but because they are hungry."

In addition, there was enmity between the north and south of the island, especially between Sassari and Cagliari. The Piedmontese, expelled from Cagliari by the local citizens in 1794, would have been pleased to transfer the capital to Sassari, where most inhabitants were immigrants from the mainland and therefore more favourably disposed towards them. "The residents of the northern half of the island regard the south as less civilised," observed Alfonso La Marmora in 1838, in his *Voyage en Sardaigne*, for which he had also prepared a map of the island, "and sometimes they refer to them as 'Sards', which the southerners take as an insult, although it is actually the name of the islanders as a whole.

"The residents of the southern part of the island, on the other hand, although prepared to recognise the superiority of their northern compatriots in certain spheres of agriculture and

which was also expressed in their native language. "Sardinia will become Piedmont, will become Italy," continued Baudi di Vesme. The powerful rhetoric of this assertion becomes comprehensible and forgivable in the light of the climate of over-enthusiastic exuberance which must have reigned in the middle of the 19th century during the creation of the Italian national state.

## Garibaldi speaks up

But Sardinia was not to become Piedmont and Italy as quickly as that – a fact which the Sardinians themselves were not slow to recognise.

trade, nevertheless consider them to be cruel and bloodthirsty."

Carlo Baudi di Vesme therefore proposed a solution: in administrative and religious affairs (except, incidentally, in sermons), the use of the Sardinian dialect should be banned and the use of Italian obligatory. "Unity of language would lead to a closer unity of spirit... thus overcoming the deep-rooted differences between the inhabitants of the various regions."

In other words: since no one really knew what to do with the island as it was at the time, the plan was to destroy its national identity – an identity to which the Sardinians had clung despite enduring centuries of foreign rule, and

Their innate mistrust of the Piedmontese was transformed in 1860 into outright suspicion and ill-feeling. A rumour began to circulate upon the island that the Piedmont was hatching plans to cede Sardinia to France.

Count Camillo Cavour, accused of secret negotiations in this respect, was energetic in his denials. He failed, however, to convince his gathering band of critics, so that eventually, after months of speculation, Giuseppe Garibaldi intervened.

Following guerrilla wars in South America, the successful defence of Rome against the French in 1848 and the death of his lifelong companion Anita, this "hero of two worlds" had settled on the little island of Caprera, off the north-eastern coast of Sardinia. The war hero had become an enthusiastic farmer. "Sardinia is the most important and strategically most significant place in the Mediterranean," he wrote in response and he expressed the conviction that as a "gentleman", Victor Emmanuel would neither agree to the cession of any more territories, nor to the division "of this Italy, which we all wish to see united".

Garibaldi remained loyal to Sardinia. Avoiding capture in 1849 after the French finally drove him from Rome, he was detained on La Maddalena by the Piedmontese government.

Caprera in 1855; one year later, he and his companions settled there. Less than four years after this he was back in politics. Although political action exerted an irresistible spell on him, he always missed his island of Caprera and visited it frequently. And it was here that Giuseppe Garibaldi, the tireless fighter for Italian freedom, died at the age of 75. In spite of its worst suspicions, Sardinia remained a part of Piedmont, albeit as a "very uncertain appendix of Italy".

On 17 March 1861 it became part of the new unified Italian state. Victor Emmanuel II proclaimed himself King of Italy, and Sardinia

From here he embarked upon his revolutionary odyssey across almost every continent. Six years later he returned to Caprera, his banishment partially lifted. He was permitted to return to Italy as a private citizen – in fact, as the captain of a small cutter – providing he refrained from political involvement.

Garibaldi's ship enabled him to establish a transport route between his native town, Nice, and Sardinia. By means of an inheritance he was able to purchase parts of the island of

**LEFT:** an historic shoulder to shoulder: Victor Emmanuel and Giuseppe Garibaldi.
**ABOVE:** the popular view of Sardinian bandits.

ceased to be the kingdom in its own right which it had been for the previous 650 years. The newly-formed nation inherited a starving and exhausted island.

## Exploitation

Camillo Cavour, who is regarded as the founding father of modern Italy, had imposed on Sardinia an unprecedented tax burden, demanding high property taxes based on a confused, incorrect and therefore unjust Land Register. He had also allowed foreign speculators to gain possession of the pastureland so essential for the Sardinian economy, and had awarded Genoese, Piedmontese and overseas investors licences for the clearing of the island's forests – an overfelling which has continued today with the development of tourism. The cereals harvested were sold to mainland traders at high prices on the open market, although food supplies on the island grew increasingly scarce.

The cost of living rose rapidly. The starving inhabitants of the towns revolted openly, whilst the impoverished country dwellers demanded a return to the old common law. The shepherds, deprived of their

railway was begun; the line was finished in 1880. But the antiquated methods of production in agriculture and the management of pastureland defied all attempts at progress. Estates were often split up into tiny parcels of land, frequently some distance from each other; additional problems were presented by plagues of locusts, a series of failed harvests, famine and the age-old menace of malaria – which spread with renewed virulence across the land deforested by foreign speculators.

> ### HARD TIMES
>
> The Sardinian population suffered famine, plague and malaria during the 17th century. In the 1650s, a quarter of the population died from plague while a famine in 1680–81 caused the death of 80,000 people.

livelihood by the ban on nomadic sheep rearing, ended up as bandits. The Sardinian senator Giovanni Siotto Pintor, who proudly insisted on wearing the local costume despite frequent exclusion from the parliamentary building in Turin, summarised the situation on his native island after its unification with the Piedmont: "They wanted to suck milk from a withered breast at any price, but what they sucked was blood!"

## Famine and plague

Even so, Italy started to improve conditions on Sardinia. The road network was completed in 1862. Shortly afterwards, work on the first

Once again the Sardinians felt they were being exploited by foreigners – this time by the investors from the mainland or overseas, whose aim was to export from the island a maximum quantity of charcoal, cheese and ore for a minimum financial investment.

One of the few bright spots on the horizon was the establishment of dairies on the island by Neapolitan and Roman businessmen. The *pecorino sardo*, the traditional Sardinian sheep's milk cheese, proved universally popular. Since this led to an increased demand for sheep's milk, there was a revival of nomadic sheep farming, which the Italian government had originally intended to abolish altogether.

## Popular bandits

Once again the island was without just and impartial rulers, so some of the local inhabitants took it upon themselves to assume the reins of power: this was the real reason why banditry escalated.

> ### HANDSOME, WILD, BOLD
>
> The Sardinian poet Sebastiano Satta immortalised the bandit as "belli, feroci, prodi" – "handsome, wild and bold". His thinly disguised sympathy echoed the sentiments of many Sardinians.

There was scarcely a village on the island which escaped the terrorisation. Berrina ruled in Dorgali; Oliena was under the sway of Corbeddu, the King of the Macchia, and Ottana under the viceroy of the Macchia, Salvatore Dettore. In Sarule, Giovanni Moni Goddi and Dionigi Mariani fought for supremacy; in Nuoro, it was necessary to obey the Carta brothers to survive.

The poems of Sebastiano Satta, like the novels of Grazia Deledda (1871–1936), who was to receive the Nobel Prize for Literature in 1926, attracted the attention of Italian intellectuals to the island's culture. Researchers began to study Sardinia's archaic language as well as its folklore, which retained numerous traces of pagan influence. And the new political parties, especially the Socialists, also began to take an interest in the island – not in the shepherds and peasants, who were still wholly wrapped up in the past, but in the miners.

## Militant miners

Sardinia's mines could have brought the island prosperity. Too small a percentage of the profits, however, was reinvested here. The novelist Grazia Deledda saw them as a factor which had a destructive influence on the primitive but harmonious island world. "The horizon spread out, broad and pure," she wrote in *Elias Portulu*, "the fragrant breeze wafted gently across the deep green pastures: an indescribable dream of peace and untamed solitude… And then, suddenly, this noble landscape, desecrated and laid waste by the black entrances and slag heaps of the mines." The miners, well known for their rebellious nature, began to voice demands for better working and living conditions. In 1900 miners went on strike in their hundreds following in the footsteps of the ferry crews of Carloforte – who had lost their jobs upon the introduction of a steamship – and the printers of Sassari. The wave of strikes reached a tragic climax in 1904 in Buggerru, when three men were killed and several more injured during violent clashes between the strikers and the army. But repression didn't change anything.The protest rallies spread from the mines to the towns, and from the towns to the surrounding countryside. The entire working population of Sardinia was in a state of unrest, and a new political awareness was dawning.

During World War I, thousands of Sardinia's inhabitants laid down their lives for their country. The dauntless men of the Brigata Sassari were mentioned in four military dispatches, and more than 13,000 of them died brutal deaths on the battlefield. Disenchantment with the government, which once again failed to keep its promises, embittered the ranks of returning troops.

Within the next few years they united to form the Partito Sardo d'Azione, the Action Party of Sardinia. At long last, after centuries of inaction, Sardinians were once more sufficiently conscious of their national identity to take their fate into their own hands. ❏

**LEFT:** women loading coal from the Iglesiente on to sailing boats.

**RIGHT:** a typical kitchen in a 19th-century farmhouse.

MARZO
APRILE
1914

# MODERN SARDINIA

*The shift from sheep rearing to tourism in the past century has had profound effects on the island's economic structure and population*

The events of World War I were to provide the main impetus for Sardinia to abandon its insular existence and enter the modern world. This transition was marked by success and failure in equal measure.

The number of Sardinians who took part in the war was unusually high. So, too, was the number of casualties. Almost one-eighth of the entire population, approximately 100,000 soldiers, saw active service; 13,602 of these never returned. This represents a casualty rate of roughly 14 percent, compared with a national average of 10.5 percent.

At the same time, these bare statistics indicate that fundamental changes in the Sardinian attitude to life had already taken place. Suddenly the island's residents saw that they could not ignore what was happening in mainland Italy if they were to rise out of the poverty they had so long endured. They realised that Italy and Sardinia shared a common heritage; and that they must also accept joint responsibility for the fate of Italy as a whole.

## Brave men

The four years of warfare in the trenches brought together for the first time officers and soldiers from the various regions of Italy. They were suddenly confronted with the necessity of learning strange new customs as they faced people whose culture and history were quite different from their own. These encounters with non-Sardinians were to leave a more lasting impression on the islanders than any others in their history to date. They fought from first to last for a country which they hoped would not forget their valour after the war was over, and which would help them end the reign of misery on their native shores.

And, indeed, their country had no choice but to tackle the problem of Sardinia and acknowledge its brave soldiers. The legendary Sardinian Brigata Sassari, which included in its ranks nine

**LEFT:** 1914 cover of the magazine *Sardegna*.
**RIGHT:** stamp celebrating the life of Grazia Deledda.

holders of the *medaglia d'oro* (corresponding to the medal "Pour le Mérite"), 450 holders of the silver medal, the *medaglia d'argento*, and 551 holders of the bronze medal for bravery, the *medaglia di bronzo*, was also awarded four gold medals for regimental courage, and was mentioned four times in dispatches.

Historians are agreed that the regiment's almost uncanny success was attributable to two factors: not only to the exemplary bravery of the individual soldiers, but also – and more importantly – to the unique spirit of warm-hearted mutual cooperation between officers and men in the illustrious Brigata. This latter quality is seen primarily as a symbol of the moral virtues of the Sardinians rather than of their military superiority.

This feeling of ethnic unity, underlined by their common cultural heritage, intensified during the postwar years. It was fanned by a renewed interest in culture and the arts as well as by various political groups and movements, especially the Partito Sardo d'Azione, the Sardinian Action Party. The men returning from the war during which they had fought so unquestioningly and uncomplainingly for so long, expected to reap in peacetime their reward for the service they had rendered their country. The encounter with other people who had already profited from economic progress and whose standard of living was much better than their own was bound to make the demobilised Sardinian soldiers ponder their lot and draw comparisons. Very soon they found that even their medals and the memories of their bold deeds could no longer console them for the fact

chance for a sufficiently powerful front to bring about a radical change in the national policy towards the island.

## The Sardinian Action Party

For Antonio Gramsci from Cagliari (1891–1937), the movement was "the first people's country party, above all in central and southern Italy". Although Gramsci was about to turn his back on the socialists in order to found the Italian Communist Party, in 1921 the Sardinian front-line fighters decided at their congress in Oristano to form the Sardinian Action Party, the Partito Sardo d'Azione. The central elements of the party

that their country did not intend to carry out its promises. Above all, the government was not prepared to grant farmers permission to till fallow land.

Many ex-soldiers joined together to form a *Movimento Combattentistico*, a movement of front-line fighters. They held their first congress in May 1919 in Nuoro. A few months later, three members of the party were elected to the Italian Parliament. Many cherished the secret hope that they would finally be allowed to carry the island's economy and society forward into the 20th century. Of course it was not only the members of the *Movimento Combattentistico* who believed that the party represented the only

programme were a varied array of demands directed towards Rome, plus the concept of self-determination for Sardinia.

One of the prime achievements of the Movimento and later of the Partito Sardo d'Azione was their encouragement of an active political awareness in large numbers of young people and peasants who had lost patience with the old liberal democratic order. As the population at large became more politically active, so their representatives put into practice with greater fervour the view acquired in the trenches, that a unified Sardinia was a powerful regional entity. And so, for the first time, Sardinia possessed a strong people's party. Tightly organised, it opened meeting rooms and local groups throughout the island and carried the political arguments from the towns to the remotest corners of the countryside. Even the rural population gathered together to form its own movement, which seemed to be in a position at last to lure the peasants and shepherds out of their traditional exile from political and social life.

Initially among the front-line fighters' movement and the rural people's movement, and subsequently in the Partito Sardo d'Azione, there was a maturing concept of a decentralised, democratic particularism. This soon led to demands for a special statute of autonomy for Sardinia, not only by virtue of its geographic location but also its specific history and culture.

The period between 1919 and 1921 was dominated by a continuous spirit of republicanism. During this time, however, the particularist doctrine flourished in many different forms: there remained a strong monarchist faction, supported above all by intellectuals and lawyers, as well as various anti-working class, anti-Bolshevist and middle-class factions.

## In the wake of Fascism

In 1923 Paolo Pili, the leader of the wing with fascist sympathies, brought about a split in the party when he and fellow-sympathisers left to join the PNF, the Partito Nazionale Fascista, the Fascist Party. That this schism should occur at all was a major setback for General Asclepio Gandolfo, Mussolini's authorised representative. He had been responsible for the island's affairs since 1922 and had been instructed to use his good offices behind the scenes with the aim of promoting unification between autonomists, fascists and militant front-line fighters in both camps.

Since the fusion of the various particularist factions with the Fascist Party had now failed, the changed allegiance of Pili's group aroused widespread interest among the population at large. Pili himself had been appointed Party Secretary of the PNF for Cagliari. Under his leadership was formed Fedlac, the Federazione delle Cooperative Lattiero-Casearie della Sardegna (Sardinian Dairy Co-operative). The

principal aim of this new institution was to protect shepherds' yields from the near-monopoly of a few large concerns.

Fedlac was an unqualified success; between 1925 and 1927 it even achieved a breakthrough with the export of sheep's milk cheese, *pecorino,* to the American market, where it was a huge success. This embryonic contact was to gain in value particularly after World War II, when cooperatives, such as the Consorzio Caseario Regionale (Regional Dairy Consortium) sprang up across the entire island.

Pili was skilful in taking advantage of fascist policies as well as part of the cooperative

programme of the Sardinian Independence Movement in order to further his own cause, until he fell from favour and was expelled from the PNF. Only a short while later, Fedlac, which had been formed on his initiative, fell victim to the world recession, followed one by one by less ambitious initiatives which had sprung up to protect wine and corn production.

The declared political aim, that of "providing a new framework for some aspects of the Partito Sardo d'Azione within the Fascist Party", was never achieved. In the 1924 elections the Sardinian Action Party did less well than the fascist unified list of candidates, but it was still represented – much to the chagrin of the

---

**LEFT:** rural workers at the end of the 19th century.
**RIGHT:** 19th-century photograph of children playing a game of cards.

fascists. Thanks to the influence of Emilio Lussu and Camillo Bellieni, the Sardinian Independence Movement became more popular and more anti-fascist in tone.

After the assassination of the socialist Giacomo Matteotti, Lussu became aware of the dangers of continued isolationism in spite of his reservations towards Marxism. He thus sought increased contact with the communists, whilst Gramsci's socialists desperately attempted to acquire the support not only of factory hands but also of farm labourers, despite their traditional suspicion of industrial workers. Gramsci made no secret of his intention of luring voters

united in a common cause proved short-lived. It was not long before the fascist dictatorship held sway on Sardinia too, despite its clearly ambivalent policy as regards the island. On the one hand, the fascists were anxious to solve Sardinia's prevailing economic and social problems, but at the same time they were also determined to quell at source even the most modest attempts at autonomy.

From 1924 the Fascist Party laid great emphasis on including in their own programme some of the characteristic demands of the Sardinian Independence Movement, e.g. the abolition of unemployment and the increasing

away from the Sardinian Action Party; at the Rural Internationale of the Fifth Sardinian Action Party Congress, he gave an inflammatory speech aimed at producing this split.

## Political extremes

During the 1924 elections, the list with the five-pointed star contained the names of candidates representing widely conflicting interests – progressive liberals and constitutional monarchists and men like Mario Berlinguer, who was able to assert himself against older, more moderate leaders, and who had won a seat whilst he was still a young man. But the hope that all these widely differing approaches might be

of productivity. On 6 November 1924, the Royal Edict No. 1931 was proclaimed. It was later to be known as the *Legge del Miliardo*, the Law of the Milliard: promulgated at the instigation of the fascists, it was designed to remove, or at least to minimise, the most glaring causes of Sardinian unrest.

Indeed, the state of the island at the time was in many respects truly wretched. In 260 of the 364 communities there was no running water; only seven communities had their own sewage system, and 156 communities had no primary school. Statistically speaking, there were not even enough teachers to allow for one per school. In 1925, an investigation of educational standards on the island revealed that more than half the 870,000 natives of Sardinia (58 percent) were illiterate. Of the 120,000 school-age children on the island, only 81,000 were registered at a school; of these, barely 60,000 attended with any degree of regularity.

Considerable efforts were made to overcome the island's chronic water shortage: in 1923 the king officially commissioned the Tirso Dam, in 1926 the Coghinas Dam was put into operation, and construction work began on the present hydraulic station on the Flumendosa. The rate at which these ambitious projects were completed was intended to put in the shade all

founded in 1938. From here coal was exported via the port of Sant'Antioco. The settlement grew rapidly, acting as a magnet for Sardinia's unemployed as well as for workers, peasants and shepherds from all over the island, who left their homes in the hope of finding permanent employment. The development naturally led to the rapid formation of a working class – the first in the country; it was well organised along trade union lines.

Nuoro became the provincial capital in 1926, but failed to develop to meet expectations and requirements. In the interior of the island things remained as they had always been: the inhabi-

irrigation projects on Sardinia, past and future. And indeed, despite the continuously increasing demand for water – a prerequisite for progress of every kind on the island – to date it has proved impossible to equal the record set by the fascists in this respect.

## Mussolini's Sardinian policy

Following Mussolini's declaration of absolute rule, exploitation of the metal and coal mines on the island was intensified, especially in the Sulcis Basin, where the town of Carbonia was

**LEFT:** coal boats on the Iglesiente beach, 19th century.
**ABOVE:** the *matanza* harvested a great many tuna.

### SARDINIAN RENAISSANCE

In 1925, the Inspectorate of Public Works was established to give priority to the Sardinian "renaissance". State undertakings, which had been put into abeyance during the war, were now revived. Progress was made especially in the region around Terralba, where 10,000 hectares (25,000 acres) of land had already been developed by the Società Bonifiche Sarde, and in the vicinity of Sanluri, where 2,000 hectares (5,000 acres) were available for development. In the Nurra, too, the town of Fertilia sprang up in the middle of 2,300 hectares (5,700 acres) of what was then agricultural land. Near Terralbas 4,000 settlers built the town of Mussolinia, known today as Arborea.

tants eked out a meagre existence as labourers and shepherds, while many of the more august leading citizens discovered an unexpected taste for fascism, using their position as head of the district council or as mayor to promote their own interests. Corruption was rife.

The efforts of the fascists to bring about a rapid integration of the island were most successful in places where economic measures were implemented and where their propaganda could reach the people. They failed utterly in the most remote country areas, where the population continued to adhere to traditional work methods and social forms, and where the

suspects lost virtually all their rights, and that they were utterly at the mercy of the whims of the prefect, quaestor, commander of the *carabinieri* or chief of the militia. Even a hint of suspicion was sufficient to put someone behind bars; informers flourished and old feuds were revived – only to be unreported by the heavily censored press. Problems swept aside in one place had a habit of reappearing again somewhere else.

In a speech delivered in Cagliari on 11 June 1923, Mussolini harangued the crowd with the message that he had not come to Sardinia merely to get to know the island. Forty-eight

restless mood of the towns could not arouse support. The fascists attempted to quash all Sardinian attempts at independence by limiting the influence of its most dangerous representatives and by encouraging the islanders to adopt a more centralised culture and way of thought.

### War against bandits

Mussolini's representatives fought with particular determination against the *banditismo*. The public safety regulations of 1931 transformed what was hitherto a compulsory domicile order under the local magistrate into house arrest supervised by the police. This meant that all

hours would hardly be long enough for that, and especially not to get to the bottom of the intractable problems of the inhabitants.

He, Mussolini, was aware of them – as all those who had ruled the island during the past 50 years had also been aware of them. Indeed, the entire nation was aware of the problems, and if no solutions had been found so far, then it was only because until that day they had lacked the iron will of renewal which constituted the heart, the essence and the credo of the fascist government. What Mussolini failed to appreciate was that even men like Cavour had had a clear understanding of Sardinia's problems. In 1849 he had replied to the urgent requests of Sardinian members of Parliament for help for their country: "I do not question that Sardinia's situation could be improved by investing a great deal of money. If the Kingdom were a great power instead of a small state, perhaps I might not blanch at demanding of the cabinet a few millions for the island's development." Even a master-demagogue like Mussolini took cover behind a torrent of words. And yet it would be wrong to maintain that the fascists were unaware of the true situation on Sardinia, or that they had failed to undertake any measures which might have improved the islanders' lot.

In 1935, 40 million lire were made available for major development projects; the money disappeared in Sassari and Cagliari. In spite of an apparent lack of interest, Nuoro managed to achieve a modest degree of prosperity and some progress during this period, whilst fascist policies were working towards independent free enterprise, especially in the agricultural sector. A few contemporary statistics will serve to prove the point.

## The economy of the 1930s

The farmers' greatest wealth lay in their live-stock, including 608,000 sheep and 160,000 goats. They made profitable harvests of barley, wheat, potatoes, oil, almonds and grapes. Of 328,000 Sardinians in full-time employment, at least 200,000 worked in agriculture and sheep farming. A further 62,000 worked in industry. The production of coarse woollen fabrics created a large number of new jobs, especially for women. In the province of Nuoro alone, 734 weaving frames produced a surplus of 100,000 metres (110,000 yds) of fabric, for the weaving factories in Prato and Biella produced cheaper fabric of poorer quality. The population increased only minimally – by 6,000 people – between 1911 and 1921.

There were numerous reasons for this unusually low rate of increase: the large number of war victims, high infant mortality – which in turn was a result of the deplorable sanitary

---

**LEFT:** Mussolini inspects the model of the city of Carbonia.

**RIGHT:** a canteen in an Iglesiente mine.

conditions and malnutrition – and, as always, a depressingly high total of malaria victims (98 deaths compared with a total of 12 for the rest of the country).

The Serpieri Laws of 1924 and 1933 were aimed at the development of all cultivable land on the island, much of which lay fallow or, if it was tilled at all, was frequently divided into uneconomically small parcels. Although pastoral agriculture and free-range cattle farming continued to predominate, in 1930 it was noted

> **RISING POPULATION**
>
> Between 1921 and 1931 the population of Sardinia grew by 1.2 percent, and from 1931 until the census in 1936 by a further 1.26 percent, resulting in a total figure of 1,004,000.

that of a total of 127,000 agricultural concerns, more than 70,000 farmed less than 3 hectares (7 acres) of land.

The fascist land reform was intended to bring about an increase in the population. This did, in fact, occur; a further change was the introduction of new crops, such as the cultivation of rice near Arborea.

In 1936, there were 351,000 Sardinians in full-time employment, of which about 16,000 were employed by transport companies, 78,000 were in industry, 211,000 in agriculture and 46,000 in miscellaneous professions. Italy exhibited a diminished concern for the island's problems for a number of years, but showed a

# Sardinian Banditry

The term *bandito* is derived from the Catalan word *bandejat*, and the Spanish *bandeado*. It is still used to describe someone who flees justice following a crime, taking refuge in the *màcchia* – usually in the company of a band of like-minded individuals. As long ago as Roman times, bandits plagued these regions. The Greek historian Strabo, writing in the 1st century BC, talks of "thwarting gangs of robbers".

For centuries the bandits' existence on Sardinia depended upon the state of tension which pre-

vailed between shepherds and peasants. Their conflicting interests – cultivation of the land on the one side and sheep and cattle grazing on the other – lay at the root of the strife. A further aspect of traditional *banditismo* is the *bardana*, which may be derived from the *gualdana* of Tuscany. It was a vendetta directed either against an entire village, or against a single wealthy landowner who possessed not only cattle stocks but also a fortune in gold – a rarity in those days. The *bardana* prevailed in Sardinia until the beginning of the 20th century, and still occurs from time to time today in the form of cattle stealing or kidnapping. Robbery usually occurred on the open road. Such attacks were commonplace in the middle of the 19th century, but

they have continued to occur sporadically until relatively recently. There were originally two reasons for cattle stealing: need on the part of the thief, or – more commonly – revenge. By taking justice into his own hands, the robber sought personal vengeance for a previous theft. By and large, Sardinian society does not regard the stealing of livestock "amongst us shepherds" as a grave offence.

Nonetheless, these basic rules of Sardinian banditry are not always strictly observed. On occasions, a moderate crime of this nature is followed by an act of far greater violence, with blood being spilt – especially if the thief refuses to offer adequate compensation for his deed. Many blood feuds originated in this kind of escalation of violence. They could last for generations.

Kidnapping is used by bandits as a means of blackmail. The theft of livestock is a relatively straightforward affair, but the abduction of a person requires much more planning and strategic ability on the part of the perpetrator. The victim must be carefully chosen and groundwork must be done. The bandits of Sardinia need the shepherds. They know every stone of the wild countryside, the gorges, caves, forests – the areas where a kidnap victim can be kept for days or months on end without being discovered Kidnappers have few difficulties organising their crimes in the inaccessible regions of the Gennargentu, or in the other hill and mountain areas, since here they are more mobile than the police or the *carabinieri*.

For many years, kidnapping was specifically a Sardinian problem: during a 20-year period following World War II there were over 50 kidnappings on Sardinia – and not a single one took place on mainland Italy. During 1966–68 alone, there were 33 on the island, but none on the mainland. But the year 1970 marked the beginning of a new, very different chapter in Italian banditry. The kidnapping of victims for ransom ceased to be confined to the island, but spread across to the mainland, where the number of cases escalated with startling speed. In the next dozen years alone there were 75 instances of kidnapping in Sardinia, and 1,378 on the mainland.

The 1990s saw a brief resurgence in kidnapping. One of the most notorious cases was of eight-year- old Farouk Kassam, who was kidnapped on the Costa Smeralda in 1992. He was held for seven months on Monte Albo, near Siníscola, where he had his ear cut off by his kidnappers. ❑

**LEFT:** detail from a mural depicting the police crackdown on bandits at Murguliai in 1899.

revived interest during the years leading up to World War II. The island acquired strategic importance, in particular as a military base and as a supplier of raw materials which were to contribute towards the realisation of Mussolini's long-held dreams of an all-powerful Italy.

The fascists were most active in the most densely populated towns. Between 1921 and 1931 the population of Cagliari almost doubled, reaching a total of almost 100,000. During the same period Sassari topped the 50,000 mark, and smaller towns – Olbia, Alghero, Oristano, Tempio, Iglesias and Carbonia – also gained in significance.

## Rural concerns

The interior of the island and the smaller towns were of no particular interest to the fascists; they left things here much as they had always been. After the *Podestà*, as the mayor was called under the fascists, the most powerful man was the Party Secretary. It was his task to supervise official duties in conjunction with the mayor, and to preserve for the principal families a certain number of privileges and a modicum of respect.

The inhabitants of the interior devoted themselves exclusively to their own problems rather than to national politics. Orgosolo was the scene of a bloody feud; between 1925 and 1935 there was further unrest, the causes of which had never really been settled. This was the heyday of the legendary bandits, who were soon translated by folk tales and popular song into resolute, philanthropic heroes. The best-known of these Sardinian Robin Hoods were undoubtedly Samuelo Stocchino from Arzana and the Pintore brothers from Bitti.

During the years leading up to World War II, the Ethiopia Campaign and the Spanish Civil War led large numbers of Sardinians to join the armed forces for the second time. There was a shortage of male labour in all areas of industry; many projects begun by the fascists were never completed, and the lack of men to work on the land made farming even less productive than it had been. Furthermore, a fresh malaria epidemic on Sardinia took a heavy toll of victims. In 1936 only some 24,620 workers were still employed in cattle farming, compared with 42,100 in 1921. A number of the Sardinian working class

**RIGHT:** basket-weaver from the Barbagia *circa* 1900.

was employed not in industry but in agricultural concerns which had sprung up as part of the land reform, or in small or medium-sized dairy farms. Few of them were permanently employed. The interior regions were firmly in the hands of semi-leaseholders, leaseholders and settlers who had been allocated their own plot of land by the fascists.

## Land reforms

The parceling out of cultivable land typical for Sardinia prevented the establishment of the semi-leasehold system in extensive regions. More common was the so-called *comparteci-*

*pazione* (leasehold cooperative). By and large the system had much in common with the tilling of land by paid hands; the *compartecipante* (co-leaseholder) usually brought neither equipment nor capital into the arrangement.

The contracts for leasehold cooperatives mostly ran for only two years. It often happened that a farmer or reaper would work virtually all the farmland in his native community during the course of his working life. Strictly speaking they were no longer sons of the soil, but could farm any of the land belonging to a considerably larger community, that of their rural district. Not only did this leasehold system allow even the poorest Sardinian peasants to make a reasonable living for their families; it also gave the landowners a greater degree of freedom in permitting them to adapt the use of their fields to the constantly changing conditions.

Serious attempts to improve Sardinian agriculture were put into operation following the Mussolini Law of 24 December 1928. More than one-third of the island was affected by the land reform. In all, 181,339 hectare (449,194 acres) of land were placed under irrigation, 725,000 hectares (1,791,000 acres) were subject to the local government reform and 7,867 hectares (19,440 acres) of mountainous territory were developed for the first time. The Land

1931 and 1932. During the final years before the outbreak of World War II, ever-increasing numbers of islanders were caught in the poverty trap or got into debt. More and more people were forced to take out large mortgages on their homes, to put their property up for auction, or even to flee the country completely.

To summarise, it would be correct to say that between the two world wars Sardinia was dominated by the fascists, who succeeded in taking the wind out of the sails of the independence movements which had arisen after World War I, the so-called front-line fighters and the Sardinian Action Party.

Reform Ordinance for the whole of Sardinia dated 13 December 1933 had the ambitious aim of developing 884,615 hectares (2,185,883 acres) of land – in other words, one-quarter of the entire island. But progress was slower than had been hoped, and by 1938 about 10 percent of the target had been developed.

## Before World War II

In general, the fascists used public works as a means of exerting direct control over the poorer classes and the unemployed. Some prefects even instituted forced labour groups for the maintenance of the roads within a community; this was the case, for example, in Cagliari in

Life in the towns followed the middle-class pattern found elsewhere in Italy, supporting fascism and being rewarded with a wide range of advantages and privileges. By contrast, life in the country retained its reactionary outlook and its own, self-contained culture, which allowed the population by and large to continue to exist in dignity.

Unrest seldom penetrated into this world, except when some ancient feud flared up again, when the alarming deeds of Samuele Stocchino, the Pintore brothers or some other bandits attracted attention, or when thousands of young men were required to join the armed forces in Ethiopia, Spain or to take part in

World War II. By an ironic stroke of fate, Sardinia had to pay a high price – two wars and thousands of dead – in order to buy its way into the 20th century.

## Sardinian autonomy

Article 116 of the Italian Constitution states that "Sicily, Sardinia, Trentino-Alto Adige, Friuli-Venezia-Giulia and the Valle d'Aosta shall be awarded particular forms and conditions of autonomy according to separate constitutional laws and statutes." At the end of World War II, the worst effects of which the island was largely spared, Sardinia felt itself more isolated than

and military administrations. Later on, six members of an executive committee assisted the High Commissioner in the performance of his duties. In December 1944 a regional assembly was created to advise the High Commissioner. It consisted originally of 18, and later of 24 members of the political parties and trades unions as well as representatives of industry and the arts. This body remained in operation until 8 May 1949 – the day on which the Sardinian people elected its first regional parliament. Shortly afterwards, following the formation of the first regional committee, the High Commissioner resigned from his post.

ever from the political and economic situation of mainland Italy, so hopes became concentrated on autonomy, universally considered to be the only way of tackling the province's numerous unsolved problems.

In 1944 the Rome government appointed a High Commissioner to supervise the running of the island. It was his task to coordinate the activities of the prefects, to act as local representative for the central government and to assume the ultimate control of both the civil

**LEFT:** today sheep are trucked around the island.
**ABOVE:** a mural known as "the land-eating landowner of Orgosolo", just outside the town.

The regional advisory committee had two main functions: to produce a draft for a Statute of Autonomy which would then be presented to the central government for approval, and in close cooperation with the High Commissioner to submit a plan to improve the island's economy as well as helping the large numbers of unemployed and needy inhabitants and malaria victims, whose position was hopeless at the time.

The final draft of the Statute of Autonomy was passed by the regional committee in April 1947 and passed on by its president to the National Constitutional Committee. On 20 June, they approved Article 116, in which Sardinia – along with a number of other regions

– was awarded special status. In a plenary session on 21 July, the Constitutional Committee discussed an application submitted by a number of Sardinian members of parliament. They came to the conclusion that the Sardinian statute should be investigated immediately.

The commission of the Constitutional Committee responsible for the statute produced a new draft, which was accepted by the full committee on 31 January 1948 – one day before the committee was disbanded. The Sardinian Statute became Constitutional Law No. 3 on 26 February 1948. The gist of the first of the 58 articles of the statute states that Sardinia and its islands is an autonomous region, which can lay claim to its own legal responsibility within the framework of the indivisible political unity of the Republic of Italy and the conditions laid down by constitutional law.

## A cherished dream

The Sardinians' hope that at some time in the future their land will see better times again is as old as the history of the island. It was a great source of strength in dark times, and supplied during the past 200 years the motivation for the best-informed and most progressive section of Sardinian society, which was in no way inferior

## THE SARDINIAN STATUTE

The Sardinian statute lists areas which the region is entitled to administer independently from central government:

● the organisation of offices and administrative bodies within the region, including the legal position and pecuniary situation of its employees

● the local districts

● the local community or town police force and the regional police force

● agriculture and forestry, small development measures and projects aimed at increased yields or soil quality improvement

● public works affecting only the region

● building construction and town planning

● public transport by bus or tram

● thermal springs and medicinal spas

● hunting and fishing

● the right of administration of public waterways as if they were public property

● the right of administration of mines, quarries and salt works as if they were public property

● customs and morals

● crafts

● tourism and gastronomy

● local authority libraries and museums.

to the intellectual and political elite of the rest of the country. Giorgio Asproni, for example, was one of Giuseppe Mazzini's most intelligent and influential advisors. He boldly supported Sardinia's interests as senator under the monarchy in Turin, opposing the centralist policies of Cavour and gaining for his native island much sympathy, especially from the Republicans and other progressives. However, what we should nowadays call an economic revival actually took place at a very slow pace indeed.

It was not until late in 1951 that the central government, with the long-awaited approval of the regional committee, at last formed an "advi-

region itself when it was required to produce a clear analysis of the most urgent tasks.

Finally, in 1958, the Commission presented its "Final Report on Investigations Preliminary to an Economic Revival". In the report, the Commission demanded the investment of 862 billion lire (at contemporary values), of which 546 billion should be made available by the state during the course of the following decade. Still no positive action was taken, however.

In 1959 another commission was instituted, with instructions to formulate a more precise plan of action. During the same year, Statute No. 7 created a regional civil service depart-

sory commission", with the task of "studying the island's resources and planning economic development in the spheres of agriculture, mining, industry, trade, transport, banking and credit, and the social structure of education". The work of the Study Commission, as it was usually called by the islanders, made very slow progress. One problem was the alterations to instructions and strategy issued by Rome; another was the difficulty experienced by the

**LEFT:** a mural of Emilio Lusso, a leading Sardinian political intellectual.
**ABOVE:** communist leader Enrico Berlinguer, who comes from Sardinia.

ment. The latter soon produced results and presented a "Final Report" during the year in which it was formed. The report demonstrated the need for measures to support 18 separate areas, especially industry. These areas would then exert a positive effect on the remaining areas, finally putting an end to the traditional economic underdevelopment of Sardinia.

Surprisingly, although several years had passed, the total sum to be invested was considerably less than that quoted in the first report. Suddenly, only 670 billion lire would be required. This did not mean, however, that action would be taken immediately to precipitate the longed-for upswing. On 17 January

1961, the Italian government agreed a draft law which was then presented to Parliament and the Sardinian local assembly. During a skilfully engineered discussion, the region insisted on the execution of the plan.

After protracted discussions between the Senate and the House of Representatives the bill finally became law on 2 June 1962, as Statute No. 522. It bore the title "Extraordinary Project to Further the Economic and Social Development of Sardinia in Execution of Arti-

### ZOLA ON SARDINIANS

"We are made from very strong rock," footballer Zola commented to the *Guardian*. "There's a very hard rock in Sardinia called *granito*. Sardinian granite is very, very difficult to wear down."

rapidly and social patterns altered considerably. The third phase, from 1966 until the present day, is characterised by a discrepancy between development as it has actually taken place and a desire to limit those aspects which have no direct relevance to the local culture of Sardinia, and which would lead to a long-term subordination to the mainland system." Despite all the mistakes and delays, for which some blame can also be laid at the door of local government, Sardinia has made remarkable

cle 13 of Constitutional Statute No. 3 of 26 February 1948". By now, 16 years had passed since the beginning of the negotiations. The sum of money to be invested had shrunk once more, to 400 billion lire, to be spread over 12 instead of 10 years.

The period after 1945, in other words the time since the implementation of the Statute of Autonomy, divides into three distinct phases according to the historian Manlio Brigaglia. During the first of these, "between 1945 and 1955, the island gradually adapted to the conditions and lifestyle of the rest of the nation. During the second phase, between 1956 and 1966, conditions on the island changed more

progress in all spheres of its public life and economy since the war, despite a growth in population from 1.27 million to more than 1.7 million.

### Expanding sectors

Considerable progress has been achieved on the educational front: the number of people without basic literacy skills in the population has fallen significantly and there has been a sharp rise in the number of students attending secondary schools. There are also more young people going on to university – although the number – 3.8 percent – is still lower than the average on the Italian mainland of 5.6 percent.

In addition, the percentage of the working population employed in agriculture dropped from more than 50 percent to around 30 percent. A high number of people are now employed in the tourism industry, although it is mostly seasonal work, and hard to quantify. In many areas Sardinia's growth rate is above Italy's national average: in the number of telephone lines in use, for example, the numbers of radios and television sets, the amount of printed matter, and the number of private cars.

There has also been a remarkable increase in sea transport. Contributing to the total were not only the increasing numbers of Sardinian emigrants returning home on holiday, but also the rising numbers of tourists.

Within a few years, it seemed as if the entire world had suddenly heard of Sardinia; businessmen were also attracted to the island and a full-scale tourist industry blossomed, enthusiastically transforming previously uninhabited or uninhabitable regions such as the Costa Smeralda – the Emerald Coast, developed by the Aga Khan and his consortium.

Booming tourism, industrialisation and the rapid transition from agriculture to the service industries, the equally rapid spread of the high-spending consumer society, and the introduction of universal education and transport systems, coupled with the population shift from the poorer regions to the industrial conurbations, have altered Sardinia's countenance more profoundly during the past 40 years than the previous two centuries had done.

But there are worrying problems, too. As in other parts of the Mediterranean, the separatist movement has been growing more vociferous in the 1990s and this, combined with a revival of kidnapping, has posed a threat to the burgeoning tourist industry.

On occasions, extra police have been drafted in to protect holiday homes on the Costa Smeralda belonging to such high-profile people as the clothing magnate Luciano Benetton and the media entrepreneur Silvio Berlusconi, who went on to become Italy's prime minister. Angelo Caria, who was the leader of the

separatist Partito Sardo d'Azione, accused such "colonialists" from the mainland of illegally installing barriers on footpaths and public land next to the beaches, preventing access to the land by local people.

## Profound changes

There seems little doubt that the lifestyle and character of the Sardinian population have undergone profound changes – unfortunately not always for the better. Particularly in the remote regions of the interior, they have precipitated a crisis in the native culture and behaviour patterns based on traditions reach-

ing back over thousands of years. The adjustment to new ways of life will take time and will not be a smooth ride. Bearing in mind the rapid pace of change typical of the last century, which has seen Sardinia enter the modern world of the western hemisphere complete with its victims, the homeless and new poor, it is uncertain whether this recent progress has been altogether advantageous for everyone at this point. With the Italian economy predicted to pick-up slightly in the short-term, Sardinia's future seems to be stable. For the time being, the fulfilment of Sardinians' long-cherished dream of independence and self-reliance seems to have been put on hold. ❏

**LEFT:** the modern port of Cagliari is Sardinia's main entry point for goods.
**RIGHT:** murals express political views and cultural identity.

# GEOGRAPHY AND WILDLIFE

*Sardinia's diverse array of geological features, natural wonders and indigenous wildlife form a treasure trove of unspoilt beauty*

Sardinia is one of the largest islands in southern Europe. Physically about the size of Wales, it has a population of some 3½ million, about half of whom are concentrated in the province of Cagliari. The island's wildlife and vegetation are genuinely unique – Sardinia's detached location in the middle of the Mediterranean has presented something of a natural barrier to cross-pollination. The land and climate help to provide the ideal habitat for species indigenous to Sardinia, some parts of the neighbouring island of Corsica and certain regions in North Africa.

Although in recent years mass tourism has played an increasingly significant role in the island's economy, it has not made quite the deleterious impact feared by some pessimistic environmentalists; many parts of Sardinia remain relatively unexplored. Covering the island's 350-km (220-mile) length, the terrain hosts a wide variety of flora and fauna.

Travel west from the millionaires' paradise known as the Costa Smeralda, with its secluded beaches, cliffs and caves, and you will find forests and vineyards surrounding the city of Sassari. Head into the central hinterland and you will probably get lost in the infamously wild and hostile hills, mountains and plateaus of the Barbagia. This image of the region has developed not only from the natural habitat, but as a result of the harsh and inhospitable living conditions of its sheep farmers, and a history of banditry. Descend southwards from the Barbagia and you enter the fertile plain of the Campidano, at either end of which are lagoons and reservoirs. The plains are bordered by the geologically fascinating high inland cliffs and table-like plateaus.

The island's habitat can be broken down into the following categories:
● coastal lagoons and wetlands, including some

of the island's, and indeed Europe's, most important wildlife parks
● *màcchia* (scrubland)
● plains and plateaus
● coasts and beaches
● mountains and woodland/forest
● caves

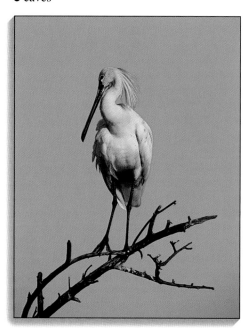

## Coastal lagoons and wetlands

Sardinia enjoys a reputation for having some of the most sublime beaches in Europe, typically featuring powdery white sands and limpid waters framed by dramatic rock formations. At key points the coastline also features lagoons, reservoirs and marshes, some of them spread over vast expanses. The most notable of these are the *stagni* (lagoons) of Cagliari.

It was the Phoenicians, who had colonised parts of Sardinia, who initiated the industry of drawing salt from the marshes east of Cagliari at Molentargius about 100,000 years ago. The name of these marshes originates from *sumolenti* ("little donkey"), the reference

**PRECEDING PAGES:** weather-worn cliffs; a rock climber stands on Mount Corrasi.
**LEFT:** porphyry cliffs near Arbatax.
**RIGHT:** a spoonbill at home in Sardinia's lagoons.

being to the donkeys on whose backs the sacks of salt were carried. The salt industry went on to become a staple of the island. It was due to this crucial source of income that Cagliari (and its sister town Quartu Sant'Elena) expanded around the waterlands, which subsequently become an integral part of the urban terrain.

The largest of the lagoons is Santa Gilla, west of Cagliari. This stretches over 4,000 hectares (9,800 acres) and incorporates the salt flats of Macchiareddu – the only area of active salt production remaining today. The land that at one time supported salt flats has been transformed into nature reserves.

once migratory birds that have settled permanently in Sardinia. As such, they can be observed all year around, both nesting and breeding in the lagoons. In a fascinating evolutionary development, they are no longer instinctively drawn to continue their seasonal passage between North Africa and Southern Europe.

The flamingo population, which now totals more than 4,000, sprung from an original colony of 1,000. The first arrivals nested in the Molentargius marshes of Cagliari in the spring of 1993, having flown from the winter-feeding grounds of the Camargue in France. These birds are a delight to observe, especially as they are

These reserves are inhabited by an incredible 200 species of birds, that is, one third of the number of species found in Europe. The bird population of Cagliari's reserves is estimated to be in excess of 100,000. This figure can be attributed to the fact that the sea-feeding bird population is attracted to the *stagni* by the abundance of shrimps (*Artemia salina*) that thrive in these waters. Some of the most noteworthy species are: avocets, blackwinged stilts, cormorants, pintail ducks, gallinule (*Porphyrio porphyrio*), and teals. Ornithologists might disagree, but to many the pink flamingo (*Phoenicopterus ruber roseus*) is the finest. The flamingos are one of a number of

easily accessible at relatively close quarters. They have become an attraction that draws professional ornithologists and amateur birdwatchers from all over the world.

Of the other lagoons, the Stagno di Sale Porcus in the centre of the Sinis peninsula (in the Oristano province) was so named because in the past the lagoon incorporated a small salt flat from which salt was extracted to conserve pork meat. Now a wildlife area protected by the Italian League for the Protection of Birds (LIPU), it is home to 10,000 pink flamingos, thousands of cranes, wild geese, cormorants, and mallards. At this, the largest lagoon in Italy, the water level changes seasonally. And, in addition to several good observation points, there is a small museum dedicated to the pink flamingo: the Museo del Fenicottero features all sorts of information about the birds.

## Scrubland and *màcchia*

Rising inland beyond the beaches and cliffs of Sardinia's coastline, the terrain consists of rocky slopes overrun by coarse scrub, that is, species of bushes resistant to strong sunlight and able to survive with little rainfall and poor soil. This scrubland, or *màcchia mediterranea* (Mediteranean maquis), flourishes in Sardinia where once there were forests. Centuries ago Sardinia was renowned for the wood gleaned from its extensive forests. But invaders and colonists, not least the ancient Romans, ransacked the forests to the point of depletion.

The denuded land gave way to erosion and a terrain insufficiently fertile for natural reforestation. In place of the once abundant trees the maquis flourished. Still today, when fires ravage the remaining forests – a regular occurrence every year – the maquis springs up. The maquis is itself vulnerable to wildfires, thus presenting the authorities with a constant hazard.

Typically the *màcchia* consists of a tangled, heavily scented and richly colourful array of plants including juniper, lentisk, myrtle and the strawberry tree (*arbutus*) or *corbezzolo* in Italian. Rosemary, heather, yellow-flowering broom and gorse, and both the pink and white flowered varieties of the cistus are all common.

From the SS 125 main road, also known as the Orientale sarda, a three-hour walk down the Codula di Luna, from Teletotem near the Supramonte to the sea, takes you to Cala Luna. This is one of the island's most beautiful and secluded beaches. The path describes a deep valley that follows the river bed, passing through aromatic maquis scrub. The surrounding land is dotted with shepherds' huts and entrances to caves that are currently being explored by speleological groups before being opened to the public.

The vegetation in the Codula di Luna valley, one of the island's wildest canyons, is quite beautiful; the oleander amid the thick Mediterranean maquis is particularly colourful. In summer, the song of the "gru-gru" of the

**LEFT:** flamingos gather at Sardinia's lagoons.
**RIGHT:** layers of *màcchia* cover Sardinia's slopes.

*bee-eaters* can be heard throughout the night and day. In the Sinis Peninsula, on the coast between S. Giovanni di Sinis and Punta Is Arutas, are more than 100 hectares (250 acres) of sandy coast with dunes covered by vegetation punctuated by cliffs and caves.

Behind the sandy dunes grows a thick Mediterranean scrub with rosemary, dwarf palm, and even an Aleppo pine wood. Declared a nature reserve in 1981, this parkland is inhabited by numerous species of birds, such as the peregrine falcon and kestrel, that nest in the cliffs. Of these, probably the most fascinating is the rare Sardinian partridge.

## The plateaus

The steeply inclining areas known as the *giare* comprise large, dark basalt plateaus formed by the lava that flowed from violent volcanic eruptions. The *giare* now appear as unique tablelands, utterly flat and supported by sheer walls of dark basalt.

The *giare* of Siddi, Serri, and especially the *giara* of Gesturi, are particularly noteworthy. They are 16 km (10 miles) long and up to 6 km (4 miles) wide. A stretch of cork forest, where the trees are all blown by the ever-present mistral wind, covers the plateau, with the exception of a few depressions called *pauli*. These *giare* are home to pony-sized horses called *achettas* that graze in fenced-off pastures. The mystery that shrouds their origins is obscured further by the *giare*'s isolation. However they got there, today these small horses romp wild along the plateau. In an ageless cork wood, on meadows dotted with white flowers, a close encounter with one of these animals is a fabulous experience.

This is also the area in which to find the prickly-pear fig (*sa figu morisca*). This frugal cactus, probably introduced by Arabs, has for centuries marked the rural landscape, often demarcating the borders of the rich landowners' territory while enriching the farms of the poor

with lush fruit. Sardinians traditionally love the ubiquitous prickly pear, whose thorns they remove with lentisk-leaf brushes. Other avid fans include blackbirds, partridges, weasels, martens, foxes and wild boars.

## Coasts and beaches

The coastline and the beaches are among the Mediterranean's most beautiful. The clean and transparent seawater laps on to a shoreline whose small coves of crystalline water alternate with rocky ravines in which the sea changes colours, from emerald green, through turquoise to a sparkling azure. The beaches are of fine golden sand, the cliffs have been smoothed and

transformed into huge sculptures by the wind. The island's various coasts all have their own particular beauty. On the western corner of the province of Sassari, the Alghero features beaches and the limestone reef of Capo Caccia. La Pelosa beach, 2 km (1 mile) from Stintino, the island's northwestern point, is one of Sardinia's loveliest beaches. White sand gradually descends into the sea, its colour giving the water some magnificent turquoise hues.

From here you can join an excursion to the Asinara island, once a prison and now a National Park. Following some 100 years of isolation, Asinara remains a mysterious island that is home to 500 mouflons (wild sheep), wild boars, hares, weasels and white (albini) donkeys. Of the bird populations, there are coarse seagulls, crested cormorants, magpies and the Sardinian partridge. In the migrating season the royal seagull stops here, too. The western coasts have long rocky tracts that lead north towards Bosa and Cuglieri. In the south, near the Sinis peninsula, Is Arutas beach features white quartz crystals that give the water its turquoise colour. The quartz at the nearby Mari Ermi beach is pink.

Further south, in the province of Cagliari, there is the Costa Verde, and in particular Piscinas, a beach of high dunes perfumed by junipers. Here, where the mistral can be quite severe, the sand gives on to an immediately deep sea. Continuing south, Cala Domestica is a narrow fjord of transparent waters set between steeply rising rocks covered in thick Mediterranean maquis.

Of the two sister islands you will find here, St Antioco has a beautiful beach that is 18 km (11 miles) long and 8 km (5 miles) wide; San Pietro is the home of the falcon *(Falco eleonorae)* that nests among the rocks every summer. Today there are more than 100 of these magnificent predatory birds, which, incidentally, were named after Queen Eleonora d'Arborea who, in 1400, declared the island's falcons to be a protected species.

Arriving on the southern part of the island, on the west coast you will find an uninterrupted series of beaches. Here natural shade is provided by the wonderful pine trees of Santa Margherita di Pula. These culminate in the well-regarded Chia beach, near the location of the Punic city of Bithia. Baia Chia is known as "the Pearl of the South", and features lovely emerald-coloured water and pink granite sand, courtesy of dunes that reach heights of 65 metres (213 ft) where the ancient gnarled junipers grow.

The eastern coast has its own beautiful and uncontaminated beaches: San Teodoro e Budoni, then Posada and Siniscola e Orosei, where the wildest terrain starts. The gulf of Orosei at Cala Gonone-Dorgali is interesting because one of Europe's last coastal forests grows here, right on the seafront. With its high limestone cliff, its grottoes and isolated beaches, this part of Sardinia is stupendously pretty. Furthermore, it offers the cleanest sea water which, with its rich colours and shades, is best appreciated from a boat.

Among the many delightful spots on this part of the island, the splendid romantic beach of Cala Luna luxuriates in the presence of six enormous caves and the oleander wood near a lagoon. The southern part of the Golfo Orosei, stretching over an area of great ecological interest, is among the best preserved in the whole island.The extraordinary union between harsh rocky landscapes and the clear trans-parency of the Tyrrhenian Sea produces a series of marvels: sheer cliffs rise from the sea, wooded slopes are inhabited by an interesting array of wildlife, and enchanting beaches can be found in such spectacular bays as Cala Sisine, Cala Biriola, Cala Marioulu and Cala Coloritzè. Overlooking them all is the unique profile of the Capo Monte Santo coast. The entire gulf is part of the Gennargentu National Park *(see Wildlife, page 99)*, which was created in order to safeguard the flora and fauna of this part of Sardinia. The monk seal is one of a number of species found here that are in danger of extinction if action is not taken soon.

One of the region's most picturesque stretches is undoubtedly the terrain around Arbatax, which is dominated by the maquis-covered Capo Bellavista. Much of the island's coast is formed by granite or limestone, but the rocks of Arbatax (whose name exemplifies the Arabic influence in Sardinia) are an exception. Composed of red granite porphyry, the rocks' astonishing red colours flare up when reflecting the slanting rays of the sun. From this point the topography changes somewhat. The terrain is dotted with wild oleaster, the "oleastru" after which the Ogliastra region is named. Further south, the stretch of coastline between Muravera and Villasimius offers a number of delightful spots.

These include the promontory of Capo Ferrato, the wild beach of Costa Rei and the fascinating inlet of Cala Sinzias. At Villasimius a very extensive and wide beach, Porto Giunco, almost gives the impression of being an African desert. This is the beach of Capo Carbonara, which is much appreciated by anyone looking for a quiet nook. The sandy shore is so wide

that one can relish the feeling of being absolutely alone. The whole region is charac-terised by a wild, sometimes quite weird, natural environment: the small, rocky islands, such as Isola dei Cavoli and Isola di Serpen-tara, are populated by rabbits and seagulls.

Finally we reach Cagliari. The Poetto beach starts in the capital, and it is easy to reach from the city centre. The beach continues for 13 km (8 miles) to Quartu St Elena, the island's third-biggest city. It is one of Sardinia's liveliest seaside stretches, from morning when families and young people meet for an hour's sun and swim-ming, to the evenings when the bars along the beach organise concerts, cabaret and cinema.

**LEFT:** the prickly pear relishes the dry conditions.
**RIGHT:** the crystalline water and rocky ravines of the island's coves.

## Mountains and woodland

Sardinia's 24,000 sq. km (9,250 sq. miles) are, the plain of the Campidano notwithstanding, made up largely of massifs. These were formed in the Palaeozoic age, and thus predate the Alps and the Appennines. The predominant rock is granite which, as a result of wind and other forms of erosion, has often come to resemble all sorts of things in people's imagination. Locals and tourists alike have spotted the bear, the tortoise, the elephant, the mushroom and the dinosaur among the rocks.

The deep, green woodlands, one of the most enchanting Sardinian features, form a heritage them unexplored. It is covered by maquis, and springs gush from a myriad of underground watercourses. The Supramonte, which is really the heart of Sardinia, features one of the most spectacular gorges in Italy – Su Gorroppu, with walls 400 metres (1,300 ft) high and the famous source of the Cologone.

The name Gennargentu derives from the Latin *Janua argenti* (Silver door), which refers to snow-capped peaks or the legend of silver in these mountains, according to whom you believe. This inaccessible area is well preserved and contains a 25 sq. km (10 sq. mile) ancient holm oak forest. Near Sassari the well-kept

of great environmental value. The Gennargentu National Park (including a 25 sq. km/10 sq. mile forest that is one of the island's most beautiful), eight regional parks and several oases of flora and fauna form a network of protected areas measuring more than 59,102 hectares (146,000 acres). The mountainous landscape dominates the central part of the island. The highest point is Punta La Marmora on the Gennargentu massif, at 1,830 metres (6,000 ft).

Serious trekkers can enjoy walks from the Supramonte di Oliena to the dense oak and chestnut forests along the old railway line near Belvi. The rough and inhospitable Supramonte is riddled with precipices and caves, many of Foresta di Burgos features oak, cedar and chestnut trees.

The Natural Reserve of Monte Arcosu–Monte Latias is a World Wildlife Fund area that climbs 1,000 metres (3,200 ft) from the sea. It includes an ancient, 3,600-hectare (8,900-acre) forest of holm oak and cork oak that is the largest green forest in the Mediterranean. Here live wildcats, Sardinian deer, hawks, kestrels, buzzards and golden eagles. Horse-riding tours, excursions and summer camps take place here.

The dark-coated Sardinian deer is the island's biggest wild mammal, though it is smaller than the mainland deer. Another difference from its larger cousin is that its mating season arrives a month earlier, around the middle of August. The Sardinian deer's favourite habitat is the thick maquis near the forest. It became almost extinct in the 1960s, when its numbers were reduced to 50 animals, but it survived with the help of WWF protection.

The Sette Fratelli Mountain, named after the seven peaks that can be seen from Cagliari, is a gigantic granite massif with wild gorges, high cliffs and fast streams shaped over the centuries by the wind. The multifarious forms of terrain found here play a contributory role in the mountain's sense of mystery.

The mountain forest covers an area of 4,000 hectares (nearly 10,000 acres), making it one of the largest – as well as one of the best preserved sclerophyll (woody plants characterised by small, leathery, evergreen leaves) forests of the Mediterranean basin. Replanted with pine, eucalyptus and cypress trees, the forest reaches an altitude of over 1,000 metres (3,300 ft). It is one of the few remaining areas inhabited by the now almost extinct Sardinian deer.

Along the streams there is a much interesting vegetation, including wild oleander, ferns, willows and alder trees. This used to be the location of royal eagle hunts and the habitat of the goshawk. The area also features the wood of Tuviois, near the Serpeddi Mount. In the torrents lives the amphibious urodele the tritone sardo (*Euproetus platycephalus*). Among the reptiles there is the rare lizard of Bedriaga, present only in the north of Sardinia, and the del Cetti snake. The real symbol of the area is the Sardinian deer, of which there are at least 700. Another distinctive animal, now protected against the threat of extinction to the extent that it thrives all over the island, is the mouflon.

The Montarbu forest is particularly rich in plant species, which give it great beauty and variety: in addition to the holm oak, you can find yews, holly, strawberry trees, phylliraeas, hawthorns, alders, and the rare peony, which is also known as the "rose of Gennargentu".

## Caves

Hidden in the mountainous landscape above the town of Ulassai, amid rocky outcrops and deep ravines, is the cave of Su Marmuri. This ranks as one of the most impressive caves in

**LEFT:** Gennargentu National Park woodlands.
**RIGHT:** the Grotta del Bue Marino, Cala Gonone.

Europe, with huge 50-metre (165-ft) high ceilings and imposing, natural limestone towers whose white peaks stand out among the dark green vegetation.

To the south of Dorgali, the Grotta del Bue Marino is so called due to the presence of the monk seal, of which there are only 500 left in the Mediterranean. This fine marine mammal dives to depths of almost 20 metres (65 ft) in its quest for fish and octopus. Also in the Dorgali area is the impressive cave of Ispinigoli. Here one can admire a 38-metre (125-ft) high stalagmite and, at the rear, the Abyss of the Virgin chasm where human sacrifices were made in

prehistoric times. Along the Codula di Luna river is the entrance to one of the island's biggest and most extensive caves, the Su Palu, which was discovered in 1980.

In the Capo Caccia area the caves include the Grotta di Nettuno, which has 2 km (1 mile) of chambers and small lakes up to 110 metres (360 ft) deep. This cave can be reached by hired boat. Other caves in the area that are worth exploring if you can are the beautiful Grotta Verde, and la Grotta dei Ricami. The Grotta Verde is so-called because of the moss which covers its stalactites and stalagmites. In the cave there is a small lake where examples of ancient graffiti have been discovered. ❏

# WHERE TO SEE SARDINIAN WILDLIFE

*Sardinia's island ecology has given rise to some unique species of wildlife, which are now protected in popular reserves and national parks*

In recent years marine and wildlife reserves have been set up to protect Sardinia's unique habitats. Diving and birdwatching holidays to the island have become increasingly popular, while more hikers and climbers are coming to Sardinia, shifting the emphasis away from sun and sand holidays to more eco-based tourism. Sardinia is on the migration route for birds between Africa and Europe; the birds often stop off at the marshes and mud flats on the outskirts of Cagliari to rest. The best time to see some of the 170 species of birds identified here is between August and March, which is also when the flamingos arrive.

Flamingos and other migratory birds can also be seen at the Sale Porcus Reserve on the Sinis peninsula, while the best place to see Eleonora's falcon is on the island of San Pietro. Places to see rare animals include the ecologically unique sand dunes on the south coast at Piscinas, where colonies of loggerhead turtles come to lay their eggs. The shy and very rare Sardinian deer is often glimpsed on the slopes of Arcosu in the Sulcis region and in the Gennargentu National Park on the east coast.

Marine life is best seen in the clean and warm waters of one of Sardinia's marine reserves. Tavolara and a couple of its neighbouring islands are due to be turned into a protected area. Dive trips (which can include equipment hire) go to the islands and to the coasts of Asinara and Gallura and the Golfo di Orosei. Dolphins can be seen in the Maddalena archipelago and you might be lucky enough to see a monk seal in the Golfo di Orosei.

▷ **NATIVE SPECIES**
Sardinia's isolation as an island has given rise to unique species of animals and birds including deer, horses and boar.

▷ **FLAMINGOS**
Pink flamingos winter in the *stagni* (lagoons) of Cagliari and Oristano during their migration to Africa. A small colony of birds now nest in Sardinia permanently.

△ **MARINE LIFE**
The warm, clean waters of Sardinia, home to many species of marine flora and fauna, are perfect for scuba diving and snorkelling.

△ **WILD HORSES**
The elusive *cavallini* (Sardinia's native miniature wild horses) can be found roaming on the Giara di Gesturi plateau and on the Capo Caccia headland.

◁ **REPTILES**
Reptiles thrive in Sardinia's typically Mediterranean climate but there are no poisonous snakes. The nifty Sardinian salamander lives the shrubby *màcchia*.

## THE GENNARGENTU NATIONAL PARK

The Gennargentu National Park in the province of Nuoro covers 59,102 hectares (146,000 acres) and includes Punta La Marmora, the island's highest peak, and the prehistoric village of Tiscali. In the valleys and lower mountain slopes are holm oak forests. Further up, maple and bay oak trees can be found with clusters of juniper, holly and yew trees towards the summit. On the mountain tops are plum trees and Corsican junipers. At spring time, peonies flower and in summer oleanders carpet even the most barren of places. *Mouflon*, marten, wild boar and foxes inhabit the mountains in large numbers. In the woods are wildcats, hares, partridges, sparrow hawks and goshawks, while buzzards and kestrels hunt in stretches of open space. Along the park's coastline can be found the rare monk seal, thought to be extinct, and the Corsican seagull and Eleonora's falcon.

### ▷ MOUFLON (WILD SHEEP)
*Mouflon* faced extinction in Italy but numbers remain high in mountainous areas of Sardinia, where they have lived since ancient times.

### ▽ SARDINIAN BOAR
*Cinghiali* (Sardinian wild boar) can be found all over the island but favour woodland areas and nut groves. Although they are hunted, their numbers are still high.

### ▷ RARE BIRD SPECIES
Rare birds such as the golden eagle *(right)*, Bonelli's eagle and the wryneck live in the mountains. The plains and plateaux are one of the few remaining habitats of bustards, while the Sardinian partridge nests in the Piscinas dunes. On the island of San Pietro, colonies of Eleonora falcon can be seen, while the European Crane nests in the Stagno di Sale Porcus.

# SHEPHERDS AND PECORINO

*The shepherds' way of life has come to symbolise Sardinia, but changes*
*are inevitable if this aspect of island culture is to survive*

Sardinia's history has always been closely bound to that of its shepherds, whose lifestyle is as fascinating as it is full of privations. The native Sardinian sheep is small and hardy, able to withstand the harsh conditions, and produces a high milk yield in spite of often poor pastures.

## Early development

Sheep rearing has a long and honourable tradition here. It was the subject of considerable attention under the Romans, in the Middle Ages and especially under Spanish rule. At other times it was further developed by various religious orders; the Benedictines, in particular, were very diligent in this respect.

Absurdly enough, it also profited from the migration from the land; previously fertile fields were left fallow and reverted to pasture which could be taken over at leisure by the shepherds and their flocks. Although the Enclosure Laws of the 19th century portioned off much of the plateau land, most of the mountainous area remains wild and unfenced. As today, these parts were largely too inaccessible and barren for any form of arable farming.

## Popular pecorino

Sheep farming enjoyed a further upsurge as a result of the involvement of a group of enterprising businessmen from Rome who established industrial cheese factories between 1885 and 1890. Here they produced on a large-scale basis the *pecorino romano* (sheep's milk cheese), popular in Italy since Roman times (Pliny refers to it in his *Historia Naturalis*). With the help of aggressive marketing, the cheese was an immediate hit in the United States where it was warmly welcomed by the large number of Italian immigrants.

Today *pecorino romano* is popular throughout the entire world. Pungent and tangy, it is eaten with bread, grated over pasta and fre-

**LEFT:** shepherd with *pecorino* moulds.
**RIGHT:** flock on its way to a feudal pen.

quently used in cooking, especially in pesto. At the turn of the century the success of the cheese transformed many of the antiquated sheep farming methods employed on the island. New production techniques and modern ideas gave the entire profession a new lease of life, forcing it out of its traditional lethargy. But – as is often

the case in times of rapid change – even as the first dairy production cooperatives were being formed, there were still extensive areas of land where farmers clung to the old order. The shepherd was upheld as a symbol of an entire culture which was in danger of disappearing as a result of the links being forged with other spheres of industry. The sinister innovations were met with reactions ranging from suspicion to outright hostility. Shepherds are deeply conservative and are extremely reluctant to have their affairs regulated by an outside force.

Sheep and *pecorino* together form one of the oldest and steadiest pillars of the island economy. Today, *pecorino* is the island's main export product and the industry remains the biggest single source of employment in the agricultural sector.

## Resistance to change

In spite of changes to the way of life elsewhere on the island, shepherds continue to live in their pastures or their sheep sheds, completely cut off from the rest of the world. They may wander for months with their flocks, and some, usually those whose pastures are particularly remote, still make the cheese themselves, in their own *ovili* (sheepfolds) – stone huts attached to brushwood milking enclosures.

Most shepherds have found that modern production techniques incompatible with their traditional methods and don't take into account variations in the local terrain. EU law has decreed the use of refrigerators to store milk and this has meant that in areas where there is no electric system, production is severely restricted. Regulations also only allow produce which maintains a continuous standard to be exported, regardless of quality. These changes to the shepherd's traditional lifestyle have to be balanced against the progression of the industry as a whole.

Improvements would involve introducing

### WOMEN IN SARDINIA

From before the nuraghic period, Sardinian women played an important role in society. In the two main archaeological museums in Cagliari and Sassari there are prehistoric bronze representations of the *dea madre* (Mother Goddess) and high priestesses. In the island's ancient pastoral civilisation typical of the Mediterranean, men would lead a semi-nomadic existence, spending long periods of time in far-off pastures with their flocks. In the shepherd's absence his wife would be left to take the dominant role in running the household and childrearing. In the 14th century the status of women was improved by one of Sardinia's most famous leaders and symbol of the island's independence –

the warrior queen Eleonora of Arborea (1340–1404). Intelligent, brave and ahead of her time, Eleonora formulated the *Carta de Logu* (legal code) in 1395, which ensured the legal status and rights of women and became the basis for the legal system in Sardinia for the next four centuries. As Sardinia entered the 20th century, the role of women in society diminished as pressure to conform to the rules of a clan or village increased and women found themselves taking more of a back seat in domestic affairs. Novelist Grazia Deledda rejected societal norms and the women in her novels are tough and independent as they struggle with their traditional roles.

higher yielding and stronger animals into flocks through selective breeding methods or working in closer co-operation with fellow-shepherds. New areas of pastureland could also be created which would not only serve as a source of food for the animals in winter, but would be available during the six- to eight-month periods of drought in the long Sardinian summer. A Sardinian flock can vary from 50 to 2,000 animals – a total which is more frequently undercut than surpassed. And yet the trade as a whole, contrary to popular impressions, is profitable and continues to attract young Sardinians, who sometimes abandon jobs in the factories and

## The products

Sardinian sheep give large quantities of milk; if the profits from this are added to those from the wool and lambs produced, the value of a sheep can double in a year. Virtually all the sheep's milk is made into cheese, either by the shepherd, co-operatives or by the increasing numbers of small companies which are flexible enough to be able to adapt to the changing requirements of their Italian and overseas customers.

The first cooperative was formed in 1907 in Bortigali, near Macomer. Its aim was to protect local shepherds from the Roman businessmen who, adept at making capital of their own

mines to wander across the countryside with their sheep. One reason why the industry is so attractive is that it has prestige. Independence is considered more valuable than monetary gain. Young urban workers are also attracted to shepherding because of the group's links to acts of banditry. Many Sardinians, not just young people, have heroic and romantic images of banditry. The Codice Barbaricino, the unwritten law of resolving conflict through brigandage, vendettas and kidnapping, is part of Sardinia's ancient culture.

**LEFT:** preparing *pecorino* cheese.
**ABOVE:** moulds in a *pecorino* dairy in Dorgali.

financial resources as well as the Sardinians' poverty and lack of unity, were poised to monopolise the sheep industry. Today there are more than 50 cheese-making factories on the island, the majority of which are situated away from the coast. Apart from *pecorino romano*, which amounts to just under half of overall production, they also make a sweet white variety of cheese known as *pecorino tipo toscanello* and *canestrato*, a delicious and strong-tasting sheep's milk cheese. The district around Gavoi is famous for its *pecorino fiore-sardo*, mostly exported to Apulia, where it is sold in quantity as a great delicacy. In the Abruzzi *pecorino fiore-sardo* is served with pears.

# The Shepherd's Knife

**M**any a Sardinian factory worker or bank employee would not dream of going anywhere without his shepherd's knife. He sees the simple pocket knife with a carved horn handle as not only a proven weapon in his fight with the canteen chop at lunchtime, but also a part of his identity – a potent symbol of a lost pastoral world. A true Sardinian loves his knife, and knives have even been immortalised in verse.

The very best knives are made by true master craftsmen who will only work to order. These men

need at least two days to make a shepherd's knife in the harmoniously classic form with a pointed blade *a foll'e murta* – "like a myrtle leaf". Should you be toying with the idea of purchasing a knife, don't be tempted by cheap imitations; they really aren't worth the money. And be sure to treat the matter of buying a knife with due respect. The careless remark by a French man of letters who, complaining about the prices of these knives, called them *couteaux de cuisine*, kitchen knives, was tantamount to an assault on Sardinian national pride.

*Sa resolza* or *sa resordza* (the Sardinian shepherd's knife), comes from the Latin word *rasoria*, knives with a swivelling sheath, and only the very finest knives have their blades protected by a

sheath of wood or horn. You will notice that anyone who brandishes a particularly fine shepherd's knife will be surrounded in a trice by a crowd of Sardinians, all proferring expert advice – and each of them purporting to be a knife specialist. The knife will be passed from hand to hand, examined and discussed, and opinions exchanged as to whether the alleged ram's horn handle might not, after all, be the latest imitation of the real thing – a theory which can only be disproved by the smell when it is heated over a naked flame. The proud owner will usually refuse to agree to such an experiment, thus inviting further taunts that in his ignorance he might have bought *i skiffu* – rubbish. The hallmark of one of the recognised master craftsmen stamped on the blade is the only thing likely to silence such conjecture.

The final test of a good knife, if you are a man, is to spit on the back of one's hand, rub hard and then check whether the knife will give a close shave. (Onlookers with no hairs on the back of their hands rarely have a place in such a circle anyhow – unless their comments indicate them to be true connoisseurs, therefore compensating for their apparent lack of virility.)

Another useful means of judging the quality of the knife is by laying the blade at a flat angle across the thumbnail and pulling it very lightly across its entire length, as far as the point. The entire movement must be executed slowly and with a look of intense concentration on the face; the consequent verdict on the "bite" of the blade is invariably restricted to an appropriately intoned and suitably meaningful "hmm" or a withering "pah!".

As recently as 50 years ago, such knives were commonly produced in pastoral communities all over the island – Arbus, Guspini, Gavoi, Fonni, Santu Lussurgiu and Pattada, to name a few. Nowadays, however, good quality knives are really only produced in the traditional manner in the last two of these villages.

The inhabitants of Pattada, a small, peaceful rural village near the town of Ozieri, are most anxious to retain the village's reputation as the knife centre of Sardinia. Knives from Pattada are considered to be the ultimate in Sardinian craftsmanship, more esteemed than any of the needlework or jewellery produced. In fact, the very name Pattada has become synonymous with the word *coltello*, or knife. ❑

**LEFT:** the making of knives in Sardinia is an art: a knife from Pattada can take up to year to produce.

The marketing of the sheep's milk cheese today is largely supervised by the Consorzio Caseario Sardegna, the consortium of the Sardinian sheep and dairy farming industry. The advantages of an organisation of this kind are obvious and it can make much more money available to the shepherds and breeders to improve their products. Medium-sized and large private cheese-making factories can claim particular success. Forty-five factories produce over half of the *pecorino romano* as well as most *tipo toscanello* and *canestrato*. Private concerns market their own products at home and abroad and many have been very successful. The *pecorino*

the milk yield is frozen during the months of highest production and turned into cheese during the summer and early autumn when milk production falls.

Ricotta, an excellent curd cheese, is also made from the *pecorino*. Light and bland, it makes a good accompaniment to *pane carasau* (traditional crisp thin bread). At one time ricotta and *pane carasau* formed the basis of the shepherd's diet; today it is mainly used in cooking. One particular use of ricotta is in the preparation of ravioli and *sebadas*, the popular Sardinian hors d'oeuvres. Initially only on the menu in a few specialist restaurants in Oliena

*romano* is still exported in the largest quantities and it is now famous not only in Italy but also in the US, Canada and parts of Europe.

## Sweet and soft cheeses

Some producers have switched to making larger quantities of sweet and soft cheeses. In spite of their relatively high price, these cheeses have gained popularity throughout Italy, and on Sardinia itself. This is due in part to the increased prosperity of the islanders and the rising numbers of tourists visiting the island. In other regions of Italy, a small proportion of

**ABOVE:** a herd of goats in the Gennargentu.

and Nuoro, *sebadas* have since won over the palates of the entire island. Fresh ricotta is also delicious served with a large spoonful of bitter-sweet Sardinian honey.

## Time for change?

It is important, however, that success to date – the relatively high prices fetched by cheese, ricotta, wool and lamb, and the favourable market situation – should not be allowed to distract attention from some of the unsolved problems in the sheep and dairy farming industry. The work environment and working conditions of the shepherds are still well below expected standards of living elsewhere in Europe, although big improvements have been a matter of course in other spheres of industry. What's more, modernisation of the industry could help to solve the problem of banditry recurring again, which in some areas was tantamount to a profitable sideline for shepherds. Even today, the increase in winter crime in lowland grazing areas corresponds with the return of the shepherds, and an increase in crime has been noted when shepherds' rents fall due.

## Government intervention

There is still plenty of room for action; an economic infrastructure must be created, and sheep

rearing must be organised differently, for – despite the financial gains to be made – at some stage in the foreseeable future there may be no one left who is willing to shepherd. The regional government has been talking for years about undertaking the necessary measures, but – as is so often the case – these good intentions are not enough. The 1950s saw substantial improvements in other areas of agriculture, with incentives for farmers, the completion of numerous irrigation projects and an increasing level of mechanisation, but the pastoral areas received little or no help. Fundamental changes must be brought about, and modern businesses created, with sufficient pasture at their disposal

and efficiently-planned livestock sheds equipped with all the latest facilities, from lighting to running water to milking machines, and regular veterinary care for the flocks.

When a parliamentary investigative committee in the early 1980s demanded the immediate implementation of some of the measures listed above it was decided that the establishment of estates or even designated areas of pasture would be a serious mistake, less from an economic than from a cultural point of view. It was considered sufficient for the government to intervene financially in the case of exceptional cold or drought, or a livestock epidemic. It is time to admit that the national and regional reform statutes of 1974 and 1976 have largely failed. Only a sensible distribution of credit and the creation of a number of medium-sized companies are likely to permit the ancient vocation of sheep rearing to survive in the 21st century. So far, membership of the EU has done nothing to improve the situation.

Quick solutions are required – ones which will break through the rigidity of established traditions while being sensitive to the shepherd's way of life. They should also guarantee shepherds (whose number fell from 80,000 to 60,000 individuals according to a recent survey) an appropriate standard of living and a niche in modern society. Only such measures can save a traditional livelihood and culture which has existed for thousands of years.

One possible solution would be to help the shepherds find new markets for their cheese and wool products among tourists. If nothing is done, the inevitable invasion of Sardinian villages by modernity, the continuing migration from the land, the industrialisation of the island and the growing numbers of local inhabitants employed in the service industries will ensure that the shepherd is increasingly isolated from society, and or even excluded altogether. With this in mind, UNESCO has been approached to protect the shepherd's unique way of life. Furthermore, a dangerous gap could arise between an impoverished interior, where sheep and dairy farming would still be the main source of income, and the wealthy tourist and industrialised regions of the island – not to mention Italy or the rest of Europe.

**LEFT:** shepherds know every animal in their flock.
**RIGHT:** an accordion player accompanies a singer.

# FOLKLORE AND FESTIVALS

*Sardinians are especially proud of their folk roots and festivals. These are celebrated and preserved island-wide by all generations*

A t the end of the 18th century, Sardinia was known as an *India de por acá*, an "India in the midst of the Western World". And thus, strictly speaking, it was to remain, at least until the end of World War I, an exotic culture about which virtually nothing was known, even by the few visitors whose spirit of adventure drove them to explore the island. Sardinia fitted into no specific category except perhaps that of "living antiquity", a place in which time had stopped dead, somewhere between the Old Testament period and Homer.

## Early visitors

It wasn't until D. H. Lawrence visited the island in 1921 with his wife and wrote *Sea and Sardinia* that it was brought to the attention of the English-reading world. Many, including the novelist and critic Anthony Burgess, have felt that Lawrence managed in six days what others failed to do in years: "A single week's visit was enough for him to extract the very essence of the island and its people." But Lawrence's conclusions were in part grounded in the inscrutability of the island and islanders that had confounded others. "Lost between Europe and Africa and belonging to nowhere... as if it never really had a fate. No fate. Left outside of time and history," he pronounced.

The geographic and cultural character of the island, noted by Lawrence, has not lost its poignancy some 80 years later. The interior of Sardinia, with its harsh, sun-drenched terrains reminiscent of North Africa, still presents an aspect of inhospitability. The lives of its people have for centuries been marked by drudgery and privation.

In addition, a diffidence towards visitors from outside these tight-knit communities completes this picture. However, do not be mistaken, this is Europe, and a region of one of the world's richest, most industrialised

**PRECEDING PAGES:** riders in the carnival at Sédilo.
**LEFT:** a masked rider at the *sartiglia* in Oristano.
**RIGHT:** the mask of a *mamuthone*.

nations. Yet, even so, a haunting paradox as to Sardinia's fate and destiny persists. Sardinians jealously guard the auto-nomous nature and character of their culture, while remaining, on the whole, committed Italians. Sardinia is, after all, both geographically and culturally separate from mainland Italy. And "Sardo" is a distinct

language, as opposed to one of Italy's myriad of dialects. It is not surprising, therefore, that you may still hear mainland Italy referred to by Sardinians as *il continente* (the continent).

## Folk roots

Traditional folklore and culture, tied as it is in Sardinia to the land and agriculture, is under threat of disappearing, as elsewhere in the developed world. What remains will inevitably loose something of its authentic value, being a celebration of the past, rather than the rituals and festivities that express the average Sardinian's real-life activities and way of living. That said, as an expression of regional pride modern generations of Sardinians (often now part of the modern urban population) have striven to keep the historic traditions of past generations alive and to preserve distinctive characteristics of the indigenous culture.

Genuine folklore and its essential links with the island's traditions are a colourful and complex aspect of the Sardinian national heritage. They are, however, all related to each other, as well as being inextricably interwoven with both the civilisation and the legal, economic and social structures of the country. It would thus be wrong simply to dismiss Sardinian folklore as a mere cultural phenom-

## The shepherd's role

All classes of society see the shepherd as a symbol of their cultural heritage. The historian Manlio Brigaglia makes an interesting observation in this respect. He reports that, shortly after World War I, the artist Mario Delitala had suggested that the Sardinian coat of arms should be changed. He proposed that the four blindfolded Moors, dating from the time when Sardinia was ruled by the house of Aragon, should be replaced by motifs representing the island's "four traditional occupations" – a shepherd, a farmer, a mountain-dweller and a fisherman. The idea found little support on the

enon, which developed among the lower social classes of the community and is of concern only to them.

To a much greater extent than in many other societies, the roots of Sardinia's cultural heritage lie in both folk culture and the customs of the so-called upper classes. Modern research has confirmed that all strata of society proudly see the cultural heritage as their common inheritance.

This is reflected in Sardinia's writers and artists. No other folkloric tradition has been so lovingly immortalised by the literature and art of its own area, whilst at the same time exerting such a profound influence on its native artists.

### 19TH- AND 20TH-CENTURY ARTISTS

Writers such as Sebastiano Satta, Nobel Prize-winner Grazia Deledda and Giuseppe Dessì all wrote about their native land, while artists like Antonio Ballero, Giuseppe Biasi, Francesco Ciusa and Filippo Figari painted it. The 19th and 20th centuries belonged to an era in the island's history characterised by an exceptional degree of artistic creativity. Alan Ross, in *Bandit on the Billiard Table – a journey through Sardinia*, said of Grazia Deledda's novels: "They are local in the best sense, touching off on almost every page illuminating truths about the Nuorese peasantry, their customs, ideas, ways of feeling… [They] are the best substitute for Sardinia landscape painting."

island and a consensus was not found for the change. So the "imported" coat of arms remained, while the figure of the shepherd is seen as being truly symbolic of Sardinia.

Intriguingly, as the figures of the Moors are blindfolded, it contrasts with one of the island's most well-known local proverbs originating from the shepherd communities: *Furat chi benit dae su mare* (He who comes from across the sea is a thief). Historically there is some justification for this attitude. Through the centuries Sardinia has been occupied (at times in total, at others in part) by a series of foreign invaders who have exploited its natural resources.

enough, another Sardinian expression describes the island as being the *Terra di Poesia* (The Land of Poetry).

It is unsurprising, then, that folkloric poetry, existing in a wide variety of genres, is such a vital part of the island's culture. A rigid metricity is particularly noticeable, even in simple incantations, curses, excommunications and *berbos* (teasing rhymes), in *ninnias* (lullabies), *attitidus* (lamentations for the dead) or *Gosos* (eulogies of the saints). It extends to various elaborate forms of love poetry such as the *mutos*, the miniature variations of which are called *muttettus* or *battorinas*. The rhythmical

## The land of poetry

One typical characteristic of Sardinian folklore is its penchant for pointed remarks. It would be no exaggeration to claim that language is the second, secret master of the island. From everyday encounters to special occasions, every event is accompanied, underlined and explained by a verbal commentary.

Few peoples possess such a broad palette of set phrases and such an extensive and colourful vocabulary as the Sardinians. Significantly

pattern of the *mutu* resembles that of the *strambotti* and *stornelli* of Tuscany (short traditional love songs written in the 17th century). It consists of two parts: the *isterria* (exposition) and the *torrada* (response). The finest *mutos* possess "a note of fantasy"; they resound with "poetic intelligence", an expression of "a higher plane and great sensitivity" which moved Italian film director Pier Paolo Pasolini (1922–75) to describe them as essentially a "female" lyric form, a form of poetry which he said "knows neither brute force nor Orgosolo".

By contrast, the lament for the dead, the *attitidu*, is often unmistakably aggressive in tone. Usually the chant of the *attitadoras* (the wailing

**LEFT:** local shepherds reminisce over photographs of people living in the area of Fonni.
**ABOVE:** a shepherd reads a book of poetry.

women who perform a similar function to the *voceratrici* of Corsica, but who in Sardinia are usually related to the deceased) is simply a tribute, complimenting the virtues of the deceased and their ancestors and imagining the great deeds they would have accomplished had death not snatched them away. If the deceased was the victim of a vendetta, however, the job of the *attitadoras* is to stir up feelings of hatred and vengeance (*attizzare*, to stir up/to fan, may well explain the origins of the word).

J.W.W. Tyndale, a 19th-century traveller in Sardinia, noted how "the feelings of the relatives are appealed to with the utmost earnest-

## Bitter honey

Max Leopold Wagner saw the *mutu* as an expression of the Sardinian tendency to melancholy, which assumes concrete form in the "grim solemnity" of the *nuraghe*, the ancient towers dating from the 2nd millennium BC that are dotted all over the island. Not every visitor, however, is of the opinion that the Sardinians are a melancholy people – although it is a trait which somehow seems in keeping with the rugged desolation of much of the countryside. Some observers maintain that the islanders are fundamentally a cheerful and out-going race. Many would say both attitudes are correct, for

ness by the Prefiche, who enumerate the murdered members of each family, recapitulate the wrongs and injuries, appeal to God, honour, and duty, and use every argument for revenge".

As long ago as the mid-19th century the government was trying to prohibit these emotional incitements to revenge the death of a loved one but the ceremony of the *attitidu*, which forms part of the *sarja* (wake), continues to be practised, particularly in some of the more remote regions of the Barbagia. Nonetheless, persistent pressure by the church has resulted in the reluctant abandoning of the most violent curses in favour of a "quieter, more sorrowful almost liturgical" lamentation (Gino Bottiglioni).

the soul of the typical Sardinian – who celebrates with such gusto, who is so full of vitality and who organises horse shows and poetry competitions between the shrewdest Improvvisatori – is remarkably contradictory.

In a work which is in essence an essay on the nature of the Sardinian, published under the meaningful title *Miele Amaro* (Bitter Honey), the writer Salvatore Cambosu maintains that the Sardinians do indeed enjoy festivals, but only because such celebrations act as an anaesthetic, numbing the painful consciousness of their tragic existence – and not because they regard them as a means of amusement. If a Sardinian actually laughs, then more often than not it is the proverbial *ghigno Sardonico* – a sardonic, spiteful laughter which is neither amusing nor an expression of joie de vivre.

Their tragedy, some maintain, is expressed by the scary masks of the *mamuthones* and those of their companions, the *issocadores*, both of which can be seen in the village of Mamoiada in the Barbagia, the heart of traditional Sardinia *(see page 275)*. (In Ottana and other villages in the same region the carnival processions are mostly dominated by the presence of *boes* or *merdùles*, wearing masks based on an ox's head.) If we are to accept the theories of researchers, these masks represent an

## The ballu tundu

Another remarkable manifestation of the contradictory combination of sadness and mirth is the *ballu*, the dance – a traditional form of expression held in high esteem by the Sardinians and still popular on high days and holidays. Though similar to the national dances of Greece and Romania, the Sardinian version is usually executed more solemnly.

Traditionally, only men and women who were betrothed or married were allowed to link fingers or touch palms – though J.W.W. Tyndale noticed that this rule was not respected in the village of Osidda in the province of Nuoro,

allegorical reference to the tragically recurring events of Sardinian history.

The wild, cumbersome *mamuthones* (who also wear sheep fleeces and huge bells on their backs), according to anthropologists, are caught by the *laccio* or *soca* (lassos) of the nimble, mocking *issocadores*, who are nothing less than images of the island's countless foreign conquerors. Francesco Masala, one of the principal writers of Sardinia's so-called *Ideology of the Vanquished*, believes this to be the case.

**LEFT:** the *ballu tundu*, a traditional round dance, in the 1950s.
**ABOVE:** a singing group *(torrone)* from Ulassai.

where "whether by uniform usage, or by a peculiar dispensation from the patron saint of the day, the greater part danced with their hands round waists".

Here, too, the observations of travellers and researchers are in blatant contradiction to each other. It is perhaps interesting to note that the comments of the "Interpreters" of Sardinia, to adopt the phrase coined by the cultural anthropologist Alberto M. Cirese, fall into two distinct categories: calumny or eulogy. Some writers – like Baldessare Luciano – regarded the *ballu tundu*, the "national dance" of Sardinia, as lascivious; others, such as Pater Bresciani, insisted that it was on the contrary dignified, serious and solemn, despite the occasional interludes of frivolity. Recently the semiologist Leonardo Sole drew attention to what he called the significant "mythical silence" which still surrounds the *ballu tundu*, and which bears a certain resemblance to a "sacred chorus". Ethnographer Francesco Alziator, who has made a study of the age of the *ballu tundu*, wrote; "Two basic features of this round dance support the theory that it is very ancient: firstly the *launeddas* (flutes), which traditionally accompany the dance throughout

> ### BALLU TUNDU ART
>
> Twentieth-century Sardinian artists Mario Delitala, Stanis Dessy and Carmelo Floris have all painted symbolic representations of the *ballu tundu*.

Como (the ruins of the adjoining historic village are now completely submerged beneath a reservoir). Aru remarks that "On the outermost right-hand pillar, on the apse side, is a painting of people dancing: tiny figures holding hands; on their heads they are wearing the *berretta* (the traditional beret of Sardinia)".

The *launeddas*, the musical instruments which provide the accompaniment for the *ballu tundu*, are thought to be very ancient indeed, possibly dating from as long ago as the time of the Nuraghi. They

almost a quarter of the island, and secondly the association of the dance with fire. For in the olden days there was almost always a fire in the centre of the circle of dancers." It is easy enough to imagine the scene; all one needs to do is to study the paintings by Mario Delitala, Stanis Dessy, Carmelo Floris or one of the other 20th-century Sardinian artists. All the painters mentioned have frequently found inspiration in the symbolic representation of the *ballu tundu*.

The art historian Carlo Aru has discovered what may be the earliest portrayal of the Sardinian *ballu tundu* in an interesting painting that hangs in the medieval chapel of San Pietro di Zuri, which was built in 1291 by Anselmo da

are a type of flute, but quite unique, occurring only on Sardinia.

## Music and culture

In a detailed study of the *launedda*, distinguished ethno-musicologists Giulio Fara and Gavino Gabriel speculate that this "triple-piped" instrument, which looks like a bagpipe without the sound bladder, might in fact be closely related to the shepherd's flute with pipes of varying length which is described by Virgil.

Tyndale worried that the "great exertion required to blow the *launedda* has considerable effect upon the health of the musicians, who frequently play for hours together". In his remarkable summary of the island's cultural heritage, a work which has assumed the form of an ethnographic stream of consciousness, Salvatore Cambosu attributes more sinister qualities to the sound of the *launedda* than the amiable Tyndale does, defining it as an existential metaphor for an "historic illness".

All of a sudden we see again before us the terrifying, grim expression of the Sardinian with the evil eye, whose character has supposedly left its ugly mark so irrevocably on the island's history.

### THE LAUNEDDA

Ethno-musicologist J.W.W. Tyndale pronounced the sound of the *launedda* (the traditional Sardinian flute) "though strange and wild, not disagreeable to the ear".

dinia: the abolition of the feudal system at the beginning of the 19th century and the monopolisation of cheese production by the large cheese-making companies on the Italian mainland during the last century. These two events challenged the basis of island society and its foundation in the pastoral culture. In an alarming, tangible way cork and plastic – the incompatible symbols of two extremely different cultures – simultaneously determined everyday life and manufacturing techniques on the island in the 1960s.

During the 20th century the cohesive strength of Sardinian culture – which is so introverted that it has earned the nicknames "Culture of Stone" and "Culture of Loneliness" – has suffered a damaging blow which threatens to destroy utterly an entire folkloric tradition.

This transformation has happened within the framework of changes that have taken place in Sardinia this century, and is, according to the ethnologist Giulio Angioni, the result of two "conspicuous historic turning points" on Sar-

**LEFT:** *launedda* players at the Sant'Efisio held festival in Cagliari.
**ABOVE:** the Easter festival at Alghero.

## Sardinia's festivals

Nowadays, Sardinia's great folkloric traditions are virtually restricted to the most important religious *sagre* (folk festivals), such as the processions of the *Redentore* (Saviour) in Nuoro in August, the *Candelieri* (Festival of Candles) in Sassari in August and *Sant'Efisio* (the biggest festival on the entire island, held in Cagliari each May), or the principal feudal tournaments such as the *Sartiglia* which takes place every spring in Oristano.

These are festivals in which sacred and profane elements coexist. Their effect is powerful. Although tourism has popularised and commercialised Sardinia's festivals, there is no better way of gaining an insight into the character and moods of the island than by taking part in these events.

Nostalgic, religious and full of contradictions, they provide an ideal starting point for an exploration of the Sardinian soul. It is remarkable how so varied a people celebrate so much within such a small area. The diverse characters of the inhabitants match the marked contrasts between the coastal region and the interior

What the descendants of settlers on the island of Sant'Antioco who arrived from North Africa many centuries ago have in common

with those of long-established residents in Alghero whose first language is Catalan, is that both communities cling to their own traditions, and not only in the food they eat – from couscous to lobster Catalane.

As already mentioned, the island's most famous festival, dating from 1656, is that of *Sant'Efisio*, the martyr and patron saint of Cagliari *(see page 162)*. On 1 May, in a grandiose procession, his statue is borne high on an ox cart from the capital to Pula, the place where he was executed. Local residents in traditional costume join his train, which is accompanied by the music of *launeddas*. The festival is an annual highlight in the lives of

many of Cagliari's citizens, but even this, the most spectacular event, isn't treated simply as a beanfeast. Sardinia's festivals are like many of the islanders themselves – frequently sombre, rarely to be taken lightly.

"None of the suave Greek-Italian charms, none of the airs and graces, none of the glamour," said D. H. Lawrence of a festa in Cagliari. "Rather bare, rather stark, rather cold and yellow," he continued. They are fiercely Christian but often their traditions make reference to pagan roots. The pre-Lenten carnivals – the best known is those of Mamoiada and Ottana – suggest more than Christian penance.

The disguise of the *mamuthones* (sinister wooden masks with twisted mouths) and the *merdules* (masks in the form of a bull's head) owe much to paganism *(see page 115)*. Equally sober are the Easter ceremonies, where the *confraternitate*, the brotherhoods, dressed in hoods and penitential robes, file solemnly through the narrow streets and alleys of towns and villages.

They give an impression of deep piety and penitence – it is not only the elderly among the spectators who genuflect before the crucifix – but again the accompanying torch processions and bonfires date from pre-Christian times.

*Candelieri*, the Festival of Candles, in Sassari in mid-August, when gigantic wooden candles are carried through the town in an ornate procession, is another authentic festival. It originated in the 13th century and is important enough for many expatriates to return home to celebrate it.

Another Sardinian characteristic, the strong element of *machismo*, can be observed in the *matanza*, the catching of the tuna in early summer when shoals of the fish migrate east. The fishermen begin their elaborate preparations for the bloody massacre weeks beforehand; their mood is one of anticipation and intense excitement. And in the equestrian festival of San Costantino, which takes place in Sedilo in July, religiosity and male pride combine. Many a rider has paid with his life for taking part in the wild horseback entry into the pilgrimage church, but there is never a shortage of volunteers. ❑

**LEFT:** the Easter festivities at Iglesiente, the origins of which date back to the 17th century.
**RIGHT:** Whitsun preparations.

# ART AND CRAFT

*Whether found in books, on the streets, or in the home, the artistry of Sardinia*

*represents cultural traditions learned orally through the generations*

The 20th century witnessed the appearance of some wonderful Sardinian literature, written for the most part in Italian. Grazia Deledda was awarded the Nobel prize for literature in 1927 *(see page 122)*, and 11 years later, Emilio Lussu's remarkable *Un anno sull'altipiano* (One Year on the Plateau), describing his

life as a fugitive and partisan, became a literary landmark. Lussu, who was a member of parliament, founded the Partito Sardo d'Azione movement in 1919.

More famous than either of these writers however was Antonio Gramsci, who was born in the village of Ales near Oristano. A leading political theorist, founder of eurocommunism and opponent of fascism, he was arrested in 1926 and spent the rest of his life in prison, where he died of tuberculosis in 1937. Only after the end of World War II was his *Lettere dal Carcere* (Letters from Prison) published. In the postwar years, Sardinian literature flourished. Gavino Ledda's autobiographical *Padre*

*Padrone* was successfully adapted for the big screen by the Taviani brothers in 1977, and Maria Giacobbe's *Diario di una Maestrina* (Diary of a Primary School Teacher) appeared in 1957. Giacobbe, who now lives in Denmark, published *Maschere ed Angeli Nudi* (Masks and Naked Angels), a portrait of her childhood, in 1999. The local book industry is currently awash with children's books. In addition to popular folk and fairy tales, these include compendiums of traditional games that have been played on Sardinian streets for generations.

## Poetry

Poetry in Sardinia has a long lineage that predates the image of the genre as a written, often romantic discipline. Given the island's rural nature, and the close-knit customs and conventions of its people, it's not surprising that the oral tradition is so prevalent. In times gone by family business, harvest details or indeed any communal news was passed down in verse. Still today, village fiestas feature popular *gare poetiche*.

These poetry contests involve two adversaries who make rhyming, and often spontaneous, comments about each other. The competitors are expected to come up with ironic, sarcastic or simply insulting repartee for the delectation of an amused audience. On a more elevated level, Sardinia's most famous poet was Sebastiano Satta (1867–1914). Though his fame did not travel very far from the island, he is still revered in his birthplace. There are numerous poetry prizes, including, since 1956, the Premio di Ozieri.

## Film

In 1953 there began an unfortunate trend that mirrored events on mainland Italy. The island's first kidnapping, at Orgosolo, was the subject of the Sicilian movie director Vittorio de Seta's *Banditi ad Orgosolo*. Made on the low budget that characterised the prevalent neo-realist genre of Italian films, it won a prize at the 1961 Venice Film Festival, but is rarely seen today. For all its international success, the Taviani brothers' *Padre Padrone* was controversial among the islanders, some of whom objected to its less than flattering portrayal of Sardinian life. This, the story of a shepherd who becomes a writer in the face of his despotic father's opposition, is nevertheless an honest, lyrical depiction of the island on which it was filmed.

## Murals

It was in the early 1970s that Sardinian artists began to create murals, usually on brick walls created by an individual or group of artists. To the islanders this was a new form of art. For all its everyday immediacy, its content could be

injustice. The murals illustrate the popular perceptions of alienation from the mainland and its cities, and at the same time express pride in the island's earthy virtues *(see pages 216–217).*

## Crafts

Authentic Sardinian crafts may have developed in conditions of poverty, isolation, oppression, fear and stubbornness, but they also represent the artists' ingeniousness, and their honest skill, pride and dignity. On an island that has long been a world of its own with little contact with outside civilisation, shepherds and farmers, miners and craftsmen had to develop their own

compared with more elevated forms, such as poetry and film. Like those art forms, murals are often used as a means to convey allegorical stories, political messages, or simply a nostalgic pride in traditional folk art. Most frequently, Sardinian artists paint murals as a commentary on the local reality. It is quite apt that, on the island that gave birth to the eurocommunism of Gramsci and the searing indictment that is *Padre Padrone*, the people have learned to use art as a way to voice their outrage at social

**LEFT:** a mural of the poster advertising the film *Banditi ad Orgosolo.*
**ABOVE:** a mural celebrating the old traditions.

creativity and construct everything they might need in their daily life. Thus from necessity they learned how to give expression to beautiful forms. Characterised by modest, simple designs, their creations depended on local nature's bounty for both raw materials and inspiration. Over the years, Sards have applied their good taste to a variety of crafts.

## Ceramics

Sardinian craftsmen have been skilled in the production of terracotta since prehistoric times. Figures and lines learned from the cultures of nations that conquered the island have been passed down the generations. The history of

# Grazia Deledda

Grazia Deledda, Sardinia's Nobel Prize-winning novelist, was born on 21 September 1871 in Nuoro, the daughter of Giovanni Antonio Deledda and Francesca Cambosu. At 15 she produced her first major work in which she painstakingly described and, when necessary, interpreted the characteristic customs of the inhabitants of Nuoro and its surroundings for the *Rivista delle Tradizioni Popolari Italiane*, Angelo de Gubernatis's periodical for Italian folkloric culture. It was an impressive work detailing all aspects of

life on Sardinia at the time. This treasure chest of knowledge, including some of the earliest records of Sardinian civilisation which had been passed down the generations for thousands of years, was to provide the basis for her books. Totalling almost 50 in number, their action nearly always takes place in Nuoro, at the very heart of the island.

Before 1900 Grazia Deledda wrote a great deal, publishing parts of her work in Sardinian or Italian periodicals. Some of her novels, such as *Fior di Sardegna* and *Anime Oneste*, reaped some harsh criticism from her fellow-citizens, but also encouraging praise from well-known Sardinian and Italian intellectuals. She was determined not to accept the role traditionally demanded of a woman in Sar-

dinian society. The customs of the time had the force of ancient, unwritten law. The man represented the family in public, tilled the fields and tried to increase the family fortune. It was the woman's duty to bear children and to bring them up to conform to the rules of the clan or village. She should be a careful housekeeper and, ideally, augment the family income by means of traditional female occupations – sewing, weaving or the cultivation of a vegetable garden.

During a visit to Cagliari, Grazia met Palmiro Madesani, a ministry official. It was not long before he asked her to marry him. Grazia agreed, on the condition that they move to Rome, and after their marriage in Nuoro, the newly-weds moved to the capital in 1900. In her luggage Grazia had packed notes and sketches for several important, as yet unfinished works, including *Elias Portolu*, which was to be published a few years later in 1903. It was followed the next year by *Cenere (Cinders)* and *Canne al Vento* (*Reeds in the Wind*, 1913) which continued the realist style of her early works. In Rome she divided her attention between her writing and her sons Sardus and Francesco ("Fran"). She wanted to describe Sardinia for posterity, as her role model, Leo Tolstoy, had done for Russia.

The move to Rome marked the start of a period of reflection on her faraway home, which she was to visit annually until 1911. The distance seemed to fuel the fires of her creativity, lending her works their characteristic depth and maturity. She wrote of stirring, sun-drenched landscapes, of the awe-inspiring solitude of some regions, of the silence pervading the island and the lives and deaths of its inhabitants, inextricably linked to the core of the earth's existence and the rhythm of the seasons.

Receiving the Nobel Prize for Literature in 1926, she made Sardinia famous throughout the world. Through her novels, European literary circles as well as Italian became aware of the unique life of the island's shepherds, of the happiness and disappointments of its young men and women, and of the lords and ladies of this ancient nation. Her characters were not presented as leading static lives, as though sitting motionless in a Homeric pastoral idyll in accordance with the popular myth, but as setting out on a journey towards the intellectual and cultural achievements of modern times. Grazia Deledda died in Rome from breast cancer in 1936. ❏

**LEFT:** Grazia Deledda, winner of the Nobel Prize for Literature in 1927.

baking clay runs parallel to that of mankind and these rustic craftsmen have remained faithful to an aesthetic standard based on simplicity and elegance. In days gone by, craftsmen were called *strexiaus*. (A *strexiu* is a craftsman who makes household crockery and domestic ceramic items such as water jugs, cooking pots, jars, and pitchers known as *marinas* for the preservation of foodstuffs, enormous bowls known as *sciveddas* that are used to prepare the dough from which bread is made, and so on.) Only at

### QUALITY GUARANTEED

ISOLA (the Sardinian Institute of Handicraft) promotes the island's arts and crafts and also acts as a guarantor of works' origins, their quality and, most vital to tourists, their authenticity.

Assemini, near Cagliari, where a large group of ceramicists display their products. Their presence here is due to the Paideia Cooperative, which has established the Assemini centre as a venue for exhibitions. This centre is also sponsored by the ISOLA (Sardinian Institute of Handicraft).

### Wickerwork

The island's rushes, asphodel, reeds, willow, myrtle, lentisk, straw and raffia have all been utilised to create a whole range of practical objects such as bas-

**ABOVE:** modern ceramic vases.

the turn of the 20th century did the practical *strexiaus* become artistic ceramicists as their pottery increasingly lent itself to the creation of modern furnishings and art objects with enamelled designs and beautiful colours. Today the ceramicists adapt the old, unchanged techniques and tools to produce modern goods. For example, contemporary pieces are still coloured by an application of the essence of fresh rockrose leaves. This is just one of a thousand ways in which "primitive" technology gives terracotta a natural colouring. One of the most popular places at which to see the results is at

kets, hampers and mats. The results typically have strong, simple structures and elegant lines. One of the best places to find basket weaving, and in particular, asphodel, is Flussio, a small village in the Planargia region. Asphodel is a plant with a long stem that grows wild in the grass pastures of the uplands and hills. Whereas skilled women weave the baskets, it is the men who pick out and uproot the ripe stems, tying them in great bundles and leaving them to dry for 10 days.

After a series of delicate operations produces fibres of different colours, they are ready for weaving. The tool for weaving is the awl, usually made from the shinbone of a cow, sharpened at one end. Among the most common motifs you'll find the arch, the Greek fret, the star, the flower, the rose, the bird, the leaf, and the dance. Baskets are displayed in front of the houses where they are sold.

Another place worth visiting for insights into basketwork is Castelsardo. You'll find the Museo dell'Intreccio Mediterraneo (Museum of Basket Weaving) in Castelsardo's castle. Exhibits here include a large assortment of utensils and tools for everyday life, all made

> ### TAPESTRY TOWN
>
> Mogoro is one of the leading centres for the weaving of carpets and tapestries in Sardinia. Every summer the town hosts an exhibition of old tapestry with a market for new products.

from locally picked dwarf-palm leaves. As you stroll along the narrow streets, you'll doubtless see women weaving baskets in the fresh air.

## Jewellery, filigree and coral

In an island known as "the land of metals", gold and silver were the driving force behind the flourishing production of amulets, talismans, necklaces and precious jewellery items *(see pages 128–129)*. The amulets and ornaments acquire significance when the silver nuggets are enriched with balls of obsidian (dark, glassy volcanic rock) that apparently give them a magical quality. Goldsmiths prospered in Sardinia in the 14th century. The workshops of that time

have left traces above all in the production of religious objects and crucifixes, candelabra, rosaries and votive offerings. The two centres that have most developed and refined this art are Cagliari and Quartu Sant'Elena, which still produce examples of rare beauty in traditional filigree jewellery. Examples include buttons shaped like breasts, earrings, necklaces, rings such as the traditional wedding band, bracelets and brooches studded with gems, pearl and coral.

From prehistoric times coral was used both as a decorative ornament and as a talisman. As a result of its colour and mysterious origin, coral has always been believed to possess magical powers. Although the entire coastline is rich in coral, Alghero is particularly famous for its beautiful jewels: necklaces, earrings, bracelets and religious statuettes all emanate from here. The windows of the workshops and shops of the old city exhibit a range of jewellery, with colourful nuances ranging from pink and deep crimson to gold.

## Carpets and tapestry

The wool of the island's numerous sheep has traditionally provided the raw material for the most successful of the small cottages industries based on the use of the old oak loom. Even today the stiff, coarse wool is used in the manufacture of carpets, wall hangings, bedspreads and furnishing fabrics. This craft also produces refined embroideries and lace that continues the techniques and the designs of an age-old practice. Motifs range from ornate geometrical patterns to designs that reveal the influence of Byzantine art, Romanesque elements, baroque art and Renaissance culture.

The hand-embroidered *a puntu de agu* technique is extremely tiring and exacting on the worker, who is required to embroider by hand using woollen or even gold or silver thread. The traditional motifs – such as brightly coloured flowers, hunters on horseback, unicorns, castles and scenes of *ballu tundu* (round dances) – remain popular, as does the technique of dying fabrics with natural colours taken from plants, infusions of leaves, flowers, bark, roots from coloured earth and even from murex. Another traditional craft product is the embroidered shawls that are made in Oliena. These typically come in dark wool, silk or linen, adorned with colourful flower motifs embroidered with gold and silver thread and embellished with gems. The shawl borders are lined with long fringes.

## Woodcarving

The craft of woodcarving developed from the peasant custom of decorating objects used in daily life with the tip of a knife; this practice has inspired the woodcarving of modern artists. Splendid wedding

## Leather and ironwork

The leather-goods tradition is almost as old as the Sardinian hills. The island's leather craftsmen are known for their high-quality harnesses and horse saddles, but they also produce belts, handbags, various clothing items, cushions and decorative objects. Leather handicrafts are usually decorated with traditional motifs and are embroidered with linen or silk thread to reproduce the typical figures of Sardinian folk art: flowers, arabesques,

chests adorned by geometric patterns and floral designs are typical. Old and richly carved chests were once the only pieces of furniture in sparsely furnished Sardinian homes. Usually made of dark chestnut wood, painted and darkened with warm ox or goat blood or with vegetable dyes, and decorated with harmonious motifs they are finely representative of the Barbagia style. Their figures – animals, birds, flowers and abstract symbols – are evidence of the mystical origin of local culture. In Sorgono you will find excellent carved wooden chests.

LEFT: a basket weaver practising the ancient craft.
ABOVE: geometric designs enliven carpets and rugs.

diverse crenellated patterns, human figurines and historical characters.

The most common iron products made in Sardinia are knives, the most popular of which – the famous *leppas* with their sharp blade and shaft of ram or mouflon horn – are made in Pattada *(see page 104)*. Other products include artistic railings, sculptures, lamp and light fixtures and assorted furniture made and sold around the island. The unmistakable style of Sardinian wrought iron recalls the arabesques of the Near East and Toledo, but most of all it is redolent of primitive early history, a time charged with magic that still enchants with the fantasy of its designs. ❑

# LANGUAGE

*The Sardinian language, made up from many dialects, has never been standardised.*
*Many fear that, unless this happens, it will be overwhelmed by Italian*

Sardinian is an old Romance language with a highly original and, in some cases, extremely archaic vocabulary. It is considered to be the most characteristic of all Romance languages, and is linked to Italian and all other Romance languages by the Latin of Roman times. During the Roman conquest of

the island Latin took over all the existing languages introduced by the Phoenicians and the Cartaginenses. Apart from its Latin skeleton, the vocabulary of Sardinian reflects the entire history of the island.

Place names, in particular, have retained roots from prehistoric times and there are a few remnants of Phoenician and Etruscan along with a handful of words with a Greek derivation dating from the Byzantine era. By the 14th century, Sardinian had developed from vulgar Latin. For the next 400 years first Catalan and then Castilian were the official languages. During the 13th and 14th centuries a quasi-official Sardinian language also established itself

through the promulgation of laws in Sardinian by the ruler-kings of Arborea. Today, the rich and complex language is an amalgam of the island's many dialects: Logudoro in the northern central region, Campidano in the south, and a number of very ancient dialects in the mountainous region around Nuoro.

All the regions are bilingual and it is only recently that Sardinian has taken second place to "standard Italian". In general, people use their dialect in informal situations only. The dialects spoken in Sassari and Gallura to the north reveal close links with the languages of Tuscany and Corsica due to waves of migration during the 17th century. On the isle of San Pietro, off the south east coast of Sardinia, a strong Piedmontese dialect is spoken, mixed with an ancient Genoan dialect dating back to the 18th century. In Alghero, people speak a variation of Spanish Catalan introduced in the 14th century. There are traces of Spanish in all the island's dialects infused from Spain's 300-year colonisation of the island. In the region of Logudoro the influence of Latin in the dialect is very strong and it is considered to be the purest form of the Sarininan dialect.

The issue of standardising the Sardinian dialect remains unresolved, although there were attempts made during the 1970s to identify the main body of the language and to introduce it to the media and literature. This fragmentation of Sardinian is a major problem for the island's writers and poets. Montanaru (1878–1957), a poet popular throughout the island, was forced to use footnotes to his verse in order to make it comprehensible to the majority of his readers, despite his efforts to write in a "Standard Sardinian" language.

All the great Sardinian writers, including Sebastiano Satta, Grazia Deledda, Giuseppe Dessì and Gavino Ledda, have felt obliged to write in Italian. Today, the main threat to the survival of the Sardinian language is undoubt-

**LEFT:** mural showing Sardinians reading the news.
**RIGHT:** the Sardinian dialect is used among friends.

edly posed by the media, which is all in Italian. More than a million Sardinians (about 80 percent of the population) speak a form of Sardinian which makes it the largest linguistic minority in Italy.

From the start of the 1970s, the language became an expression of pride and identity and Sardinian people called upon the national and regional authorities not only to recognise the Sardinian people as an ethnic and linguistic minority but also to recognise Sardinian as the national and official language of the island. During the 1970s the Partito Sardo d'Azione launched campaigns to persuade the regional authorities to put Sardinian on an equal footing with Italian. Sardinian with the passing of time has became more and more an Italian *patois* under the label of regional Italian.

The fact that the Italian language is increasingly asserting itself in the conversational language of the young and that the use of Sardinian is declining in rural areas is resulting in the gradual reduction in the number of Sardinian speakers. But despite this constant regression, Sardinian remains a living language and it is estimated that half of Sardinian families were still speaking the language in the second half of the 1990s.                    ❏

## SARDINIAN PROVERBS

Proverbs are the expression of the defining culture of a country. In an agropastoral world like that of Sardinia, language is usually very simple and direct but full of meaning. As Sardinians say *"Su tropu istorpiat"* (too much disturbs). Elderly Sardinians often make use of proverbs in reference to situations in daily life, eg. *"Bene narat su diciu"* (the saying speaks well). Proverbs are collective observations about life and death, philosophy and the meaning of life. Sardinian society is very individualistic and when it is hard to find a consensus people will often say *"Centu conca centu berrittas"* (a hundred heads for a hundred hats). Sardinians value their social life, family and friends highly. Proverbs about friendship include: *"su bisonzu a connosches sos amigos"* (a friend in need is a friend indeed) or *"Mezus bastonadas de amigu chi non lusingas de inimigu"* (better to have blows from a friend than compliments from an enemy). Belief in the traditional laws of vengeance to find justice are reflected in the saying: *"Justizia pronta, vinditta fatta"* (ready justice, revenge done) while Sardinia's traditional values, rooted in the soil and farming, gives rise to the highest personal compliments to be paid from one person to another: *"Bona commenti su pani"* (good as bread) because bread is essential for life.

# SARDINIAN COSTUME AND JEWELLERY

*The wearing of traditional costume and jewellery is still very much an integral part of the island's festivals and feast days*

At festival time in Sardinia the streets of the villages and towns become ablaze with men and women wearing highly coloured traditional costumes. Intricate and flamboyant, the costumes are in stark contrast to the surrounding countryside. Sardinians are big festival-goers; in the past highdays and feast days were an opportunity to meet people from other villages and mark important occasions. In this closed island society costume and jewellery were not only indicators of where you came from but of social standing and wealth as well. Regional variations in costume are still apparent today and are worn with pride by village members. In general, traditional dress for women consists of beautiful red waistcoats edged with gold filigree work cut away at the sleeve, and worn over white blouses with lace cuffs and collars, decorated with an elaborate brooch. Full-length layered dresses of white, black and red are worn; in some areas a blue apron is added to the red outer skirt. A black or white embroidered headscarf is also worn; in Desulo and some other mountain villages embroidered caps are favoured. Beautifully embroidered black shawls with silk fringes are drawn across the shoulders. The costumes are accessorised with rings, brooches, necklaces, cuff-links, bracelets, pendants and intricate buttons. Traditional costume for men is far less elaborate but still very colourful. It consists of a red waistcoat, white shirt, red neckerchief and a black skull cap called a *berreta*. The best collection of traditional costumes is at the ethnographic museum at Nuoro *(see page 279)*.

▷ **DECORATION**
Hand-made shoes are decorated in the same manner as costumes, using techniques handed down from mother to daughter. Many items take years to complete.

△ **MALE DRESS**
The lead male rider in the Sa Sartiglia festival in Oristano is sown into a white shirt by a group of girls and he wears a woman's mask, bride's veil and a black hat.

◁ **THE PARAPETTU**
*Parapettu* is a traditional item of clothing worn by women to cover their breasts. It dates back to 1852 when the Jesuits decided that displays of flesh led to temptation.

◁ **EASTER IN SASSARI**
Festival jewellery includes *su Giunchigliu* necklaces and filigree *sos breves* pinned to clothing containing images, prayers and magic spells.

△ **OLIENA CRAFTS**
A woman from Oliena wearing pieces of traditional jewellery, including buttons inset with turquoise and a velvet choker with a gold pendant.

# TRADITIONAL JEWELLERY

Sardinian *prendas* (jewellery) is intrinsically linked to traditional costume. Made of gold, silver or very fine filigree, it is handed down through the generations and reflects life, fertility and love in its design. The quality and amount of jewellery is an important indication of social status. Worn on a dress or waistcoat, buttons have a small cylinder inlaid with a semi-precious stone at their centre. Necklaces come in two types: *su Giunchigliu*, a long gold chain wrapped several times around the neck, or *su Ghettau*, which has links adorned with large filigree balls. Precious stones are worn from a dark velvet choker. *Maninfide* rings, featuring two clasped hands, are given by a fiancé to his intended. The most distinctive design for brooches is the *Sinnai*, which has a large ruby or cameo set in the centre of a sunflower design. Typical feast-day earrings are shaped in a bow with a pendant of a semi-precious stone, or are butterfly-shaped and made of gold leaf. Earrings with figures of a bird, peacock or hen and joined by two cones or pyramids are also worn, as are earrings in the shape of bunches of grapes.

▽ **ORGOSOLO PARADE**
The village of Orgosolo has two popular festivals in which all the inhabitants, including children, take part by dressing up in traditional costumes.

▷ **DESULO DRESS**
Many of Sardinia's traditional costumes feature elaborate embroidery and *petit-point*, as this superb tunic and head dress from Desulo show.

▽ **HEADDRESS**
Sardinian women use a heavily embroidered shawl to cover their heads. They are the result of years of work and are worn with pride.

# FOOD AND DRINK

*Eating and drinking in Sardinia is a treat. The food is simple, good value and gutsy, while the wines are some of the best produced in Italy*

Sardinian cooking comes from an agri-pastoral past, poor and simple. It is the cooking of shepherds and farmers who have never been rich but have made their simple dishes tastier by the use of aromatic herbs offered by the earth. An ancient inscription in the Grotta della Vipera in Cagliari mentions the use of saffron, the violet stigma of the crocus flower, in cooking. Other common aromatic herbs are the black berry of the myrtle, rosemary, laurel, mint and many others.

Sardinian cooking may be poor in some respects but it is extremely rich in others, for it has flavour, intelligence, versatility and an exotic nature. Some recipes are still prepared in the same way as they were thousand of years ago. The native cuisine of the island has also been influenced by other Mediterranean cultures such as the Arabs. For example, in the isle of San Pietro a popular dish is *cas-cas* which is the same as North African and Arab couscous. Another is the couscous-like dish, *fregula,* which originated in ancient Rome and is a fusion of these three cultures.

In ancient times meat requirements were met by hunting or by keeping animals such as pigs, sheep, cows and goats or occasionally horses. White meat, especially poultry, was eaten only in small quantities: roast or boiling fowl was regarded as food only for invalids or pregnant women. Surprisingly for an island, fish fared no better (though the island did give the name to sardines, fished in copious numbers).

It is possible that the lack of appetite for seafood is explained by the fact that the Sardinians have never been a nation of seafarers. They have always regarded the sea as an enemy, ever bringing new waves of conquerors to their island. Even today the owners of the fishing fleets operating in Sardinian waters tend to come from Ponza, Naples, Genoa or Carloforte. The annual *matanza*, the tuna harvest, an event dating from Roman times, is

these days mainly to supply the export market and is by and large backed by Japanese funds. That said, recent trends have led to a greater emphasis on fish in restaurants on the coast; around Cagliari, in particular, you will find excellent lobster, red and grey mullet, and in the Oristano-Cabras region, eel.

## Breads

A variety of kneading techniques, handed down by women from generation to generation, and widely differing forms and contrasting types of leavening explain the remarkable range of breads available on the island. The artistically shaped loaf of bread is a typical example of Sardinia's culinary heritage.

At festivals, people try to outdo one another with the intricacy of their designs. Each area in the patchwork of regions has its own characteristically shaped loaf, so it would be difficult to attempt to produce even a semi-complete list. The best-known – not least because it is successfully marketed on the mainland – is the

**LEFT:** cheese is still made by hand.
**RIGHT:** picking olives in the time-honoured tradition.

*pane carasau* (sheet of music) – two crisp, round, flat loaves. As this type of bread keeps fresh for long periods, shepherds have traditionally taken a few *pane carasau* with them as provisions on their long wanderings. *Su pistoccu, su infraxiu* and *su cocoi* are sold in bakeries all over the island. Most restaurants serving typical Sardinian cooking list various types of breads among their specialities.

## Roast specialities

Deserving of more detailed study are the *arrosti*, the roast and grilled meat specialities which are a highlight of Sardinian gastronomy,

particularly in the island's interior. The principal characteristic of these dishes is that only the meat of young animals – lamb, kid, suckling pig and veal – is used.

There are two main methods of preparation. In the first, shared by other Mediterranean countries (in particular Turkey), a hole is dug in the ground (stakes are laid on its base and driven round the inside to shore back the earth) and a deep trench is then dug round the hole, leaving about six inches of soil as a "wall". The meat, usually the whole carcass, is placed inside the hole (which is liberally lined with herbs), and a fire is lit above. When this is sufficiently hot, the live ashes are raked into the trench. The heat bakes the meat evenly; the herbs lend it a delicious aromatic flavour.

In the second method, the suckling pig, lamb, kid or veal is placed on wooden or metal spits. These are then positioned vertically or horizontally around the central fire. The spits are turned from time to time to ensure that the meat cooks evenly.

In some districts the finishing touch is provided by a lump of bacon fat, which is wrapped in paper and then ignited. As it drips down on to the spit, the fat colours the meat golden brown and makes it crisp. One of the few good things D. H. Lawrence had to say about Sardinia was about such a kid roast.

The most impressive *arrosti* are those served on special occasions: country festivals, saints' days or weddings. For the Sardinians, any cause for celebration naturally presents a social duty to provide good and plentiful food. You can sample an *arrosto*, usually described as a typical Sardinian speciality, in nearly every restaurant on the island. Although not the only true Sardinian dish, the *arrosti* have a centuries-old tradition.

## Antipasto

The most popular *antipasto* (hors d'oeuvre), the *antipasto di terra*, offers a selection of ham, smoked sausages, olives, chicken liver, heart, *sa cordula* (lamb tripe, served rolled up and grilled or fried with peas), mushrooms and brawn. As well as *antipasto di terra* there is *coccoi e sattizzu* which is bread with sausage or Sardinian *prosciutto*, a cured ham often made of wild boar. Visitors who want to eat seafood can usually opt for a sophisticated but unfortunately not typically Sardinian *antipasto di*

### HONEY

Sardinia produces excellent honey. Flavoured by its native flowers, many different varieties of honey are available. Among them are eucalyptus, orange blossom and wild lavender. There is also a bitter honey made from the strawberry tree *(arbutus unedo)*, which is prepared in December and is thought to prevent bronchial asthma. *Millefiori* or *miele della flora mediterranea* is made from a mixture of all the honey made throughout the year and is a good choice if you're looking for a pot of honey to take home with you. Honey can be bought in supermarkets, local shops or, best of all, at festivals and local fares from the people who make it .

*mare*, a recent innovation designed with tourists in mind. *Antipasti* usually are extremely simple and all the products are homemade. For example, olives in brine are always present, delicious after a period of seasoning in salted water with wild fennel seeds. Black olives in brine and sautéd in oil, garlic, and chopped parsley and a sprinkling of vinegar are another favourite.

A superb appetiser, *bottarga* is made from slated grey mullet roe which has been pressed and dried. *Bottarga* (often called Sardinian

## Pasta and soup dishes

As elsewhere in Italy, in Sardinia a meal without pasta is unthinkable. Here it is almost always home-made; the three most popular types are *malloreddus* (small wheat and potato flour dumplings), *maccarrones cravaos* (dumplings) and *maccarrones de busa* (a type of very fine cannelloni). All three are served in a sauce of fresh tomatoes with chunks of meat or pieces of smoked sausage and herbs and accompanied with a condiment of cheese melted in a bain-marie.

caviar) is served cut in thin slices covered in olive oil. When it is grated on pasta it makes an delicious first course.

Other starters include *merca*, a dish of grey mullet simmered in salted water and wrapped in marsh grass, and *bocconi*, which consists of whelks simmered in salted water served hot. *Sa burrida* can be eaten as an appetiser or a main dish. It is made of dogfish, boiled in slices and then marinated for at least 24 hours in a sauce made of garlic, parsley, walnuts, vinegar, and the chopped dogfish livers.

---

**LEFT:** Sardinian honey is a regional speciality.
**ABOVE:** roasting a pig on a spit for *arrosti*.

Equally common are thick broths of vegetables, meat and herbs; they are substantial, often meals in themselves. You could try *pecora in cappotto*, boiled mutton with potatoes, onions, celery and dried tomatoes prepared in Barbagia, or *suppa cuatta* (Italian *zuppa galllurese*), a dish with regional variations but generally made with large slices of bread and cheese arranged in a pan, sprinkled with grated *pecorino* and finely chopped garlic, drowned in a hot meat broth. Or in Moni *favata con lardo*, a soup of broad beans with sausage, lard and wild fennel. Another famous *primi piatti* (first course) are *angiulotts*: ravioli-like parcels stuffed with ricotta or fresh cheese, spinach and saffron. *Culungiones* are large ravioli stuffed with potato purée, mint and a little cheese, served with tomatoes or meat sauce; while the delicious *pane frattau* is made of *pane carasau,* softened in stock flavoured with *pecorino* cheese, tomato sauce and a pouched egg on top. *Fregula* is a granular pasta, similar to couscous. It is served with steamed clams, like pasta, or in broth as a thick soup.

## Seafood dishes

Seafood cuisine is a recent addition to the menu; in fact, until recently *su pisci* was the main food only in Cagliari and a few other coastal places. Today there are a lot of tasty fish dishes on the menu to choose from, starting with the famous *ziminu* or *ssaa cassola*, a fish stew. Among the many different types of fish available in Sardinia, mullet, red mullet, *ghiozzi* (small fish cooked in semolina and then fried) and eels, both barbequed and fried, deserve a special mention. All of them may be cooked and eaten as a main course if they have been marinated in *scabecciu*, a sautéd sauce of oil, garlic and vinegar.

Barbequed mullet can be prepared in two ways: either with a laurel leaf stuck into the fish's belly and left there for the cooking time,

or by immersing the fish, before cooking, in a brine made from water, garlic and an abundance of salt. Barbequing is also perfect for white bream, gilthead and seabream; bass, on the other hand, should be simmered and seasoned with olive oil and lemon. Lobster and crabs can also be cooked in this way.

Popular regional fish dishes include *l'aragosta alla catalana* (Catalan-style lobster), served with oil, vinegar and onions; *polpagliara*, small octopus simmered in a spicy

### MAIN DISHES

Main dishes are usually *an arrosto* made from suckling pig, lamb, kid or veal or wild boar, served with a spicy sauce. Vegetable side dishes include lettuce, fennel, celery, radishes and globe artichokes.

products for more than 5,000 years, so it is not surprising that the range of fine cheeses made from sheep's, goat's or cow's milk is extensive. Gourmets will delight in the discovery of *caprino, fiore sardo, semicotto, caglio, casagedu, casu marzu, pepato* and *romano*.

All types of cheese are available, from soft curd to hard, with flavours ranging from slightly acid to mild and aromatic to piquant. Some are eaten simply with bread; others are grated generously over pasta.

sauce; *fregula cun cocciula* (baby clams), best eaten in Cagliari; *orziadas*, sea anemones rolled in semolina and fried, also from Cagliari; roasted mullet and eel-soup from Oristano; fish casserole and *musciamme* (dried tuna fish fillet), a speciality of Carloforte; stuffed squid from Olbia; and roast cuttle fish from Dorgali.

### Desserts and cheeses

A traditional lunch *alla sarda* – Sardinian style – will conclude with cheese and dessert. The islanders have been manufacturing dairy

**LEFT:** a shop sign for a rustic bakery.
**ABOVE:** *merca*, grey mullet wrapped in marsh grass.

Desserts are another Sardinian speciality; one particular favourite, *sebada*, consists of two circles of pastry the size of a fruit plate; dipped in honey and sometimes sprinkled with sugar, they are filled with a layer of curd cheese and fried in deep fat. Invariably, a selection of fruit is offered at the end of a meal. This varies according to season. Popular, too, are dried fruits and nuts: almonds, hazelnuts and dried figs. A favourite confection at festival time consists of shelled almonds and orange peel dipped in honey.

The most commonly served digestif has always been *aquavite*, an aromatic grappa with a high alcohol content. Sardinians settle down for a glass or two at any time of day. Another powerfully flavoured liqueur has also become popular among Sardinians in recent years: *liquore di mirto*, distilled from myrtle. It is red in colour when it is manufactured from the berries, and clear if only the leaves of the plant are used.

## Wines

The origins of Sardinian wine go back to the century BC. The old *nuragus* vines (the name most probably comes from the nuraghe) together with the Vernaccia vines are the oldest on the island. The *cannonau, giro'* and *torbato*

vines date back to the time of the Catalans and the Aragonese; the *monica* and *malvasia* vines to the Byzantines, Vermentino vines to the Ligurians and the first *moscato* and *nasco* vines to the Romans.

There is a wide variety of local wines; most have a high alcohol content and are full-bodied, smooth, and deeply coloured. The best-known bear the description Cannonau. Wines bottled in the cooperative cellars bear the DOC, a label guaranteeing quality; this certificate of authenticity is only awarded to wines from specific wine-growing areas. The varieties available range from heavy and lighter red wines, through rosés to whites. Most tend to be on the dry side rather than sweet or heavy; some are decidedly tangy. Cannonau wines are grown in the eastern provinces and Dorgali. A lot of vineyards produce these wines; some have outlets where you can buy and taste wines. One of the popular places for tastings is retail shop at the Cantina Sociale di Jerzu co-operative in the Ogliastra.

Three wines from the district around Cagliari – Girò, Monica and Nasco – are red all fairly sweet or sweet. The popular Moscato di Cagliari and Malvasia are available from the Cantina Sociale di Quartu Sant'Elena. Nuragus, from the nearby Monserrato winery run by the Cantina Soicale di Monserrato, is an excellent accompaniment to pasta, rice dishes, soup, white meat, fish and seafood. Meloni wines, produced by the Meloni Vini, come from vineyards located in different areas of the island. At Selaargius, the Santa Rosa estate specialises in dessert wines.

Vernaccia, perhaps the most famous Sardinian wine, is served as a dessert wine or as an aperitif and tastes rather like a dry sherry. It comes from the Cantina Sociale della Vernaccia, founded in 1953, and is grown in the fertile lower valley of the Tirso river.

Mandrolisai (red or rosé) wine from Sorgono is traditionally drunk during the feast of San Mauro and Santu Antine. The Cantina Sociale del Mandrolisai was formed in 1952 to improve the quality and distribution of the wine. Semidano, a white wine with a fruity and intense bouquet, is excellent with shellfish and also comes from this area. Another good wine to go with shellfish is Vermentino, which can also be drunk as an aperitif. It is a light wine and has an aroma of quince with a hint of bitter almond.

From the provinces of Oristano and Nuoro comes Malvasia, a sweet dessert wine. Look out for Malvasia di Bosa, one of the most outstanding DOC Sardinian wines. The Malvasia white grape is common throughout the Mediterranean and is thought to have come from the Greek port of Monemvasia, in the Peloponnese. Returning to red wines and moving to the Sulcis in the southwest of the island, we find Carignano, a ruby red-garnet with an excellent consistency.

In restaurants the local wine *(vino locale)* is often served from jugs. It is usually very drinkable and is cheaper than buying by the bottle. ❏

**LEFT:** a bottle of wine from Sassari.
**RIGHT:** fresh *pecorino* cheese in a farmhouse kitchen.

# PLACES

*A detailed guide to the entire island, with principal sites clearly cross-referenced by number to the maps*

One can never go by appearances alone in Sardinia. By way of example, this book's first editor cited a vivid memory from his first visit to the island, way back in 1972, when he met some village youths in Orgosolo, who showed him their pistol and insisted on arranging "safe" accommodation for him. In the end, they all finished the evening eating spaghetti, drinking rough wine and playing cards – and it didn't seemed to matter that everyone else in the bar carried shotguns.

Since those days, much has changed. Mass tourism has made its impact on the north coast, and the Costa Smeralda has been taken over by the international jet set. However, for the individual traveller with initiative there are still many beautiful things to discover on the island, and they are covered in the following pages.

We begin with Cagliari, one of Europe's oldest cities. It has a little bit of everything: the cosmopolitan character of a port city, the luxuries of an Italian shopping mecca, Spanish ambience in the old quarter and the village-like character of a small Sardinian town. It has a warm atmosphere, is open and accessible, and is backlit by the wonderful Mediterranean sun. "Lost between Africa and Europe" is how D. H. Lawrence described the capital of the island, set atop its 10 hills.

We then travel up the east coast to Olbia, a fast-growing commercial centre which is also the gateway to the the Costa Smeralda, where, according to legend, the wind was born. We then take in Gallura and the north before reaching Sassari. With its rather unattractive outlying districts, its skyline of tall buildings, superhighway and shopping malls, Sassari may not instantly appeal, but it does have a cosmopolitan, big-city character which many may welcome after a spell at the beach. Finally, we proceed down the west coast, from Alghero to Oristano, through the southwest, and on to the Barbagia, a hilly and sometimes bleak terrain which the Romans named after the "barbarians" they found there.

Sardinia is justly famous for its beaches. The algae which plagues so many Mediterranean beaches has not yet arrived here, and there are the added enticements of white sand, rose-coloured cliffs and water of the deepest blue. Many beautiful beaches and inlets are still freely accessible, and there are still coastal regions which have not been opened up to mass tourism. Driving many kilometres in order to discover a secluded little beach of your own is therefore unnecessary. But remember two important points: the closer you are to one of the larger ferry harbours, the more crowded the beaches, and the closer to the Costa Smeralda, the more expensive is everything on offer. ❏

**PRECEDING PAGES:** taking in the view on the Gennargentu massif; stairs on the Capo Caccia leading to the Grotta di Nettuno; Cagliari at dusk.
**LEFT:** the rugged landscape of the Barbagia.

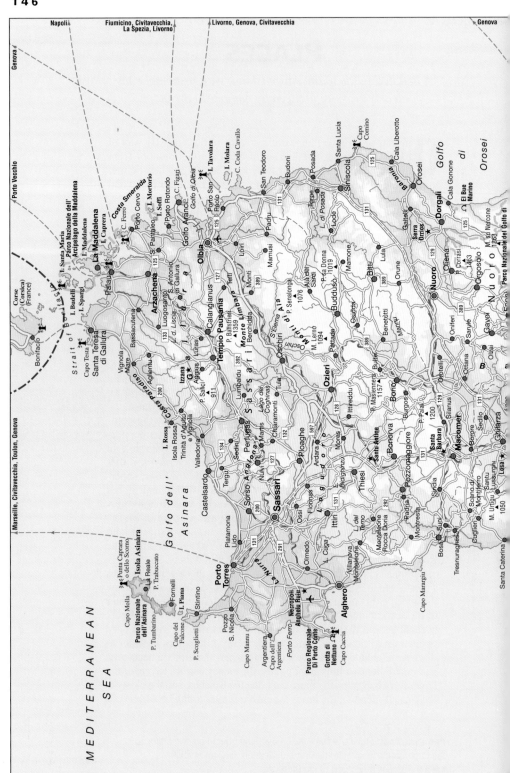

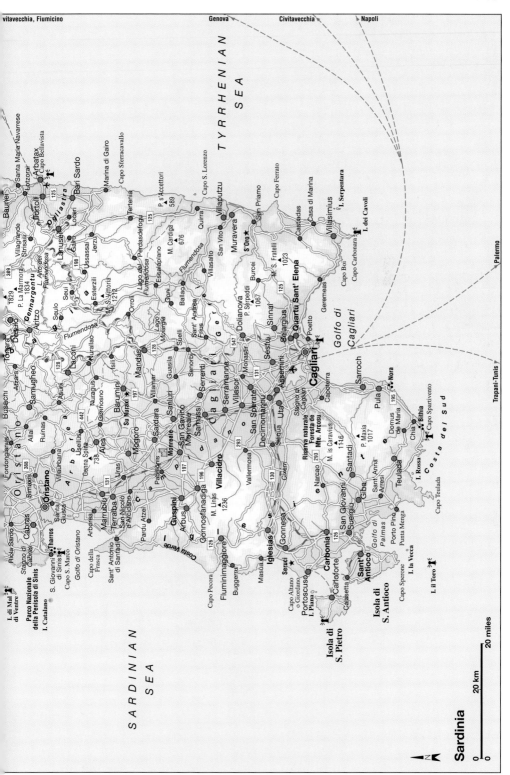

**Sardinia**

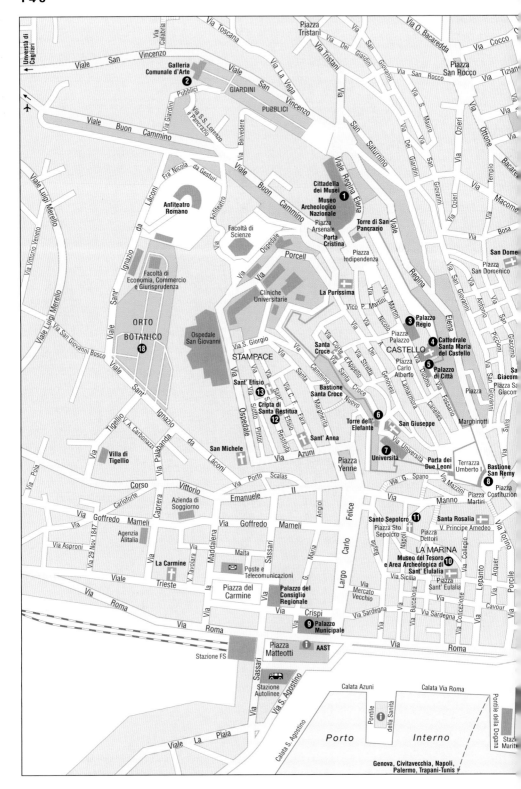

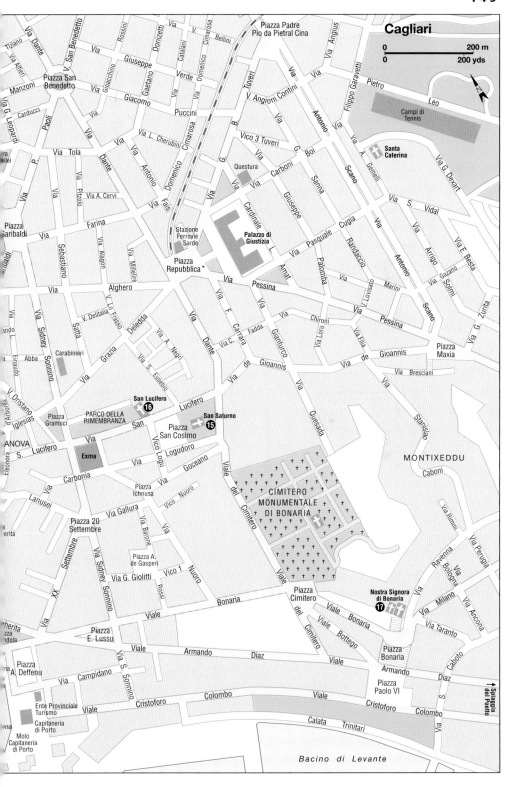

# CAGLIARI

*The name Cagliari is derived from the 12th-century Spanish callaris or callari, which comes from "karalis", "karale" or "karali" – older expressions meaning "a rocky place"*

Map on pages 148–49

L ooking across to the limestone hill of the Castello from Sant'Elia, the observer can see how appropriate the name of Cagliari is. Accurately dated archaeological finds from Sant'Elia, Santa Gilla, San Bartolomeo and Calamosca prove beyond doubt that the first inhabitants settled on this part of the island at the end of the 3rd millennium BC. The Phoenicians, plying their trading routes between their native shores (the present-day Lebanon) and the Iberian peninsula, moored their ships in Cagliari in the Golfo degli Angeli. The coast here formed a perfect natural harbour which afforded their fleet not only a safe and sheltered anchorage, but also the opportunity to take aboard fresh provisions. The Phoenicians colonised the area and built a series of trading ports along its coast. Cagliari soon developed into one of the most important trading centres on the East-West Mediterranean axis. Ships laden with goods from the East dropped anchor here in order to exchange some of their cargo for local products such as wool, cheese, minerals and cereals.

In order to accelerate the spread of their culture across the island, the next conquerors – the Carthaginians, descendants of the sea-faring Phoenicians – criss-crossed Sardinia with an important network of roads radiating from Cagliari. Evidence seems to indicate that the structure of the town administration here was modelled on that of Carthage itself: two *Sufeti* – native members of the urban aristocracy – were given the task of ruling the city. This was a clever move on the part of the invaders, for they chose two governors who belonged to families that had made their fortunes from trading (and were thus likely to be amenable to the Carthaginians), and who were also held in high esteem by the rank and file of the populace.

**LEFT:** the bastion of San Remy.
**BELOW:** balcony talk.

## Roman Cagliari

When the Romans arrived, the castle area must have formed the heart of the city under the Carthaginians, as it was to do later under Pisan rule. The Carthaginian town was delimited on one side by the extensive **Necropoli Tuvixeddu** and on the other by the **Necropoli Colle di Bonaria**. The discovery of the necropolis on the Colle di Bonaria was a particular source of jubilation in archaeological circles, as the site yielded numerous ancient inscriptions.

Not until the arrival of the Pisans would foreign invaders feel at home here. Following the decline of the Roman Empire, the town entered a prolonged period of stagnation. Since the Roman towns were more complex in design and of greater architectural merit than those of their successors, the colony they built on the coast was doomed to remain isolated and untouched by the newcomers whose more modest accommodation would have looked as out of place as the

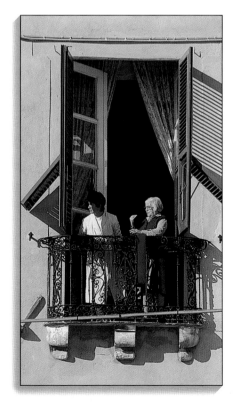

The Punic Necropoli Tuvixeddu (temporarily closed for renovation) has some interesting murals. The Anfiteatro Romano in Viale Sant'Ignazio da Láconi (open Nov–Mar 10am–4pm, Apr–Oct 10am–1pm, 3–6pm; entrance fee) was built in the 2nd century AD.

**BELOW:** the Palazzo Municipale serves as the town hall.

new residents in such splendid surroundings. Archaeological excavations and sporadic findings have verified the presence of the Roman town under the modern city. Remains of the Roman city include the Villa di Tigellio (not open to the public), a complex of three Roman houses dated from 1st century AD; the **Anfiteatro Romano** (Roman amphitheatre), built directly in the rock of a natural valley, and the recently discovered archaeological area of Sant' Eulalia in the Marina quarter. The extensive distribution of Roman artefacts and indication of the town's structure through archaeological remains bare testimony to the town's prosperity and vitality. It is estimated that 20,000 people lived in Cagliari during this period, their daily need for water satisfied by an aqueduct which carried water from a source 45 km (28 miles) away.

## Cagliari in the Middle Ages

During the Byzantine era and the occupation by the Vandals the town continued to grow in importance, so that it was on the point of dominating the entire southern half of the island. The spread of Christianity rapidly elevated Cagliari to a sort of spiritual and moral capital. This occurred long before it was created the official capital of the *giudicato* of the same name. The most significant traces of the period when the Vandals ruled Sardinia (AD 455–553) bear witness to the triumphal march of Christianity. The Vandal king Thrasamund banished all strict Catholic bishops whose views he did not share to southern Sardinia. They were not permitted to leave.

The year AD 704 marked the beginning of Saracen incursions along the south west coast of Sardinia. In 733 Cagliari was sacked and its inhabitants forced to pay a tribute. Fear of the sea and the invaders it carried to the island wrought

fundamental changes in the character of this typical coastal town; they were to prove so long-lasting that for almost three centuries Cagliari was to remain cut off from world history. This isolation may have been why Sardinia's first *giudicato,* a defensive alliance with its own jurisdiction, was formed around Cagliari. It was not until the arrival of settlers belonging to various religious orders, such as the Benedictine monks from Montecassino, or the followers of St Victor of Marseilles, that the town seemed prepared to open itself once again to Western influence. Mindful of its commercial history, it established contact with the French towns along the Mediterranean coast and began trading with the city states of Genoa and Pisa, which were subsequently to dominate the history of Cagliari and even Sardinia itself, first as partners and then as conquerors.

Under Pisan rule, the town enjoyed a considerable demographic, artistic and economic revival. For the Tuscan visitors the town's layout had a familiar air, and they expanded it enthusiastically. It became one of the most important ports on the Tyrrhenian Sea; secular and sacred buildings such as the new cathedral were erected, and the three defensive towers were built around the castle.

Map on pages 148–49

*The Exma building (the town's former abattoir) is decorated with cow's heads.*

## The Spanish conquest

In 1326, following the decline of Pisa, Cagliari fell into the hands of the royal house of Aragon. Their first action was to expel all native Sardinians from the castle, and it was occupied by foreign noblemen whose mission it was to decide the fate of the town. In 1418 it became the official residence of the Viceroy of Sardinia, who replaced the Governor General. In 1421, in the presence of the King of Aragon, Alfonso V "The Magnanimous", the Viceroy of Sardinia, Bernardo de Centelles, inaugurated the island's first parliament. Under Aragonese rule the city's administrative system built up by Pisa was dismantled and replaced by a new arrangement resembling that of Barcelona. The administration of justice was in the hands of a governor and a *Bàilo,* who later assumed overall control of the professional associations and the guilds, and eventually also of customs and excise. The *Amostassen* was responsible for the town's food supplies; he was assisted by two *Clavari,* who were in charge of the slaughterhouses and the granaries. Public works were carried out by *Obrieri,* and a consulate for marine affairs dealt with matters concerning overseas trade and regulated disputes between merchants.

Under Aragonese and Spanish rule, Cagliari's position as an important port and trading town was reinforced. Such was its expansion that the neighbouring *Villae* of Stampace and Villanova were completely swallowed up by its suburbs, thereby losing their original function as refuges or *Oppida.* Between 1620 and 1626, Philip III encouraged the foundation of a university. At this time, too, Cagliari was the scene of feuds, sometimes bloody, between powerful local families and the Spanish newcomers. This violence culminated in 1668 in the assassination of the Viceroy, Camarassa and the Marchese di Laconi. One of the Viceroy's murderers, Castelvì, Marchese di Cea, was sentenced to death and beheaded in 1671 on what is now the Piazza Carlo Alberto. In due course the other

**BELOW:** Piazza Carlo Alberto.

conspirators were also arrested and handed over to the executioner. The plot against the Viceroy was the most obvious manifestation of the latent tension smouldering between the Sardinian populace and the Spanish colonial power. What's more, the ruling Spanish tried to introduce a number of unwelcome minor administrative reforms, which aggravated matters further. As a consequence, the population, in the northern half of the island in particular, openly supported Austria in its ambitions to make Spain part of the vast Habsburg Empire.

On 12 August 1708, the British naval fleet under Admiral Lake approached the town of Cagliari and opened fire. Following the Peace of Utrecht, signed in 1713, Duke Victor Amadeus II of Savoy became the sovereign of the Regno di Sardegna, the Kingdom of Sardinia. On 4 August 1720 Sardinia, along with Naples, Milan and the Spanish Netherlands, was formally handed over to the Austrian Empire by the Spanish; on 8 August the island was passed on to Luigi Departes, the emissary from Savoy.

## The House of Savoy

As part of the Kingdom of Savoy-Sardinia, Cagliari suddenly became an international political arena. On 28 January 1793 it was forced to fend off an attack by the French fleet under Lorenzo Giovanni Truguet. Following heavy fire from the ships' cannons and an attempted landing, the invaders were repulsed by the hastily summoned militia under the command of Gerolamo Pitzolo. In the wake of the turmoil which Napoleon spread across the whole of Europe, including Italy, Cagliari was to become the refuge of Charles Emmanuel IV of Savoy, the King of Sardinia. He lived for seven months in the Viceroy's palace on the Piazza Palazzo. On another occasion the town was again called upon to provide a king of Savoy with hospitality and protection (which unfortunately was not always reciprocated). On this second occasion, the recipient was Victor Emmanuel I, returning from exile in Gaeta and Rome following the abdication of his weak brother, Charles Emmanuel IV. He was a guest in the Viceroy's palace from 17 February until 7 May 1814.

**BELOW:** Tuscan facade of the Santa Maria Cathedral.

The town chronicles relate a series of dramatic events in the middle of the 19th century: there was a succession of famines and epidemics which plagued the inhabitants, exacerbated by the indescribable sanitary conditions under which the population lived, a series of violent riots, and hangings ordered without ceremony by the increasingly nervous rulers and their bands of compliant henchmen. In spite of these drawbacks, during this period the town gradually acquired its modern appearance. The new buildings erected after 1840 and designed for purely peaceful purposes helped to shake off the image of "fortress Cagliari", an image that the city had endured since Roman times.

The town and its surroundings offer sights of every kind, including the Golfo degli Angeli and the *bastioni*, overlapping fortifications belonging to different ages that completely surround the Castello quarter. These gracious defences seems to hover weightlessly above the town, surveying one of the loveliest natural landscapes in Europe. The views over the city are breathtaking.

## Castello quarter

Cagliari is the island's capital and largest town, with a population of almost 250,000. The wealth of precious objects and architecture to be found here tells of the city's complex history, which on more than one occasion has determined the fate of the entire island. A good place to start a tour is from the Castello quarter, the large ancient stronghold of town, over which the two medieval towers of Torre di San Pancrazio and Torre dell'Elefante rise.

For many visitors the highlight of the Castello quarter, and indeed of the town itself, is the the city's museum complex, the **Cittadella dei Musei ❶**, situated on Piazza Arsenale in the heart of the old town. Until 1966–67, when it was allocated to its present role as a documentary and cultural witness of local history, the building itself experienced a very turbulent past. The present structure rises above the remains of the ancient Piedmontese fortress and arsenal. Standing on the highest point of Cagliari, it affords a spectacular view over the town and the bay. The two architects of the Cittadella, Gazzola and Cecchini, were successful not only in creating a harmonious blend of elements from a number of different architectural periods, but also in adapting historic elements to new uses, as can be seen particularly in the case of the fine Renaissance portal and splendid statue of Santa Barbara.

The Cittadella complex houses four museums. The **Pinacoteca Nazionale** (National Art Gallery ; tel: 070 674054; open Tues–Sun 9am–8pm; entrance fee) contains an important collection of *retabli* polyptychs. Polyptychs were introduced by the Aragonese during their conquest in the 14th century. The huge paintings were used as altarpieces, usually divided into three sections and placed behind a main altar, or acted as the main focus of a side chapel. Intended to be

Map
on pages
148–49

*The Torre di San Pancrazio, the northern gate of the Castello quarter.*

**BELOW:** clothes hung out to dry.

instructive visual depictions of religious themes and the lives of saints, the central panel of a polyptych often features the most important events in a saint's life. Most of the *retabli* in the collection come from the church of San Francesco in Cagliari and are attributed to painters known only by the title of Master and the village in which their work was first recognised. The *retablo della Porziuncola* by the Master of Castelsardo, painted in 1492, is probably one of the best examples of this particular period and style of painting.

Also contained in the Cittadella's complex is the **Museo d'Arte Orientale Stefano Cardu** (tel: 070 651888; open Tues–Sun, summer 9am–1pm, 4–8pm; winter 9am–1pm, 3.30–7.30pm; entrance fee). The collection was bequeathed to the town by Stefano Cardu, a Sardinian at the court of the king of Siam in the 19th century. The collection contains Chinese and Siamese *objets d'art*, dating back to the 11th century. One of the most unusual museums in the complex is the **Mostra di Cere Anatomiche** (tel: 070 6757627, open Tues–Sun 9am–1pm, 4–7pm; entrance fee), which displays 23 disquietingly realistic anatomical wax models based on originals made by Clemente Susini in 1803.

### Inside the Museo Archeologico Nazionale

Contained within the complex is the city's best museum: the **Museo Archeologico Nazionale** (tel: 070 655911; open Tues–Sun 9am-8pm; entrance fee). The exhibition rooms contain displays of prehistoric and early finds as well as a large number of objects illustrating the long history of the island. The first appearance of human beings in Sardinia dates to the early Palaeolithic Age (350,000 years ago) but the earliest material displayed in the museum dates back to the Neolithic period (6000–2700 BC), including pottery, obsidian tools and small fat

**BELOW:** Museo Archeologico Nazionale.

Map on pages 148–49

female statuettes, which formed part of the Great Mother Goddess cult, often found in *domus de janas*. Of particular interest are the *bronzetti* (recent and late Bronze Age bronze statues) representing people in religious contemplation, along with those depicting archers, *navicelle nuragiche* (small boats) and votive gifts from nuraghe and nuraghic villages, grave temples and sacred springs. The majority of human figures represented are males but among the female representations there are some extremely expressive female figures, the so-called "mothers". Seated on round stools, the figures embrace their sons on their laps. One female figure holds a naked adult in her lap instead of a male infant. This figure is interpreted as being a a nuraghic Madonna with her dead son – God.

The Phoenicians' time on the island is marked by a collection of valuable objects discovered in sites scattered along the coast: imported Etruscan Bucchero vases found near Cagliari, Phoenician ceramic pots with mushroom-shaped rims and Greek cups and plates. Of great value is the fabulous Carthaginian glass paste necklace found in Olbia, which has large beads representing colourful human faces and animals. The juniper-wood statuette of a *kore* (a girl wearing festive dress) was discovered in the former Punic settlement of Olbia, as was a particularly well-preserved example of the apotropaic terracotta masks which were manufactured extensively by the Phoenicians to ward off malevolent spirits.

The Roman period in Sardinia is represented by glass vases and bottles, used to import wine from central Italy. Sigillata Italica or Arretin ware, a new type of tableware, was adopted during this time by those who could afford it. Lead ingots with the seal of the Emperor Hadrianus produced in the south of the island and exported to Rome have also been found.

The last section of the ground floor contains a collection of Early Christian and medieval artefacts which includes metal objects such as jugs, lamps, incense burners, silver and bronze fibulae and a number of Afro-Mediterranean clay oil lamps with varied decorations and designs. It provides a rare opportunity to appreciate the culture of the Byzantines and Vandals, the island's early invaders. The other two floors of the museum have displays relating to particular sites or areas.

*The term* domus de janas *derives from an ancient folk superstition, according to which the modest graves or "houses" hewn from rock by the island's early inhabitants were in fact the homes of* janas *– supernatural beings, usually referred to as fairies.*

**BELOW:** Museo d'Arte Orientale Stefano Cardu.

## The Galleria Comunale d'Arte

At the foot of the Piazza Arsenale, walking downhill into Viale Regina Elena, you will come to the pleasant **Giardini Púbblici** (open daily), in the middle of which lies the **Galleria Comunale d'Arte ❷** (tel: 070 490727; open Wed–Mon, summer 9am–1pm, 5–9pm; winter 9am–1pm, 3.30–7.30pm; entrance fee). The gallery has a collection of modern works by Sardinian artists and stages exhibitions of contemporary artists. Among the most notable works in the museum's collection are paintings by Tarquinio Sini from the 1920s and Giuseppe Biasi. Early 20th-century work by Francesco Ciusa is also on show here – particularly impressive is his piece *La Madre dell'Ucciso*. Ciusa gained international recognition and was honoured at the 1907 Venice Biennale.

*The Palazzo Regio (Piazza Palazzo; open Tues–Sun 9am–1pm, 3–7pm) was once the official residence of the Piedmontese monarchs.*

**BELOW:** Cattedrale Santa Maria del Castello.

## Palatial splendour

From Piazza Arsenale outside the Cittadella and passing under the Palazzo delle Seziate, you arrive in Piazza Indipendenza. On the right is the building which housed Sardinia's mint during the 14th century. It also functioned as an archaeological museum and you can still see the inscription for the museum above the main entrance. Following Via Martini, the former Pisan blacksmiths' road, to the left is the small square bearing the same name with an open view over the eastern part of the town, the lagoon of Molentargius, the salt works and Cagliari's long beach, Il Poetto. The Piazza Palazzo, created after the removal of bomb-damaged World War II buildings, has always been the centre of civil authority on the island. The **Palazzo Regio** ❸ (Royal Palace or Palazzo Viceregio; open daily 9.30am–1.30pm, 4–7pm) is the seat of the prefecture. An older building, home to the Viceroy sent to rule the island by the king of Aragon, stood here from the 14th to the 18th centuries. The present building was constructed in the 18th century on the orders of the Kings of Sardinia. Inside, it is worth taking a look at the fine staircase leading up to the *bel-étage* designed by the military engineer De Guibert, as well as at Bruschi's allegorical and realistic frescoes in the Provincial Assembly Chamber.

The **Cattedrale Santa Maria del Castello** ❹ (open daily 8am–12.30pm, summer 4–8pm; winter 3.30–7pm) was built in the 13th century but only the belfry and the supporting beams of the main doorway remain from the original building. The cathedral has been remodelled on a number of occasions, finally receiving its Romanesque facade in 1930 in the style of Pisa and Lucca. The Catalan Gothic-style chapel in the right transept is evidence that the building plans were changed when the invading forces of Aragon conquered the town in 1326. Inside the cathe-

dral are two works of art of particular interest. The first is the carved reliefs of the two stone pulpits by Guglielmo da Pisa which flank the main doors. The engravings were originally commissioned in 1160 for Pisa's cathedral and later donated to Cagliari. During modernisation of the church in 1600 the original pulpit, formed by eight panels, was split into the two we see today. The engravings show 16 scenes from the life of Christ, including the *Last Supper* and the *Sermon on the Mount*. In the Gothic-Catalan chapel on the right transept is a copy of a 15th-century triptych, the *Trittico di Clemente VII*, attributed to the flemish Rogier van der Weyden (1399–1464), the official painter of Brussels. The painting originally belonged to Pope Clemente VII, but during the *Sacco Di Roma* in 1527 it was stolen and ended up in Cagliari where the original can still be seen in the cathedral's Treasury. Next to this is a six-panelled polyptych the *Retablo della Crocefissione* by Michele Cavaro (1517–84). Under the cathedral is the crypt, which contains the tombs of many notable people including the wife of Louis XVIII of France. The crypt is carved out of the rock that forms the foundation of the cathedral and decorated with depictions of saints by local artists.

The **Palazzo di Città** ❺ (currently being restored), the old town hall, today has an 18th-century facade but the original building existed during Pisan rule. For centuries it was the seat of one of the branches of Sardinia's Parliament. The whole of the quarter is crossed by the long Via Lamarmora, where the street level rooms of nobiliary buildings, once used as stables and store rooms, have been transformed in quaint antique shops and artisan's workshops.

## Towards the Bastione San Remy

The quarter is delimited to the west by the imposing **Bastione Santa Croce**. The view of the gulf, of Santa Gilla lagoon and of the Stampace quarter is breathtaking. The **church of Santa Croce** (currently being restored) was built in 1661 over a synagogue abandoned after the edict of Ferdinand the Catholic in 1492, which expelled all Jews and Muslims from his land, which at the time included Sardinia.

The **Torre dell'Elefante** ❻ (open summer 9am–1pm, 3.30–7.30pm; winter 9am–5pm; entrance fee) at the end of the road is the obliged passage from Via Università into the quarter. It owes its name to the little elephant carving placed upon a plinth on its facade, under which the head of Marchese di Cea was displayed for 17 years after the tower was built. The tower was designed by Giovanni Capulain in 1307, a local architect, who also built the Torre di San Pancrazio in 1305. The gate mechanism and the gate of the Torre dell'Elefante can still be seen.

The **Università** ❼ along Via Università, was established in 1606 and today the Rectorship, together with the library, is housed in the former Tridentine Seminary building, which dates to 1700. The noteworthy **Collezione Sarda Luigi Pilloni** (tel: 070 6752420; open Mon–Fri 10am–1pm) is also kept in the same building. The collection contains 206 geographical maps of Sardinia dating from the 16th century, 54 paintings covering the same period by painters local to or related to the island, prints and drawings of 19th-century Sardinian costumes and a valuable collection

Map on pages 148–49

**BELOW:** strolling along the Via Roma.

of local carpets, packsaddles and chest covers. The museum is a very good source of information on local culture. The **Museo di Geologia e Paleontologia D. Lovisato** (Geology and Palaeontology museum) and the mineralogy museum, **Museo di Mineralogia** (both museums in the Earth Sciences Department, Cagliari University, Via Trentino 51; open Mon and Fri, tel: 070 6757753 for an appointment) are devoted to the geological history of Sardinia. The displays include fossils and rocks gathered in the first half of the 19th century and a splendid collection of minerals from Sardinia's mines.

At the end of Via Università, on Piazza Costituzione, is the **Bastione San Remy** ❽ which was used to defend the castle to the south. The bastions were built in the early 18th century after 400 years of Spanish rule, by the Baron de San Remy. He became the first Piedmontese Viceroy of Sardinia and made his name by enlarging the island's fortifications. The interior of the bastion has recently been renovated. It can be reached via a magnificent staircase built in 1902, and the view from the top of the ramparts is spectacular. The bastions are popular on Sundays because of the bric-a-brac market that takes place here every week. Overlooking the terrace is Palazzo Boyl (1840), built over what remained of the Torre dell'Aquila, one of the ancient towers surrounding the quarter. Its balcony is decorated with four statues representing the seasons.

## La Marina quarter

The narrow Marina quarter, originally surrounded by walls, has always been tied to the ups and downs of the port's commercial activities. Today it is a poor but very lively area. Its alleys are lined with a succession of welcoming little *ristoranti*. Their menus are not restricted to fish but if you are in search of first

**BELOW:** the bastion of San Remy has fantastic views over the city and out to sea.

class sea food, try here. The quarter is more or less a rectangle closed on one side by Largo Carlo Felice and the elegant building of La Rinascente store, on the other by Piazza Amendola with its enormous Ficus trees, palms and jacarandas. To the north the quarter ends with the pedestrian street Via Manno, under the Bastione San Remy.

Map on pages 148–49

Via Roma, parallel to the port, contains the **Palazzo Municipale ❾** (or Palazzo comunale; tel: 070 6777067; open Mon–Fri 9am–1pm; by appointment only), which was built at the end of the 19th century and serves as the town hall. Nearby is the **Palazzo del Consiglio Regionale** (Regional Government offices) in Via Sassari– a hideous and frequently criticised building. The only mitigating factor is the fine series of sculptures by the Sardinian artist Costantino Nivola, who died in America in 1988, his adopted homeland, after a career spanning several decades.

Via Roma enjoys a sunny position overlooking the sea. By day a multitude of little cafés under the porticos are crowded and lively. The weather is mild all year round so that the tables on the pavements and squares are left outside even in winter. The main harbour nearby provides a link with the Italian mainland and other Mediterranean ports, including Tunis. The **Via Manno**, the **Largo Carlo Felice** and some sections of the **Via Roma** have become important shopping streets. The modern stores and clothes boutiques radiate chic. If you are in search of Italian fashion you can find it here, but be prepared to pay high prices for the best designer labels.

*Underneath the church of Sant'Eulalia is a museum and archaeological area.*

Today the main historic and cultural reference point in La Marina is the 14th-century parish **church of Sant'Eulalia** in Piazza Sant' Eulalia. Under the church, recent archaeological excavations have discovered parts of the old Roman town, which can now be seen as part of the **Museo del Tesoro e Area Archeologica di Sant'Eulalia ❿** (MUTSEU, Vico del Collegio; tel: 070 663724; open Tues–Sun 10am–1pm, 5–8pm; entrance fee). The museum is housed in part of the underground complex found under the altar of the church. Apart from containing part of the Roman town, the museum contains wooden sculptures, silver objects, vestments and paintings, some of which come from the two nearby churches of Sant' Lucia (today in ruins) and Santo Sepolcro.

**BELOW:** Via Roma and the town hall.

The **church of Santo Sepolcro ⓫** (Piazza Santo Sepolcro, off Via Dettori; open daily 10am–1pm, 5–8pm) belonged to the Templars from 1248 to 1311. It was then entrusted to the main confraternity of the Cross, which took care of the burial of the poor and those the condemned to death. In 1538 lumps of earth coming from the Holy Sepulchre in Jerusalem were scattered here.

In the church is an octagonal chapel donated in 1686 by Viceroy Ayala as a votive offering for the recovery of his daughter from illness. From the small stairs on the side of the church you arrive in Via Manno, the favourite pedestrian street of young people in the area. This street and Viale Regina Margherita join at Piazza Martiri, a meeting place in the past for writers and travellers such as D.H. Lawrence and Grazia Deledda.

**TIP**

The very popular Festa di Sant'Efisio takes place during the first four days of May. If you are thinking of staying in Cagliari during this time it is a good idea to book accommodation in advance.

**BELOW:**
the steps of the Basilicai di Nostra Signora di Bonaria.

## Stampace and Villanova

Stampace is one of the four historical quarters of Cagliari, it is easily reached by foot from Piazza Yenne, under and west of the castle. In the past it was inhabited by artisans and artists, who congregated around Via Azuni and what is today the Corso Vittorio Emanuele.

Stampace has many churches including the Jesuit complex of the **church of San Michele** (open daily), built at the end of the 17th century in a Spanish-baroque style. Right at the centre of Stampace, in Via Sant'Restituta, is the **Cripta di Santa Restituta** ⓬ (tel: 070 6776400; open Tues–Sun 9am–1pm, 3.30–7.30pm). It is a large room with traces of Punic and Roman presence later transformed into a palaeochristian church. The crypt is tied to the worship of Saint Restituta, whose statue, dating from the 5th century, was found during excavations. The nearby **church of Sant'Efisio** ⓭ (open Tues–Sun 9am–1pm, 3.30–7.30pm) was built in 1700 and is the headquarters of the Gonfalone brotherhood which organises the colourful **Festa di Sant'Efisio**, the famous folk festival in honour of Saint Efisio, at the beginning May each year. The festival is the biggest in Sardinia and the whole town is involved in its preparations. Saint Efisio, is credited with saving Cagliari from the Black Death, and is revered throughout the island. During the festivities the saint's statue is carried to a tiny church in Pula which stands on the exact spot where he was martyred. Garlanded oxen draw the statue through the town on a richly decorated cart, escorted by elegantly costumed riders and followed by a vast crowd. The sound of *launeddas*, Sardinian flutes, accompany the party.

The **Villanova quarter** is made up by small houses originally inhabited by farmers that cultivated the fields on which the modern town has developed. Today the houses are part of a labyrinth of narrow and long alleys which give Villanova a lively and colourful atmosphere. The 15th-century **church of San Giacomo** ⓮ (open daily 7.30–11am), on the piazza of the same name, is an important centre for the traditional and folkloristic liturgical rites that take place during the Holy Week.

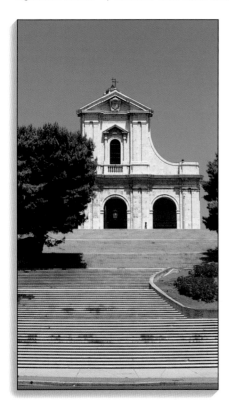

## Other churches in Cagliari

Outside the four historical quarters there are some very important churches in Cagliari: one is the **Basilica di San Saturno** ⓯ (tel: 070 2010302; open 9am–1pm) on the newly developed Piazza San Cosimo, just off the Via Dante. Built on the site of an early Roman necropolis, this Romanesque basilica is the oldest church in Sardinia. Saint Saturno was beheaded in 303 during a time of Christian persecution. His body was buried in a crypt over which the Basilica di San Saturno was built. The first mention of a church dedicated to Saint Saturno is in the *Life of Fulgenzio*, written in 533–34. What can be seen today is the result of a 20-year-long restoration programme. At the corner of the same square is the **church of San Lucifero** ⓰ (tel: 070 656996; at present visits only by appointment). The side door of the church bears the coat of arms of Aragonese Cagliari, placed next to two dogs, symbols of the Dominicans. Excavations have revealed a palaeochristian complex formed by three chapels dating from the 5th–7th century under the church. On Via San Lucifero is the **Exma building** (tel: 070 666399; open Tues–Sun, summer 10am–2pm, 5–12pm; winter 9am–8pm), which served as the town's slaughter-house before its conversion into a stylish exhibition centre holding concerts and exhibitions of Sardinian art.

In Piazza Bonaria on Viale Bonaria is the **Basilica di Nostra Signora di Bonaria** ⓱ (open 6.30–12am, summer 5–7.30pm; winter 4–6.30 pm), built in 1704. The basilica dominates the skyline as you approach Cagliari from the sea and is believed to give protection to sailors. A flight of steps leads up to an impressive neoclassical facade. Next to it is the less impressive but older **church of Bonaria**, built in 1326, which contains the 14th-century wooden Madonna – the centre of devotion on its main altar. This was the first church to be built in Sardinia in an Aragonese-Gothic style immediately after the arrival of Alfonso d'Aragona to commemorate the conquest of Cagliari. In the cloister of the convent is the entrance to the interesting **Museo del Santuario di Nostra Signora di Bonaria** (tel: 070 301747; open daily 9–11.30am, 5–6pm; entrance fee), where religious objects and ex-voto are kept, many of them in the shape of boats and ships and dating from the 18th century. The museum also contains finds from local excavations and the mummified bodies of a family who died from the plague in the 17th century.

## Green spaces and beaches

If you want to find out more about Sardinia's flowers, trees and plants, Cagliari contains one of Italy's most famous botanical gardens, the **Orto Botánico** ⓲ (Viale Sant'Ignazio; tel: 070 6753501; open summer 8.30am–1.30pm, 3–7pm; winter 8am–1.30pm; entrance fee, guided visits every second and forth Sunday at 11am). Founded in 1858 by the town's university, it is divided into three climatic – environments: Mediterranean, Tropical and Rocky-Arid. A visit to the garden is pleasant not only for the variety of plants and their surroundings but also for the presence of a Punic water tank, a Punic Roman quarry, the remains of a Roman aqueduct and, if you wish, a visit to the nearby Roman amphitheatre *(see page 152)*.

The hill of **Monte Urpino** rises for over 100 metres (330 ft) between the modern quarters of eastern Cagliari and the Molentargius coastal marshes. Covered by pine trees, it is, together with the **Colle di San Michele**, one of two parks in town. In the park is the recently restored castle bearing the same name. It was built in the 10th century to defend the capital against the Giudicato of Cagliari. It is currently used for exhibitions. A panoramic road leads to the top of the hill where there is a stunning view over the town and the lagoons that surround it. If your itinerary can fit in a day at the beach then head for **Poetto**. To get there take the Via Roma and stay on it until it turns into the **Viale Diaz**, then follow the coast until you reach Poetto and one of the longest beaches in Italy, with views across to the foothills of the Sella del Diavolo. The Marina Píccola, at the southern end of the beach lined with restaurants and bars, has a lively atmosphere. ❏

**Map on pages 148–49**

**BELOW:** cacti growing in the Orto Botánico.

# CAGLIARI TO OLBIA

*This varied route covers the southeast and northeast of the island, taking in varied landscapes, villages and historic sites along the way*

Map on page 166

**T**he road from Cagliari to Olbia, the Eastern Trunk Road or SS 125, is known as the **Strada Statale Orientale Sarda**. It is one of the main traffic arteries in Sardinia, leading north. A few kilometres after leaving **Cagliari ❶** the road runs past the **Monte dei Sette Fratelli** (Seven Brothers), a small range of mountains with peaks up to 1,000 metres (3,280 ft) high. The ancient village of **San Gregorio** at the 27-km (17-mile) mark is the first stopping off place in the new Sette Fratelli Regional Park, which is due to open in the near future. The area, characterised by a forest-maquis formed by holm oaks, cork trees and arbutus (strawberry trees), is already part of the Foresta Domaniale dei Sette Fratelli, which covers 6,200 hectares (15,320 acres). There is also a protected area for the rare *cervo sardo*, the short Sardinian stag. Following the gorge of the Rio Cannas, the SS 125 arrives at San Priamo and connects itself with the coastal road a few kilometres before Muravera *(see page 166)*.

## Villasimius and the Isola dei Cavoli

Setting off from Cagliari via the Viale del Poetto you will come to **Quartu Sant'Elena**, where the **Museo Contadino sa Domue Farra** (Via Eligiu Porcu; tel: 070 811627; currently closed for restoration), an original Campidanese farmhouse displaying traditional agricultural implements and domestic tools, is well worth stopping off for. An alternative museum of the same nature is on Via Eligio Porcu (tel: 070 812462; open summer 9.30am–1pm, 5–10pm; winter 9.30am–1pm, 4–7pm; entrance fee).

The next important stop (about 32 km/20 miles) is **Villasimius ❷** (archaeological museum; open June–Sept Tues–Sun; entrance fee), lying some 40 metres (128 ft) above sea level. It has enjoyed a remarkable boom in recent years and is now dotted with holiday complexes, apartment blocks, hotels and villas catering to large numbers of Italian and foreign tourists during the summer months, when the population expands to three or four times its off-season total. Scuba divers will enjoy the sea around the headland, an area which is rich in vegetation and marine life. Villasimius, and in particular the Albergo Stella d'Oro, achieved literary fame through *By The Saracens' Tower*, a novel written by Ernst Jünger.

Villasimius lies in exceptionally lovely countryside; approaching from Cagliari along the road to **Capo Carbonara**, the visitor will be enchanted by breathtaking views of the sea and a scattering of tiny islands, the largest of which are the **Isola Serpentara** and the **Isola dei Cavoli ❸**. The island is dominated by an imposing lighthouse, which houses a sea research centre. The islands are part of the Capo Carbonara

**LEFT:** a local agricultural worker.
**BELOW:** boats in the marina at Villasimius.

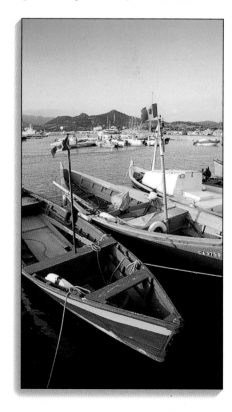

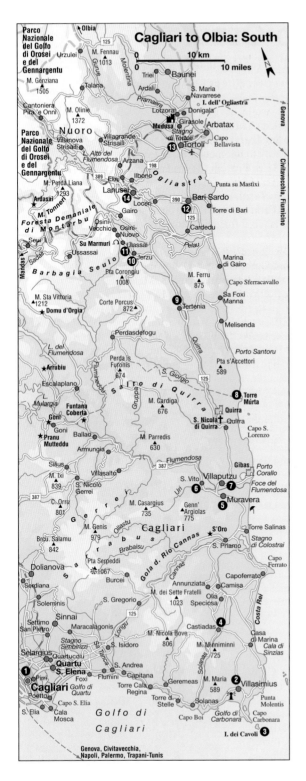

Parco Nazionale del Golfo di Orosei e del Gennargentu

**Cagliari to Olbia: South**

0    10 km
0    10 miles

sea reserve, recently established by the Italian government to preserve and explore the marine life and environment in this area. It is possible to visit the island, and sea research centre, by boat as part of an excursion package.

Back on the main island, the coastal margin is overshadowed by granite cliffs polished smooth by the sea over millions of years. It is possible to find chlorite, biotite, orthoclase, muscovite, pyrites and quartz among the rocks. Unfortunately, the lovely setting has been marred by some tourist developments that have failed to respect the countryside. To the south of the town, however, some efforts have been made to repair environmental damage; for example, new groves of pine trees have been planted. Villasimius' 17th-century **Fortezza Vecchia** (Old Fortress) rises up above the harbour. Built for military purposes and coastal protection, since 1982 it has housed an international centre for experimental art, attracting many European artists of stature. Their works are exhibited in the town hall or outside. Worth mentioning is the moving *Sagra* festival held in Villasimius in honour of Our Lady of the Shipwrecks (*Madonna del Naufrago*), celebrated in mid-July in the sea by the Isola dei Cavoli. It is marked by a procession of fishing boats and the scattering of flowers on the sea in commemoration of lost lives.

## The Costa Rei and the Sarrabus region

Before rejoining the SS 125 the traveller passes through the hamlet of **Castiadas** ❹, surrounded by a vast agricultural area created by a penal colony that was established in 1875. At the time, open-air convict colonies were common in Europe and were founded on the assumption that hard work would aid rehabilitation. The convicts constructed all the buildings in the colony, including a hospital. The result is the small, partially restored hamlet we see today. Back on the SS 125, the road follows the coast and then heads back inland to **Muravera** ❺. The town is surrounded by extensive, and in spring wonderfully fragrant orange groves. It lies approximately 11 metres (35 ft) above sea level; it has a population of about 5,000 and a modern tourist infrastructure. Hotels, holiday villages, campsites, elegant villas and lodgings in private houses provide accommodation for thousands of visitors every summer. The atmosphere is very relaxing. The seemingly endless beaches of **Costa Rei** reach right up to the foothills of **Capo Ferrato**, the lagoons of **Feraxi** and **Colostrai**, and the salt-works of the **Peschiera**, which contains coastal marshes of noteworthy naturalistic interest because of the presence of many different species of birds including flamingos, white egrettes and herons. The flat coastal strip gradually gives way to the mountainous foothills of the Sarrabus region, through which, flanked by fields and citrus plantations, meander the **Flumendosa** and the **Picocca** rivers. Although no larger than 179 sq. km (69 sq. miles) the area includes a range of stunning landscapes, encompassing plains and ranges of mountains as well as lakes and superb stretches of coast. Instead of ousting agriculture tourism has regenerated it by creating demanding new markets.

Map on page 166

*The tourist town of Muravera makes an ideal starting point for trips into the interior or along the coast.*

Muravera was inhabited at the time of the Nuraghi civilisation; later on, under the Romans, the town must have acquired a certain importance in view of its situation on the Roman road to Olbia. During the Middle Ages, in 1258, Muravera was transferred from the *giudicato* of Cagliari to that of Gallura. In 1324 it fell into the hands of Pisa, and at the end of Pisan sovereignty it was given in fief to Carroz, Count of Quirra, and then to de Centelles and de Osorio.

The community is divided into the three districts of Castiadas, San Pietro and Costa Rei. In the vicinity, near Piscina Rei, there are 22 Neolithic menhirs; six of them are still in their initial vertical positions. Their original signif-

**BELOW:** defensive towers dot the coastline.

icance remains unclear. Comparisons with similar ancient structures on other sites in northern Europe seem to indicate that their purpose was to mark the passage of the seasons. A further 42 menhirs can be seen on the site of the **Nuraghe Scalas**. Of artistic interest is Muravera's 16th-century church of **San Nicola di Bari** (open daily), which was built in a slightly self-conscious Catalan Gothic style.

The little town itself has retained numerous folkloric customs and every year various festivals take place. The **Sagra degli Agrumi** (Citrus Fair), which takes place on the first or second Sunday before Easter, features processions of folk groups wearing traditional embroidered costumes and playing traditional instruments such as the prehistoric launedda, a flute-type instrument consisting of a number of pipes, traditionally used by shepherds.

## Villages along the Flumendosa river

The village of **San Vito ❻**, northwest of Muravera, has approximately 4,000 inhabitants and a parish extending over an area of 230 sq. km (89 sq. miles) of mainly mountainous countryside. To the south are woods and oak groves; in the middle rise the peaks of the Monte dei Sette Fratelli; in the north lie the mountains of the Sarrabus. The entire area is a refuge for wildlife: the Sardinian partridge, ring and turtle doves, wild boar and rabbits, the hobby and the Sardinian deer all inhabit the area in large numbers. Mining – for silver, and other minerals – was once a major industry in the area and as a result the village enjoyed a fourfold increase in its population at the turn of the 17th–18th century. Large numbers of convicts were used as forced labour in the mines. Since the completion of the **Flumendosa Barrage** the river valley – previously subject to frequent flooding – has been exploited more intensively for farming, in particular horticulture.

**BELOW:** wall shrine to the Virgin Mary.

In a field near San Vito an ancient grave containing 14 skeletons and a rich store of funeral gifts was unearthed. The collection of gold and silver earrings, bangles, fibulae and pottery dating from the 5th and 4th centuries BC can be seen in the archaeological museum in Cagliari. Worth seeing, too, is the San Vito parish church; it has a fine facade, twin belfries, and a fine crucifix in one of the side chapels. In mid-June the village celebrates an interesting traditional and religious festival in honour of St Vitus, the local patron saint.

There is a festival in honour of St Mary on 3 October, when the community gives thanks for the wine harvest. The district has a rich craft tradition and produces some excellent handicrafts, such as colourful embroidery and basketwork. The local cuisine is also justly famous. It includes Sardinian specialities such as roast kid, *is culingionis de patata* (a type of ravioli filled with cheese) and *is perdulas cum meli* (pastry cases filled with a delicious mixture of honey, egg and curd cheese).

**Villaputzu ❼**, a small town of 5,000 inhabitants, lies along the SS 125 (about 3.5km/2 miles north of Muravera) on a small plain formed by the detritus deposited by the Flumendosa river. Views extend across to the Mediterranean *màcchia* on the hills of

Map
on page
166

the Sarrabus, a tangle of wild strawberries, mastic trees, phyllirea, juniper bushes and low-lying holm oaks. A closer look reveals the remains of two silver mines: **S'Acqua Arrubia** and **Gibbas**, which lie in the middle of the small coastal marshes of **Porto Corallo**. Both were in operation until the beginning of the 20th century.

In the Middle Ages Villaputzu belonged to the Sarrabus district of the *giudicato* of Cagliari. Its name at the time was Villa Pupussi or Villa Pupia. Later, together with l'Ogliastra, it was annexed by the *giudicato* of Gallura under Giovanni Maria Visconti. At the end of the 14th century it was the scene of the fierce quarrels between the Sardinian rulers of Arborea and the Aragonese. During the 16th century the **Fortezza Gibas** and the **Porto Corallo** were constructed to protect the town from the increasingly persistent attacks of the Turks operating off the North African coast.

## Around Torre Murta

Near **Torre Murta** ❹ can be seen the remains of a settlement dating from the 3rd millennium BC, including a *domus de janas*. In 1966, during excavations on the Santa Maria Hills, the archaeologist Francesco Barrecca discovered the ruins of a Phoenician settlement. It is likely that the site of the Acropolis of Sarcopos, a Phoenician-Carthaginian temple-fortress, must also have stood somewhere near here. The Latin *Itinerarium* of Antoninus, written at the beginning of the 3rd century BC, refers to the town of Sarcopos as being situated 32 km (20 miles) from Porticenses (Tertenia) and Ferraria (San Gregorio). North African pottery finds in the area probably date from the 6th and 7th centuries AD; local clay artefacts in the shape of combs and two bronze and clay fibulae indi-

**BELOW:** sunset on the Costa Rei.

cate that the area was inhabited during Vandal and Byzantine times. There are two important buildings worth visiting nearby. Some 15 km (10 miles) from the centre, on the SS 125, stands the pretty little Romanesque church of **San Nicola di Quirra**. It was built entirely with bricks, very rare in Sardinia, by the Pisani in 12th century and is surrounded by *cumbessias* (shelters for pilgrims). On a broad plateau demarcated by precipitous cliffs perches a grim fortress, the **Castello di Quirra**. The view is breathtaking. Folk festivals are still important in the area and during the Sagra di Sant'Antonio del Fuoco a giant bonfire is lit on the village square in accordance with an ancient pagan rite.

Along the SS 125, just before the Rio Corr'e Cerbu, a dirt road on the left leads to the 450 metre (1,476 ft) lead and arsenic mine of Baccu Locci, which remained active until 1950. The road then climbs up to the **Salto di Quirra**, a very large, high plateau with scenery of great natural beauty. The plateau can be reached more easily by following the panoramic road that goes up to Perdasdefogu and leads to Monte Cardiga. The road remains at a constant altitude and runs past the base of many *tacchi* (high limestone plateaus often separated by deep canyons).

## The Ogliastra region

The landscape of the southern part of the Ogliastra region is characterised by *tacchi*. The gateway to the Ogliastra and the Province of Nuoro is **Tertenia ❾**, which lies in the middle of a largely uninhabited region divided into three main districts: Sapala, Quirra and Villamonti. There are many springs in the vicinity, as well as a mountain torrent, the Sibiri or Rio Sibi, and a number of mountain peaks such as the San Giovanni. Between the two regions of the Sarrabus

**BELOW:**
a contented cow.

and the Ogliastra, at the southern end of the Jerzu district, you may be lucky enough to come across a *Petra Fitta*, a monolith usually in the form of a phallus, or a flat, altar-like *Petra de s'Altari*.

There are a number of well-preserved *nuraghi* in the region around Tertenia, although others have been almost completely destroyed. Some of the best examples are the **nuraghe su Concali** and the **nuraghe Longu**, along the coast of the Marina di Tertenia south of the coastal tower of Sarralá. Travellers interested in churches will enjoy visiting those of the Beata Vergine Assunta, Santa Lucia, San Pietro, Santa Sofia or Santa Teresa. The most colourful festivals include that of the *Vergine Assunta* (Assumption) and those in honour of St Sebastian and St Sophia. The festivities attract visitors from the surrounding villages as well as foreign tourists.

Further to the west, a few miles from the SS 125 between Tertenia and Bari Sardo on a long ridge surrounded by hilly country lies the slightly larger town of **Jerzu** ❿. By sheer determination it seems to survive despite the poor quality of the soil. Jerzu's schools – primary, middle and upper – show it to be a modern, progressive place. A noble *Cannonau* vintage is produced in its vineyards; in former times the farmers themselves would make the wine, but nowadays this is undertaken almost exclusively by the cooperative wine cellars, which are also responsible for marketing the product at home and abroad. The neighbouring countryside is mostly mountainous. The cone-shaped **Punta Corongiu** affords a spectacular view of the Tyrrhenian Sea; on clear days one can even see the summits of Villacidro on the other side of the island, towering above the smaller mountain peaks and wooded slopes.

Jerzu's most important festival of the year is the **Sant'Antonio di Padova** held on 13 June in honour of St Anthony of Padua, to whom one of the town's churches is dedicated. Other buildings of note which are worth a quick visit include the churches of St Sebastian and St Erasmus.

The picturesque town of **Ulassai** ⓫ is situated in a canyon which formed itself between two *tacchi*. Of great interest for its beautiful concretions is the **Grotta Su Marmuri** (opening hours vary, tel: 0782 79859 for details; entrance fee), part of the limestone massif at the back of the village. The grotto has a large entrance and long caves where the constant 12°C (53°F) temperature requires the use of a pullover even in summer. Continuing towards Gairo in the Rio Pardu Valley one finds the ghost village of **Osini Vecchio**, abandoned in 1951 because of the collapse of buildings caused by landslides. In front of the village on the opposite slope are the ruins of two other villages also abandoned because of landslides.

Returning to the SS 125 and continuing northwards, the traveller arrives in **Bari Sardo** ⓬. The origin of the name lies in its *abbari* (marshy ground). Historically the town enjoyed considerable importance, for the jurisdiction of its courts extended as far as Lotzorai, Girasole and Loceri. Today the town derives most of its income from agriculture and cattle breeding; in former times it was also famous for flax and the manufacture of linen, when it had 250 looms. Bari Sardo's best agricultural products are its red and white

**Map on page 166**

**BELOW:** a farmer from Arbatax.

wine, and various types of fruit: lemons, oranges, pears, plums and apricots. In the mountains there are still many species of wild animals: rabbits, ring and turtle doves, partridges and wild boar. The stretch of coast near **Marina di Cea** has become a popular with tourists.

## Tortolí and Arbatax

**Tortolí**  lies further to the north in a small, fertile plain surrounded by fields. Sheltered from the westerly winds by the hills of the Barbagia, Tortolí is equally sheltered from northerlies by Cape Montesanto near Baunei. In former times the marshes and lakes surrounding Tortolí increased the risk of malaria infection and gave the town a reputation for being an unhealthy place to live.

To the south of Tortolí, which has seen rapid expansion during the past 30 years, flows the river of the same name, fed by a number of smaller tributaries coming from Arzana, Elini, Ilbono and Lanusei. Its banks are a haven for various species of water birds, including cranes and flamingos (*Phoenicopterus ruber)*, whose more usual homes are Andalusia, the South of France and the lagoons of Cagliari. Tourism, the port, the industry of nearby Arbatax, a new airport and the fertile surrounding countryside make Tortolí one of the liveliest towns in the Ogliastra region – a fact evinced by its numerous schools and hotels. In the past, Tortolí was a bishopric and before that the seat of the margraves of Quirra. It was spared, however, the cruel and detested forms of feudalism which prevailed elsewhere on Sardinia.

The suburb of **Arbatax** is on the coast a few miles further on. It is a well-known seaside resort with a small harbour used by both commercial and pleasure craft, with connections to the Italian mainland as well as other ports on the

**TIP**

Food and drink are not served on board the Trenino Verde so bring your own supplies for the journey.

**BELOW:** ancient shoreline defence.

island. Industrial drilling platforms are produced in the port of Arbatax and this industry, along with tourism, has brought the district regular employment and prosperity. The small **Trenino Verde** (Green Train), formed by a 1930s steam locomotive and two vintage carriages, leaves Arbatax and follows the winding narrow gauge railway track built in 1894 until it reaches Cagliari. The railway was built so that the heart of the wild southern parts of the island could be accessed and the rich mineral deposits and forests of the region could be exploited commercially. As the Trenino Verde slowly climbs through the mountains it sometimes stops to avoid wild animals on the track, reminiscent of D. H. Lawrence's train journey described in his book *Sea and Sardinia*, written in 1921.

## Lanusei

The little town of **Lanusei**  lies away from the coast, perched on the eastern foothills of the Barbagia a few miles from Tortolí. The surroundings are mostly mountainous; the principal peaks are those of Cardiga, Fenurau and Tissidu.

General Alfonso La Marmora – geologist, geographer, anthropologist and explorer – travelled the length and breadth of the island, recording his impressions in his *Voyage en Sardaigne*. In 1833 he remarked that the Ogliastra region must be rich in copper deposits, for in ancient times local tribes used the metal in the production of their idols and simple artefacts (examples of these are on view in the Museo Archeologico Nazionale in Cagliari). He later concluded that copper was mined at Funtana Raminosa (Copper Spring) in the heart of the Barbagia region. Lanusei, now a bishopric and the seat of the local courts, has a long and venerable tradition. It is the proud setting of the first Salesian-

*Young men carry the Virgin Mary to the incontro in Arbatax.*

**BELOW:** observing the Easter procession in Arbatax.

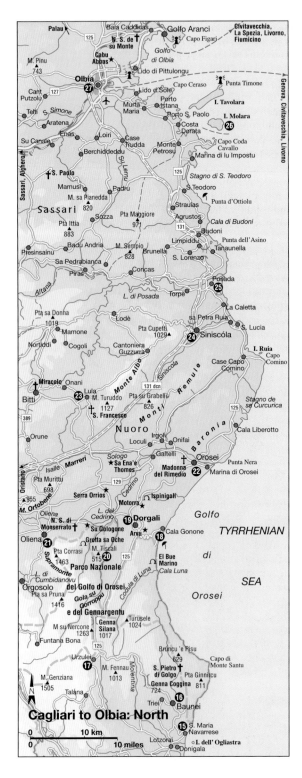

Cagliari to Olbia: North

0        10 km

0        10 miles

Sardinian foundation (established by the followers of St John Bosco). The town also possesses numerous schools and colleges. A handicraft fair is held in summer on the main square (selling crafts, pocket knives and wood carvings) but in the near future the fair will become a permanent feature inside the town's museum. In the **Duomo** (Cathedral of St Mary Magdalene; open daily) are some interesting paintings and canvases of Delitala, an important 20th-century Sardinian painter.

The **church of Santos Cosma e Damiano** (dedicated to two brothers, the patron saints of doctors, who were canonised following their martyrdom in the 4th century) is in the neighbourhood of Lanusei on the way to Bosco Selene. If you have a packed lunch, a good place to stop is in the picnic area in the **Selene Wood**, the town's surrounding holm oak forest which, at 1,000 metres (3,280 ft) above sea level, has some commanding views of the valley below as it descends to the sea.

The wood also has numerous walking trails of varying difficulty. The **Bosco Selene Archaeological Park** (open daily; entrance fee) consists of two Giant's Tombs and part of a large nuraghic village.

## From Baunei to Urzulei

A charming little village by the sea, **Santa Maria Navarrese** ⑮ forms part of the community of Baunei. It developed around the church of the same name which has an olive tree in its courtyard said to be over a thousand years old. According to legend, the church was founded by one of the daughters of the King of Navarre in gratitude for being saved from a shipwreck. The church stands on the site where she reached land. The town lies on the southern coast of Montesanto and contains hotels, restaurants and holiday villas.

Its environs are wild and untouched and stretch in the east as far as the cliffs overlooking the Tyrrhenian Sea. Goat and pig herds still wander among the

Map on page 174

holm oaks, arbutus and the shrubs of the *màcchia*, to feed on the profusion of berries and acorns. Boat trips can be made from the port of Santa Maria Navarrese to various destinations including Cala Luna, Cala Sisine and Cala Goloritzè in the Golfo di Orosei.

The town of **Baunei** ⓰ is famous for its hard-working population. In the *Dizionario Geografico Storico del,* written in 1833, it is recorded that "Leisure is a crime" here and "in the fields, men and women's hands compete for the most calluses". Local residents still bake acorn bread, at one time prepared all over the island. The local recipe goes something like this: soak some clay and wood ash particles in water, decant and pour the water into a large pot. Place the pot on the stove and add some shelled acorns (the ash particles act as a leach and remove the bitter taste from the acorns, while the clay softens them). A smooth paste will gradually form. Stir continuously, and cook until it is dark red, almost brown in colour. Allow the mixture to cool and solidify. Place the dough in the sun to dry. Today, few local residents pursue the area's traditional occupations of woodcutting or weaving; most are employed in jobs associated the regional tourism industry, the manufacture of sweets, or wine production. Tourism has also resulted in a return to the simple cooking methods and traditional fare based on goat, kid and lamb, or occasionally wild boar or other game hunted in the surrounding countryside.

*Ham, a popular antipasto (starter), is left to cure to improve its flavour.*

The vast area surrounding Baunei is of exceptional naturalistic interest. It is in Baunei that the shape of Ogliastra region becomes apparent – defined by the Supramonte mountains and the Codula di Luna river to the north, the Gennargentu mountains to the west, and the hills of the Salto di Quirra to the south. The coastline looks like a huge mountainous amphitheatre looking out towards the Tyrrhenian Sea. The landscape is very varied and has remained largely untouched due to its long isolation and difficult terrain.

**BELOW:** river and rock of the Gola su Gorroppu.

The coast is characterised by high cliffs, false inlets and beaches with crystalline water. The **Altopiano del Golgo** (1,000 metres/3,280 ft) is a large depression in the limestone rock covered by a flow of basaltic lava, where the enormous **Golgo Ravine** (295 metres/967 ft) opens up. Not far away is the simple church of San Pietro di Golgo, built in the 18th century, and surrounded by rustic *cumbessias* (pilgrim's houses).

From the plateau it is possible to walk down the **Codula de Sisine**, a narrow limestone canyon formed by the Supramonte di Baunei that ends at the sea in the Golfo di Orosei. The Codula de Sisine is 4 km (2½ miles) of low-difficulty track of great natural beauty ending at Sisine beach surrounded by majestic cliffs. The **Cala Coloritze** is dominated by l'Aguglia, an enormous pinnacle reaching 100 metres (328 ft) high. L'Aguglia has become popular with free-climbers who come here to test their mountain climbing skills.

From Baunei the main road, the SS 125, continues northwards. On one side is the **Gola su Gorroppu**, a spectacular canyon 500-metres (1,640-ft) deep and 4-km (2-miles) long in it's most spectacular part. On the other side is the **Genna Silana Pass** (1,017 metres/3,336 ft at its highest point). About 25 km (16

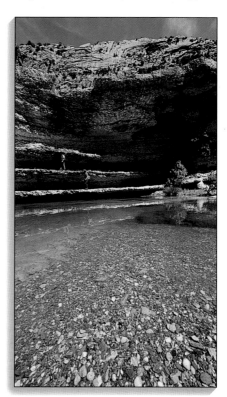

*Boat tours from Cala Gonone take you to Grotte di Cala Luna, and the beautiful Cala Luna beach.*

**BELOW:** the nuraghic village of Serra Orrios near Dorgali.

miles) after Baunei on the SS 125, the Hotel Genna Silana (closed for restoration) is a lovely spot to stop for refreshment and makes a good base for excursions in the area. It is possible to follow the Gola su Gorroppu on foot but in the final section it is necessary to use ropes to get over some vertical cliffs and ponds, so take equipment with you.

The path that leads down the large canyon of Cala Luna, the Codula di Luna, is about 8 km (5 miles) long and starts from the Supramonte di Urzulei. It takes about three hours to walk the easy-to-follow path, which passes through *màcchia* scrub and the entrances to many caves. The village of **Urzulei** ⓱ is on the left-hand side, clinging to a wooded hillside and sheltered from northerly and south-westerly winds. It lies at the foot of **Punta is Gruttas**, in the midst of varied terrain where the shepherds allow their flocks to roam wild. Continuing towards Dorgali, beyond Urzulei the road is full of nasty bends but these are more than compensated for by the awe-inspiring views.

## Dorgali and surroundings

Barely 2 km (1 mile) before Dorgali, there is a road tunnel through the Monte Bardia. At the far end lies the densely populated Dorgali suburb of **Cala Gonone** ⓲. The views as you exit the tunnel are magnificent: a gentle limestone hill falls away towards the sea. Juniper, rosemary and other aromatic Mediterranean plants blossom under ancient holm oaks. Spreading out in the distance, Cala Gonone is a former fishing village whose original inhabitants were not natives of the island. Nowadays it is a sizeable town with hotels, villas, flats, apartment houses and campsites. With views extending across glistening emerald waters it is easy to see why it has become so popular with tourists. Cala

Gonone is the starting point for boat trips along the 40 km (25 miles) of wild cliffs, interrupted by small bays and beaches with emerald water that reflects the rich vegetation (junipers, holm oaks, lentisc and oleander). Many grottos with little sandy beaches are visible at sea level.

Map on page 174

The most famous grotto of all is the huge **Grotta del Bue Marino**, renowned for its spectacular caves which are thought to extend for about 8 km (5 miles), although only 1 km (½ a mile) of the caves is open to the public. The grotto was also home to Sardinian monk seals until the 1950s and people still come here in the hope of catching sight of one. The most popular beach in the area is **Cala Luna**, described as one of the most beautiful beaches in the Mediterranean because of the flowering pink oleanders that reflect themselves in the tiny fresh-water lagoon behind the beach. The beach is surrounded by six grottos and high rocks. A daily boat service allows you to reach parts of the coast which are otherwise only accessible by long and tiring walks. Tickets for boat rides can be arranged at the Porto Turístico through various agencies. Prices vary according to the trip; it is possible to get a boat only to the Grotta del Bue Marino or you can go as far as Arco di Goloritzè with stops at Cala Sisine and Cala Luna.

**Dorgali ⑲** extends along the foot of the Monte Bardia, which protects the town's inhabitants from the sea breezes. Cattle farming and agriculture have been practised here since the earliest times; the vineyards of the nearby community of Oliena to the west are famous for their noble *Cannonau* vintages. Dorgali itself thrives on a flourishing handicrafts industry: cork, wood, wool, gold and silver items are all produced by a variety of medium-sized firms, most of them are also involved in local tourism.

The principal sights in and around the town include the nuraghic village of **Serra Orrios** (open daily 9am–noon, 4–6pm; entrance fee) 11 km (7 miles) northwest of Dorgali near the SS 125. This is one of the best preserved nuraghic villages in Sardinia, dating from the 10–12th centuries BC. The 70 round huts in the village are grouped in six clusters, each with a central well. A small temple area has also been discovered. About 15 km (9 miles) northwest of Dorgali is the Marreri valley, near the village of La Traversa. On the road that connects Dorgali with the SS 131 you will see signposts to the giants' tomb of **Sa Ena'e Thomes.** The tomb has a high stela carved in granite.

Heading north from Dorgali, about 4 km (2½ miles) on the right-hand side of the SS 125 you will see a sign for the **Grotta di Ispinigoli** (open daily; entrance fee). The cave contains a 38-metre (125-ft) stalagmite – the highest in Europe. Some interesting archaeological finds dating from the time of the Phoenicians have been discovered in the cave.

Four km (2½ miles) from Dorgali, on the road that connects the SS 125 with Cala Gonone and not far from the tunnel, is the turn off for the **nuraghe Mannu** (open daily; entrance fee), a recently excavated site and in a panoramic position over Cala Gonone. Archaeological finds dating from Palaeolithic times have also recently been discovered in the **Grotta Corbeddu** in the Lanaittu Valley, which during the 19th century was used as a shelter for the

**BELOW:** inside the Grotta di Ispinigoli.

*If you are visiting the Su Gologone spring, bring some food with you and enjoy lunch at one of the picnic tables in the eucalyptus wood surrounding the spring.*

**BELOW:** standing at the entrance of the nuraghic village of Tiscali.

bandit of the same name. With the assistance of the community of Oliena and the Principal Office for Archaeological Cultural Remains in the Provinces of Sassari and Nuoro, a group of students from Utrecht has been carrying out excavations which have unearthed plant and animal fossils proving beyond any doubt that the island was inhabited by man during the Old Stone Age, and not merely – as was previously assumed – since the Neolithic Era.

## The Valle Lanaittu to Oliena

The gateway to the Supramonte, the Valle Lanaittu, is covered by holm oaks and juniper bushes, which provide shelter for the mouflon that roam the hills. The valley also contains **Monte Tiscali** ⓴ (515 metres/1,690 ft). At the top of the mountain a wide crater opens up and inside is the hidden nuraghic village of **Tiscali** (open daily; entrance fee). Discovered in the 19th century, Tiscali consists of a number of round dwellings with limestone walls. It is thought that the village was inhabited up to the time of the Roman invasion and its high walls and surrounding terrain acted as natural defences. To get to Tiscali, take the turn off on the right near Su Gologone and leave your car about 2 km (1 mile) after Grotta sa Oche following the main dirt road. Follow the red and white marks on the rocks to the chasm of Tiscali. The walk to the crater village takes about 1¾ hours. In the nuraghic village of **Sedda e sos Carros**, also in the Valle Lanaittu about 100 metres (328 ft) away from the Grotta Corbeddu, in spring 2002 the sacred font was vandalised and decorations were stolen; it has been reconstructed and will open again to the public in 2004.

Returning to the SS 125 towards Olbia, a few kilometres past Dorgali you can turn off towards **Oliena** ㉑. The little town lies at the foot of Punta Corrasi, sep-

arated from Dorgali by the Valle Lanaittu. The most noteworthy sight in Oliena is **Su Gologone**, a spring situated near the hotel and restaurant of the same name. Gushing in a torrent from the limestone cliff, it is the most important spring in Sardinia, flowing at 400 litres (106 gallons) of water per second before joining the Cedrino river. Part of the river lies within the parish boundary of Galtellìs, an important town in Sardinia in ancient times. After being transferred to the *giudicato* of Gallura, it subsequently became a feudal estate under the name of Baronia; the surrounding area is still called by this name today. Oliena is a centre of apiculture and horticulture, but its main claim to fame within the province of Nuoro is as a producer of olives and wines.

The beauty of the surrounding countryside, coupled with the open character and hospitable nature of the inhabitants of Oliena, is famous in Sardinia. Within Oliena itself and its environs there are numerous late Romanesque and Pisan-style churches, all completed before the 14th century. The town centre is dominated by the **Chiesa di Santa Maria** (open daily); at Easter this is the scene of one of the most popular religious ceremonies in Sardinia. **S'Incontru** (which means the encounter) marks the meeting between the Virgin Mary and the resurrected Christ. The brightly coloured costumes, shawls, and filigree jewellery for which the town is famous are all on display during the festival. Ancient but well-preserved are the churches of **Santa Croce** and **San Lussorio**; from 21 August the latter forms the setting for a festival combining both sacred and secular elements, which attracts visitors from miles around.

*The traditional dress of Oliena includes lacework blouses and Sard jewellery.*

The Jesuits played a key role in the town's history. They were responsible for establishing the parish **church of St Ignatius Loyola** (open daily), named after their founder, and the associated boarding school, which previously housed a

**BELOW:** farmhouse in the Supramonte.

*The church of
Rosario in Orosei,
the historic centre of
the Baronia region.*

**BELOW:** marble
quarry in Orosei.

school of rhetoric. During the 16th and 17th centuries, the Jesuits painstakingly undertook the development of 16,000 hectares (39,500 acres) of mountainous countryside; some of this was later sold off to local farmers but 4,000 hectares (9,900 acres) are still in the possession of the society today. They grew wheat, barley, broad beans and several varieties of fruit trees. Thanks to their skills and their diligence, Oliena is now a thriving agricultural community. Take the time to see the church offices, where a varied collection of paintings, a number of old manuscripts and some exceptionally well-preserved church utensils are on display.

## From Oliena to Orosei

The SS 129 to Orosei is a pleasant road, bordered by pretty hills covered with olive and almond trees. Short lowland stretches occur from time to time, mostly given over to viticulture except when the local livestock farmers use them as grazing for their animals, principally sheep. Now and again the way leads through rough countryside, where the parched clay soil supports oleander, *màcchia* scrubland vegetation, arbutus and the thorny Sardinian gorse, the flowers of which blossom in spring and early summer, covering the landscape in a magnificent carpet of yellow.

The valley of the **River Cedrino** is marked by a mighty dam constructed to prevent the regular destruction caused by flooding when the river bursts its banks. On one occasion, however, the dam was unable to contain the deluge; the waters devastated the valley and the ancient villages of **Galtelli**, **Loculi**, **Irgoli** and **Onifai**. Of the four settlements, Galtelli lies on the right bank; Loculi, Irgoli and Onifai are on the left. In spite of the importance which this valley possessed in the years when it was the diocesan seat of the bishopric of Galtelli (which was transferred to Nuoro in 1779), it was infested with malaria and offered little employment; for a long time its population lived in poverty.

The houses and churches of the four villages, especially those of Irgoli and Galtelli, bear silent witness to a peasant culture and its religion, displaying fine examples of a formal but modest Mediterranean architectural style: tiled roofs, courtyards, archways, and belfries which – large or small – seem to cling to the ground rather than soar heavenwards. A good example of a 17th-century house is, Casa Marras in Galtellì, which is also an ethnographic museum, (open May–Sept 10am–1pm, 4–8pm or tel: 0784 90005; entrance fee), an architectural complex that covers 800 sq m (957 sq yards) transformed into an ethnographical museum.

The small town of **Orosei ㉒** is located on the final section of the SS 129. Situated on the plains on the right bank of the Cedrino river, the village is overshadowed by the **church of San Gavino** on the top of a hill, and by the vantage point **Gollei**, from where there is an idyllic view across the district's fertile flower gardens and orchards. The parish church of **San Giacomo Maggiore**, placed at the top of a large flight of steps, has an 18th-century facade and is surmounted by an unusual group of small domes.

Not far are the "palatzos Betzos", ancient homes belonging to noble families. Among them is the recently opened **Museo Don Nanni Guiso** (tel: 0784

997084; open summer daily am–pm; winter Sat and Sun 4–7pm; entrance fee), the first Italian museum to be opened in the 21st century. The Don Guiso collection displays surprising small miniature theatres from the 18th century, antique books on Sardinia, 19th- and 20th-century dresses and drawings of important Italian artists. The **church of Sant' Antonio Abate** is enclosed in a large courtyard with a Pisan tower, and contains 15th-century frescoes. Every year on 16 January a big bonfire is lit at the centre of the courtyard in honour of the patron saint. Further celebrations are held in the parish **church of San Giacomo** in honour of Nostra Signora del Mare (Our Lady of the Sea) the second week in May and, at the pilgrimage place of the same name to the west of the town, the festival of Nostra Signora del Rimedio (Our Lady of the Healing). This last occasion, which takes place in September, was recorded for posterity by the Nobel Prize-winning writer Grazia Deledda in her novel *Canne al Vento*; pilgrims come from near and far to take part. Orosei is clearly prospering. Its agriculture is sound, and it derives a steady income from its marble quarries. Above all, its seemingly endless beaches (Cala Liberotto, Cala Ginepro and several others which are less well known but no less attractive) have been opened up to tourism.

Map on page 174

## Around Orosei

About 30km (19 miles) inland from Orosei is the village of **Lula ㉓**, near the Monte Albo woods, where the important sanctuary of San Francesco di Lula stands. According to tradition it was founded by bandits in 1600. San Francesco was believed to be their protector, and anyone experiencing difficulties obtaining justice now goes to consult him. Near the sanctuary there is a church and a

**BELOW:** along the Orosei coastline.

*The name of Posada's Castello della Fava translates as "bean castle". It gained its name during the time of the Moorish invasion.*

**BELOW:** the village of Posada sits on a picturesque mountain.

number of *cumbessias* (pilgrim's houses). It's an interesting spot, and becomes very lively in the first week of May when thousands participate in a pilgrimage to the shrine, where plentiful free food and wine is available for everyone. North of Orosei the SS 125 follows the coast. The invitingly clear sea here is as unpolluted as it looks. After driving for a short while through pine groves and characteristic Mediterranean vegetation, you will reach the twin villages of Capo Comino and Santa Lucia, before arriving in **Siniscola** ㉔, and its coastal suburb, La Caletta, with its own harbour and a pretty beach.

During the latter part of the 20th century, tourism and a number of small industries – including a lime kiln and a cement works – have resulted in a more rapid population growth rate in Siniscola than in any of the other towns or villages within the province of Nuoro, apart from the regional capital itself. Today Siniscola, which lies on almost level terrain, has some 10,000 inhabitants.

Some 5 km (3 miles) in front of the town lies the sea; behind, to the west, lie the parallel mountains **Remule** and **Monte Albo**. What these mountains lack in height they more than make up for by their awe-inspiring, strangely shaped limestone cliffs. At dawn they greet the day with a shimmering pale pink hue; by midday they are a dazzling white; and as dusk falls they are suffused in a blaze of crimson. On a number of occasions Siniscola was the victim of attacks by raiding Turks. In 1512, 150 inhabitants were captured and carried off as spoils of war before being sold into slavery. Later on the citizens built two defensive towers, Santa Lucia and Caletta, which are still in good repair today, as well as constructing a fortified wall around the perimeter of the town.

The 12th century ruins of Castello della Fava is a daunting fortress some 20 metres (66 ft) high on the hill above the town of **Posada** ㉕ (entrance fee).

Stairs lead to the top of the castle's tower where there is a panoramic view of the surrounding countryside, the sea and the Posada river. In earlier times Siniscola was the seat of the barons of Monte Albo, under whose jurisdiction also lay the towns of Lodè and Torpè in the interior and Posada and San Teodoro on the coast. Nowadays Posada and San Teodoro, together with Budoni, are in the midst of rapid economic and touristic expansion.There are numerous hotels, apartments and rooms in private houses to accommodate the hordes of visitors who come every summer to the beaches between Siniscola and Olbia.

Map on page 174

## Beaches and bays

The most beautiful beaches to be found along this stretch of the east coast are **Su Tiriarzu** at Posada, **Budoni**, the sandy beach of **l'Isuledda** on the peninsula of the same name, and the beach of **La Cinta**, a narrow strip of sand 3 km (2 miles) long that separates the coastal marsh of San Teodoro from the sea, not far from the mighty foothills of Punt'Aldia. The remaining stretch of road as far as Olbia is some 35 km (22 miles) long and leads through one of the most enchanting regions in the whole of Sardinia, past the Cala Coda Cavallo, the Spiaggia di Salinedda beach, and a succession of bays – Cala Ruia, Cala Suaraccia and Cala Purgatorio to the foothills of Monte Petrosu and the picturesque beaches of Porto Taverna, Porto San Paolo and Porto Istana.

The silhouette of **Isola Molara** 🔞 and the forbidding cliffs of Isola Tavolara are right in front of you. Tavolara, a limestone mountain island 4 km (2½ miles) long and just 1 km (½ mile) wide, towering to the height of 564 metres (1,850 ft) can be reached either by private boat (enquire among the local fishermen) or by one of the small ferries which leave from Porto San Paolo. To the west soar

**BELOW:** beach on the southern Costa Rei.

Map on page 174

the shimmering red and white granite peaks of the mountains of the interior, while in the foreground groves of holm oaks and cork oaks stretch out before them, rising above an undergrowth of myrtle, arbutus and buckthorn. Here and there blackened stretches resembling a lunar landscape are the result of fires which regularly afflict Sardinia during the summer months.

## Olbia

Thanks to a remarkable expansion of both population and the local economy during the past decade, **Olbia** ㉗ has a modern airport and a flourishing port despite the proximity of the harbour at Golfo Aranci, only 15 km (9 miles) away. It is the main arrival point for people staying on the Costa Smeralda – except for those arriving by yacht. Its first population boom occurred during the years 1921–31, when a group of foreign industrialists developed local cheese production and mussel farming. Despite its Greek name (*Olbius* means happy), the town was not founded by the Greeks. There is no doubt that the Carthaginians once lived here; when the Romans conquered Sardinia (238 BC), Olbia ceased to rely purely on its economic value and acquired military power as well as strategic importance. In those days the town was connected to the rest of the island by three roads; they served as highways for the legions as well as for the transport of goods. Later, during the Christian era, they were a great aid to the Christian missionaries in their progress to convert the islanders. In Carthaginian times, Olbia extended more or less from the site of the present-day Via Asproni to the Piazza Matteotti. But the town's Golden Age occurred under the Romans, from the last century of the republic to the end of the first century of the empire. In 1904 a hoard of money was found in the necropolis; the 871 gold coins bear the portraits of 117 different Roman families and include 312 different currencies. The break-up of the Western Roman Empire during the 5th century BC marked the beginning of a long period of decline in the fortunes of Olbia. The town repeatedly fell prey to Arab raids from the 8th century onwards and many of its inhabitants fled to the interior. It was not until the turn of the millennium that it began to flourish again, initially as the first capital of the *giudicato* of Gallura, and later under Pisa, when it acquired the status of a free city. During this time the town was rechristened Terranova, a name which it bore until 1939. The kings of Savoy were responsible for the road linking Olbia to what is now the main highway, the Superstrada Carlo Felice, as well as the railway link with Chilivani, and for a marked increase in the trading links with Marseille, Sicily and the Italian mainland.

Worth a visit is the Romanesque **Basilica of San Semplicio** (open daily 6.30am–12.30pm, 4–7pm), on the street of the same name built between the second half of the 11th century and the beginning of the 12th century. It contains frescoes of the same period that represent two bishops (San Semplicio and San Vittore) and a fragment of a fresco depicting only the heads of a group of people. A huge three-day festival is held in mid-May in the basilica to commemorate San Semplicio's martyrdom in the 14th century. ❏

**BELOW:** a Roman aqueduct, Olbia. **RIGHT:** catching up on the gossip.

# COSTA SMERALDA

*The elite Costa Smeralda, the Aga Khan's playground
for the beautiful and wealthy, makes up for what it lacks
in atmosphere with undiluted luxury*

Map
on page
190

I f you drive directly north from Olbia Airport you will reach the place where Sardinia is at its most beautiful, the **Costa Smeralda ❶**, the Emerald Coast. Olbia, blighted by urban pollution, bunker-like concrete hotels and endless advertisement hoardings, couldn't be more different. Here the sea shimmers in hundreds of shades of aquamarine, your lips taste of salt, and your hair is tousled by a breeze fragrant with the scent of the *màcchia*, a heady mix of forest, aromatic rosemary, lavender and myrtle. According to Sardinian legend, this is where the wind was born. High wind-eroded cliffs, wild mountain terrain, 80 stunning bays and a string of idyllic coves make this 55-km (35-mile) coastal strip in north-west Sardinia one of the most attractive holiday destinations in the world. It is also one of the most exclusive. It was discovered at the start of the 1960s by His Highness Karim Aga Khan. Although scarcely out of his teens at the time, he was able to see the potential of this demi-paradise at the very heart of Europe's already overcrowded Mediterranean region. In conjunction with some of his wealthy friends, he set about creating a holiday resort for the world's wealthiest people. Over the next 20 years the Aga Khan created one of the most expensive and prestigious holiday regions in the world.

**PRECEDING PAGES:**
Cala di Volpe hotel,
Costa Smeralda.
**LEFT:** rock and sea,
Costa Smeralda.
**BELOW:** windsurfing.

## Cardinal rule

The Aga Khan's **Consorzio Costa Smeralda** was a non-profit organisation which ensured with utmost strictness that the harmonious relationship between nature and the works of man remained intact. One cardinal rule was that no villa, hotel or apartment block could be visible above the tops of the typically small holm oaks and tamarisks. Jacques Coelle, architectural genius and member of the Académie Francaise, designed the elegant houses surrounding the Piazza in Porto Cervo. The facades are endowed with the pastel-coloured patina that glow authentically at sunset. Land prices on the Costa Smeralda rose by 600 percent over a period of 10 years. Potential developers today must reckon with meteoric prices. During the peak season, which reaches its climax in July and August, some 12,000 people, mainly Italians, flock to Costa Smeralda: owners and tenants of the luxury villas, hotel guests, visitors in their private yachts.

In 2003 the Costa Smeralda was sold for 290 million euros to Tom Barrack of the US property development group, Colony Capital although the Starwood Hotels & Resorts still manages the major hotels. A coalition of Sardinian and Italian groups tried to outbid Colony Capital but failed. The group has recently detailed plans to build two luxury hotels, 100 villas and a golf course on the island. Objections to the

scheme include the fact that a golf course already exists and its maintenance during the summer months is extremely high and in conflict with the founding principals of the development.

Until recently, most of the houses along the Costa Smeralda were constructed with natural building materials available locally: stone and granite. Their roofs are covered with grass, so that they were hardly noticeable until you are standing before the front door. Even then, they mostly look like oversized kennels rather than houses, although inside they may contain up to 20 rooms. All telephone wires and electric cables run underground, waste water from the villas, the hotels and even the yacht harbour is processed by the most expensive treatment plant in the world. If a boat-owner is caught emptying his chemical toilet into the harbour or into some lonely bay, he can expect draconian punishment. The fines lie between $2,000 and $5,000; in the case of a second offense, exclusion from the marina and the loss of mooring privileges is the rule. The laws are enforced by a special Costa Smeralda Consortium task force, but their role is to provide security as much as to punish misdemeanours. The Costa Smeralda is a sanctuary for the very rich; there are no paparazzi, and they can rely on silent discretion and watchful eyes at all times.

*"This is obviously a place for people with above-average material possessions – I wouldn't even want to have the others here as guests." – the Aga Khan gives his view on the Costa Smeralda.*

## Beaches and boats

A private yacht is the ultimate status symbol on the Costa Smeralda. People manage without their expensive cars but they are reluctant to hide all evidence of wealth. During the winter months the yacht basin is scoured by a natural current. Except for *ferragosto* (15 August), when Italian high society swoops in from Milan and Rome, hiring a boat or obtaining a mooring in the harbour

**BELOW:**
Porto Cervo Marina.

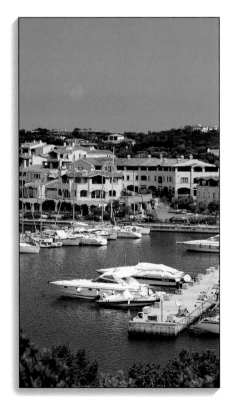

Map on page 190

should present no problems – but paying for it might be more of a deterrent. The Costa Smeralda **marina** was completed in 1975; its wharf is among the best functioning in the world. Altogether there are 650 berths here for boats between 12 and 55 metres (38–176 ft) in length. There is also a special dry dock. The best skippers in the world, from America and Australia, all converge on the Costa Smeralda. Nowhere else in Europe will yacht owners have so little difficulty finding experienced yachting crews to help them win one of the Costa's many regattas: the *Settimana della Bocche* at the end of August, and the competition for the largest yachts in mid-September. The Sardegna Club is an annual event, and the Premio Offshore is the race for the fastest motor boats (known as "cigars"). Stefano Casiraghi, who was married to Princess Caroline of Monaco, was a regular competitor here, and died while participating in a race of this kind.

Beaches are one of the highlights of the Costa Smeralda. If you don't have access to a private yacht then you can still visit some of the beautiful beaches on the mainland. You can enjoy diving in style, for example on **Long Beach**, or head for the the the sheltered **Petra Manna Beach** or **Capriccioli Bay** on windy days. The **Romazzino Beach** (also known as Princess Beach) is highly secure and at lunchtime you can eat in the Romazzino Hotel. You will need a boat, however, to get to the **Spiagga Rosa**, where the soft sand has a rose tint *(also see page 198 for details of the Maddalena Islands).*

The sea is not the only attraction of the Costa. International golfers regard the **Pevero Golf Course ❷** (above the Cala di Volpe hotel) as one of the loveliest and most challenging (18 holes, par 72) in the world. It was designed by Robert Trent-Jones on a raised spit of land; from each hole players enjoy spectacular views of the coast and the sea. The setting recalls Palm Beach. At the 19th hole there is an excellent restaurant and a luxurious indoor and outdoor swimming pool. Those who are not content with the swimming, sailing and golfing facilities can practise their tennis on one of the nine courts at the plush **Porto Cervo Tennis Club**.

*The harmonious relationship between nature and the works of man remains intact on the Costa Smeralda.*

**BELOW:** Porto Cervo shopping precinct.

## Porto Cervo

Little happens in **Porto Cervo ❸**, the focal point of the Costa Smeralda, before late afternoon, but at sunset the beautiful people flock for a sundowner on the **Piazzetta** or to shop at the designer boutiques at the **Sottopiazza**. The atmosphere at Porto Cervo is glamorous but a little surreal. Anyone can wander around its pristine streets but only the super rich can afford to stay for longer than a drink or a modest bite to eat. The main attraction of Porto Cervo, apart from the people and yachts, is the pretty **Stella Maris church** built on a hill above the marina. Designed in 1968 by architect Michele Busiri Vici, the whitewashed church contains the *Mater Dolorosa*, a painting by El Greco, a valuable 16th-century organ from Naples, a German altar cross from the same period, and two outsize Polynesian shells which serve as baptismal fonts.

## Where the wealthy stay

Most regulars on the Costa Smeralda are the proud owners of their own holiday residences; the loveliest

Map on page 190

houses are on Romazzino Bay at **Cala di Volpe** ❹. The finest houses for rent are on Petra Manna Beach. It was clear from the beginning, when the Aga Khan discovered the area in 1961, that, as well as the multi-million pound villas, hotel accommodation of an appropriate kind would also be required. The **Pitrizza** is the smallest of the big names, but by far the best. It lies in a rustic and romantic setting on the bay known as **Liscia di Vacca**. The **Cala di Volpe Hotel**, the most famous hotel in the area, looks like a medieval castle, and tends to be filled with wealthy Americans. Although luxurious, only the older part of the hotel (including the bar), built by Jacques Coelle, is really attractive. Coelle's son added a wing like a casbah and a marina like Port Grimaud.

The **Hotel Cervo** is less expensive than the other establishments, but it is very charming. All rooms have a spectacular view of the harbour, the decor is rustic-elegant, and it is conveniently situated – you can reach anywhere in Porto Cervo on foot from here. It is a particular favourite of boat owners who want to spend a night on *terra firma* whilst keeping their boat under close surveillance.The **Terrace Bar**, overlooking the piazza of Porto Cervo, serves as a meeting place for the whole resort. The restaurant is better than at Cala di Volpe, and the view is priceless. The **Romazzino** directly overlooks the beach, only separated from it by gently sloping, carefully manicured lawns. The hotel, also decorated in rustic elegance, is a favourite of Swiss families with children.

**BELOW:**
one of the plush
hotels in the area.
**RIGHT:**
Stella Maris church.

## Eating and drinking

You can eat and drink pretty well on the Costa Smeralda, but one thing is quite clear: apart from a few notable exceptions it is no mecca for gourmets. Specialities always include fish, *spaghetti aragosta*, roast suckling pig from the barbecue and smoked wild boar ham. Everything is accompanied by warm *pane carasau*, the ultra-thin bread which is seasoned with salt and rosemary and sprinkled with best olive oil, and which "makes music" – a crunching sound – when you bite into it.

Port Cervo doesn't have much to offer in terms of nightlife, but a short drive away is the very chic **Sottovento**, a nightclub which looks rather like an elegant barracks located outside the domain of the *consorzio* on the road to Cala di Volpe. North of Porto Cervo towards Baia Sardinia lies **Ritual**, the training ground for the new generation of the Costa's millionaires. Those who prefer more peace and less stress should take their after-dinner *digestivo* in **Il Portico** on the Piazzetta. The bar is very attractive and decorated in Moroccan style.

Alternatively, you can escape to **Porto Rotondo** ❺ (a miniature Porto Cervo), only 20 minutes from Porto Cervo by car, or 10 by boat. Built in 1963, though less attractive architecturally, it is also a stylish resort. It lies in a little bay, with tiny piazzas, a handful of designer boutiques, a small harbour and two white sandy beaches.

The pretty granite church of San Lorenzo, up the steps leading off the central Piazzetta San Marco, was designed by the architect Andrea Cascella. An open-air theatre which holds concerts during the summer months is nearby. ❑

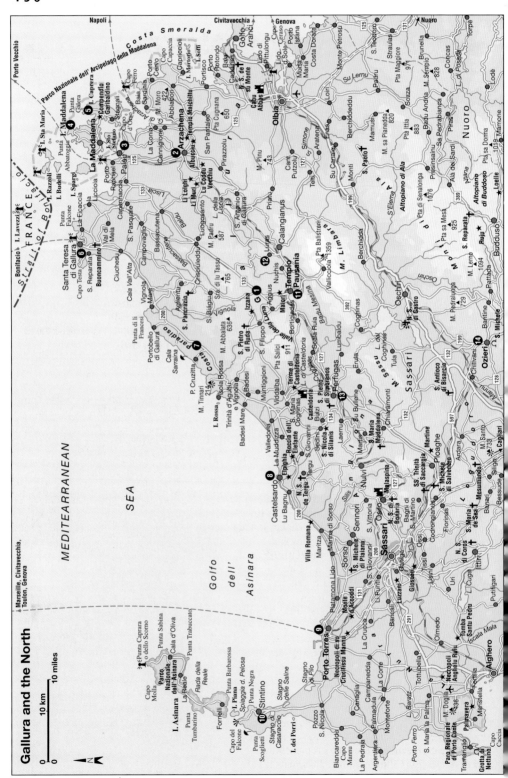

## Gallura and the North

# GALLURA AND THE NORTH

*This itinerary takes in Gallura's dramatic coastline, the islands of Maddalena, the town of Stintino and then travels through the interior of the region*

Map on page 196

A journey through the Gallura promises the traveller a full and varied experience. The island's most extensive oak woods surround Monte Limbara and the little town of Tempio Pausania, and the shores of the Costa Paradiso form part of one of its loveliest stretches of coastline. What's more, at Arzachena there are two of Sardinia's best-preserved *tombe dei giganti* (tombs of giants).

Gallura ❶ is a north-eastern sub-region of Sardinia defined to the west by the river Coghinas, to the south by the Monti di Alà and to the east by the village of San Teodoro. Its principal characteristic is defined by the granite rocks which determine its landscape. The countryside is punctuated with *stazzi* (traditional houses). These are low, elongated buildings usually formed by three aligned rooms: the central room is both the entrance and dining room with a bedroom on each side. Placed at the centre of a vast land, *stazzi* are surrounded by the necessities of family life (a kitchen garden, an orchard, vineyard and maybe a small patch of wheat) and grazing ground for cattle. Built from the 18th century by shepherds that were looking for new lands to settle, they slowly transformed themselves into farms, which are still inhabited.

**PRECEDING PAGES:** the coast around Gallura. **BELOW:** Capo Testa.

## The Golfo di Arzachena

The fashionable atmosphere of the Costa Smeralda fades as one drives away from Porto Cervo, but the first place of any size on the Golfo di Arzachena is the elegant seaside resort of Baia Sardinia, whose string of luxury hotels are almost as expensive as those on the Costa Smeralda. Just across the bay, however, the small fishing port of **Cannigione** offers the first campsites in the region, and the air of exclusivity quickly becomes a thing of the past. The town itself has little to offer but some of the beaches to the north of town further up the coast are pleasant.

The steep cliffs surrounding **Arzachena** ❷ lend the little town the appearance of a village in the Dolomites rather than one on a Mediterranean island. However, the rapid development of the Costa Smeralda over the past few years has brought economic benefits to these neighbouring regions. The bleak, poverty-stricken Sardinia associated with the Gennargentu has now completely disappeared; the area looks now prosperous, without having lost its rural character.

## Arzachena's archaeological sites

Around Arzachena are a number of important remains from the time of the Nuraghi. They have given their name to the civilisation which they represent: the Li Muri or Arzachena Culture. Some 3,000 years BC, the

**BELOW:** Garibaldi memorial, Isola Maddalena.

Gallura was inhabited by groups of semi-nomads and shepherds. Witnesses to this epoch are the stone box graves of **Li Muri** (Coddu Vecchiu; tel: 336 869619 or 338 3672646; open daily 9am–1pm, 4–7pm; entrance fee), each of which was found to hold a single corpse buried in a squatting position. The graves themselves were surrounded by concentric circles of stones. More famous, and easier for non-specialists to appreciate, are the two *tombe dei giganti* near the village on the road to Luogosanto.

**Lu Coddu Vecchiu** is one of the best-preserved *tombe dei giganti* in existence. A stela, 4 metres (13 ft) high and subdivided into two sections – a square unit and a half-arch – stands sentinel in front of the grave. Through the semicircular opening at ground level, which repeats the contours of the stela, sacrificial offerings could be presented to the dead person. Flat stone slabs positioned vertically form a semicircle demarcating the ceremonial and sacrificial arena. Li Muri and Lu Coddu Vecchiu can be reached by following the signs to the town of Luogosanto and taking a dirt track signposted to "Coddu Ecchiu".

On a hill a few kilometres further on, also marked by a signpost on the Luogosanto road, lies the *tombe dei giganti* of **Li Lolghi.** The form of this grave is very similar to Lu Coddu Vecchiu. The stone box graves of Li Muri are also not far from here. The traveller approaching the region via the SS 125 from Olbia will find the **Nuraghe Albucciu.** It is signposted about 3 km (2 miles) before Arzachena, but is in any case impossible to miss because of the **Ristorante Nuraghe** nearby. The most interesting feature is the fact that the *nuraghe* itself is not constructed in the familiar tower form. It is one of the very few corridor *nuraghi* in Sardinia. Close by stands the **Temple of Malchittu**, which formed part of the Nuraghi settlement. The **Roccia Il Fungo** (Mushroom Rock) is a weathered granite rock near Arzachena. Like the spectacularly-shaped Roccia dell' Elefante (Elephant Rock) near Castelsardo and the Roccia L'Orso (Bear Rock) near Palau, it features on many postcards.

## Palau and Arcipelago della Maddalena

Continuing along the SS 125, the traveller passes first through the little port of Palau and then through **Capo d'Orso**, where a weathered cliff formation resembles the eponymous bear (*orso* means bear). As far as Cannigione the coast road skirting the Golfo d'Arzachena is in excellent condition, but after that the surface is poor until Palau. On the way are a number of pleasant campsites with good facilities, offering overnight accommodation. **Palau ❸** itself is a little coastal town dominated by its harbour, from which ferries leave regularly for Caprera and La Maddalena. Apart from the ferry port and the Roccia L'Orso ("Bear Rock"), the town offers visitors few attractions of particular note. It is easy enough to find boats to take you to any of the offshore islands (just ask around at the quay; the fishermen will advise), but at **Palau Mare** in Palau's Via Nazionale you can hire everything you might need to explore the archipelago independently – from a rubber dinghy to a yacht.

The island of **La Maddalena ❹** is formed of granite and is the only island in the archipelago with an urban centre. Lying only a few kilometres from the mainland, together with the other islands of the archipelago of the same name, it represents what remains of the land link that once existed between Sardinia and the island of Corsica. Sea level eustatic movements were responsible for the formation of this miniature island chain, consisting today of more than 50 islets.

On the largest island, almost 50 sq. km (19 sq. miles) in size, lies the town of **La Maddalena**. Its fashionable atmosphere underlines the elegance of its architecture. Also on the island is the interesting **Museo Archeologico Navale Nino Lamboglia** (Maritime Museum; Giardino, Strada Panoramia; tel: 0789 8736423; due to reopen soon) which contains the remains of a Roman cargo ship dating from the 2nd century BC. Thanks to its advantageous strategic position, the island often played an important military role in the past. Even today, it is the site of bases of both the Italian and US navy. Unfortunately for visitors, the presence of the latter's nuclear submarines has resulted in a considerable proportion of La Maddalena being declared a prohibited area.

The fame of the other large island, **Isola Caprera** ❺ is largely due to its famous resident, Giuseppe Garibaldi (1807–82), for whom it was home for many years, the refuge to which he always returned, and the place where he died. Garibaldi created a model farm on the island; his memorial museum, the **Compendio Garibaldino** (tel: 0789 727162; open Tues–Sun, summer 9am–6pm; winter 9am–1pm; entrance fee), has the air of a place of pilgrimage, and is well worth visiting.

The Maddalena archipelago is formed by seven major islands, of which **Budelli** is the best known with its famous **Spiaggia Rosa** (Pink Beach), made famous by the 1965 film *Il Deserto Rosso* (Red Desert) directed by Michelangelo Antonioni. The stop-off point on the island of **Santo Stéfano** is the Spiaggia

Map on page 196

*The archipelago of La Maddalena has been a national park since 1998. Together with the French national park of the Arcipelago di Lavezzi, it will, by 2005, form the international park of the Bocche di Bonifacio.*

**BELOW:** Roccia Il Fungo – "the mushroom rock".

*The belltower of the church of San Vittorio in Santa Teresa di Gallura.*

del Pesce beach; most of the rest of the island is a military base. All the islands in the archipelago can be reached by boat from Palau.

**Santa Teresa di Gallura** ❻ lies at the northernmost tip of Sardinia. Its harbour is the starting point for ferries across to Corsica. The twin approach roads – the SS 133 from Tempio and the SS 200 from Castelsardo – both pass through attractive countryside. The most noteworthy sights here are the bizarre rock formations along the cliffs near **Capo Testa**. From the **Torre Longosardo** there is a spectacular view of the wild and often inaccessible coast of the Gallura, whose waters and sea-beds provide ideal conditions for deep-sea diving and the white cliffs of Bonifacio. Also in the vicinity of Capo Testa are two quarries dating from Roman times.

## Along the coast

The road from Santa Teresa to Castelsardo passes through what is undoubtedly one of the loveliest regions in Sardinia, with stretches of outstanding coastline – the most famous of which is the aptly-named **Costa Paradiso**. The steep precipices typical of the northern coast force the road inland. Running parallel to the coastline, it follows a serpentine course through untouched *màcchia*. Travellers will notice the reddish peaks of the Monte Pitrighinosu and the Monte Puntaccia on the horizon.

The sparsely populated area between the SS 200 and the SS 133 has a wild charm. Along the lonely stretch of road to **Tempio** you will see cork oaks, their trunks, with patches of freshly peeled reddish bark, gnarled and misshapen by the wind. An enduring impression of these regions is of the impenetrability of the *màcchia*. In places, however, it is dissected by routes to the sea which are

**BELOW:** the coastline of the Costa Paradiso.

welcome to the hot and weary motorist. Some 10 km (6 miles) past Santa Teresa, the **Spiaggia di Rena Maiore** and the **Cala Vall'Alta** offer some of the best opportunities for bathing.

The situation on the lovely **Costa Paradiso ❼**, whose turning lies about 25 km (16 miles) from the main road, is quite different. The development consists of an extensive, well-planned holiday park. In fact, it comprises several little *villagi*, hidden away in dense thickets. Its architects made great efforts to make the complex as unobtrusive as possible. But their aim that the buildings should blend harmoniously with the countryside has been only partially successful. Inevitably, development has meant the destruction of the natural equilibrium of another lovely stretch of coastline. Critics worry, believing traditional Sardinia will die in the stranglehold of its *residencias* and *villagi*. The choicest land has been snapped up by the tourism industry, the loveliest beaches bought by big private hotels for the exclusive use of their patrons. Whether a development is constructed in a traditional Sardinian style which harmonises well with the countryside, or takes the form of a vast concrete hotel complex, or even a string of sugar-cube-style villas, seems almost irrelevant.

The two smaller beaches of the **Baia Trinità** are open to the public; overlooking them is the **Isola Rossa**. From here there is also a long sandy beach stretching almost as far as the rocky promontory overlooking **Castelsardo ❽**, a town perched on a trachyte cliff, looking as if it might be the very source of Sardinian folklore – and kitsch, to judge by the large number of shops (including a hypermarket) offering souvenirs and handicrafts for sale. Castelsardo was founded in 1102 by the Genoese Doria family. First known as Castel Genovese, the settlement's name was changed after the Spanish conquest to Castel Ara-

Map on page 196

**BELOW:** traditional design in a carpet from Castelsardo.

*The aptly named Roccia dell'Elefante. A nearby* domus de janas *has a carving of an elephant on its walls.*

gonese; in 1796 the King of Sardinia gave it the present name of Castelsardo. Nowadays, during the summer months at least, the town is usually too full of tourists to make a visit here entirely pleasurable, but the castle hill has managed to retain its attractive atmosphere and it is worth venturing up its steep, narrow alleys. The fortress at its summit houses the **Museo dell'Intreccio Mediterraneo** (tel: 079 472380; open Tues–Sun, summer 9.30am–1pm, 3–8.30pm; July 9am–12pm; winter 9.30am–1pm, 3–5.30pm; entrance fee). The museum displays a collection of basketwork and weaving. Other attractions in the town include the **Cattedrale di Sant'Antonio Abate**, inside is a 16th-century altarpiece; *Madonna with Angels,* by a 15th-century painter known as Maestro di Castelsardo.

Outside on the twisting road to Perfugas lies the **Roccia dell'Elefante**, a curiously shaped outcrop of rock which resembles a young elephant with its trunk raised. Castelsardo is well known for its Easter procession, which takes place on the Monday of Holy Week. Interspersed with ancient rituals and traditional songs, the ceremony has retained all its original medieval character; *Lunissanti* (Holy Monday) in Castelsardo is generally regarded as one of the finest examples of Easter festivities to be found anywhere on the island.

Continuing south the SS 200 follows the outline of the coast once more. Some 15 km (9 miles) from Castelsardo it arrives at the **Punta Tramontana**. By taking the route via **Sorso** and **Sénnori,** the traveller can very quickly reach Sassari. The SS 200, however, carries on along the coast through the *pineta*, beyond which lies the **Platamona Lido,** the favourite beach of the inhabitants of Sassari, though not one that can be recommended to visitors with the time and means to go elsewhere. Over 20 km (12 miles) long, the beach stretches as far as the industrial port

**BELOW:** Castelsardo from the water.

of Porto Torres. Its backdrop of pine groves makes for an attractive setting, but the proximity of Sassari has somewhat marred its beauty. Campsites alternate with discotheques and beach cafés. However, none of this seems to deter the local residents; the Platamona Lido is to Sassari what the Poetto Beach is to Cagliari.

Map on page 196

## Porto Torres and Stintino

It makes no difference from which side you approach **Porto Torres** ❾; it is an unattractive little town dominated by vast oil refineries. Since Roman times it has been famous as the home of seafarers; even in those days the inhabitants conducted lively trade with the mainland. Nowadays container ships and tankers have taken over. The principal port in northern Sardinia, Porto Torres is one of the main gateways to the island, with ferry links to Civitavecchia and Genoa. It also has a thriving oil industry.

*The Regata della Latina takes place in Stintino at the end of August, with vintage boats and colourful yachts taking part.*

The town has impressive remains from its early Roman history – ruins of the original trading post and the former *Turris Libisonis*, the Roman colony founded in 27 BC. Near the present railway station lie the **Terme Centrali** (Roman Baths), with mosaics dating from the 3rd–4th century BC. There is also a seven-arched bridge from the same period and a museum, the **Antiquarium Turritano** (Via Ponte Romano; tel: 079 514433; open Tues–Sun 9am–7.30pm; entrance fee) that contains finds from archaeological excavations in town and on its outskirts. The **Basilica di San Gavino** (open 7am–noon, 4–7.30pm; entrance fee) was completed in the year 1111; it houses the tomb of the martyr of the same name and is one of the most important Romanesque buildings to be found on Sardinia.

Following the main highway to Sassari, the SS 131, you will arrive at the sanctuary of **Monte d'Accoddi**, (open 9am–6pm; entrance fee), an early altar shaped like a truncated pyramid with a large access ramp. Similar to a mesopotamic *ziggurat*, it dates to approximately 2500 BC. It is the only structure of this kind to be found in the Mediterranean area.

**BELOW:** the Basilica di San Gavino.

The most northwesterly point of the island is a small triangle of land bounded by the towns of Porto Torres to the north and Alghero to the south. With the exception of Porto Conte on the Capo Caccia and the little resort of Stintino, the entire area is as yet virtually untouched by tourism. The drive from Porto Torres to Stintino passes through fertile, sparsely-populated farmland; unfortunately vast chemical complexes dominate much of the landscape, and as a result, the long expanse of beach between the two towns is not particularly attractive.

Stintino ❿ is a small, unaffected place consisting of holiday cottages, a few hotel complexes and two marinas. Founded at the end of 1800 by fishermen and shepherds forced by the state to abandon the island of Asinara, the town is one of Sardinia's major touristic destinations. The **Pelosa beach**, at Rada dei Fornelli between Capo del Falcone and the island of Asinara, is regarded as being among the most beautiful beaches in Sardinia. The island of **Asinara** was expropriated in 1885 to set up a hospital and a penal colony. In its recent history the Fornelli prison on the

# The Cork Oak

French traders introduced industrial cork processing to Sardinia in the 1830s. Spread across what remains of the once-magnificent cloak of woodland are three different species of oak tree. Up to an altitude of 1,200 metres (3,900 ft) on the more exposed upper mountain slopes is the deciduous down oak (*Quercus pubescens*), while two evergreen species, the holm oak (*Quercus ilex*) and the cork oak *(Quercus suber)* grow at lower altitudes (up to about 700 metres/2,240 ft) in more sheltered positions. The holm oak thrives on limestone and karst soils, while the cork oak – which is found only in the Western Mediterranean – prefers the earth of slate, granite and volcanic regions.

Extensive woods of cork oaks are found on the acid basalt and trachyte uplands of the island, such as the Giara of Gesturi, or on the infertile granite wastelands of the Gallura in northeast Sardinia. The various dialect names for the cork oak – *suberju, suelzu, suveliu, suergiu, suaru* or *cortigu, ortigu, orteghe* – are derived from the Latin *suber* or *corticulum* – "cork" or "bark".

The thick cork bark protects the tree from damage, cold, heat and drying out. Today, large specimens – which may be 200 to 300 years old and up to 20 metres (65 ft) tall, with a trunk diameter of as much as 1 metre (3 ft) – are only encountered in the remotest areas of the island.

A cork oak can produce bark until it is about 125 years old if the peeling is done correctly. Peeling requires considerable skill and experience, in order to avoid harming the bright red cambium, the growing surface for the next layer of cork.

When stripping is done properly, the bark is peeled from a cork oak for the first time when the trunk is 1.3 metres (4 ft) from the ground and has a circumference of at least 60 cm (24 inches). This is usually when the tree is about 15 years old. A tree will be peeled about eight times during its lifetime, usually at intervals of 9 to 12 years, or until the quality of the cork declines below an acceptable level.The sections of stripped bark are transported to one of the cork factories in the towns of Tempio and Calangianus. Here they are graded according to quality. The poorest quality consists primarily of the first peeling of the wild "male" cork oak. This is processed straight away into cork waste for the building industry, where it is used as insulation material.

The elastic "female" cork from later peelings is left to mature in the open air for at least six months. During this process the sun and rain, heat and cold removes most of the red powder and other impurities from the cork's pores and makes it lighter in colour. The cork is then soaked in enormous vats of hot water for about an hour. This process removes most of the tannic acid, and the cork swells up and gains the requisite elasticity. Bottle corks are then stamped out from the sheets of bark, which are pressed flat as they dry. Corks for bottles are cut parallel to the annual rings of bark growth, and barrel corks at right angles. ❑

**LEFT:** cork bark is put out to dry in the open air for months.

Map
on page
196

island was used to confine Italian *brigatisti* and *mafiosi*. The penal colony was closed in 1997 and a year later the island became the Parco Nazionale dell'Asinara. Although access is still restricted, it is possible to arrange a guided tour of the island to see the wide range of wildlife.

Just before Stintino lies the Tonnara Saline, formerly an important tuna fishing station which has now been converted into a well-designed complex of holiday homes. Industrial developments of the past century possess a certain charm of their own, and travellers who appreciated the unique attractions of the abandoned mines near Sulcis and Iglesiente may also find it worthwhile to drive across to **Argentiera**. Since ceasing to serve their original purpose the little miners' cottages have undergone conversion into comfortable modern homes; additional groups of houses have also sprung up overnight. The main shaft, however, has been retained in its original form, as has the heart of the mining village, which recently gained protected status.

## The interior of the Gallura

The road No.133 makes its way towards the inner part of the Gallura where the gentle countryside is punctuated by large heaps of granite blocks, inselbergs (granite towers) and cork tree woods. In villages like **Luogosanto** (350 metres/1,148 ft above sea level) the archaic features of the local regional culture have been retained. Continuing south, **Aggius** lies at the foot of the impressive granite mountains (Monti di Aggius) and is connected via a panoramic road to the **Valle della Luna**, a vast plain with an incredible scenery of weathered granite blocks, piled one on top of the other.

The little town of **Tempio Pausania** ⓫ lies at the heart of the Gallura, at the foot of the granite peak of **Monte Limbara**. Irrespective of the direction from which you approach this area, you cut through dense oak forests unlike any to be found elsewhere in Sardinia. Tempio Pausania itself lies at an altitude of 555 metres (1,820 ft), giving it the air of a mountain resort – an impression underlined by the town's atmosphere. Lately Tempio (in competition with Olbia) has been campaigning to become the island's fifth provincial capital. The ancient rivalry between the two towns, dating from the time of the Spanish occupation, is still strong today.

Visitors wishing to spend some time in Tempio can visit its 15th-century cathedral and **Museo Bernardo De Muro** (open daily 8am–2pm, 4.30–7.30pm, tel: 079 679952 for an appointment), dedicated to the famous tenor who was a native son of the town. Ideal for a rest and refreshment is the **Café Gabriel** in the Via Mannu (currently closed), which serves excellent Sardinian food: *suppa cuata, ravioli dolci di Tempio, pane frattau* or *cordula* – the latter a popular dish of lamb offal and peas in a tasty sauce.

A short distance from Tempio lies the centre of the Sardinian cork industry. **Calangianus**, some 10 km (6 miles) away, is the cork capital. Two km (1 mile) away from Calangianus, in the village of **Luras** ⓬ are four *dolmen*; the most important is *dolmen* Ladas, which has a structure that is similar to *tombe dei giganti*. There is also an ethnographic museum, a

*A cork oak with its bark stripped down to the red inner bark.*

**BELOW:** the abandoned mine of Argentiera in the Nurra.

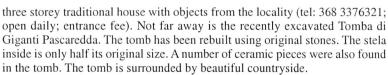

Map
on page
196

three storey traditional house with objects from the locality (tel: 368 3376321; open daily; entrance fee). Not far away is the recently excavated Tomba di Giganti Pascaredda. The tomb has been rebuilt using original stones. The stela inside is only half its original size. A number of ceramic pieces were also found in the tomb. The tomb is surrounded by beautiful countryside.

Leaving Tempio and travelling towards Sassari, the road No.127 crosses the Coghinas river, the natural border between Gallura and the subregion of Anglona, and reaches **Perfugas** ⓭. The oldest man-made lithic tools of Sardinia, dating back to the Palaeolithic period, have been recently found in this territory. The **Museo Archeologico e Paleobotanico** (Via Nazario Sauro; tel: 079 564241; open Tues–Sun, summer 9am 1pm, 4–8pm; winter 9am–1pm, 3–7pm; entrance fee) displays the abundant prehistoric and nuraghic material found in the many sites in the area. The Palaeobotanical section has a small collection of vegetable fossils while the Palaeolithic section displays Clactonian-type tools, which are thought to come from an open-air workshop that was abandoned leaving everything in its place.

Following side roads through a mountainous area you will reach the **Lago del Coghinas**, the second-largest lake in Sardinia. It was dammed in 1927 and provides one of the island's main supplies of drinking water. The journey is delightful if you don't mind the serpentine nature of the road. A good place to have a picnic is at the site of the Romanesque church of **Nostra Signora di Castro** (open daily) because of its position dominating the plain and Lake Coghinas. It was built in the second half of the 12th century and was the seat of the bishopric of a medieval hamlet until 1505. Passing through **Oschiri** and taking the SS 199 you will finally arrive in **Ozieri** ⓮, a prosperous and attractive little town lying on a fertile plain supporting crops and cattle farming. The most impressive feature of the town is its magnificent range of neoclassical houses. They outshine those in many of the other, larger towns on the island.

**BELOW:** street with café in Ozieri.
**RIGHT:** winter on Monte Limbara in the Gallura.

### Prehistoric finds

Not far from Ozieri lies the **Grotta di San Michele** (guided tours Tues–Fri 9am–12.30pm; entrance fee), the scene of some of Sardinia's most important archaeological finds. The name of the town was given to the prehistoric period which they represent, which is now known as the Ozieri Culture. Part of the excavated material can be seen in the **Museo Archeologico** (Convento Clarisse; tel: 079 7851090; open Tues–Sun 9am–1pm, 4–7pm; entrance fee), housed in the 17th-century cloisters of the convent annexe of the church of San Francesco. In the same square is an interesting 16th-century noble house. The **Cattedrale dell' Immacolata** (open daily) has a neoclassical facade and an interior with Gothic vaults. There is also an important polyptych, the *Madonna di Loreto*, the work of a 6th-century Sardinian artist known as the Maestro di Ozieri. The nearby village of **Pattada** is the best place to buy a genuine hand-crafted shepherd's knife *(see page 104)*. If you are not yet tired of winding roads you are recommended to tackle the lonely, sinuous and unforgettable stretch of road from **Buddusò** to **Bitti** and **Nuoro**. ❑

# SASSARI

*If you arrive in Sassari at the end of a tour of Sardinia, you will probably feel as if you have returned to the Italian mainland without actually crossing the sea*

Map on page 212

I n **Sassari** there there is no trace of the island's rural soul, which is usually evident even in the island's larger towns and cities. The town wears an urban, worldly countenance. In fact, a great deal of mainland blood flows through their veins. In the early 13th century the merchants of Genoa and Pisa – both cities of international importance in medieval times – transformed an insignificant peasant village in the hinterland of Porto Torres into a flourishing commercial town. Even today, the citizens of Sassari are proud of being a "community of shopkeepers". Trade enabled them to free themselves from the dependence on Porto Torres which had dogged their existence since Roman times. Their only regret is that throughout their long history they have never quite managed to oust Cagliari from its position as the most important town on the island. During the 17th century it was a close-run thing, as Sassari almost managed to overtake its arch-rival in the south. In 1617 the university of Sassari received its charter, three years before that of Cagliari. Such was the town's prosperity that private citizens donated enough money to build or renovate nine churches and monasteries. However, the plague in 1652 and the subsequent fall in population shattered the hopes of Sassari's inhabitants. It seemed that thereafter their town was fated to remain the perpetual runner-up.

**PRECEDING PAGES:** rooftops near Sassari. **LEFT:** washing in the old town. **BELOW:** old clashes with new.

## The modern city

Today, with its population having reached 120,000, Sassari is again able to show that it is at least as good as the capital. Three of the most famous Sardinian politicians of post-war times – Communist Party leader Enrico Berlinguer, the former presidents Antonio Segni and Francesco Cossiga – are all natives of Sassari.

In the sphere of arts, too, Sassari succeeded in finding its own individual style – possibly the only Sardinian town to do so. Many of the churches are the work of local stonemasons, known as *picapedras*, who gave the basic architectural styles imported from the mainland a popular, Sardinian touch. This tendency also applied to the sculptors of Sassari, who during the 17th century adorned the town's numerous new churches and monasteries with countless statues and altars. They also carved the *candelieri*, enormous wooden pillars shaped like candles which every year on 14 August are carried through the old town from the Piazza Castello to the church of Santa Maria di Betlem (St Mary of Bethlehem) by the members of the various craftsmen's guilds. The I candelieri (Feast of Candles), whose origins appear to lie way back in the 13th century, has remained an authentic folk festival, for which some expatriates even return home from overseas.

During the Cavalcata Sarda (usually held in May), however, the local population prefers to leave the

town to foreigners and tourists. The Cavalcata, one of Sardinia's best known festivals, features a horse-back parade of riders in traditional costume who later take part in a daring horse race. The participants are drawn from surrounding villages and it is an excellent opportunity to see the traditional costumes of the region. Over the weekend, folk groups perform traditional song and dance in the Piazza d'Italia during the evening.

### The Piazza d'Italia

The spacious **Piazza d'Italia ❶** covers an area of precisely 1 hectare (2½ acres); framed by official buildings dating from the 19th century such as the **Palazzo della Provincia** and the neo-Gothic **Palazzo Giordano**, it is an ideal starting point for a tour of the town. It is a good idea to visit the square during the daily *passeggiata*. This evening stroll is a custom in every Italian town and takes place between business closing time and dinner. The traditional rigid segregation of the sexes, still strictly observed by the older generation, seems to have

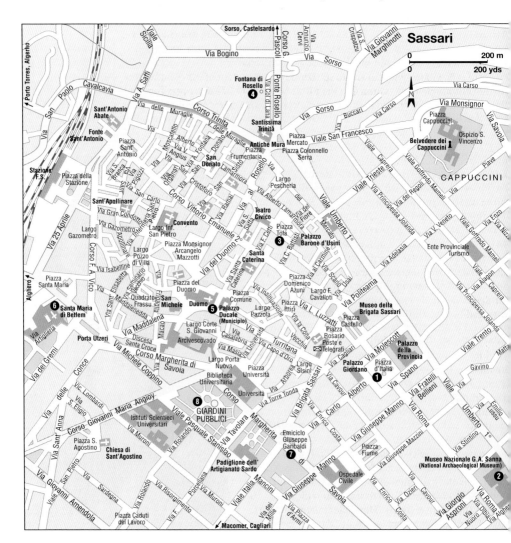

lost its significance for the youth of the town. In times past, some 150 years ago, sheep still grazed on this piazza, in whose numerous banks and administrative buildings the financial and political fate of the town is now decided. Until well into the 19th century there seemed no necessity to expand the urban area beyond the limits set by the 13th-century city walls. For 600 years, under the Spanish and the Piedmontese, the entire area was compressed within an area of some 30 hectares (75 acres).

Providing a link between the Old Town and the newer districts is the **Piazza Castello**, which lies next to the Piazza d'Italia. In the1870s, whilst new buildings in the architectural style of the Italian mainland were sprouting up on the Piazza d'Italia, on the Piazza Castello they were demolishing the fortress after which it is named. The castle was built in 1330 by the Aragonese; for centuries afterwards it served as a symbol of foreign rule and oppression.

Map on page 212

## Two museums

The military barracks attached to the castle house the **Museo della Brigata Sassari** (Piazza Castello; tel: 079 233303; open Mon–Sat 9–noon, 3–4.30pm). The museum is dedicated to the Sardinian regiment who endured heavy losses during World War I fighting against the Austrians. The museum's collection includes military items and memorabilia from the conflict.

There is one more essential site to see before making a tour of the old town: the **Museo Nazionale G.A. Sanna ❷** (Via Roma 64; tel: 079 272203; open Tues–Sat 9am–8pm; entrance fee). It's 17 immaculately-ordered galleries present a summary of the most important aspects of the island's interesting archaeology. The **ground floor** is dedicated to a complete vision of the island's prehistory and history up to medieval times; a room is dedicated to the prehistoric altar of Monte d'Accoddi (about 2500 BC), followed by showcases that display objects coming from *tombe dei giganti* (giant's tombs) and natural caves (from the Neolithic to the Bronze Age, 6000–1800 BC). The **upper floor** is entirely dedicated to the Nuraghic civilisation and includes a collection of 2,000–3,000-year-old bronze statues, among which is the realistic bronze ox found in the sacred well of Perfugas. There is also a collection of imported Etruscan and Greek pottery and equally fascinating pieces of gold and silver Carthaginian and Roman jewellery, which is still worn with traditional Sardinian costumes.

**BELOW:** Corso Vittorio Emanuele II.

## The heart of the Old Town

Through the middle of the Old Town runs the **Corso Vittorio Emanuele II**. The town's long-standing residents, ever conscious of tradition, still call it the Plath de Codinas (the Street of Stone) because the thoroughfare was once lined with elegant *palazzi* and the residences of wealthy merchants. Apart from the Corso, the citizens of Sassari have given other streets and squares local dialect names. The **Via Lamarmora**, which runs parallel to it, is known to locals as the Carra Longa; leading off the Corso is the Carra Pizzinna (today's **Via Battisti**), which links up with the Carra Manna (the **Piazza Tola**). The dialect names – "little bushel" and "large bushel" – refer to the fact that these

*The baroque facade of the church of Sant' Antonio Abate.*

**BELOW:**
Sassari's Duomo.

measures were once in use here. Rising above the **Piazza Tola** , invariably overcrowded with cars and market stalls, is the monument to the historian Pasquale Tola (1800–74). Today the square has a neglected, down-at-heel look. Even the long, winding Via Lamarmora scarcely hints that it has seen better days; the local aristocracy once held court behind the crumbling stucco and seedy-looking facades. But the rather splendid looking **Casa di Maramaldo** (not open to the public) at No. 81, dating from the 17th century, at least gives some indication of the noble magnificence which once characterised the street.

The most popular street in the Old Town is the **Via al Rosello**. The silversmiths after whom the alley was named are a rare species today, and most of them have moved into more modern, more elegant quarters. Here and there you'll see the the odd cobbler and carpenter at work, latter-day representatives of a once-thriving craft tradition. In one cheese store, which offers an enormous choice within a very small space, you can be sure of finding genuine Sardinian cheese, sold with a wealth of original cooking tips. It's an excellent place to buy *pecorino romano*, the famous Italian sheep's milk cheese *(see page 101)*. The picturesque Via al Rosello leads – as the name indicates – to a spring and the **Fontana di Rosello** , the island's most famous monumental fountain. The 12 stone lion's heads adorning the Renaissance fountain are surrounded by statues symbolising the four seasons. The statue in the middle of the fountain represents a divinity called Giogli, and a statue of San Gavino is at the top of the fountain. The viaduct was erected during Fascist times. Beyond the bridge lie the densely populated districts of town. They provide typical examples of Italian government-financed housing of the pre- and postwar periods. Here on the outskirts of Sassari, the suburbs are as characterless and monotonous as those

of any other town. Your best bet is to return via the **Ponte Rosello** to the **Nuovo Mercato**, the New Market, where mountains of fresh fish from the Gulf of Asinara are on sale every morning.

## The cathedral

Continuing along the Via al Rosello and across the Corso, you will come to the Cattedrale or **Duomo** ❺ (open daily). The ornately carved facade was added around 1700 to a Gothic structure which was itself built on to an 11th-century Romanesque church. Its interior shows strong Gothic influences and houses the most valuable painting in town: a Processional Standard by an unknown master, dating from the late 15th century. In the vicinity of the cathedral there is a church every few yards. It is as if the Corso Vittorio Emanuele divided the Old Town into two sections – a secular northern district completely devoted to trade, and a nobler, more contemplative southern area where attention was focused entirely on spiritual matters. Opposite the cathedral stands the desecrated Manneristic Chiesa di San Michele (Church of St Michael).

*A statue in the Giardini Pubblici overlooking the pleasant grounds.*

Not far from the Duomo is the **Palazzo Ducale** (Ducal Palace); built for the Duke of Vallombrosa from designs of Valino between 1775 and 1805, it was one of the island's most important architectural models. It has housed the Town hall since early 20th Century. Following the main road in front of the palace is the Jesuit College built between 1559 and 1605 together with the annexed **church of San Giuseppe**. In 1617 it became the first university in Sardinia. The college has recently been bought and restored by the Soprintendenza and is used for temporary art exhibitions.

On the far side of the broad expanse of the **Piazza Mazzotti**, during the construction of which some 50 years ago a large number of historic houses were demolished, rises the church of the Convento Cappuccini, which houses a number of altars carved by local artists.

**BELOW:** Santa Maria di Betlem.

Across the **Corso Vico**, outside the city walls, stands the church of **Santa Maria di Betlem** ❻ (open daily), with its striking silver dome. After its consecration in 1106 it was tended first by Benedictines and then by Franciscans. The church is held in high esteem by local residents; it is here that the 3-metre (10-ft) huge wooden candles used in the *I candelieri* festival are stored. Inside the cloister is a 14th-century fountain which once supplied the town with water.

Passing along the **Via Maddalena** and the **Via Turritana** in the Old Town, where there is a succession of modest inns and restaurants, you will arrive in the bustling **Via Brigata Sassari**, named after the heroic Sardinian brigade which saw action during World War I. Continuing across the semi-circular **Emiciclo Garibaldi** ❼, dominated by the statue of Giuseppe Mazzini (1805–72), the politician instrumental in the unification of Italy in 1861 – you will soon reach the **Giardini Púbblici** ❽ (Municipal Park), a refreshing place to cool down and unwind. The park contains a modern pavilion, the **Padiglione dell' Artigianato** (open Mon–Fri 9am–1pm, 4–8pm), which displays a selection of Sardinian handicrafts of high quality.     ❑

# THE ART OF
# THE MURALES

*As a true form of public art, murals communicate directly to a wide audience. In Sardinia they are becoming an artistic tradition*

Brilliantly coloured *murales* (murals) on satirical, political or social themes are a popular form of expression in Sardinia and can be found in many villages around the island. The tradition of mural painting in Sardinia dates back to the 1960s and reached a peak in the mid-1970s in the town of Orgosolo in the Barbagia region. The Italian Association of Painted Towns was formed to preserve and publicise towns with murals and to promote cultural and creative links between the regions. Perhaps the most famous touristic murals are to be found in the village of San Sperate, about 8 km (5 miles) northeast of Uta, which contains works by the local artist Pinuccio Sciola. The murals here are not as vibrant, numerous or political as they are in Orgosolo. Instead they are painted in the muted tones of the Sardinian countryside and represent bucolic and domestic scenes. Just before you reach the village of Orgosolo there is a mural painted on a large rock by the side of the road known as "the greedy land-owner of Orgosolo". Orgosolo has about 150 murals in various conditions dotted along its main streets. It all started back in 1975 when the local art teacher Francesco del Caslon and his students decided to fill the town with murals on local and universal themes.

Other artists involved in painting the murals include Pasquale Buesca and Vincenzo Floris.

▷ **POLITICAL MESSAGES**
Murals are often used to express political opinion. In Sardinia the themes range from local to international. This mural is about the coup d'état in Chile.

△ **LOCAL HEROES**
Orgosolo's murals have many different subjects but one common theme: the adjustment between traditional values and the modern world.

▷ **ANTI-MILITARISTIC**
A painted mural in cartoon form protesting against military industrialists making money from the war in Vietnam in Orgosolo.

## △ OLIENA

Oliena has fewer murals than Orgosolo and, although they are less well-executed, they are still worth a look for their overt political content.

## ▽ INVITATION TO PEACE

One of the most famous murals in Orgosolo features a Charlie Chaplin figure in an anti-war protest "Another war? No thanks."

# MURALS IN ORGOSOLO

If you're travelling in the Barbagia region, make a detour to Orgosolo to see some of the town's 150 murals. On Via Deledda there are characters drawn from the books of Grazia Deledda. Along Via Gramsci is a mural depicting the life of the politician, one of the founders of the Italian Communist Party; at No. 60 another depicts the tragic events leading to the end of the Baader-Meinhof Group and at No.166 is a mural showing shepherds protesting against not being able to leave their pastures fallow in the spring with the slogan "*vardamos o non vardamos?*" (to keep or not to keep?). Opposite is a mural with the message "the young want to work, not shoot" – a reference to the town's reputation for banditry. Further on is a mural protesting against noise pollution. On Via Mercato on the walls of the library are paintings by local artists; in front of the parish church is a scene from a bandit hunt. In Piazza del Popolo a mural depicts shepherds' protests against industrialists, while other murals indicate strong opposition to war and militarism.

## ▽ FOLKLORE FIGURES

A mural depicting the Mamuthones carnival at Mamoiada. The Mamuthones are among Sardinia's most famous folk figures.

## ▽ TRADITIONAL IMAGES

An old woman dressed in the traditional clothes of a widow looks out from her front door in this naturalistic mural in the town of Fonni.

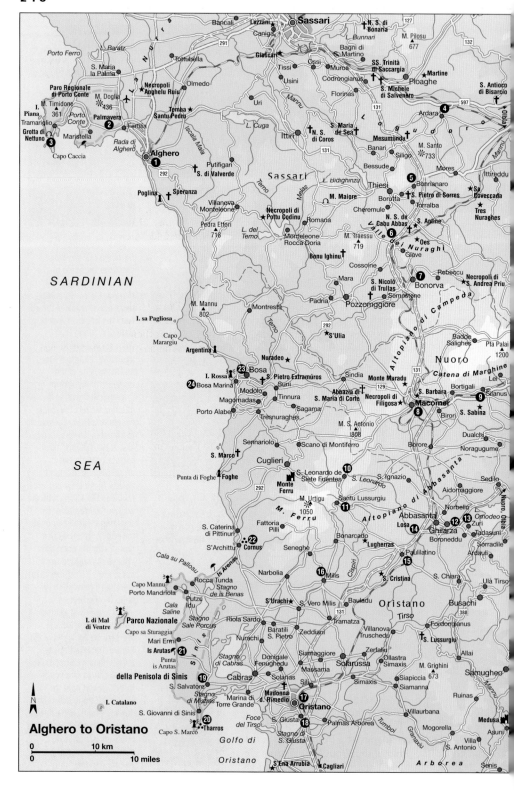

**Alghero to Oristano**

# ALGHERO TO ORISTANO

*The western coast of Sardinia has beaches, nature reserves, caves,
hiking trails, splendid towns, Romanesque architecture
and Roman remains to explore*

Map
on page
218

**S**trongly influenced by Spanish culture, **Alghero ❶** has the most Spanish feel of any Sardinian town. The city is generally considered to have been founded in 1102. However, long before the dawn of the Christian era the Phoenicians set up a trading post on this exposed bay in western Sardinia. In the early Middle Ages fleets of marauding Arabs also maintained a base for their fleets here, from which they could set out on their raids on the southern coast of France. Nonetheless, it was not until the beginning of the 12th century that settlers fortified the little peninsula on which the Old Town remains huddled to this day.

## Spanish loyalty

It was at this time, too, that the place received its somewhat inauspicious name, Alghero, which translated means "full of algae". For 250 years the Doria family from Genoa was in power here, but in 1353 they were forced to cede the town to the forces of Aragon. With the arrival of the first Aragonese-Catalan officials came the first Catalan settlers. Following an uprising against harsh Aragon rule, the resident Sardinians and Ligurians were all driven out of Alghero, and were replaced from 1372 by settlers from Barcelona, Valencia and Mallorca.

 Alghero was transformed into an urban fortress in which only citizens whose loyalty to the regime was proven were allowed to live. The town was closed in on all sides by walls, towers and bulwarks (the fortifications on the landward side were demolished during the 19th century to provide work for the inhabitants of a nearby penal colony). The citizens were not allowed to travel further than about 3 km (2 miles) beyond the city boundaries, in fact as far as a number of churches in the surrounding countryside. The dominant influence in Alghero came not from the mainland but from the sea – or, to be more precise, from the Iberian peninsula. To this day it has remained the most Spanish town in Sardinia.

 Although one soon becomes accustomed to the coexistence of two languages on the rest of the island, the situation in Alghero is considerably more complicated. Here one will hear Catalan in addition to Italian, which virtually all Sardinians speak perfectly even if it is not their mother tongue, and the archaic-sounding Sardinian, which is comprehensible only to the initiated. The visitor will often hear local inhabitants using Catalan in conversation, and will notice that it is used with increasing frequency on the streets, in the squares and, for some reason, in relation to buildings of interest to tourists. Perhaps the local inhabitants think Prassa del Pou Vel, Carrer de Bonaire and Les Quatre Cantonades sound more invit-

**BELOW:** Alghero's
festivals have a
Spanish influence.

*A Catalan shield in Alghero. The Catalan culture deeply influenced the town and its people.*

**BELOW:** the battlements of Alghero Old Town.

ing than **Piazza Civica**, **Via Umberto** and **Via Carlo Alberto**. In the general wake of all stronger minorities the citizens of Alghero have revived an interest in their Catalan roots, founding parties to promote the interests of their minority culture and various folklore groups to breathe new life into their traditional folk music. It is not surprising, therefore, that the town's most famous culinary speciality is Catalan-style lobster.

## Alghero Old Town

The Old Town of Alghero covers barely one-tenth of today's total city. It is, however – apart from the beaches and hotels located beyond the city limits – the only part of the town worth exploring. It is surrounded on three sides by towers and fortifications; the best introduction to the town can be gained from a walk along the old **Battlements**.

Setting out from the massive round **Torre dell'Espero Reial** (The Tower of Royal Ambition), the visitor can stroll past the lively **Piazza Sulis** in the southeast, fringed by cafés and trees, to the half-ruined but still impressive Forte de la Magdalena lying right beside the harbour in the north. En route is the octagonal **Torre de Sant Jaume** (St James's Tower) and the circular **Torre de la Polvorera**, which is situated on the north-westerly tip of the peninsula. From the fortifications along the **Lungomare Marco Polo** there are spectacular views across the Bay of Alghero as far as Capo Caccia. Finally, via a narrow battlement walk, you reach **Forte de la Magdalena**, which dates from the 16th century. It is no less impressive because the town's fishermen now use its base as a workshop where they repair their boats. The local inhabitants enjoy taking a walk along the three-sided seafront promenade, especially the **Lungomare Colombo**

to the south; during the height of the holiday season it is as busy here as on any metropolitan boulevard. The fascinating alleys of the Old Town, tall and narrow like dark mountain gorges, finger off the promenade. The Old Town itself is best entered through the **Porta a Mare**, the Sea Gate, on the north side. Another entrance is in the **Porta a Terra**, the original main entrance to town. The door still bears the stone coat of arms of the crown of Aragon and used to be closed at dusk. Inside there is a reception centre where the visitor can access information about Alghero's history.

## Duomo di Santa Maria

The **Duomo di Santa Maria** (Cathedral of Our Lady; open daily 6.30am–noon, 5–8pm) is reached by crossing the long, funnel-shaped main square – the **Piazza Civica**. Its style evolved over 200 years, from the mid-16th to the mid-18th century; unsurprisingly, in most observers' opinion, the result, a late Baroque-Manneristic superstructure on top of the late Gothic main building, lacks unity. Attached to the Duomo is the **Museo Diocesano d'Arte Sacra** (tel: 079 9733041; open daily; entrance fee) inside the church of Nostra Signora del Rosario. On display is a collection that forms the town's liturgical treasure.

In front of the cathedral, on either side of the **Via Sant'Erasmo**, lies the former Jewish quarter; the Jews formed an essential part of the community in every trading centre of international importance during the Middle Ages and often rose to positions of influence. In the middle of the 15th century, with the necessary permission of the king of Aragon, Alghero's Jews raised the necessary finance for the construction of the **Torre des Hebreus** (The Jewish Gate). It provided a second point of access to the town on the landward side; until well into

Map
on page
218

TIP

The tourist office in Alghero is at the airport, in Fertilia, tel: 079 935124. It is open Mon–Sat 8.30am–8pm (11.30pm during August), another tourist information office is near the Porta a Terra (Piazza Portaterra 9; tel: 079 979054; open daily).

**BELOW:**
a view of Alghero.

the 19th century it was closed every evening at dusk with the traditional cry "All those outside must stay outside!"

Fanning out behind the cathedral are the most elegant streets of the Old Town: the dignified **Via Umberto**, in which the aristocracy and clergy resided under the rule of Spain and Savoy, and the **Via Carlo Alberto** (Carrer Major), where you will find the finest and most expensive shops in town. Dominating the end of the street is the sumptuous Baroque Chiesa di San Michele (open daily), built by the Jesuits. Its coloured majolica dome rises above the exquisitely restored monastery complex of San Francesco (built during the 14th and 16th to 17th centuries); during the summer months the Romanesque cloisters form an atmospheric setting for classical music concerts. Some of the alleys of the Old Town have a distinctly southern flair; here, unlike in other, more restrained towns on the island, one is sometimes struck by resemblances to Naples. For centuries Alghero, as the capital of the Coral Riviera, has attracted fishermen from the Naples area, especially from Ponza and Torre del Greco. They have traditionally specialised in the hazardous business of fishing for coral.

The combination of this influx from Campania, linked to the Catalan influence already mentioned, has given the townspeople their characteristically cheerful temperament. As far as the coral is concerned, despite being promoted as the town's emblem by the tourist industry, nowadays only a small proportion of the coral used in the decorative items in the local shop windows actually originate off the Sardinian coast. The coral reefs have long been depleted.

## Excursions from Alghero

For the traveller wishing to get to know the northwest of the island there is no better starting point than Alghero, with its excellent tourist infrastructure. Moving north from the town and passing the Bombarde beach, on the right the Nuraghic complex of **Palmavera** ❷ (open Mar–Sept 9am–7pm, Oct–Feb 9.30am–4pm; entrance fee; guides available) lies surrounded by a village of round huts that includes one used as a meeting house, with a stone bench along its perimeter that could seat up to 43 people.

Continuing along the same road the bay of Porto Conte, the ancient Roman **Portus Ninpharus**, appears in front of you. It's the only true natural port in Sardinia, where Charles V's fleet was harboured on its way to Tunis; it is closed on one side by the promontory of Capo Caccia, which houses the **Grotta di Nettuno** ❸ (open summer 9am–7pm; winter 9am–2pm; entrance fee; *also see page 278)*. To get to the grotto you need to take a boat from Alghero port. The boat ride takes about 30 minutes and departs at 9 and 10am in the summer and 3 and 4pm in April, May and October.

North of Porto Conte is the inaccessible **Cala dell'Inferno** (Hell's Bay) set in a limestone cliff shaped by erosion. The surrounding flora is made up of a low Mediterranean bush that includes many different endemic plants. From Porto Conte to the north it is easy to reach Argentiera and Stintino.

Taking the road through Sassari, one soon reaches the **Via Carlo Felice**, the SS 131, which passes through a region full of historical interest. In this area

**TIP**

Alghero is arguably the best place on the island for fresh seafood. Stop at the market in Via Sassari for lobster, sea urchins and squid, or try the local restaurants.

**BELOW:** Tuscan-style stripes on the Santissima Trinità di Saccargia.

there are several of the 20-odd Romanesque churches founded on the island between the 12th and 14th centuries. The majority of them were constructed by master craftsmen summoned from Tuscany – often at the behest of the wealthy mainland merchants who imported large quantities of minerals, coral, hides, cattle, cheese, salt and cereals from Sardinia.

One of the finest and best-preserved churches is the **Santissima Trinità di Saccargia** (Church of the Trinity of the Spotted Cow; open daily; entrance fee). It stands near the village of Codrongianus, some 15 km (9 miles) from Sassari. According to local legend a gentle, pious cow played a significant role in the church's foundation – though, with its distinctive walls of alternating layers of dark-coloured basalt and light-coloured limestone, it resembles a zebra more than a cow. The construction of religious buildings on Sardinia was nearly always politically inspired. The ruling families from the mainland hoped that the influence of the church on the island, boosted by impressive decorative arts, would secure and strengthen their political influence. But whatever the reason underlying the foundation of the Spotted Cow church, there is no denying the splendour of its position.

Inside, the apse contains the only existent cycle of 13th-century frescoes on Sardinia. Only 3 km (2 miles) from the Santissima Trinità di Saccargia stands the **Chiesa di San Michele di Salvènero** (open daily). Although it also dates from the 12th century, its design seems less elaborate, more traditional.

## From Ardara to Borutta

Some 14 km (8 miles) further along the road is the village of **Ardara ❹**, a fascinating stop for anyone interested in the Hohenstaufen dynasty. Here, in 1239,

Map on page 218

*The sharp descent of the Escala del Cabirol leads to the Grotta di Nettuno.*

**BELOW:** a stone carving on the Santissima Trinità di Saccargia.

in the **Santa Maria del Regno** (the Black Cathedral; open daily) – built of black basalt in about 1100 – Enzo, the son of the Hohenstaufen Emperor Frederick II, celebrated what was to prove a short-lived marriage to Adelaida. Since his wife's dowry included a sizeable proportion of the island, in the form of the *giudicati* of Torres and Gallura, Enzo proclaimed himself king of Sardinia. He soon abandoned both his wife and the island (he seems to have been unable to stand life on this rough and lonely island for any length of time), but he refused to relinquish his royal title, which he held until his death in a dungeon in Bologna, where his enemies kept him prisoner for 23 years. In the same cathedral is Sardinia's largest retablo: a polyptych measuring 10 by 6 metres (32 by 20 ft), painted in 1515 by Giovanni Muru, hanging behind the main altar and formed by various wooden panels.

## Romanesque churches

From Ardara continuing east on the SS 597 there are two other important Romanesque churches: **Sant'Antioco di Bisarcio** (open daily), built in 1065–1153, with an unusual asymmetrical facade, and **Nostra Signora di Castro** (open daily 9–12am) situated in a panoramic position and enclosed in a small court. Twenty km (12 miles) from the tranquil village of Ardara, with its sad memories of the Hohenstaufens, the highway rejoins the Carlo Felice Superstrada at the farming village of **Bonnànaro** ❺. The effects of the steady migration from the land during the past decades have been particularly noticeable here. The settlement has given its name to an advanced culture (the Bonnanaro culture 1600–1800 BC) which preceded the nuraghic period. It must have been an austere civilisation based on the bare essentials of life – in keeping with the harsh, unyielding nature of the island interior – and yet, according to archaeological evidence, it was sufficiently sophisticated for the performance of complicated surgical operations such as trepanation, the drilling of the skull.

*BELOW: a farmer's weathered face.*

Another Romanesque church lies in the vicinity of Bonnànaro. **San Pietro di Sòrres** (open daily), in the village of **Borutta**, stands perched at a height of 520 metres (1,665 ft) on a little plateau. Its location amid the bleak limestone landscape is breathtaking. Situated on another limestone plateau nearby is a largish village, **Thiesi**, whose inhabitants make a living from arable and livestock farming. A mural in the local middle school illustrates the part played by chauvinism and exploitation in Sardinian history. Those of the island's politicians who support Sardinian autonomy accuse the Italian state of the same attitudes. The mural, by Aligi Sassu, a well-known artist of Sardinian extraction, represents the "Year of the Attack" – 1800, when the Duke of Asinara launched an attack on the villagers who refused to deliver his feudal dues.

## Along the Carlo Felice

From Thiesi, a road crossing pretty countryside passes under the Carlo Felice Superstrada and leads into the **Valle dei Nuraghi** ❻ near **Torralba**. The name sounds as though it is a slogan coined by the tourist office, but it is authentic. The hollow contains a large number of mysterious megalithic nuraghic constructions. The finest, the **Nuraghe Santu Antine** (open daily 9am–sunset; entrance fee includes admission to Museo di Torralba), stands in the middle of the valley. Its main tower, now some 17.5 metres (56 ft) high, may well have measured as much as 20 metres (68 ft) before the top courses of stones were dismantled during the 19th century to build the village well in Torralba. The *nuraghe* is of a highly complex construction; built of layers of basalt blocks, it includes – apart from the 3,500-year-old main tower – three lower and less ancient subsidiary towers arranged in a clover-leaf shape. In later times, the local population was so impressed by the *nuraghe* that it called it Sa Domu de Su Rei, the Royal Palace. Strangely enough, the king referred to was actually the Roman emperor Constantine, who is revered throughout the island as a courageous fighter of holy wars and a protector of the Sardinian people. You can discover more about the Nuraghe Santu Antine – its labyrinthine interior structure of walls, corridors and rooms as well as the remarkable construction of the main tower, which consists of 28 courses of stone blocks, mounted upon each other without the use of mortar – at the **Museo di Torralba** (tel: 079 847298; open daily; entrance fee) where excavated items and other interesting exhibits are on display.

Also famous for its *nuraghe*, as well as its attractively coloured hand-woven carpets, is **Bonorva** ❼, a small agricultural market town lying further to the south on the Carlo Felice. The territory surrounding the town is rich historically. One of the most famous sites is the **Sant'Andrea Priu** necropoli (open daily), a prehistoric ipogeic tomb formed by 18 rooms that in Palaeochristian, Byzantine and medieval times was used as place of worship. Frescoes have recently been discovered on the walls and are in the process of being restored. The town's archaeological museum (tel: 348 5642611; open daily 10am–1pm,

Map on page 218

**BELOW:**
waiting patiently.

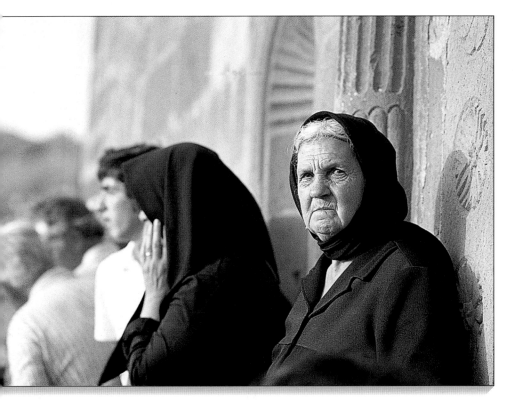

3–7pm; entrance fee) contains a wing of the former conventual complex of Sant' Antonios' church, dating from the 17th century. The museum also features an informative virtual journey through the history of central Sardinia. Other ancient ruins lie at an altitude of approximately 650 metres (2,080 ft) on the **Su Monte** plateau; they can best be reached on foot with a guide hired from the village; the walk takes about an hour. Here the Nuraghi must have made their last desperate stand against the incursions of the Carthaginians.

## Macomer

In 1478 yet another Sardinian dream of maintaining the island's independence was shattered near the little town of **Macomer ❽**, which lies some 15 km (10 miles) further southwards. The soldiers of Leonardo Alagon, Margrave of Arborea, were defeated by a vast army sent by the new rulers from Aragon. It was this Spanish victory that broke the last remaining pocket of resistance on the island. Macomer lies on a trachyte ledge which slopes away to the south. The panorama from the town sums up the island's geological history. It stretches from the basalt plateau in the foreground to the granite and limestone mountains of the interior on the horizon. The town itself has a gentle and lively atmosphere in which the visitor will feel instantly relaxed and at home: as an ancient trading centre and road junction, Macomer has a long tradition of extending hospitality to strangers of every kind.

The area was settled in ancient times by the Nuraghi, who were followed by the Carthaginians and the Romans. They found it an agreeable site, especially compared with the rough, often inaccessible land that characterises much of the interior. The roads radiating from Macomer follow tracks used since time immemorial: east through the village of **Silanus ❾**, with the Byzantine-Roman-

**BELOW:**
flock of sheep
near Macomer.

esque **Chiesa di Santa Sabina** and the *nuraghe* of the same name, and west through **Sindia** with its nearby Romanesque-Burgundian Cistercian Abbey Church to Bosa.

Map on page 218

## On the way to Zuri

Alternatively one can take the road to Santu Lussúrgiu, which runs through the hills to the southwest of Macomer; after 15 km (10 miles) of lonely countryside one reaches the hamlet of **San Leonardo de Siete Fuentes** ⑩, whose *siete fuentes* (seven springs) rise in a shady park. In summer people come to take the waters, which have a diuretic effect. The parish church, the Chiesa di San Leonardo, built of dark-coloured trachyte rock, dates from the 12th century. It was originally constructed in Romanesque style, but extensive Gothic additions were built at a later date.

Along the barren rocky cliffs of the Monte Ferru, the traveller passes an extinct volcano. The region's topology shows the traces of past eruptions. The little market town of **Santu Lussúrgiu** ⑪ spreads out across a former crater. Livestock farming is the main source of livelihood for the inhabitants, and its handicrafts are closely linked with sheep rearing: the women weave rugs and blankets from the wool, and the men produce the sharp knives which they need for shearing in the spring. The town also has a reputation for excellent wood-carving, a skill which in days gone by occupied the shepherds in the long days and weeks as they grazed their flocks. From Santu Lussúrgiu to Abbasanta the road descends the barren slopes of the Monte Ferru and then passes between an endless succession of *tancas*. These plots of land demarcated by stone walls are an essential characteristic of the Sardinian countryside, giving it a geometric

**BELOW:** many farmhouses are far away from the nearest village.

chequerboard appearance. When the land was parcelled out during the 19th century to enable more peasants to become landowners, the construction of these walls marked a revolution in land use. For thousands of years – since the earliest days in the island's history – the Sardinians enjoyed common land that was worked by the community as a whole. From this point on, however, this quasi-communist concept of property ceased to exist.

In the tiny village of **Sant'Agostino**, modest cottages and guest houses for pilgrims, known as *muristenes*, are clustered round a basalt church. The same dark stone was used for the buildings forming the heart – the oldest part – of **Abbasanta**. This village possesses a pseudo-Renaissance parish church which lends it a certain dignity, but it remains merely a simple, sprawling community of farmhouses and shepherds' cottages. **Ghilarza ⑫**, which today forms part of the Abbasanta built-up area, appears to have a much more urban air, an impression due in part to the large number of churches within the town limits. They include **San Palmerio**, **San Giorgio**, **Santa Lucia** and the **Carmelo**. In addition there are several picturesque medieval country churches. There is the small **Casa di Antonio Gramsci** (tel: 0785 54164; open 10am–1pm, 4.30–7.30pm, closed Tues) on the Corso Umberto, which provides an insight into the life of the Marxist writer, philosopher and politician. Gramsci was born in 1891 in the village of **Ales**, attended the school here in Ghilarza for 10 years and died in 1937 after enduring a lengthy prison sentence for his anti-fascist views.

From Ghilarza it is only a stone's throw to the tiny hamlet of **Tadasuni**. The local priest, Don Giovanni Dore, founded its **Museo degli Strumenti della Tradizione Sarda** (by appointment only, tel: 0785 501 13), one of the most complete Italian collections of traditional musical instruments. Housed in rather

**BELOW:** man playing the *launeddas* – the traditional Sardinian flute.

cramped conditions in the priest's house (the Casa Parrochiale, Via Adua 7), the collection stands and falls by its founder, Don Dore, whose indefatigable enthusiasm led him to make a study of the sophisticated construction techniques employed in the seemingly primitive musical instruments of Sardinia – above all, the *launedda*, the shepherd's flute, the *serraggia* fiddle and the *tumbarinu* drum. Don Dore's authoritative explanations and demonstrations provide the best possible introduction to the island's musical tradition. Although traditional music is still frequently performed at folk festivals, the archaic tone patterns make it largely inaccessible to the uninitiated.

The village of **Zuri** ⓭, near Tadasuni, is also worth visiting. During the 1920s, when the Omodeo Dam was under construction, the entire settlement was moved to its present site. Not only the inhabitants but also the lovely Romanesque Gothic parish church of **San Pietro** was relocated: the pink trachyte blocks were painstakingly dismantled, one by one, and then reconstructed here. The village of **Fordongianus** lies south of Tadasuni and offers the only possibility to visit the ruins of Roman thermal baths where hot water still flows (tel: 0783 60157; open summer 9.30am–1pm, 3–7pm; winter 2.30–5pm; entrance fee). The name comes from the Latin Forum of Traiani, an important Roman settlement which controlled the movements of the local population from the mountains to the east. Not far below, **Samugheo** has an important **Museo dell'arte Tessile** (Textile museum; tel: 0783 631052; open Wed–Sun 10am–1pm, 4–7pm).

## Water temples and nuraghe

Before leaving this densely populated region on the edge of the basalt plateau of Abbasanta, it is well worth making a slight detour to view the well-preserved

Map on page 218

*One of the three interior chambers of the Nuraghe Losa.*

**BELOW:** the exterior of Nuraghe Losa.

*A ceramicist puts the final touches to a vase in a workshop in Oristano.*

**BELOW:** statue of Eleonora d'Arborea in Oristano.

**Nuraghe Losa** (tel: 0785 54823; open 9am–1pm, 3–7pm; entrance fee), located some 3 km (2 miles) southwest of Abbasanta. The ivy-clad ruins exude a nostalgic air; naturally enough, in this volcanic area, the walls are constructed of dark basalt blocks. The main tower is estimated to be approximately 3,500 years old; the subsidiary towers and exterior walls were built a few centuries later. Even if you are not particularly interested in *nuraghe*, you should include this megalithic construction near Abbasanta in your tour of the island. The Nuraghe Losa, the fortress of Santu Antine near Torralba, and the settlement Su Nuraxi near Barumini are all quite different constructions, and represent excellent examples of the *nuraghe* – some 7,000 in all – which can be found all over Sardinia. Some are in good condition, but many are decayed almost beyond recognition. The *nuraghe* lend the landscape an aura of archaic melancholy, in which all attempts at progress seem out of place. All the more powerful, therefore, is the impact of the Nuraghe Losa, standing in peaceful timelessness on a small rocky eminence just a few dozen yards from the noise and frenzy of the traffic ploughing up and down the Carlo Felice superstrada below.

Visitors are frequently surprised by the obvious parallels between the religious rites of the Nuraghi and those of present-day Christianity. Three thousand years ago, the Nuraghi used to gather to celebrate their festivals around **Il Pozzo di Santa Cristina** (Water Temple of Santa Cristina; tel: 0785 55438; open summer 9am–9pm; winter 9am–5pm; entrance fee), which lies a few miles south of **Paulilatino** on the stretch of the Carlo Felice between Abbasanta and Oristano. The elegantly constructed well shaft of the ancient sacred spa is surrounded by walls which archaeologists believe to be the remains of former pilgrims' huts. The **Museo Archeologico-Etnográfico** (open Tues–Sun daily; entrance with water temple ticket) in the centre of the town has a collection of finds from Santa Cristina. The rural **Chiesa di Santa Cristina**, situated not far from the ruins of the *nuraghe* spa temple, is similarly encircled by simple dwellings for worshippers. Here, as so often on Sardinia, there is no clear distinction between the pagan and the Christian. Anyone who comes here in May or October, when the local inhabitants gather to celebrate their festivals, which are a potent mixture of the secular and the sacred, will have plenty of opportunity to experience Sardinian hospitality.

On the road to Oristano, one more detour remains – a short side-trip to **Milis** . On the edge of the village stands the Romanesque **Chiesa di San Paolo**, dating from the 12th–13th centuries. The houses are surrounded by the citrus orchards which the French poet Paul Valéry described in his *Sardinian Journey*.

## Oristano – the small capital

Regardless of the direction from which you approach the town of **Oristano** , it is easy to fall under the impression that you are entering an overgrown village rather than the capital of Sardinia's smallest province. The town has become the focal point of western Sardinia, a region it governed during the period of the medieval *giudicati*. Until well into the 15th century the town was the capital of the judicature of Arborea, which was subjugated by the rulers of Aragon later

than the other three *giudicati*. It is possible that the Aragonese were in no particular hurry when it came to conquering this province – the ruling family of Arborea was itself originally of Catalan descent, although they had been resident on Sardinia for many years. The dominant personality of the house of Arborea was the *Giudichessa Eleonora*, who died in 1404. Her seat of government is commemorated by the name of the main square; during the 19th century it was also decided that a somewhat pompous statue should add to the tribute. Surrounded by figures of lions, the lovely Eleonora strikes an elegant attitude. The descendants of her subjects love to gather at her feet, especially in the evening, to meet their friends and lovers, lick ice creams, exchange gossip or just to see and be seen. From **Piazza Roma** you enter the pedestrian area in the historical centre, once completely surrounded by medieval walls of which today only the **Torre di Mariano II** (the Torre di San Cristóforo), built 1291, remains. It once served as the main gate to the city. The small pedestrianised area has new, elegant shops.

Lining the main road are various buildings, among which is Palazzo Arcais with its wrought iron balconies. In Palazzo Parpaglia is the **Antiquarium Arborense** (tel: 0783 791262; open 9am–2pm, 3–8pm, closed Sun am; entrance fee) which features a picture gallery and a large and wide-ranging archaeological collection, including some Roman artefacts from the excavations at Tharros and Sinis. There is also a large reconstruction of Tharros in the 9th century AD.

Dominating the Piazza Eleonora is the **Palazzo Comunale** (town hall, not open to the public). It is a former Piarist monastery, whose (desecrated) church, with an unusual oval ground plan, now serves as the local council chamber. Despite the increase in population to just over 30,000 over the past 30 years, Oristano has none of the sophisticated flair of Cagliari, Sassari or even Alghero.

Map on page 218

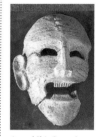

*An exhibit from the Antiquarium Arborense in Oristano.*

**BELOW:** exterior of the church of San Francesco.

The **Duomo** (open summer 8am–1pm, 4–7pm; winter 7am–1pm, 3–6.30pm) was built in a mixture of architectural styles; of the original complex, dating from the 13th century, only the Gothic Cappella di Rimedio in the right aisle remains. Parts of a Romanesque ambon, created by Pisan craftsmen during the 2nd century and used as a chapel balustrade, are now displayed in the first chapel of the right aisle. Nino Pisano, whose name indicates that he, too, was a native of Pisa, carved the coloured Gothic wooden statue of *The Annunciation* in the cathedral, as well as a statue of St Basil standing in the nearby Church of St Francis. Nino Pisano was a craftsman who lived and worked during the 14th century, when Pisa was still anxious to maintain its links with the *giudicato* of Arborea and its capital.

Next to the Duomo is a good example of 18th-century architecture, the **Seminario Tridentino** (open daily), and along the same road is the church of San Francesco, with a neoclassical facade, where you will find the *Crocifisso di Nicodemo* (Crucifix of Nicodemo) in a side chapel. The colourful wooden crucifix is generally considered to be one of the finest examples of Spanish sculpture. Following in the footsteps of the Pisans and other Tuscans, who had been instrumental in bringing about a unique blossoming of the skills of Romanesque church builders on the island, the new Spanish colonial rulers began to show their determination to excel in the realm of the arts as well. The best way of establishing contact with the people and buying their loyalty was undoubtedly via the churches and the art treasures they contained; they enabled them to impress and surreptitiously influence the masses. Also clearly of Spanish origin is the *Sartiglia*, a spectacular competition for mounted riders which takes place on the last Sunday before Lent and on Shrove Tuesday. Cervantes describes a *Sortija* of this kind (even the name is very similar) in his world-famous

**BELOW:** rider
in the Sa Sartiglia
carnival in Oristano.

Map
on page
218

picaresque novel, *Don Quixote*. The event is a riding competition between two leading riders and their attendants, masked and wearing typical Spanish dress, with lace mantilla and top hat. Lances at the ready, they are required to gallop at and pierce a hanging star. Magical powers are ascribed to the two leading riders, who are known as *componidoris*. It is said that the success of the next harvest can be predicted from the number of times they manage to strike the star.

To the south of Oristano the **Campidano** is a vast alluvial plain, in part still covered by coastal marshes and lagoon. The fertile alluvional soil and the abundance of water make this a very important region for Sardinian agriculture and excellent vegetables, rice and wines are produced here. In the inner part of the plain, villages have an agriculturally based economy, while fishing is the major activity for communities living near the lagoons, for example Santa Giusta and Cabras.

## A bird paradise

The **Chiesa di Santa Giusta**, 3 km (2 miles) south of Oristano, was built when Pisan influence on the region was at its zenith, not only in politics but also in the arts. Standing on an eminence, the 12th-century trachyte basilica served as a model for many Romanesque-style churches in Sardinia. The interior, with its triple nave, is supported by granite and marble columns which are far older than the church itself: they were filched from the Carthaginian-Roman settlements of Tharros and Othoca (a common practice at the time). Latest archaeological investigations indicate that Othoca, once a prosperous town, must have been located on the site of the present village of Santa Giusta.

The village of **Santa Giusta** ⓲ lies between two coastal marshes which are havens for island wildlife. The first, the **Stagno di Santa Giusta**, covers an area of some 900 hectares (2,200 acres) and is well-stocked with fish. There are, however, plans to reduce its size by half – which would mean a death sentence for much of its wildlife – to create room for an industrial plant.

Somewhat confusingly, the second lake, the **Stagno Pauli Maiori** (Big Swamp), is smaller than Santa Giusta (although still very large). It lies to the east, with its dense reeds, interspersed with tamarisk, providing a home for mallards, coots and marsh harriers, bitterns and the rare purple heron. Ruddy shelduck, which are already extinct in mainland Italy, can still be spotted in parts of the **Stagno di Cabras**, a lake lying to the west of Oristano. Its vast size – 2,000 hectares (5,000 acres) – helps to make it one of the most fascinating ecological wetlands in the whole of Europe.

Although it is directly linked to the sea, the lake displays a relatively low level of salinity; for this reason, the flamingos prefer the saltier waters of the **Stagno di Mistras**. In autumn they settle in their hundreds – even thousands – when they migrate from the Camargue in the South of France to spend the winter months in Sardinia. A wealth of unexpected discoveries awaits nature-lovers in the region surrounding Oristano. They should try to hire a local guide for a tour of the Stagno di Cabras. Until recently, the fishermen here used *fassonis* narrow, one-man boats made of reeds similar to those that are still used on parts of the Nile and Lake Titicaca.

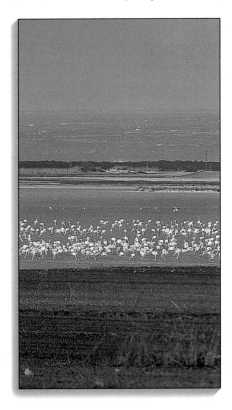

**BELOW:**
flamingos in the
Stagno di Mistras.

## Silent churches

Those heading from Cabras to **San Salvatore**  will feel themselves transported into another world as they approach the village isolated between the lagoons. For most of the year the village-sanctuary is utterly deserted but it comes to life during the summer months when tourists arrive and at the beginning of September when pilgrims from the surrounding villages come to take part in the nine-day Sagra di San Salvatore (Festival of the Redeemer). During the festival they live in *cumbessias* (pilgrims' houses) praying, eating and sleeping in the company of the other visitors over a period of several days. The statue of Christ is borne in procession from Cabras to the church of San Salvatore, accompanied by youths in white robes, running barefoot.

It is noteworthy that here, too – as in Santa Cristina near Paulilatino – a Christian place of pilgrimage coincides with a pagan holy site. Beneath the present building lies a *hypogaeum* (ancient burial chamber; tel: 347 8184069; open at irregular times, call for details) constructed by the first inhabitants of the area, the Nuragic, as a water temple. Carthaginians used the three underground cellars as storerooms for their wares (the flourishing trading centre of Tharros lay only 5 km/3 miles away); the Romans used them as a dungeon, and from the 4th century AD the Christians turned them into a catacomb church, which they decorated with monochrome wall paintings with divinities related to water worship: Venus, Mars, Eros, *nymphs*; the punic writing of the word *rufus*, meaning "heal" is also frequently seen.

Not far from San Salvatore, the church of **San Giovanni di Sinis** also has a long history. A simple 6th-century building was extended into a triple-naved edifice during the 9th–11th centuries, or possibly even earlier; the barrel vault-

**BELOW:**
*cumbessias*
(houses for
pilgrims) at
San Salvatore.

Map
on page
218

ing of the roof rests on short, massive pillars. The stone blocks needed for the conversion were brought from nearby Tharros. *Portant de Tharros sa perda a carros* is an old Sardinian proverb, "They carry stones away from Tharros," for from the 11th century onwards the once-magnificent Phoenician and Carthaginian trading city served only as a quarry – not only for the extension of San Giovanni in Sinis, but also for **Christano**. Here magnificent medieval buildings were constructed using marble and stone blocks already hewn into the appropriate shapes and often decorated with splendid carvings.

## Tharros

The town of **Tharros ⑳** (tel: 0783 370019; open summer 9am–8pm; winter 9am–5pm; entrance fee), which was founded by the Carthaginians during the 8th century BC, soon achieved incomparable prosperity. In the 3rd century BC it came under the rule of the Romans, who extended it considerably. During the 8th and 9th centuries the inhabitants started to leave the town – possibly because of the Saracen raids, which were an almost daily occurrence, but conceivably also because of the malaria which had reached epidemic proportions in a marshy district of the peninsula. Later, during the 11th century, when an attempt to resettle Tharros ended in complete failure, the new and rapidly-growing town of Oristano finally wrestled supremacy from its declining neighbour.

It was a Punic custom to bury the dead with rich funeral gifts: exquisite gold jewellery, precious stones, valuable glasses and fine pieces of pottery. Many such items can be seen in the principal archaeological museums of the island, especially in Cagliari and Sassari. But as organised excavations did not begin until recent times, in many cases not until the 20th century, some archaeologi-

*The Corinthian columns at Tharros, the symbol of the town.*

**BELOW:**
the church of San Giovanni di Sinis.

cal treasures inevitably fell into the hands of plunderers. An English aristocrat, Lord Vernon, removed the contents of 14 graves during the 19th century; and neither Charles Albert (1798–1849), the king of Savoy and Piedmont-Sardinia, nor the French novelist Honoré de Balzac (1799–1850), could resist the temptation to take a few precious "souvenirs" home with them. Of the magnificence of former days, only ruins and the remains of walls are left – the best-preserved dating from Roman times. Visitors with little experience of archaeological sites may find it difficult when confronted with these abandoned ruins to imagine a living town with residential districts, temples, public baths, streets, shops and a colourfully mixed population. But even non-experts can appreciate the magnificent setting of the ruined city on its narrow peninsula jutting out into the Gulf of Oristano, and of the Phoenician-Carthaginian *tophet*, in which until the 2nd century BC first-born children were buried with animal sacrifices to the gods in times of war, famine and pestilence.

## Sinis Peninsula

The **Sinis Peninsula** lies between Capo Mannu in the north and Capo San Marco in the south. The beach of **Is Arutas** ㉑, northwest of San Salvatore, consists of glittering round grains of quartz. The beach is now a protected zone after visitors started to take sand home as a souvenir. Further to the north, by the **Capo sa Sturaggia**, the coast becomes steeper as it plunges seawards down yellowish-brown cliffs. Here the flocks of cormorants reign supreme, building their nests on the rocky crags.

**BELOW:**
the coastline
of Is Arutas.

A short distance further on is **Putzu Idu**, which has become a popular place to buy a holiday home for people living in Oristano, although the inauguration of the **Parco Nazionale della Penisola di Sinis** (Sinis Peninsula National Park) has put an end to the unco-ordinated building proposals which threatened the area. **Santa Caterina di Pittinuri** is an unpretentious modern seaside resort situated on an attractive rocky inlet, near which interesting examples of coastal erosion, such as the rock arch **S'Archittu**, are in evidence. Near the town lie the ruins of **Cornus** ㉒, probably founded by the Carthaginians during the 5th century BC.

During the First Punic War the native Sardinians and the Carthaginian immigrants, among whom relations had not always been convivial, joined together in an anti-Roman alliance – but this did not prevent their being defeated by the legions of Rome. Cornus remained a town of some importance even in Roman times; in about AD 1000 it was nonetheless abandoned by its inhabitants, who probably found a new place to live in Cuglieri, 15 km (10 miles) away.

The road to **Cuglieri** climbs along the sides of Monte Ferru. The town has been the seat of old religious orders, a bishops' headquarters and the site of an important seminary. In days gone by there were no fewer than three monasteries in this farming village, and in **Scano di Montiferro** nearby. The region also has other remains bearing witness to even older civilisations: *tombe dei giganti* and the ubiquitous *nuraghe*, of which there must have been three (hence

the name) in **Tresnuraghes**. From here it is worthwhile climbing down to the crystal-clear sea and the enchanting coastal strip. The leafy branches invariably lying on the village streets of **Flussio** and **Tinnura** tend to remind visitors of preparations for Palm Sunday. In fact, they are fronds of bog aspho-del grass, spread out to dry before being woven into attractive basketwork, which is then offered for sale in the doorways of the houses along the main street. Passing through **Suni**, with its characteristically squat houses, the road continues downhill into Bosa.

Map on page 218

## Bosa

The little town of **Bosa** ㉓ lies on the banks of the Temo, the only navigable river in Sardinia. The town has two major districts: Sa Costa and Sa Piana. A residential area grew up and formed a link between the two districts; the main characteristic of Sa Piana is that the buildings are rather higher and the alleys narrower than in any other town on the island.

The district of the town known as **Sa Costa** clings with a succession of par-allel rows of houses to the side of an 80-metre (260-ft) hill, the summit of which is crowned by the **Castello Malaspina** (open daily 10am–noon, 4–7pm; entrance fee), which was built by the Malaspina family in 1112 and later extended by the rulers of Aragon. This district has no church of its own, since the residents were dependent on the castle in religious as in other affairs. They were permitted to use the castle chapel, **Nostra Signora di Regnos Altos**, where in recent years a cycle of 14th–15th century frescoes of the Spanish school was discovered. If the church is open (it has been undergoing restoration) climb to the top of the ramparts for a magnificent view. Beneath the maze of

*Bosa's coat of arms. Bosa became a royal city under Spanish rule.*

**BELOW:** Chiesa di San Pietro in Bosa.

Map on page 218

alleys and stairs which make up the streets of Sa Costa, the former free town of **Sa Piatta** sprawls across the plain by the river. The **Corso Emanuele II** contains some elegant patrician houses and the imposing **Cattedrale** (open 7am–12.30pm, 3–7pm), which contains a 16th-century marble statue of *Madonna col Bambino*. There is a small, picturesque river port by the bridge over the Temo river. Beyond the bridge extend the unusual terraced houses of **Sas Concias** – former tanneries which present an interesting example of industrial architecture of a bygone age.

In idyllic isolation on the left bank of the Temo, 2 km (1 mile) from the town centre, stands the Romanesque-Gothic **Chiesa di San Pietro**. Constructed in the 11th century, the church formerly served as the cathedral of Bosa. As the presence of the necropolis indicates, it occupies the site of the Roman town. Thanks to its attractive urban architecture and the gentle green of the surrounding countryside, Bosa is one of the most attractive towns in Sardinia.

Be sure to take a gentle stroll up to the fortress – wandering aimlessly through the Sa Costa district before climbing a further 111 steps between olive, fig and almond trees to the summit of the castle hill. In the alleys of Sa Costa black-clad women produce beautiful embroidery and sell it outside their homes – although the women are supposed to sell all their exquisite needlework to cooperatives, which buy up their work in order to sell it at set prices in the main tourist towns. Along with gold and silver filigree work, coral jewellery and wood carving, this so-called *Filet de Bosa* is eloquent proof of the craftwork tradition still practised here.

The nearby seaside resort of **Bosa Marina** ㉔ has a beach of dark, radioactive sand which contains a high proportion of iron. It has been proved to possess healing properties in the case of rheumatic illnesses. Today the beach is a more popular venue for windsurfers and equipment can be hired locally in the summer months.

**BELOW:** a fish trap weaver in Bosa.
**RIGHT:** the rocky coast between Alghero and Bosa is a last resort for vultures.

## An endangered species

From the town of Bosa, a road leads northwards in the direction of Alghero. It passes through an austere landscape with eroded slopes and strangely-formed trachyte rocks. Skirting round the villages of **Montresta** and **Villanova Monteleone**, it then descends to the plain of Alghero via a series of vertiginous bends and switchbacks. Since the 1960s Bosa and Alghero have also been linked by a new coastal road. Environmental lobbyists have been vociferous in their criticism of this traffic artery, since they fear its impact on what has been until now a lonely and untouched stretch of countryside, which has served as nesting territory and sanctuary for many species of coastal and sea birds.

They fear, too, that increased numbers of tourists will drive away the huge but rare griffon vulture from this habitat, perhaps condemning it to extinction. However, this hasn't yet happened, thanks to local naturalists who have devoted much time to solving the problem. Nonetheless, the stretch of coastline made accessible by this road, arouses a wonderful sense of solitude more intense than almost anywhere else on the island; driving or hiking through the region is a real pleasure. ❑

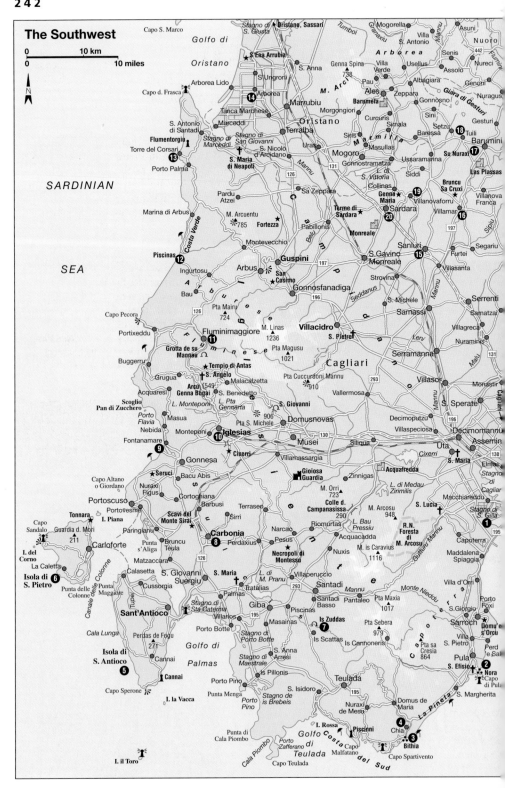

# The Southwest

0      10 km

0      10 miles

N

SARDINIAN

SEA

Capo S. Marco

Golfo di
Oristano

Stagno di
S. Giusta

Oristano, Sassari

Tumboi

Mogorella

Villa

Asuni

Nuoro

S'Ena Arrubia

Genna Spina
738

Villa
Verde

S. Antonio

Usellus

Senis

Nureci

442

Arborea Lido

S. Anna

Albagiara

Genoni

Giara di Gesturi

Capo d. Frasca

Arborea

SI'Ungroni

M. Arci

Pau

Ales

Zeppara

Gonnosno'

Nuragus

14

Marrubiu

Villa
Verde

Morgongiori

Barumela

Gonnosno'

Tanca Marchese

Oristano

Curcuris

Simala

Sini

Gesturi

S. Antonio
di Santadi

Marceddi

Terralba

Uras

Siris

Masullas

Setzu

Tuili

18

Barumini

Flumentorgiu

Stagno di
Marceddi

Stagno di
San Giovanni

S. Nicolò
d'Arcidano

Mogoro

Gonnostramatza

Ussaramanna

Su Nuraxi

17

Torre del Corsari

13

S. Maria
di Neapoli

126

131

L. di
S. Vittoria

Siddi

Las Plassas

Porto Palma

Collinas

Bruncu
Sa Cruxi

Pardu
Atzei

Sa Zeppara

Genna
Maria

19

Villanovaforru

Villanova
Franca

Marina di Arbus

M. Arcuentu
785

Terme di
Sardara

Sardara

20

Villamar

16

Costa Verde

Fortezza

Pabillonis

Monreale

Sanluri

Furtei

Piscinas

12

Montevecchio

Balu

S. Gavino
Monreale

Strovina

197

Villasanta

Segariu

Arbus

Guspini

197

15

Ingurtosu

San
Cosimo

Seddanus

S. Michele

Serrenti

Bau

Gonnosfanadiga

196

Samassi

Samatzai

Capo Pecora

Pta Mairu
724

M. Linas
1236

S. Pietro

Len

Villagreca

Nuraminis

Portixeddu

126

Villacidro

Serramanna

131

Fluminimaggiore

11

Pta Magusu
1021

Cagliari

Buggerru

Grotta de su
Mannau

Pta Cuccurdoni Mannu
910

293

Villasor

Monastir

Tempio di Antas

S. Angelo

Arcu
Genna Bogai

549

Malacalzetta

Vallermosa

S. Sperate

Grugua

S. Benedetto

906

Decimoputzu

195

Acquaresi

L. Monteponi

L. Pta
Gennarta

S. Giovanni

Villaspeciosa

Decimomannu

Scoglio
Pan di Zucchero

Pta S. Michele

Domusnovas

Siliqua

R.N.

Assemini

Porto
Flavia

Masua

130

Uta

130

Nebida

Monteponi

Iglesias

10

Musei

Cixerri

S. Maria

Stagno
di
Cagliar

Fontanamare

9

Villamassargia

Einnas

Gonnesa

Cixerri

Stagno di
S. Gilla

Capo Altano
o Giordano

Seruci

Bacu Abis

Gioiosa
Guardia

Zinnigas

Acquafredda

S. Lucia

Macchiareddu

Nuraxi
Figus

Cortoghiana

M. Orri
723

L. di Medau
Zirimilis

Stagno di
S. Gilla

1

195

Portoscuso

Barbusi

Terraseo

Colle d.
Campanasissa
290

M. Arcosi
948

Capoterra

Portovesme

I. Piana

Scavi del
Monte Sirai

Sirri

Biomurtas

L. Bau
Pressiu

R.N.
Foresta
di
M. Arcosu

Maddalena
Spiaggia

Capo
Sandalo

Tonnara

Guardia d. Mori
211

Páringianu

Carbonia

8

Narcao

Pesus

Acquacadda

M. is Caravius
1116

Villa d'Orri

I. del
Corno

Carloforte

Bruncu
Teula

Perdaxius

Nuxis

Necropoli di
Montessu

S. Giorgio

Porto
Foxi

La Caletta

Punta
s'Aliga

126

Villaperuccio

Sarroch

Isola di
S. Pietro

6

Matzaccara

S. Giovanni
Suergiu

S. Maria

L. di
M. Pranu

Santadi

Monte Nieddu

Domu
s'Orcu

Calasetta

Tratalias

293

Mannu

Villa
S. Pietro

Punta delle
Colonne

Punta
Maggiore

Cussorgia

Palmas

Giba

Santadi
Pantaleo

Pta Maxia
1017

Perd
e Sa

Canale delle Colonne

Villanos

195

Masainas

Piscinas

Is Zuddas

7

Pta Sebera
979

Pula

2

Cala Lunga

Sant'Antioco

Stagno di
Sta Caterna

Porto Botte

S. Anna
Arresi

Is Scattas

Is Cannoneris

Pta sa
Cresia
864

Nora

S. Efisio

Capo di Pula

Isola di
S. Antioco

5

Perdas de Fogu
271

Cannai

Golfo di
Palmas

Stagno di
Porto Botte

Stagno di
Maestrale

Is Pillonis

Teulada

195

Domus de
Maria

S. Margherita

Cannai

Porto Pino

S. Isidoro

La Pineta

Capo Sperone

I. la Vacca

Punta Menga

Porto
Pino

Stagno de
is Brebeis

Nuraxi
de Mesu

4

Chia

Punta di
Cala Piombo

I. Rossa

Piscinni

3

Bithia

I. il Toro

Porto
Zafferano

Golfo
del
Sud

Costa

Capo
Malfatano

Capo Spartivento

Cala Piombo

Capo Teulada

Teulada

# THE SOUTHWEST

*A tour of the southwest takes the traveller through attractive countryside, crossing the former mining regions of the Sulcis and the Iglesiente*

Map on page 242

Sassari

Cagliari

The stretch of coastline along the Costa Verde is as yet still largely untouched, and the two islands of Sant'Antioco and Isola di San Pietro each possesses a charm of its own. The alluvial plains known as the Campidano, which sometimes call to mind the valley of the Po, divide the southwest from the rest of the island. The most important north-south highway in Sardinia, the Carlo Felice, which links Cagliari with Sassari, runs across the plain and makes it possible to cross the region in a few hours.

## The coastal route

Leaving Cagliari on the SS 195 – the well-maintained road leads southwards towards the **Capo Malfatano**. To the north lies the lagoon of the **Stagno di Santa Gilla ❶**, a area of international interest which has managed to survive despite the surrounding industry, aircraft noise and other unfavourable conditions. The lagoon and ancient Macchiareddu salt flats extend over 4,000 hectares (9,800 acres). The Molentargius marsh, to the east of Cagliari, attracts many species of migratory birds including large numbers of fen-birds, and, during August and March, flocks of nesting flamingos. The Macchiareddu salt flats have been used since nuraghic times for the production of sea salt. They constitute the second most important salt pan in Italy, containing characteristic evaporating basins.

**PRECEDING PAGES:** the Costa del Sud. **BELOW:** sliding down sand dunes.

Although the only salt works left in the area are those that operate in Macchiareddu, it is in the **Golfo di Cagliari**, and particularly here in the **Golfo degli Angeli**, that the impact of recent environmental damage can be seen.

About 30 km (18 miles) from Cagliari you will reach **Pula**. Close by, perched on a small peninsula, lies the Roman town of **Nora ❷**. It was here that the oldest Phoenician inscription was found, dating from approximately 1000 BC. In 238 BC Nora was chosen as the capital of the Roman province of Sardinia, largely due to its favourable location and a fine natural harbour. From the 5th century AD the town sank into insignificance, to be reawakened after centuries of oblivion by archaeological excavations during the 1950s. They revealed what is thought to be a Phoenician temple to the fertility goddess Tanit, a 2nd-century Roman temple, a theatre and on the *sa punta 'e su coloru*, the Cape of Snakes, a Phoenician-Carthaginian holy place.

It is possible to take a free guided tour (in Italian) of Nora's remaining excavations contained within an **archaeological site** (tel: 070 9209138; open 9am–sunset; entrance fee). On the beach at Nora is the church where the 350-year-old May procession of Sagra Sant' Efisio ends. According to tradition, the underground crypt preserves the remains of the saint.

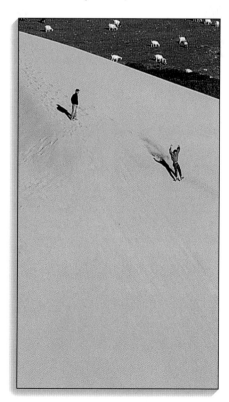

TIP

The Ristorante Sa Cardiga e su Schironi, by the turning to Capoterra, is considered to be one of the best places to eat fish on the island.

In contrast to the north of the island, the south coast of Sardinia has not yet been properly opened up to tourism. The five-star hotel **Is Molas** offers luxurious recreation facilities including an 18-hole golf course. Between Santa Margherita and Bithia stretches **La Pineta**, 10 km (6 miles) of sandy beach. The next port of call along the coast is **Bithia** ❸, accessible via the nearby village of Chia. In addition to the watch-tower, a so-called Saracen Tower built in the 17th century to defend the island against the Turks, there is also the site of a Phoenician-Roman township with a temple complex where a likeness of the archaic deity *Bes*, originating in Egypt, was discovered.

In **Chia** ❹ there are fine granite sand dunes that can reach up to 24 metres (75 ft) and upon which ancient juniper trees grow. In front of the beach, surrounded by shallow emerald and deep blue water, is the small island **Su Giudeu**, which is accessible on foot. The coastal road now becomes the Strada Panoramica della Costa del Sud, and goes past **Capo Spartivento** with views over some of the most beautiful spots of the largely unspoiled southern coastline, through a sparsely populated area to a lighthouse and then on to the **Capo Malfatano**. The rocky headlands are emphasised by additional watch-towers, such as the 17th-century **Torre Piscinni**, which was built over a Roman quarry.

Near the little hamlet of **Porto di Teulada** the road leaves the coast, skirting the **Monte s' Impeddau** (267 metres/876 ft), a vast area used by NATO forces for target practice. Near **Sant' Anna Arresi**, which holds an annual international jazz festival, a little side road leads back towards the coast, to the seaside resort of **Punta Menga**. Perhaps more interesting than these little villages are the many coastal marshes hereabouts: the **Stagno de Is Brebéis, Stagno di Maestrale, Stagno Baiocca**, and the **Stagno di Santa Caterina** shortly before you arrive in

**BELOW:** column in the Phoenician town of Nora.

Sant'Antioco. For bird-lovers, there are plenty of flamingos, herons and cormorants. In the old ghost village of **Tratalias** stands the Pisan-Romanesque church of Santa Maria (open Tues–Sun 9am–1pm; entrance fee), built in 1213 in grey-trachyte and stone featuring a little staircase leading from the roof.

Map
on page
242

## The Isola di Sant'Antioco

At 109 sq km (42 sq miles), the volcanic **Isola di Sant'Antioco ➎** is the largest island lying off the coast of Sardinia, and the fourth-largest in Italy. It can be easily reached by means of a causeway; just before entering the village of Sant'Antioco itself you can see the remains of an old **Roman bridge**. The semicircular arch looks somewhat lost beside the main road, but it proves that in former times the offshore island was linked to Sardinia. Sant'Antioco is a bustling little port with a picturesque old town centre. Its main street, the **Corso Vittorio Emanuele**, is sheltered from the searing sunshine by a dense avenue of pine trees. During the Phoenician era, in the 9th and 8th centuries BC, the former town of **Sulcis** was one of the most important cities in the Mediterranean area. It was used as the port of dispatch for the ores mined in what is now the Iglesiente region. The town covered a much larger area than its present-day successor. The **Museo Archeologico** (open daily 9am–1pm, 3.30–7pm in summer; 3.30–6pm in winter; entrance fee) has displays of recent excavations and information about the archaeological site where they were found. Additional relics of the past are to be found in the catacombs underneath the parish church (open 9.30–noon, 3.30–6pm; entrance fee). On the way to the Necropolis, in an early 20th century farm house in Via Mazzini, is the ethnographic museum Sa domu Antiga (open Tues–Sun 9am–1pm, 4–7pm; entrance fee).

*The church of Sant'Antioco stands on the site of a 6th-century church.*

**BELOW:** the coast close to Calasetta on Sant'Antioco.

Not far away lies the **Tophet** (Via Castello; open daily; combined entrance fee with Necropolis), the ritual ground of the Phoenicians where their deceased children were cremated. Countless urns containing children's ashes stand on the archaeological site close to the vast **Necropolis**. Additional relics of the past are the catacombs underneath the parish church. During the First Punic War, Sulcis acted as a Carthaginian naval base, which in turn led to harsh retaliatory measures by the forces of the Roman Empire. Under the emperors the town regained much of its former importance, but it was plundered on several occasions by the Saracen hordes. During the 16th century virtually all the inhabitants abandoned the city. Only in the 19th century did it rise again from oblivion, a trend which has continued as a result of the local tourist industry.

More attractive is the little port of **Calasetta**, which lies on the northernmost tip of the island. The chequerboard street layout and the low houses recall the Arab influence during the 18th century. The local popularity of couscous is a culinary relic of this time. Any tour of the island should include the **Tonnara** on the **Punta Maggiore**. During the *Matanza* – which takes place in about May, depending on when the schools of tuna pass by the island – a complicated system of nets is erected in order to lure the fish into the *camere della morte*, in which the sea turns crimson with blood as the tuna are killed. Processing takes place in the *tonnara* itself. The entire procedure attracts large crowds of onlookers every year.

Calasetta is also the starting point for the crossing to the pretty **Isola di San Pietro ❻**. Its area of 50 sq. km (20 sq. miles) makes it the third-largest of the offshore islands. The only place of any significance is **Carloforte**, founded in 1738 under the King of the House of Savoy, Charles Emmanuel III. As in the case of Sant'Antioco, the island was settled by Ligurians; during the 16th

**BELOW:** children's urns at the *tophet* near the Phoenician town of Sulcis.

century many of them were kidnapped and borne off to Tunisia, but were later set free. The island has volcanic rock formations and pillars such as the Punta delle Colonne and Capo Sandalo, and myriad species of birds, among them Eleonora's Falcon, which was named in honour of Eleonora D'Arborea who first declared that the bird should be protected in the 14th century. For years Sardinian conservationists have been lobbying to have the island declared a national park. Apart from a grotta in the south, San Pietro can also offer the visitor a *Tonnara* in the north of the island. The Ristorante Da Nicolo on the **Corso Cavour in Carloforte** is recommended for somewhere to eat.

Map on page 242

## The inland route

Leaving Cagliari in a northwesterly direction on the SS 130, pass **Elmas Airport** and continue towards Iglésias and Sant'Antioco. To the west in the mountainous area is **Monte Arcosu** (open Sat and Sun, June–Sept 8am–8pm, Sept–June 9am–6pm; entrance fee), the largest World Wildlife Fund Reserve in Italy, covering 3,000 hectares (7,413 acres). It is one of the last habitats for the Sardinian deer. About 15 km (10 miles) from the capital lies the village of **Uta**, which is worth a short detour. Some way outside the village itself lies the church of Santa Maria (built in AD 1140), which is without doubt one of the loveliest Romanesque country churches in southern Sardinia. A few miles from Siliqua stands the **Castello di Acquafredda** (open daily, summer 9am–1pm, 3–7pm; winter 9am–1pm, 2–5pm; entrance fee) on a volcanic outcrop overlooking the Cixerri river. The castle is a picturesque fortress dating from the 13th century. A particularly scenic route is the winding SS 293 as it passes over the Colle della Campanassissa and beyond to **Villapéruccio** and the Monte Pranu. The abandoned stations and marked-out route of the erstwhile **narrow gauge railway** criss-crossing this mining region of the **Sulcis** recall the long-since uneconomic industry. Visitors wanting to enjoy a stroll through the oak woods of the *màcchia* are recommended to park by one of the stations and walk along the routes of the former tracks.

*Trachytic stacks in the Cape of Columns, off Isola di San Pietro.*

**BELOW:** street on Isola di San Pietro.

Near **Nuxis** stands a rare example of Sardinian Byzantine architecture: the country church of **Sant'Elia** (open daily), dating back to the 8th century, with a Greek cross plan and central ogival dome. If you're stopping off for lunch, the Restaurant Letizia in Nuxis uses local herbs (wild fennel and borrage) in traditional Sardinian recipes. North of the village of Villaperúccio is the site of the most important rock necropolis in Sardinia: the **Montessu Necropolis** (open daily 9am–1pm, 2pm–sunset; entrance fee). Dating from prehistoric times, it contains almost 40 *domus de janas*, the so-called "house of the fairies", some of which retain their original walls in red and yellow. From here you can drive up to the vast rocky plateau of **Monte Essu**, on which is situated the extensive Ozieri Culture complex.

The territory of **Santadi** belongs to the part of the island which emerged from the sea in the Lower Cambrian Era (Sa domu Antiga, ethnographic museum; Via Mazzini; open Tues–Sun 9am–1pm, 4–7pm; entrance fee). Characterised by the presence of limestone and schist, the area has abundant natural caves with a wide variety of unique concretions and crystal

# Mining

Extensive areas of Sardinia, especially the southwest (Sulcis and Iglesiente), the southeast (Gerrei and Sarrabus) and Nurra in the northwest consist of limestones and slates from the earliest periods of the earth's existence. These areas are considerably older than the other principal mountain formations in the Mediterranean; their rich mineral deposits, especially lead, zinc, silver, copper and iron, made Sardinia the first and largest mining region in Italy.

Over 4,500 years ago the island's early settlers began to extract and smelt metals (copper, lead and silver). There seems little doubt that the Nuraghi civilisation flowered 3,500 to 2,500 years ago largely as a result of their trading links and metalworking skills. Evidence of the degree of mining activity in Phoenician, Carthaginian and Roman times can be found in the tools and oil lamps discovered in mine shafts, as well as in vast slag heaps such as the one at Campo

Romano near Iglésias. During the Roman Empire, Christians were often exiled to the mining areas of the Iglesiente. Under Pisan rule, silver casting around Iglésias (Monteponi, Campo Pisano) became prevalent. During the 13th century Iglésias, the former city of Uilla Ecclesiae, received its charter as a "silver town" with exemplary mining regulations and municipal rights under Pisan law, including that of minting its own coins. In 1343, 20 years after their conquest of Sardinia, the rulers of Aragon imported Sardinian mineworkers to Spain in order to improve the silver mining industry on the Iberian peninsula.

Sardinian mining enjoyed a further upturn in the 19th century – thanks to increased mechanisation and the use of explosives, and also to the introduction of the Piedmontese Mining Laws of 1848, which permitted foreign investors to circumvent the property rights of Sardinian landowners. In 1871 the College for Mining Engineers in Iglésias was set up and is still in existence today.

At the turn of the last century, with falling prices on the world market and the declining productivity of the Sardinian mineral seams, the heyday of the island's mining concerns was over. Under Mussolini an artificial boom was created with the intention of making Italy strong and independent. The coal town of Carbónia was founded to produce sulphurous lignite (with a combustion rate scarcely above that of peat) which was elevated to the title of "Sulcis coal" for Mussolini's propaganda purposes.

Iglésias, once a wealthy town, with its charming historic centre and Pisan city walls, is well worth a visit. The traveller arriving in Buggerru will have difficulty imagining that not much more than 100 years ago this mining community, complete with hospital, schools, library, concert hall and a little theatre, was the first town on Sardinia to have electricity – before both Cagliari and Sassari. Even outside the town limits, in the workers' housing estates and the opencast mines of Malfidano, there is hardly a trace left of the living and working conditions which in 1904 led to bloody unrest and the first general strike in Italy's history.  ❑

**LEFT:** Miners' memorial in the mining town of Carbónia.

formations. Particularly worth a visit for its fine stalagmites and stalactites is the **Grotte di Is Zuddas** ❼ (open daily, summer 9.30am–noon, 2.30–6pm; winter 12am and 4pm; entrance fee), 8 km (5 miles) south of Santadi. The economy of the region is based on sheep rearing and agriculture, as is demonstrated by the existence of numerous *furriadroxius*. These are small rural hamlets, one of the four types of traditional Sardinian houses which were created by shepherds in order to protect their flocks from Saracen incursion during the 18th century. They are a form of scattered housing not common in the rest of Sardinia's countryside. The *Matrimonio Mauritano* (Mauritano wedding) on the first Sunday in August in Santadi represents a genuine example of traditional Sulcis countrylife: a wedding ceremony celebrated according to centuries' old customs, an ancient propitiatory rite.

Map on page 242

## Miners' towns

At the centre of the Sulcis region is the town of **Carbónia** ❽ (Villa Sulcis, archaeological museum; Via Napoli; open Tues–Sun 9am–1pm, 4–7pm; entrance fee), planned during the fascist era. Following the international boycott of Italy as a result of the 1936 Abyssinian campaign Mussolini instigated the building of the mining town of Carbónia. Within just two years it was completed. The sulphurous "Sulcis coal" subsequently produced was virtually useless but was supposed to ensure self-sufficiency as far as Italy's energy was concerned.

The monotonous fascist architecture of the blocks of flats and the monumental central square, the **Piazza Roma**, still dominate the town today. Infinitely more interesting than Carbónia itself is **Monte Sirai** (archaeological site; open summer 9am–1pm, 3–7pm; winter 9am–5pm; entrance fee), which lies directly outside the town and which is the setting for one of the most important archaeological sites in Sardinia. The former Nuraghe settlement was destroyed during the 7th century by Phoenicians from Sulcis (Sant'Antioco), who then constructed a fortress here. Today the complex includes the remains of an acropolis, houses and a necropolis. From the summit one has an undisturbed view of the havoc wrought throughout the countryside by the nearby industrial complexes – one of the less attractive aspects of Monte Sirai. From the nearby harbour of **Portoscuso** one can set sail for the Isola di San Pietro.

Continuing along the road in a northerly direction, strike off westwards towards **Fontanamare** ❾ soon after the **Gonnesa** turning. Driving through the district surrounding the reedy estuary of the **Torre Gonnesa**, the road eventually reaches the sea. Of the former coal port very little remains today; only the buildings still standing serve as reminders. Nowadays the coast here is an extensive bathing beach. And yet, it is hard to escape the relics of the region's mining past; the few intact quarries and slag heaps take on the appearance of prehistoric ruins.

From Fontanamare there is a breathtakingly beautiful corniche leading to the mining villages of **Nebida** and **Masua**. Directly ahead is the **Scoglio Pan di Zúcchero**, a vast rocky outcrop rising suddenly from the sea. In this area there are many mines or part of mines which can be visited with specialised guides: for example Porto Flavia in Masua (contact Igea, tel:

**BELOW:** oxen are still used for fieldwork.

0781 491300), where minerals were directly taken from tunnels to ships for export. Or Galleria Henry, in **Buggerru** (tel: 339 8848962, 0781 54023), a mine dating back to 1865 situated on a cliff above the sea on Planu Sartu plateau.

The mountains of the Sulcis and the Iglesiente show the scars of centuries of exploitation: huge craters dug into the mountainside, the removal of half an entire mountain and ruined 19th-century mines. There are countless ruined complexes such as these. To a greater extent than the other towns, villages and tourist sights, these mineworks provide an eloquent record of Sardinian economic and social history. All the mines of the region are becoming part of the Parco Geominerario Nazionale and although there have been great delays, it has been recognised that the infrastructure of the mining industry should be preserved as a part of Sardinian social history, while also attracting tourists. On the road back to Iglésias is **Monteponi**, one of the most important mines on the island and well worth a visit.

The most important town in the southeast of the island is the mining town of **Iglésias ⓾**, situated at the heart of the zinc and lead quarrying district. The town's name is derived from its local church (*ecclesia* is Latin for church). Founded in the 13th century, it was a significant silver mining centre; the community was even awarded the right to mint its own coins. Do not be deterred by the somewhat desolate outskirts, instead head immediately for the interesting historic town centre. The Old Town was built according to a chequerboard plan; it is clustered around the Gothic-Romanesque **Cattedrale di Santa Chiara** (open daily except Thursday) on the Piazza Municipio. On the same square stands the Ristorante Villa di Chiesa, which serves good Italian food at an acceptable price. Also worth seeing are the pretty little townhouses of the Old Town, many with wrought-iron balconies. The **Museo delle Arti Minerárie**

**BELOW:** disused railway in the area of Iglesiente.

(open July–Oct Fri–Sun 7–9pm) displays a collection containing over 8,000 rare stones and fossils discovered during the excavations throughout the Iglesiente and various pieces of mining equipment. The **Grotta di San Giovanni** (open daily; entrance fee) near **Domusnovas** was the only cave in Italy into which you could drive by car. A road, some 900 metres (3,000 ft) long, follows the course of the river through the picturesque grotto. At the end of the tunnel there is a restaurant, a bar and a picnic area. If you contine on you find yourself in the vast **Foresta demaniale Marganai** (Marganai forest) where a botanical garden (Giardino Montano Linasia) has all the main endemic plants and 100 species of other plants, (open Tues, Thur, Sat and Sun 9.30am–1pm; entrance fee).

Map on page 242

## Iglésias–Costa Verde–Oristano

Before embarking upon the trip from Iglésias to Oristano, consider whether you have enough time to take it easy, and whether your stomach is strong enough for the hairpin bends. It is not a road to hurry. Immediately after leaving Iglésias, the SS 126 climbs up the mountain in an endless series of tight curves. It passes through acres of oak forests which can compete with those of the Barbagia in terms of both remoteness and beauty. The region itself is virtually unpopulated, allowing the visitor to appreciate Sardinia's famous timeless charm. At the top of the pass, at the **Arcu Genna Bogai**, marked by a small convent, the view of the valley below suddenly opens up to include the pillared temple of Antas (open summer daily 9am–1pm, 3–8pm; winter Sat and Sun 9am–1pm; entrance fee), where Sardus Pater was worshipped. A Roman place of worship during the 2nd century, it was built on the site of a much earlier Punic temple. According to Sardinian mythology, Sardus Pater is the original ancestor of the island's inhabitants. He reputedly came from Africa to populate the island, but the origins of the deity can be traced back to a Punic god. Today, remains of pillars and the partially-restored floor plan of the temple remain; its undeniable attraction is derived primarily from its unusual site.

**BELOW:** handling the hairpin bends.

Following the course of the **Rio Antas**, you will pass the **Grotta de su Mannau** (tel: 0781 580189; open summer daily 9.30am–6.30pm; winter by appointment only), of geological and archaeological interest, and the town of **Fluminimaggiore** ⓫. The SS 126 winds on its way, climbing from the level of the river to the next eminence before entering the village of **Arbus**. Here you will find the first museum dedicated to Sardinian knives from the 16th century knives and a reconstruction of a blacksmith's workshop (Via Roma; tel: 070 975220). Shortly before doing so it passes a small side turning which leads down to the mining communities of **Ingurtosu** and **Naracáuli**. The industrial ruins consisting of miners quarters (open but not secure) and management headquarters (closed to the public) are worth seeing, if only from the outside. The dirt road continues down to the sand dunes of **Piscinas** ⓬ that cover about 30 sq. metres (almost 12 sq. miles). The 100-metre (330-ft) high dunes of fine sand are being continually reshaped by the strong sea breeze; on them grow scattered groves of coastal juniper and various forms of wildlife make their home in the sands. For this reason this is a protected area. **San Cosimo** is a

well-preserved *tombe dei giganti* by a little road leading from Arbus to **Gonnos-fanadiga**. It lies immediately before the bridge over the stream running down into the valley.

## On the Costa Verde

A small, winding road leads from Gúspini along the ridge of the **Montevecchio** and then down to the **Costa Verde**. Montevecchio's lead and zinc mines, were some of the most important in Europe until 1960. It is possible to have guided tours to the 1876 Liberty style pit (tel: 335 5314198; guided tours June–Sept 10am, 10.45am, 5.30pm, 6.15pm; entrance fee). The name refers more to the hinterland than to the coastal margin itself, for its massive sand dunes recall a desert rather than a green and pleasant land. From **Marina di Arbus** the coastal strip is open to vehicles in both directions. The sand dunes near **Torre del Corsari** ⑬ are particularly magnificent. But even this maritime landscape, as yet largely untouched, seems to be endangered by the speculators.

The few fishing villages are already beginning to sprout holiday complexes, most of which, sadly, are being built without much concern for the environment – and this is despite a law passed in 1990 forbidding development of this particular coastal strip. An alternative means of exploring the coast is on horseback; mounts to suit all ages are available for hire in the village of Torre del Corsari. After negotiating an arduous series of bends the traveller arrives some 30 km (20 miles) later at the **Golfo di Oristano**, behind which lie the **Stagno di Marceddi** and the **Stagno di San Giovanni**. After rejoining the SS 126, your next town along the route is **Arborea** ⑭, also built during the fascist era and originally called Mussolinia in honour of Il Duce. Arborea was laid out

**BELOW:** the sand dunes of Piscinas.

along new-town principles in 1928 in order to populate the plain of Oristano, which had been made agriculturally viable by the construction of irrigation canals. It was decided to introduce settlers from Venetia and the plain of the Po; they defied the endemic malaria and transformed the region into fertile land. The little town possesses a few fine Art Nouveau houses as well as a well-run hotel and restaurant – the Ala Birdi, which serves as the equestrian sports centre for the surrounding area, and the Ristorante Al Pavone. The present-day name of Arborea recalls the old *Giudicato* of Gallura, Torres, Cagliari and Arborea. It also serves as a reminder of Eleonora d'Arborea, the former *Giudicessa*, who refused to acknowledge the sovereignty of the Aragonese, uniting virtually the whole of the island in her resistance. Today she is celebrated as a national heroine. In 1392 she was responsible for the famous *Carta de Logu*, a comprehensive legal code which governed the lives of the islanders and which prevailed until the 19th century.

Map on page 242

## Su Nuraxi and surrounds

Following the SS 131, take the exit to **Sanluri** ⓑ where, in 1409, the Aragonese troops led by Martin the Young won the battle that put an end to Sardinia's independence. It is possible to visit the Castello di Eleonora d'Arborea that houses the **Museo Risorgimentale Duca d'Aosta** (tel: 070 9307105, www.sabattalla.it; open July–Sept 4.30–9pm, Oct–June Sun 9.45am–1pm). The museum contains mostly military exhibits from the 19th century but there are some Napoleonic memorabilia to look out for and some pieces of fine furniture. On the upper floor is the Museo della Ceroplastica, which contains miniature 16th-century wax sculptures. Also in Sanluri is the **Museo Storico Etnografico** (Via Cappuccini; tel: 070 9307107 for an appointment, open daily 9am–12am, 3–6pm; entrance fee), attached to the Convento dei Cappuccini. Dedicated to the Capuchin friars, the convent contains local archaeological finds. On the way to Barumini is the village of **Villamar** ⓰. The parish church contains a large polyptych, painted in 1518, situated behind the main altar, which was the most important work of the Sardinian painter Pietro Cavaro. Just after the village, a road on the left leads to the nuraghic site of **Bruncu Sa Cruxi** (open daily).

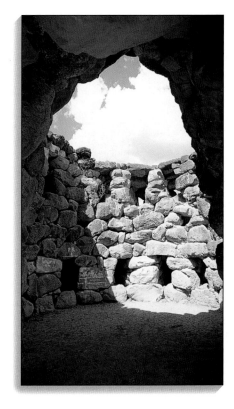

**BELOW:** the ruins of Su Nuraxi.

**Su Nuraxi** ⓱ (tel: 070 9368128; open daily 9am–dusk; guided tours every 30 minutes; entrance fee) about 1 km (½ mile) to the west of Barumini, consists of a large Nuraghe fortress dating from the 13th to the 6th century BC, surrounding a massive round defensive tower with a well. The layout of the complex is still clearly visible today; it is easy to recognise the different phases of construction. The main central tower was built between the 15th and 13th centuries BC, and the further fortifications with four round towers were constructed about 300 years later.

The connecting walls, of massive lumps of solid rock, as well as five further towers, date from the period leading up to the 7th century BC. Outside the fortified walls arose a village of more than 200 circular huts; during their construction in the course of the 7th century BC the main complex itself was destroyed. During a fourth phase it was rebuilt, before being

**Map on page 242**

abandoned by all inhabitants during the 5th century BC. Walking through the village of round huts, the visitor is struck by the cramped and self-contained style of building. The entire complex was excavated as recently as 1949 and has been recently listed as a World Heritage Monument.

## Outside Su Nuraxi

South of Su Nuraxi, the appropriately-named Marmilla (from the word bosom) rises out of the plain. Perched on top is an ancient fortress marking the frontier where the territory of the former *giudicato* of Arborea met the *giudicato* of Cagliari. The ruins of the castle of **Las Plassas** date from the 12th century. Between Barummini and Las Plassas is the **Sardegna in Miniatura** park where the island's most important archaeological sites and monuments are reproduced in 1:20–25 scale (tel: 070 9361114; open Mar–Oct daily 9am–dusk; entrance fee).

From Barumini it is possible to reach the Giara di Gesturi, following the signs from Tuili. **Tuili ⑱** itself is a delightful small village, probably the best preserved in all the Campidano-Marmilla area, where visitors can walk through the recently restored Old Town and feel the spirit of the island's old way of life. The polyptych of San Pietro, painted by Maestro di Castelsardo (1500) in the parish church of San Pietro, is one of the most significant 16th-century paintings in Sardinia and fills a chapel on the right-hand side. The **Giara di Gesturi**, a volcanic high plateau, is one of the major environmental attractions in the area. World famous because of the presence of some 500 wild horses (*cavallini*), the isolated table mountain is covered by myriad large and small rainwater ponds that in the spring are covered by various *ranunculi* (aquatic plants), creating a unique and enchanting scenery. The plateau has also become home to a variety of birds, some of which are migratory. It is possible to hire a guide to take you on a horseback tour of the area.

Returning to Tuili and following the signs for Villanovaforru, the traveller will find in the open countryside the **Museo Naturalistico di Sa Corona Arrubia** (tel: 070 9341009; open Mon–Fri 9am–2pm, 3–8pm, Sat and holidays 9am–8pm) where fossils are permanently displayed together with other temporary exhibitions. In the town of **Villanovaforru ⑲,** the **Museo Archeologico** (Viale Umberto; tel: 070 930050; open Tues–Sun 9am–1pm, 3.30–7pm; entrance fee with Genna Maria complex) is housed inside a nicely restored 19th-century building on Piazza Costituzione, and displays nuraghic artefacts found in the nearby *nuraghe* complex of **Genna Maria** 1 km (½ mile) west of the town. Genna Maria was discovered in 1977 and is still being excavated.

Sardinia has a number of springs which have been exploited for thermal cures. The town of **Sardara ⑳** was famous in Roman times for its healing spas, and today they are used in the treatment of rheumatic illnesses. Sardara also contains an important sacred spa from the era of the Nuraghi; it rises near the **Chiesa di Sant' Anastasia**. The new **Civico Museo di Sardara** (Piazza Libertà; tel: 070 9386183; open Tues–Sun 9am–1pm, 5–8pm; entrance fee) displays material ranging from pre-nuraghic pottery to objects belonging to the Giudicati period. ❑

**BELOW:** local farmer. **RIGHT:** holm oak stripped to the dark red cambium.

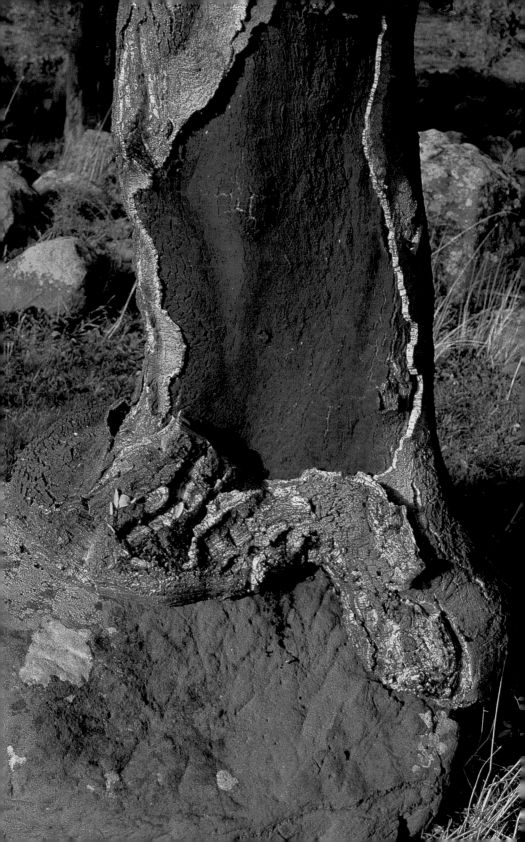

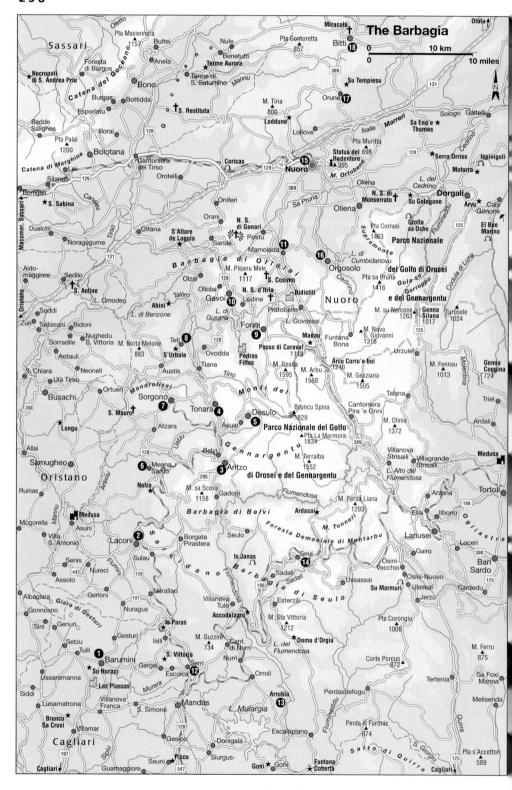

The Barbagia

0        10 km
0        10 miles

# THE BARBAGIA

*Hikers and climbers appreciate the dramatic beauty of
the Barbagia, while other visitors are intrigued by
the region's strong cultural identity*

The Barbagia, which runs almost parallel to the mountain range of the Gennargentu, is the highest of the sub-regions of Sardinia. The name is of Roman origin and is derived from the Latin *Barbaria* or Barbaricum. The Roman conquerors described as Barbarians any people whose culture was based neither on the Roman nor the Greek civilisations, and whose social order and lifestyle were markedly different from their own (the people here resisted Roman colonisation for longer than those in any other Sardinian region). It was probably a *giudice* from the *giudicato* of Arborea who first subdivided the region into five sections: Barbagia di Ollolai, di Seui, di Seulo, di Belvì and Supramonte.

## Prehistory and history

Remains of antiquity, bearing witness to the early settlement of the area, can be found here as elsewhere in the form of the *nuraghe*, which date from the 15th to the 2nd century BC. Estimates put the total number on the island between 7,000–8,000; some 200 to 250 of these are situated in the Barbagia. Unlike those to be found elsewhere on Sardinia, where human hand or inclement weather has wrought extensive damage or even removed them from the landscape altogether, most of the *nuraghe* in this area are remarkably well preserved.

Some of the *nuraghe* in the Barbagia still have exterior walls standing, linking several towers or small cone-shaped buildings by means of corridors which were designed to provide a means of internal communication. A wall some 7–10 metres (20–30 ft) high surrounded the earth bulwark at the height of the living accommodation of the main *nuraghe*. People entered an oval room connected by means of a spiral staircase with the two upper-floor rooms and eventually with the terrace on top of the flat-roofed cone.

The existence of the Nuraghe Longu in the Samugheo district and the Nuraghe Nolza in the vicinity of Meana was known even during the 19th century. Archaeologists are still unable to agree as to the original purpose of these buildings. The hypotheses range from simple clan dwellings to fortifications.

Further evidence of the region's early history can be found here, as in other districts of Sardinia, in the shape of *Sas pedras fittas* massive standing stones, firmly anchored in the ground. These stones exist in the vicinity of Gavoi-Lodine, not far from the original Byzantine cemetery of Nostra Signora d'Itria, as well as in the Grillu district (near Fonni), or in the mountainous forests of Ovodda. They may be sacred stones which were worshipped as late as the 6th century AD, before local inhabitants and their chieftain Ospiton

**PRECEDING PAGES:** festival procession in the Barbagia.
**BELOW:** Whitsun preparations.

were converted to Christianity by Pope Gregory I. Also dating from prehistoric times are the *tombe dei giganti* (giants' graves). They are to be found scattered across the entire island as well as here in the Barbagia. These graves – which, according to legend contain men of enormous stature, the mythical first inhabitants of Sardinia – are often situated remarkably close to *nuraghe* or on the outskirts of a Nuraghi village.

The *tombe dei giganti* are rectangular constructions of worked stone that range from 8–28 metres (26–92 ft) in length. Characteristic of these tombs is the vertical stela, whose size is proportional to that of the grave (the longest is more than 4 metres/13 ft) and is placed over the entrance of the tomb. One of the best-known *tombe dei giganti* in the Barbagia region is the S'Altare de Lògula near Sarule. It was discovered during the 19th century by General Alfonso La Marmora who travelled the length and breadth of the island, exploring as he went, and recording his findings in his *Voyage en Sardaigne*. The interest aroused by his findings prompted the search for further sites.

Also worth visiting are the *domus de janas* (fairy dwellings), dating back to the neolithic age (3500 BC). Again local tradition ascribes a supernatural origin. Legend maintains that they were inhabited by fairies or virgins; they took the form of small houses or caves hewn from the bedrock and measured about 1–2 metres (3–5 ft) in height.

## Fact and fable

Ancient scientific and historical texts describe the inhabitants of the Barbagia as "the people from Ilion" or "the descendants of Iolaos", who bravely fought against the Carthaginian and Roman hordes in an attempt to preserve their free-

**BELOW:** the region has many *nuraghe*.

dom and independence. One derivation of the name indicates a link with Troy ("Ilion"), and refers to a maritime people originally from Asia Minor who had come to Sardinia in order to found their own colony. The other harks back to Iolaos, the legendary Greek hero who is purported to have reigned over a Greek colony with the assistance of the sons of Hercules.

Pausanias, an early chronicler, confirms that in the interior of the island and in the mountains of the Barbagia there are many place names which are derived from the Iolaos of antiquity. Two examples are the villages Ollolai and Artilei; according to the historian Angius the latter stems from Arx Jolai.

It is claimed that the Carthaginians attempted to subjugate the inhabitants of the Barbagia on several occasions, but that they were never able to achieve a clear-cut and therefore final victory.

When the island came under Roman rule in 238 BC, the new conquerors, while trying to bring the entire island under their sway, encountered determined resistance in the Barbagia. In view of this, the Roman government sent men of the stature of Publius Cornelius, Marcus Pomponius, Tiberius or Sempronius Gracchus with instructions to subjugate the Barbagia in order to bring the entire country under the control of the Empire.

Under the rule of the Emperor Tiberius a large number of exiled Romans, possibly as many as 4,000, were dispatched to Sardinia. They were sent to prevent the attacks by the Barbaricini on other regions of the island which had already been pacified and brought under Roman rule. Under the Emperor Justinian the Barbaricini started up their raids once more, and the emperor was forced to give orders for the Roman legions to set up camp at the foot of the rough mountains of the Barbagia. It was during this period that the name Barbaricini

Map on page 258

**BELOW:** the Barbagia converted to Christianity in the 6th century AD.

occurred for the first time. Scarcely 50 years after Justinian, the Sardinian tribe at last found a leader and general in King Ospiton, whose reputation owes as much to legend as it does to historical veracity. He possessed the ability to guide his people with a firm hand. By all accounts they were a nomadic tribe whose only interest lay in tending their flocks, and who had no interest in the arduous tasks associated with agriculture, although it is possible that the large numbers of discontented Roman refugees may have taught them the rudiments of farming and other manual skills.

### Christianity arrives

During the 6th century AD the Barbaricini were converted to Christianity. Pope Gregory I sent Felix and Cyriacus to the Barbagia to spread the gospel throughout Sardinia. Under the influence of the commander-in-chief of the army, Zabarda, King Ospiton became a follower of the new faith. From this point on he tried to win the tribes under his sovereignty over to Christianity and to discourage them from the worship of pagan idols, the practice of superstitious rites and pagan customs.

The Barbaricini embraced the new faith with fervour. It seems possible that their passionate enthusiasm for the new beliefs encouraged them to desecrate the symbols of their former religion, as other Sardinian tribes before them had done. There is some evidence to support the theory that at this time they began to overturn and in some cases to destroy the *pedras fittas*, or to tear apart the holy places of their pagan gods.

During the Saracen invasion many Sardinians fled deep into the interior of the island in the face of the brutality of the advancing foe, finding refuge with the Barbaricini and thus augmenting their numbers. Although contemporary sources provide no information on the matter, it seems possible that the inhabitants of the Barbagia, true to their reputation as indomitable warriors, may have played a decisive part in the crushing defeat of the Saracen Prince of Mogeid-al-Amiri, referred to in ancient chronicles as Museto. After the victory over Museto (AD 1015–16), the history of the Barbagia becomes progressively more integrated into that of the island itself.

It passed through the period of the *giudicati*, became the scene of violent struggles and was ruled in turn by the Genoese, Pisans, Aragonese and Spanish. In the face of the frequent unjust tricks played on them, the people of the region never abandoned their guard and maintained a rebellious attitude. This can be witnessed in an episode dating from 1719, when a sudden doubling of taxes prompted the Barbaricini, and in particular the citizens of Olzài, to revolt against Spanish rule.

### Mountain peaks

The Barbagia consists almost entirely of mountainous and hilly country, which rises towards the east as it approaches the massive ranges of the Gennargentu. Some of it is very bleak. Its highest peak is named after General Alfonso La Marmora. The summit of **La Marmora** reaches 1,834 metres (6,017 ft) above

**BELOW:** traditional costume plays an important role in festivals.

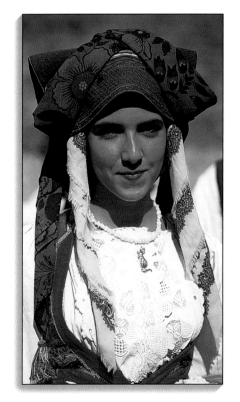

sea level; the neighbouring peak of **Bruncu Spina**, which for several months each year is capped with snow, is more than 1,829 metres (6,000 ft).

On a fine day with little cloud, the view from the highest peaks of the Gennargentu is overwhelming and confounds the sense of bleakness that the region so often inspires. It extends across the mountains, which imperceptibly fall away towards gently rolling hills; in their folds lie densely wooded valleys snaked by streams that become transformed into rushing torrents in times of flood. In particularly clear conditions one can see as far as the Tyrrhenian Sea on the distant horizon.

The peak of **Monte Spada** lies in the region known as **Barbagia di Ollolai**. It marks the end of an extensive mountain range which stretches eastwards as far as the **Corru'e boi** (Cattle Horn) gorge and the pass of the same name on the main Nuoro-Lanusei-Ogliastra road. Then the highland area winds on further to Monte Novo S. Giovanni in the district of Orgosolo, where the River Cedrino rises, and on as far as the limestone escarpment by Oliena and the Lanaittu Valley, which marks the boundary between the administrative districts of Oliena and Dorgali.

Throughout the region there are springs fed by the mountain snows. Their fresh water is popular all over the island; healing powers are even attributed to some of them, such as the springs of **S'Abba Medica** near Gavoi, or the spring water from the **Guppunnìo** spa and the **Regina Fontium** (Queen of the Springs) in Ollolai. The most famous healing spas are those of **Monte Spada** and **Campu Maiore** in Ortueri. People come to sample them from all over the island.

There are only three rivers of any significance: the **Flumendosa**, the **Talòro** and the **Araxisi**. The Flumendosa rises in the southern gorges of the Corru'e boi,

Map on page 258

*Climbing in the region has become increasingly popular.*

**BELOW:** the snow-covered countryside.

collecting the water of the eastern Gennargentu and numerous smaller tributaries from the Mountains of the Ogliastra before flowing into the Tyrrhenian Sea. The Talòro, a tributary of the Tirso – the island's biggest river – has its source in the Barbagia di Ollolai, expanding between the districts of Gavoi, Ovodda and Olzai to become the lake of the same name, after which it flows across the Plain of Ottana and the central Tirso Valley before joining the main river.

## Plants, trees and flowers

The Barbagia still retains some of the luxuriant vegetation, especially the forests, which at one time made Sardinia one of the greenest spots in the entire Mediterranean.

In the mountains, acorn-bearing oak trees still grow up to an altitude of 1,200–1,300 metres (3,800–4,200 ft) above sea level. By far the most common species is the holm oak, followed by pedunculate and cork oaks. The latter supply the cork industry, an important factor in the Sardinian economy since the 19th century *(see page 204)*.

The cork, stripped from each tree every seven to eight years, is exported in a raw and processed state. The numerous forest fires which plague the region in the hottest summer months and uncontrolled overfelling have led to a drastic reduction in the tree stocks. At the beginning of the 19th century they were estimated at 66 million. The millenary woods of Sardinia were cut down by charcoal burners from the Italian peninsula and transformed into railway sleepers, charcoal for domestic heating or wood to feed steam engines. The protests of locals went unheard and in a few decades the island became unrecognisable.

Apart from the incalculable ecological and aesthetic damage, the fires have

**BELOW:** *màcchia* in full blossom.

a deforesting effect which has led to a shortage of food for livestock, particularly for pigs, which produce excellent meat for the manufacture of ham and sausages when fed on acorns. Visitors who appreciate the natural wealth of the coastal regions of Sardinia will be further delighted by an excursion into the woods and meadows of the Barbagia. They will discover, apart from areas of natural or specially-planted new forests, specimens of holm oaks which have stood there for several centuries – if not millennia.

As far as flora is concerned, the Barbagia is especially well-endowed: broom, oleaster, yew, ash, tamarisk, willow, elder, alder, poplar, holly and laurel grow in abundance. *Màcchia* shrubs – blackthorn, myrtle, arbutus and numerous other species – are one of the reasons that many visitors come to this part of Sardinia and scientists from Italy and abroad come to study the environment.

Many of the plants bear berries or wild fruits with a slightly bitter taste, for instance, the sloe. Others, such as the arbutus, produce delicious fruits; it is from the blossoms of the arbutus that bees collect nectar for the famous, pungent-tasting Sardinian honey. The fruits are red and are about the size of a morello cherry. They are eaten raw or made into jam, and are known for their laxative effect. In former times it was common for locals to distil them to make a schnapps-like drink.

Chestnut woods and hazelnut bushes are chiefly found around Desulo, Tonara, Aritzo and Belvì. The inhabitants of these districts include the fruits of the forest in their diet to some extent, albeit less than in days gone by. Nowadays much of the produce is exported to other regions of the island. Almonds and hazelnuts are the principal raw ingredient required by the confectionery industry for the production of *torrone* (nougat with nuts), eaten in great quantities

Map on page 258

**BELOW:** acorn bread is still made in some areas.

*A storage chest, made from local wood, with traditional carvings on the front panel.*

during festivals. For generations it has been manufactured in Tonara, Aritzo and Belvì. The chestnut trees used to supply excellent wood for a variety of purposes, and still do to some extent. In the old days (and occasionally still today) craftsmen used it to make items for everyday use, such as doors or windows. More stylised objects, too, are produced – also functional, but requiring a greater degree of artistry – such as benches with built-in storage chests (the front panel of which is almost always decorated with stylised illustrations of birds, flowers, leaves or the landscape of the place of manufacture), looms, spindles, distaffs and other items for the processing of wool. Tables, plate racks, kitchen furniture and beds were usually made of a softer wood, in particular that of the pear tree.

Among Sardinia's plants and herbs are thyme and rosemary – both of them common in the South of France and Spain – as well as wild lavender, gorse with its characteristic yellow flowers and sharp thorns, brambles (laden with blackberries during September), pink and red rock roses, heathers and a wide variety of forest ferns. Unforgettable in spring and early summer are the seemingly endless fields of daisies, corn poppies and bog asphodel. The latter is one of the typical plants of the *màcchia*; it produces long, thin stems with small white flowers in late spring.

## Birds, beasts and bees

The island has relatively varied fauna. Eagles, falcons, vultures, red kites, partridges, ring doves, thrushes, magpies, quail, turtle doves, snipe, blackbirds and buzzards all live and breed here. On the mountain slopes, where acorns and berries are plentiful, or even near vineyards and vegetable gardens, one will

**BELOW:**
mountain goat.

often encounter wild boar – a robust species which breeds easily in spite of environmental damage, in contrast to many others whose numbers have declined or are threatened with extinction. In recent years they have become a popular addition to the Sardinian menu. The most common wild animal on Sardinia and in the Barbagia used to be the mouflon, a wild short-fleeced mountain sheep. In former times it wandered the mountains in herds, but sadly today it is becoming increasingly rare. Only walkers crossing the crests of the Supramonte near Oliena and Orgosolo, or wandering through the heart of the Gennargentu may be fortunate enough to see this magnificent creature. It looks like a ram, but has the coat of a deer.

Also of interest are the beehives. Apiculture (bee-keeping) was once more widespread than it is today, but the increased number of uninhabited areas given over to protected flowering plants has led to a revival of the ancient occupation. As in the old days, walkers can once again delight in the unexpected discovery of a honeycomb tucked away in a tree hollow which one of the many swarms of wild bees has converted into a hive.

## A journey into the Barbagia

An expedition into the Barbagia is recommended to every foreign visitor; it is a truly wild spot which even many Sardinians haven't explored. This region, which forms the very heart of the island, is accessible only by road, by public or private transport.

In general, the road network and the public transport available are adequate, but one obviously enjoys a greater degree of independence when travelling by private car. The Strada Statale 131 has been improved and is now of motorway standard, but has remained toll-free; by taking it, the visitor can soon reach Nuoro, one of the possible starting points for a tour of the Barbagia. The following route, using the island capital, **Cagliari** – with the largest harbour and the principal airport – as the point of departure, is only one of the many possibilities available. It is very difficult to organise a single itinerary that covers the Barbagia, because of the great morphological variability of the region. Deep valleys, high plateaus, and mountain peaks and ridges, which are at times difficult to get over, take turns to provide the dominant geographical feature. In some places there is no asphalt road, only a dirt track to follow.

After leaving the town on the Carlo Felice (SS 131), you will soon arrive at the right-hand turning of the SS 197 between **Serrenti** and **Sanluri**. Here a detour is recommended to the remarkable *nuraghe* complex of **Barumini ❶** and the **Giara di Gesturi**, a vast table mountain of basalt which is as geologically interesting as it is picturesque, and which is the home of wild Sardinian ponies.

After about 10 km (6 miles) on the SS 128 one reaches the village of Laconi, which is still in the **Sarcidano**, but which lies on the edge of the Barbagia. **Laconi ❷** the largest town in the Sarcidano, enjoys an attractive situation. It is the birthplace of St Ignatius of Laconi; the saint's meagre possessions are preserved in the house where he was

Map on page 258

*Peregrine falcons are just one of the birds of prey to be found in the region.*

**BELOW:** the Barbagia is accessible by a network of roads.

born, Casa Natale di Sant'Ignazio (tel: 0782 86902; open Thur and Sun 9am–12am). Apart from the 16th-century bell tower, you can also visit Castello Aymerich (open 8am–sunset); its magnificent park not only contains flowers native to Sardinia but also bay trees, horse chestnuts, pedunculate oaks, beaches and cedars from the Himalayas and the Lebanon.

Some of the most important decorated menhirs of Sardinia have been found a few kilometres away from the village and have been gathered in the newly created **Museo delle Statue Menhir** (tel: 0782 866216, email: menhirlaconi@tiscali.it; open Oct–Mar 9am–1pm, 4–6pm, Mar–Sept 9.30am–1pm, 4–7.30pm) in the basement floor of the Town Hall.

The route continues northwards from Laconi and reaches **Aritzo** ❸. An important mountain resort surrounded by chestnut and hazelnut woods, the town still has some interesting buildings, including a 17th-century Spanish prison and an Arangino "castle", which became a private home at the beginning of the 20th century. The town has a good regional Museo Etnografico (tel: 0784 627200; open Tues and Sun 10.30am–1pm, 4.30–7pm; entrance fee), which has displays of craft, costume and domestic and agricultural machinery.

The Sagra delle Castagne (Chestnut Fair) held in the town at the end of October attracts people from all Sardinia. Aritzo is also the starting point for many excursions that can be done by four-wheel drive vehicles provided by local hotels or on foot, with a local guide. The **Tacco Texile** (975 metres/3,199 ft), an unmistakable limestone rock at the top of a conical hill, is the destination of many walkers. Not far away is the village of **Belvì**, which holds its Cherry Fair in June and has a small but interesting Museo di Scienze Naturali e Archeologiche (tel: 0784 629806; open by appointment).

**BELOW:** even the smallest of towns have churches.

## Tonara and Desulo

The towns of Tonara and Desulo nestle in the western foothills of the Gennargentu massif, along the mountain route. These are some of the highest villages on the whole island. The town of **Tonara ❹** is known principally for its production of *torrone* (nougat), which is sold throughout the island at fairs. Honey is one of the prime ingredients of *torrone* but it is also used to make the majority of Sardinian cakes. Sardinian honey is prized for its quality and huge variety, largely determined by the diversity of wild flowers on the island, which give each honey its distinctive flavour. You can choose between perfumed citrus fruit honey, delicate asphodel or balsamic eucalyptus. The rare strawberry tree honey with its unique bitterness is highly sought after.

It is in the area surrounding the Gennargentu massif that Sardinia's traditional culture of sheep herding is most apparent. Visitors can still find a network of ancient footpaths, many of which are still in use by shepherds and their herds. These paths connected pasturelands and, in the 19th century, mountains, before they were deforested by charcoal burners. Today the paths are used by hikers. As the paths are not signposted, many people use local guides or walk the paths in groups. Hikers often come across *pinnette* (ancient round huts with thatched roofs) which are used by shepherds for shelter, especially during the lambing season when shepherds cannot leave their flocks.

The village of **Desulo ❺** (Casa Montanaru, ethnographic museum; tel: 0784 619624; open by appointment), at an altitude of 895 metres (2,900 ft) is one of the few villages where you can still see some women wearing the traditional costume of the region. The costume here is remarkable for its simplicity of design and use of bright colour: orange, red, blue and yellow. Many excursions start from Desulo.

Map
on page
258

*Locally produced honey is used to make* torrone *(nougat), a speciality of Tonara.*

**BELOW:** the mountain-top village of Tonara.

*A woman from Desulo in traditional costume with a plate of festive food.*

Footpaths beaten by local shepherds lead walkers to **Bruncu Spina** (1,829 metres/6,000 ft) and **Punta La Marmora** (1,834 metres/6,017 ft), the highest peak on the island. On the northern side of Bruncu Spina a ski lift has been in service since the 1990s. It is used for short periods of the year after major snowfalls. For several months of the year large quantities of snow fall on the summits and gorges of the Gennargentu, where it continues to lie for some time. Winter sports complexes and hotels are being built in the area to attract skiers. There is no suggestion that the Gennargentu can compete with the more famous ski resorts of the Alps or the Appenines, nor is it likely to be able to in the future. Nonetheless, it is recommended for a skiing holiday with a difference or, for those who have time, just as an interesting place to spend an extra week after a stay on the coast.

The Italian Alpine Club (CAI) built a shelter house on the island's highest peak, Punta La Marmora (Rifugio La Marmora) which is used as a landmark and for its good spring water by hikers even though today only ruins remain. Alternatively, by following the SS 128, you can reach Tonara and then Desulo, from Laconi passing through Meana Sardo, Atzara and Sorgono, and then a number of minor roads should you want to get off the beaten track. Between villages grapevines and fruit are cultivated in fields. Here orchards reach as far as the eye can see: cherry and almond trees, plum, fig and pomegranate trees, olives, hazelnuts, walnuts and chestnuts.

## Meana and Sorgono

**BELOW:** snow-topped mountains.

The village of **Meana ❻** is not usually part of regional itineraries. Pleasantly placed between mountains at 600 metres (1,969 ft) above sea level, it preserves the feeling and quality of life of the Sardinian mountain people. A few

kilometres above the village is Nuraghe Nolza, presently under restoration but nonetheless open to visitors. In a dominating and extremely panoramic position, it is different from most *nuraghe* in that it was built using clay to cement the space between stone blocks – a revolutionary idea that caused instability and many structures to collapse. The nearby village of **Atzara** has a late Gothic parish church with a Romanesque bell tower and side chapels decorated with precious wooden altars.

**Sorgono ❼**, part of the subregion of Mandrolisai, is in a valley surrounded by woods and orchards. It is a popular place to visit during the summer months because of its pleasant climate, which also allows for the cultivation of grapes for the famous Cannonau wine. Seven kilometres (11 miles) outside Sorgono is the **Santuario di San Mauro**, one of the most interesting rural sanctuaries on the island. Built in the 16th century, in an Aragonese-Gothic style, it has a Renaissance door with a carved Gothic rose window above it. Inside is an impressive staircase and a single vault. Surrounding the church are *cumbessias* (pilgrim shelters) that were used as lodgings during the feast day of San Mauro, held on the first day of June each year.

The festival is still popular today and its religious ceremony is accompanied by a fair at which local handicrafts and produce are sold: iron, copper, leather and terracotta goods, walnuts, hazelnuts, dried chestnuts and honey as well as different varieties of sweetmeats. During the 19th century the fair also provided an opportunity to purchase foreign-made goods like linen, woollens and leather items, silk, *majolica*, china, and thoroughbred horses. Just outside the church courtyard is a new restaurant run by a cooperative of locals which has an interesting menu and, surprisingly, serves some very good fish dishes.

Map on page 258

*When D.H. Lawrence arrived in Sorgono during his* Sea and Sardinia *trip he described the village as being similar to "some little town in the English West country".*

**BELOW:** village in the Barbagia.

Before arriving in Fonni via Ovodda, first visit the small archaeological museum in **Teti** , the **Museo Archeologico Comprensoriale** (Via Roma; tel: 0784 68120; open Tues–Sun 9am–12.30pm, 3–5.30pm; entrance fee). The museum has a collection of objects found in the nearby nuraghic archaeological site of S'Urbale, and an interesting reconstruction of a round hut from 1000 BC with some sleeping niches and domestic articles inside.

About some fifteen kilometres (9 miles) to the north of Teti in a very isolated and difficult to find valley, are the remains of the large nuraghic village of **Abini**. A number and variety of bronze votive figurines were found here, representing hero-warriors with four eyes or arms, that can now to be seen in the archaeological museum in Cagliari. Daggers, votive bronze swords and other small objects are displayed in Teti's archaeological museum.

## Changing times

The past few decades have seen some rapid changes in the customs and lifestyle not only of individuals but also of entire communities in Sardinia. Contrary to first impressions, this is as true of the Barbagia region as it is of other regions of the island. Only the shepherds with their flocks have managed to retain the old way of life. They have become symbolic of the nomadic lifestyle which was once typical of the land.

Pasture land is not always in ample supply, but the grass and wild herbs available contribute to the taste – even the consistency – of the meat and the milk products of the shepherd's flock. Gone are the days when every shepherd wandered the countryside on foot with his dog. Today most shepherds use a car or a jeep for transport when they have errands in the village or want to visit their sheep. Their vehicles also enable them to transport wood or food for their livestock, to deliver the milk to the cheese factory, and lambs, kids or pigs to the butcher. Visitors may still occasionally see a mule or a donkey carrying goods. At high altitude, in the remotest, most inaccessible places in the mountains, they are still irreplaceable. However, for everyday transport purposes over long distances they have been superseded by vehicles.

**BELOW:** flock of sheep on the move.

Modernity has arrived even in the furthest corners of the Barbagia, as the inhabitants demand their right to share in the comfort of the present day with its achievements and new products. Most of the single- and two-storey houses found in villages are still of the traditional variety, with ancient moss-covered tile roofs. In some places they have been renovated with much imagination and personal effort, enabling them to meet modern requirements. Sometimes, however, they have simply been demolished to make way for new housing which is out of keeping with the traditional appearance of the town or village.

Migrant workers and traders who sought employment in the more prosperous regions of the island, such as Nuoro, Cagliari or Sassari, often return eventually to their native mountains, where they invest part of their savings in the construction of a new house or the renovation of an old building. Today, in the agricultural estates of the parishes of the Barbagia, vegetable fields, vineyards and orchards which had been allowed to lie fallow since the 1960s are being revived by owners who have become disillusioned by jobs in the service industries or in one of the factories in the faraway towns. The future also looks increasingly rosy for the groves of oak and chestnut trees and the large areas planted with hazelnut bushes, which have retained their original charm despite the recurring fire hazard which lays waste vast tracts of land: oak and pine woods, groves of cork oaks and the *màcchia*, where heathers, rosemary, thyme, rock roses, arbutus trees with their red berries, mastic shrubs and black-berried myrtle flourish.

The mastic shrub is the principal source of food for both goats and pigs; it is also used to yield an oil for household use. Myrtle berries and juniper are used to distil *mirto*, a schnapps. At the beginning of the century there were entire woods of juniper bushes several hundred years old. Today the stands are much younger, although in the valleys of the Barbagia you may still come across an ancient specimen which is as big as a tree.

## Fonni – the highest village

At 1,000 metres (3,280 ft) **Fonni ❾** is the highest village in Sardinia. It is also one of the region's biggest centres and is popular with hikers and walkers, who use the town as a base for excursions into surrounding countryside and mountain peaks. The town's most interesting monument is the 17th-century church of San Francesco (open daily), also called the sanctuary complex of Nostra Signora dei Martiri. The complex is surrounded by porticos and the interior of the church is remarkable for the 1,700 religious frescoes and late Baroque altars. On Whit Monday (the first Sunday in June) and on 24 June for the festival of San

Map on page 258

**BELOW:** the countryside surrounding Fonni attracts many walkers and hikers.

Giovanni, local people wearing traditional costumes parade through the streets on horseback and visitors from the surrounding countryside join in pious tribute to the Virgin Mary. The festivals are well known throughout Sardinia and were described by Grazia Deledda in her novel, *Canne al Vento*.

## Sites around Fonni

From Fonni it is only 35 km (22 miles) to Nuoro via Mamoiada along the 389 road or, in the opposite direction, just a few kilometres to reach the **Corru'e boi Pass** (1,246 metres/4,086 ft), a passage between the inner Sardinia of the Barbagie, the Nuorese and the planes of the Ogliastra on the eastern coast. The well-preserved Tombe dei Giganti Madau (open daily) is an indication of the historical importance of the area.

Just west of the pass, the *tombe dei giganti* are noteworthy because of their position and good condition of their burial corridors. East of the pass is a nuraghic village with a temple where excavations are still in progress. The road meanders between long rows of vineyards, orchards of fruit trees, past newly planted groves of cork and holm oaks and flowering *màcchia*. Flocks of sheep and herds of cattle graze between fragrant violets and heather; the rich supply of wild mushrooms are a welcome treat for the wild boar – which, however, remain largely unseen.

If you want to, it is possible to continue from Fonni to Nuoro by means of an alternative route. On the road heading towards Gavoi is the **Lago di Gusana**; shortly before reaching the lake the road joins the 128 road, an attractive route skirting the right hand shore. The lake is pleasantly surrounded by trees and it is used for canoeing and camping. The hotel Talòro, on a small peninsula, has

**BELOW:**
the traditional
costume of Fonni.

a restaurant with excellent regional cooking. From the lake the next stop on the route is **Gavoi** ❿, an important centre dominated by the 16th-century church of San Gavino with a Gothic rose window in trachyte stone. From the village it is worth making a short detour to see the large sanctuary of **Madonna de Sa Itria** (open daily) where, not far from the church, a 3½-metre (5-ft) high neolithic *menhir* bears witness to the continuous use of the sanctuary as a place of worship throughout many millennia.

Continuing north from Gavoi through **Sarule**, **Orani** and **Oniferi** the road links up with the SS 131 from Abbasanta to Nuoro. Not far from the junction several *domus de janas* are set into the hillside. Part square and part concave, some of the individual chambers are linked to one another by means of low doorways or windows. The pilgrimage church of **Nostra Signora di Gonari** (open daily) lies between Sarule and Orani on an unmistakable wooded cone-shaped hill, from which talc is quarried. The building is unadorned and dates from the time of the *giudicati*. The festival of dedication, which is celebrated in appropriate style, falls on 8 September each year. During the Roman occupation Orani may well have been one of the most densely populated villages in the Barbagia. Many of Sardinia's artists, including the well-known contemporary painter Costantino Nivola, have hailed from Orani.

In **Mamoiada** ⓫ (644 metres/2,060 ft), a predominantly agricultural village producing vegetables, wine and fruit, one of the most original, fascinating and famous carnival processions in Sardinia takes place on Shrove Tuesday. The *Mamuthones* of Mamoiada, as frequently happens elsewhere in Sardinia, don special disguises for the carnival (in Orotelli they become *Thurpos*, in Ottana they are known as *Boes* and *Merdules*). The *Mamuthones* hide their faces behind

Map on page 258

**LEFT:** carved *Mamuthones* masks.
**BELOW:** a Mamuthone.

black carved wooden masks and wear sheepskin or occasionally goatskin fleeces reaching down to their knees, with breeches of coarse velvet and traditional shepherds' knee-high leather gaiters worn in the Barbagia until about 30 years ago. The *Mamuthones'* scary appearance is enhanced by the bunch of clanging cow bells weighing up to 50 kg (110 lb) hung over their shoulders and carried on their backs. They walk in procession accompanied by *Issohadores* (young escorts) in bright costumes and carrying leather lassos, which they use to capture astonished spectators or – better still – their beloveds from the crowds watching the procession. A good place to experience the atmosphere of the festival out of season is at the Museo delle Maschere Mediterranee (www.museodellemaschere.it; open Tues and Sun 9am–1pm, 3–7pm; entrance fee), which displays a collection of traditional masks aided by a video which introduces visitors to carnival. Another major festival in the town is held in honour of saints Cosimo and Damian. It takes place in the little country church of the same name, which stands on a fertile upland plain near Mamoiada directly opposite the picturesque Gennargentu Massif.

## The Barbagia of the South

The village of **Serri** ⑫ is best known for its position near the Giara di Serri, a basaltic plateau on which the nuraghic site of **Santuario Nuragico di Santa Vittoria** (open daily; entrance fee) is situated in a panoramic position. The archaeological complex is divided into three major sections: a temple area that includes a sacred well, a temple and a small church; a public area with a large courtyard for nuraghic festivals; and market and living quarters that include a chief's hut. About 5 km (3 miles) southeast of the town of **Orroli** is the **Nuraghe Arrubiu** ⑬ (open daily; entrance fee), one of the largest nuraghic complexes

**BELOW:** the simple elegance of the landscape.

in Sardinia dating back to the Bronze Age. It is formed by a tall central tower which today measures 16 metres/50 ft high, although it is thought to have been 21 metres (67 ft) high when it was originally built. The tower is surrounded by a bastion with five towers, which is surrounded by a lower wall with eight towers. The name Nuraghe Arrubiu, which means Red Nuraghe, comes from the lichens that cover the complex – at sunset the complex becomes bright red. Nuraghe Arrubiu is situated on a high basaltic plateau (500 metres/1,600 ft) near the edge of the canyon of the Flumendosa river, that here is more than 300 metres/960 ft high.

The Flumendosa is the second longest river in Sardinia and flows to San Vito, on the eastern coast. Along its course it is interrupted by three dams that form as many lakes. The river creates a natural barrier with its deeply cut gorge between regions. The historic centre of **Sadali** was built around the 13th-century church of San Valentino, next to which a beautiful karstic spring bearing the same name erupts out of the rock as a 7-metre (23-ft) waterfall. The surrounding area is very rich in water – not common in Sardinia – and it has created an unusual landscape in the limestone rocks. The **Grotte de Is Janas** (Fairy Caves; open daily) are surrounded by a holm oak wood. This section of the Barbagia is characterised by what is known as *Solitudini*, lonely, uninhabited expanses of land. The average population density in this region is less than 60 people per sq. km (150 per sq. mile) and can decrease in times of austerity.

The next village along the road is **Seui ⑭**. Of great interest in the town is the **Museo della Civiltà Contadina** (Rural Life Museum; tel: 0782 54611; open daily) that displays many objects reflecting the history and traditions of the village. Along the SS 198 from Seui is the unmissable **Foresta Montarbu** (Montarbu forest), reachable by a long dirt road that winds into the vast, wild area, or by getting off the Trenino Verde at the stop for San Girolamo. Footpaths in the forest are well signposted and lead to Monte Tonneri, where it is possible to see deer and mouflons. The Perda Liana, about 1,293 metres (4,242 ft) high from its base, is, together with Tacco Texile of Aritzo, one of the most characteristic peaks of the island.

## Nuoro, heart of the Barbagia

**Nuoro ⑮** lies under the same spell of enchantment as the Barbagia itself, caught between reality and myth, a passive witness to history and to the fate of its shepherds, peasants and poets. D. H. Lawrence reckoned there was nothing to see in Nuoro, though he did admit: "I am not Baedeker." Today Nuoro has put on a guise of modernity. On every corner public-and privately-owned buildings have sprung up; new schools have been built. An expanding services industry and tourism have led to the town's rapid growth over the past 30 years.

Since 1926 Nuoro has been the provincial capital again, as it was under the Sardinian monarchy. At the beginning of the 19th century approximately 3,500 people lived here. Today the population is between 35,000 and 40,000, and the upward trend continues. No other town within the province can compete on a cultural level, although the economy, work situation, tourism and trade have resulted in greater fluctuations than

Map on page 258

**BELOW:** visitors to Nuoro.

# Caves and Caving

Sardinia's rocks are the oldest in Italy. Karst formations cover a relatively small area – only about 6 percent of the island, mainly along the coast – compared with the more extensively occurring metaliferous rocks and granite, The quality and exciting variety of forms, however, serve to compensate for the relatively small size of the area involved. The underground world of grottoes and caves that characterise Sardinia's karst limestone was created almost 500,000 years ago, during the epoch of prehistory known as the Palaeozoic Era.

Ever-new shapes were formed during the geological periods which followed: the Mesozoic, Tertiary and Quaternary Eras. The result is a truly remarkable variety of forms. The inroads made by the sea also lend the grottoes a completely individual character, making them attractive to geohydrologists, palaeoclimatologists, biologists and tourists. The study of Sardinia's caves didn't start until the 1950s. In 1954 a British team of explorers discovered and investigated the Grotta di Nettuno on the Capo Caccia, a formation of red limestone rising 180 metres (600 ft) above the sea. Today, over 100,000 people clamber into the bowels of the earth via the Escala Cabirol, the so-called Deer's Steps, each year. Many more visit by fishing boat from Alghero harbour. The cave contains a small lake (La Marmora), which – like the lake in the Grotta del Bue Marino in Calagonone (Dorgali) – provides a perfect miniature example of the vast underground lakes of Europe. It is thought that these, along with other caves on the island, had magico-religious significance during the Ozieri period. More recently, but sadly no longer, the two caves were home to a colony of rare monk seals, the last colony of seals to be found on the Mediterranean.

Passing through the Hall of Ruins (Sala delle Rovine) of the Grotta di Nettuno into the Palace Hall (Sala della Reggia), the visitor ascends the Music Tribune (Tribuna della Musica) from which there is a view into the Organ Hall (Sala dell'Organo) and the Domed Hall (Sala della Cupola). In some of the caves stalactites and stalagmites have assumed the most bizarre shapes over the course of millions of years and shimmer in a range of beautiful colours.

Sardinia's caves were more frequently discovered by accident rather than as the result of specific exploration by archaeologists searching for prehistoric bronze statues and jewellery or human or animal remains; others were discovered by engineers searching for karst springs to increase the island's scarce water supplies, or by workers collecting guano – the dried excrement of seabirds, used in fertilisers – and miners involved in the extraction of lead or zinc.

During the 19th century, General Alfonso La Marmora made a detailed study of the island's caves, documenting their formation, their geomorphology and their exploitation. Scientifically based speleology as such has been applied to Sardinia only since the end of World War II. To date, only a small proportion of Sardinia's caves have been studied. ❏

**LEFT:** the stalactite and stalagmite formations of the Grotta di Ispinigoli near Dorgali.

were the rule in the not-so-distant past, when small independent businesses flourished by making and selling only the essential requisites of life. Traces of vanished peoples in the form of remains from the Nuraghe era and later epochs are to be found not only in the surrounding district but also close at hand: towards **Monte Ortobene** or in the direction of **Valverde** and **Badde Manna** (The Big Valley), from which one can see in the distance the plains and the mountain peaks of Oliena and Orgosolo. Nuoro's position as the centre and symbol of the entire Barbagia was assumed at the beginning of the 20th century; the region itself extends considerably beyond the boundaries laid down over the years, encompassing such places as **Orotelli, Orune, Bitti, Onanì** and **Lula** to the north.

Map on page 258

## Sites to see in Nuoro

Famous sons and daughters of Nuoro, such as the poet Sebastiano Satta, the Nobel Prize-winning novelist Grazia Deledda *(see page 122)* and many others are responsible for the town's amazingly rapid rise to cultural and social prominence. Travellers can visit the final resting place of Grazia Deledda in the eastern district of town, on the way to L'Ortobene: the **Chiesa della Solitudine** (the memorial hall in which one finds solitude; open daily). The leading citizens of the town have erected a museum in the house where the famous woman of letters was born. In the **Museo della Vita e delle Tradizioni Sarde** (Via Antonio Mereu; tel: 0784 257035; open daily Oct–June 9am–1pm, 3–7pm, June–Sept 9am–8pm; entrance fee), also known as the Museo Etnográfico, visitors can examine a varied and well-chosen collection of folkloric items from all over the island: traditional costumes for both men and women from various towns and villages, matching jewellery – valuable filigree work in gold or silver or of coral, and works of art by skilled goldsmiths whose families in many cases have plied the trade for generations. Apart from costumes, the museum displays a large number of exhibits illustrating the ancient craftsmanship of the island, which even today produces magnificent rugs and wall hangings, exquisite shawls, scarves and linen and silk embroidery. Also on display are a collection of traditional musical instruments; a room devoted to festival costumes and masks and a section devoted to the sweets, cakes and breads found throughout the island. The museum complex is designed to evoke a Sardinian village.

*Piazza Satta contains artworks by local artists Costantino Nivola and Francesco Ciusa.*

**BELOW:** buildings in Corso Garibaldi.

Another museum worth a visit in Nuoro is the **Museo d'Arte di Nuoro** (tel: 0784 252110; open Tues–Sun 10am–1pm, 4.30–8.30pm; entrance fee); housed in a 19th century building between Corso Garibaldi and Piazza Sebastiano Satta in the Old Town. The museum displays a collection of Sardinia's best known artists, featuring important painters such as Biasi, Ciusa and Nivola. It also organises various temporary exhibitions often dedicated to art of the late 19th and early 20th century, poetry readings and jazz evenings. There is also a new National Archaeological Museum, close to the cathedral (tel: 0784 31688; open Tues–Sat 9am–1pm).

Further sights in the town centre include the **Cattedrale di Nostra Signora della Neve** (Our Lady of the Snows; open daily) erected during the 19th century on the foundations of a considerably older,

*The Nuraghe Tanca Manna in the province of Nuoro.*

**BELOW:**
delicate embroidery
from Oliena.

smaller place of worship. It houses a large number of valuable art treasures of interest to the visitor. Then there is the **San Pietro** district of town, where the birthplaces of Grazia Deledda and Francesco Ciusa are situated, and the **Chiesa delle Grazie** (Church of the Graces; open daily) – both the old and new buildings – which owns a boarding school run by the Brothers of the Order of Giuseppini d'Asti. The monks also take care of the pilgrimage chapel which attracts large numbers of the faithful from surrounding districts, especially during the *Novene,* held in November each year.

## Excursions from Nuoro

Two of the rural churches in the vicinity are worth an excursion: the church of **Nostra Signora di Valverde** on the wooded northern slopes of the Ortobene, from where there is a magnificent panoramic view right across to **Orune** and the lovely Valle di Marreri, and the **Cappella di Nostra Signora di Monte Ortobene**, lying about 8 km (5 miles) from Nuoro at an altitude of some 1,000 metres (3,200 ft) above sea level. It is accessible by car, public transport and on foot via a long and twisting road which climbs some 400 metres (1,280 ft) above the town.

From the **Belvedere**, the observation platform on the Monte Ortobene, there is a breathtaking view in all directions. There are also hotels, restaurants and bars (although fewer than in Nuoro itself) and a massive bronze Statue of the Redeemer, the work of the sculptor Vincenzo Jerace, dated 1901. During the last few days of August (26–30) each year, the *Sagra del Redentore* is celebrated in its honour. The festival is one of the most famous and impressive on the entire island as it demonstrates not only the colourful costumes, the traditional danc-

es and music, but also the deep and sincere piety of the Sardinian people. Nuoro is a good base for excursions into the surrounding countryside – to the towns and villages of Orotelli, Orune, Bitti, Siniscola, Orosei, Dorgali, Irgoli, Galtellì – all of which are described elsewhere in this book.

**Oliena** *(see page 178)* and **Orgosolo** in particular, which lie 10 km (6 miles) and 16 km (10 miles) respectively from Nuoro, are worthy of a more extended visit. Each of the little towns has both cultural and historic attractions as well as strong traditions of hospitality. Both lie on the Supramonte, the first limestone mountain range within the Gennargentu southeast of Nuoro. The murals in the village of **Orgosolo** ⑯ are famous *(see page 217)*. Nowadays the original political message concerning the struggle against powerful landowners and government repression is played down by the villagers. The film *Bandits at Orgosolo*, directed by Vittorio e Seta, dubbed the town the bandit capital of the island, a label that has been hard to shake off. The bandit Graziano Mesina, known as the Scarlet Rose for robbing the rich to give to the poor, was born in Orgosolo.

## Mountain walks

The **Supramonte**, which contains the communities of Oliena, Dorgali, Orgosolo and Urzulei, can be approached from a number of directions – albeit in general only by foot, on horseback or in a cross-country vehicle. In each of the four villages, but in particular in Oliena and Orgosolo, walkers will find good accommodation and well-run guided tours – in short, everything to meet a trekker's needs. The tourist information office in Nuoro has produced a free touring map for trekkers and walkers detailing 10 alternative routes. The Supramonte is clad in unspoiled holm oak woodland. Broom grows between giant tree trunks felled

Map on page 258

**BELOW:** hikers taking the easy way down Punta Corrasi.

*Barbecued meat on a spit – a traditional part of a shepherd's meal in the Barbagia.*

**BELOW:** putting the finishing touches to *pane frattau* – carasau bread soaked in tomato sauce with pecorino and egg.

by age or lightning, but from which fresh shoots are already beginning to grow. Others have been transformed into pillars of charcoal by some long-past or more recent forest fire. In the half-shade of day or on bright moonlit nights they stand there like secret beings, monsters or devils from Dante's Inferno. Walkers be warned: grottoes and gullies open up without warning (across the millennia they may have swallowed up animals or even men); today speleologists are discovering their secrets.

The mountain itself is not high; its loftiest peaks scarcely reach 1,500 metres (4,921 ft), with **Punta Corrasi** at 1,463 metres/4,800 ft) and **Monte Ortu** at 1,340 metres/4,396 ft. They lie on the northern boundary of the Supramonte, between Oliena and Orgosolo. In the southwest, within the district of Orgosolo, rise a number of ridges. They, too, are not particularly high, but, like the **Monte Novo San Giovanni**, they are steep and picturesque. Changing light conditions and the natural texture of the rock make the limestone shimmer – sometimes blue-grey or green, then silver, copper-coloured or chalky-white.

The way into the secret, enchanted world of this part of the Barbagia is via ancient footpaths or old, unmarked tracks made originally by the wild boar, mouflons, goats and pigs who even today roam through the dense undergrowth of woods and clearings in search of food. The further one goes, the more overwhelming is the feeling that time has stood still. The impressions which visitors take home with them from the Supramonte are of relics from an Arcadian past: the cottages *(su pinnettu)*, built of largely untreated, massive trunks of oak, yew or buckthorn, the stalls for livestock and goats, the pigsties *(s'edìle)*, and the few *nuraghe* constructed of white blocks (Nuraghe Mereu), defying decay. And then there are the innumerable underground springs and rivers, crystal-

clear especially in the caves, disappearing underground only to resurface either in **Su Gologone** in the Oliena Valley, or else in the heart of the Supramonte, maybe in the **Gorroppu**, the wild gorge of the same name.

Map on page 258

Even the everyday food is natural and simple in the Barbagia: roast suckling pig, wild boar, goat, sheep and goat's milk cheese, ham – perhaps from the local pigs which are often crossed with wild boar and fed on acorns. Since time immemorial every meal has been accompanied by one of the traditional breads such as *pane carasau* (a flat crisp bread consisting of two wafer-thin layers); to drink there is fresh spring water from one of the many caves, or a powerful wine from Oliena, Orgosolo, Dorgali or Mamoiada.

## Festival dance and song

Following a meagre harvest or a year with too little rain, after a seemingly end-less period of breathless anticipation, tensions are released in a festival. As well as being celebrations they express confidence in the future and faith in a deity. In this traditionally poor country, a concentrated effort was required to wrest from the soil the bare essentials of life. It was an existence made doubly diffi-cult by the island's long history of foreign rulers.

Festivals were a means of expressing – at least for a short while – all the plans, ideals and dreams conjured up by human fantasy and limitless imagi-nation. A festival also provided an opportunity to give vent to a basic melan-choly within a circle of friends. A people like the Barbaricini, living amidst the noble silence of mountain, hill and valley, where every stone is a witness to ancient times and forgotten secrets, are a people who often prefer to commu-nicate by gestures rather than words, a tendency that has often led to them being described as taciturn.

**BELOW:** a traditional *coros* (choral) group from Fonni.

Feelings and attitude to life are expressed by a look, perhaps by a smile or a scarcely articulated word. But one of the festivals particularly loved by the inhabi-tants of the Barbagia is the so-called Poetry Contest. To the universal delight of their audience, two or three speakers supply an impromptu commentary on life in general or aspects of Sardinian history in particular; the delight of the listeners increases in proportion to the elaborateness of the performance.

Dance is an essential component of every celebra-tion in the Barbagia. Indeed, dance formerly held an even more important role than it does today. It is governed by strict rules, which may vary from one village to the next. The musical accompaniment is provided by a single instrument, the accordion. The young men begin and are followed by the girls.

Traditionally, the dancing takes place in front of a church or at country places of pilgrimage, or in the village square. Nowadays performances for visitors are held in amphitheatres and theatres, and the indi-vidual communities include dancing as part of the principal *Sagre* (folk festival). Sometimes the musi-cians may strike up spontaneously during a wedding or carnival celebrations, but not as frequently as in the past when, on hearing the strains of a familiar melody, men and women formed a circle, the size of which depended on the number of dancers and the

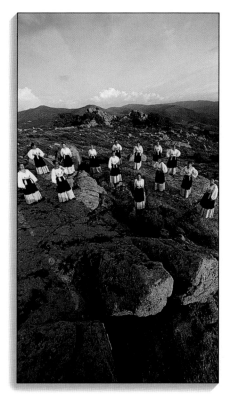

rhythm of the music. Church festivals assume a particular religious and social value in the Barbagia. The celebrations, which are part of the region's traditional folklore, take place either at places of pilgrimage dedicated to the saint in question or to the Mother of God, or else in the villages themselves. The festival is held in honour of the local patron saint, or another saint, or the Madonna, who is particularly revered in Sardinia. In some churches or country places of pilgrimage the pilgrims, some of whom may have travelled great distances, recite their prayers in novenae, in a cycle of nine consecutive days. By this means they fulfil a vow or thank God for His mercy. In the larger and major festivals, the faithful still sleep in the *cumbessias* (also called *muristenes*), which are built in an arc around the church or in a circle at a discreet distance.

Many village and country festivals are still observed with great ceremony, sometimes even with pageantry. Wealthy men and women of good reputation assist the priest. Sometimes these helpers are known by the title of prior or prioress; more commonly, however, they become the president or member of a committee. Priors and committees alike are invariably determined to do everything better than their predecessors. Sometimes the limits of friendly competition are overstepped, and the event degenerates into an image-building exercise for the organising families or clans.

## Festive food

As in days gone by, vast quantities of meat, wine and food are stockpiled for such occasions. It is considered essential that every guest, be they invited neighbours, travellers from further afield, or a chance tourist, should have more than enough to eat and drink. The entire contents of kitchen and cellar will be

**BELOW:** traditional festival cakes.

wheeled out as hosts try to outdo each other in their hospitality, pressing visitors with genuine warmth to taste all the dishes on offer, and sample the local wines. If you are very lucky, and turn up at festival time, you may be invited to visit the home of one of the local families.

The young people of the community organise entertainments. The *Morra* is a game in which two players have to stretch out simultaneously some of the fingers on one hand, calling out a number between two and ten. The player who guesses the number wins. And then there are the *Ballu Tundu*, the "national" dance of Sardinia, poetry competitions, guitar competitions and horse racing.

At every place of pilgrimage, usually immediately in front, until very recently you would find a little market, a tradition which dated from the Middle Ages. The shepherds and farmers, and above all the craftsmen, used to sell their goods or exchange them for others. Thus the festival acquired the character of a fairground. Today, because of regulations endorsed in recent decades, only professional traders can offer their goods for sale. *Torrone* (nougat) can be purchased, along with cow bells and a variety of small kitchen utensils of wood, copper or bog asphodel leaves manufactured in Tonara, Desulo, Aritzo, Belvì, Isili, Ovodda or Ollolai.

The most attractive festivals in the western Barbagia are the *Feste-Fiere* (the church dedication festivals) in Samugheo, Ortueri and Sorgono. The first festival is that of St Basil; the second is the Birth of the Virgin Mary, the *Natività della Vergine*, on 8 September; the third is the festival of St Maurus Abate (1 June), held in the church of the same name, a building with a single nave and situated some distance from the village. In Sorgono the *Assunzione della Barbagia Vergine* (the Assumption of the Virgin Mary) and the Festival of the Redeemer (*Salvatore*) on 9 November are celebrated with due style.

**Map on page 258**

**BELOW:**
a game of *morra*.

## Festivals of Barbagia

Among the many festivals *(sagre)* celebrated in the rural areas or the towns of the Barbagia di Seulo, the following are particularly worth catching: the festivals of St Mary Magdalene, patron saint of the parish church of the same name, and that of Corpus Christi, in mid-June, and St John the Baptist (23–24 June). The festivals provide an excuse for a huge common feast for villagers and visitors, further evidence of the importance the Sardinians attach to hospitality and community spirit.

In the past, the more isolated churches of the Barbagia have often offered sanctuary to bandits, who could be as pious and affable as they were cruel and bloodthirsty. This sometimes resulted in clashes with church authorities. For example, a decree issued in 1832 forbade the celebration of Mass in the Church of St Christopher near Seui, since it had been desecrated by a group of bandits who had turned it into their home. Magnificent festivals are celebrated in Esterzili in honour of the patron of church buildings: St Michael the Archangel in the village and St Sebastian, the Assumption of the Virgin and St Anthony of Padua outside the gates.

Apart from Christmas, a festival observed with special attention everywhere on the island, the festivals are scattered at random throughout the year. A disproportionate number occur in spring, when the shepherds and their flocks return from the plains of the Campidano or the Nurra, and in summer, when the expatriate workers from the Italian mainland come home to see their families.

**BELOW:** festive meal for shepherds at Oliena.

The inhabitants of the Barbagia love to celebrate their delight at seeing them again. Shared memories are revived, and for the duration of a short summer or festival day the melancholy and the loneliness of the too-cold or too-dry winter

are dispelled, along with worries about the livestock and the success of the harvest or the problems of living in economic exile. Visitors will not be excluded from these festivities, but they should possess the gift of being good listeners to really get the most out of them. Then they may even gain an insight into subtle, deeply felt and inexplicable *Mal de Sardegna*, the very soul of the island.

Map on page 258

## The Nuorese

North of the Gennargentu mountains, the region of the high granite plateaus extends itself. It gets its name from the town of Nuoro. The **Nuorese** is a territory covered by vast cork and oak woods, inhabited in nuraghic times, and today sparsely populated by shepherds living in isolated villages.

Orune ⑰ is one such village, situated at 765 metres (2,510 ft) above sea level on the edge of the plateau and dominating the Isalle valley. A few kilometres out of the village at the end of a specially built road (10 minutes' walk downhill on a path) is the sacred spring of **Su Tempiesu**, the most beautiful and refined water temple in Sardinia. It is an architecturally unique, a small temple with perfectly cut stones, monolithic small trachyte arches that have only a decorative function, and dates from 1,200 BC.

From the positioning of the springs it seems clear that the spring did not attract large of numbers of people, as in the case of the sanctuary of Santa Vittoria di Serri. The large number of nuraghic springs and their distribution on the island demonstrate the great reverence the people had for water; so great that springs became sacred places of worship. For this reason, while the houses and even *nuraghe* seem to be primitive in their construction, in water temples a high level of craftsmanship in stone cutting and evocative and refined design is demonstrated.

Continuing north on the plateau, at 800 metres (2,600 ft) above sea level, one encounters the village of **Bitti** ⑱, famous for the production of sheep's cheese and more recently for being the home town of the *Tenores di Bitti*. It is thought that the local dialect is the closest to resembling Latin on the island. In its territory there are the remains of many important nuraghic settlements.

A large nuraghic village called Romanzesu has recently been found on the granite plateau. The complex covers an area of 7 hectares (17 acres) and is characterised by buildings used for worship. A sacred well has been excavated, together with two *megaron* temples (rectangular temples preceded by a vestibule), a vast ceremonial space placed inside a large enclosure wall and a structure of concentric walls, of unknown function. The dating of materials confirm that the site was in use from the 13th century to the 9th centuries BC. The complex is very interesting because of its position inside a cork tree wood (open daily, summer 9am–1pm, 3.30–7.30pm; winter 8.30am–1pm, 2.30–4pm; entrance fee). Moving towards the western border of the plateau, above the Tirso river, is **Benetutti**, a village well-known for its thermal waters, one of the few thermal waters exploited in Sardinia. The most important spa is that of the Aurora or of San Saturnino on Benetutti, with sulphuric water and a temperature between 34°–43°C (93°–109°F). ❏

**BELOW:** filling bottles with spring water.

# ✶® INSIGHT GUIDES
# TRAVEL TIPS

# ✸ INSIGHT GUIDES Phonecard

## It's a global phonecard

One global card to keep travellers in touch. Easy. Convenient. Saves you time and money.

Save up to 70%* on international calls from over 55 countries

Free 24 hour global customer service

Recharge your card at any time via customer service or online

## It's a message service

Family and friends can send you voice messages for free.

Listen to these messages using the phone* or online

Free email service - you can even listen to your email over the phone*

## It's a travel assistance service

24 hour emergency travel assistance – if and when you need it.

Store important travel documents online in your own secure vault

For more information, call rates, and all Access Numbers in over 55 countries, (check your destination is covered) go to **www.insightguides.ekit.com** or call Customer Service.

## JOIN now and receive US$ 5 bonus when you join for US$ 20 or more.

### Join today at

### www.insightguides.ekit.com

When requested use ref code: **INSAD0103**

### OR SIMPLY FREE CALL
### 24 HOUR CUSTOMER SERVICE

| | |
|---|---|
| UK | 0800 376 1705 |
| USA | 1800 706 1333 |
| Canada | 1800 808 5773 |
| Australia | 1800 11 44 78 |
| South Africa | 0800 997 285 |

### THEN PRESS **0**

For all other countries please go to "Access Numbers" at **www.insightguides.ekit.com**

* Retrieval rates apply for listening to messages. Savings based on using a hotel or payphone and calling to a landline. Correct at time of printing 01.03

(INS001)

*powered by* **ekit**

"The easiest way to make calls and receive messages around the world"

# CONTENTS

# Getting Acquainted

## The Place

**Area**: 24,090 sq km (9,309 sq miles).
**Coastline**: 1,850 km (1,150 miles).
**Capital**: Cagliari.
**Population**: 1.7 million.
**Language**: Italian and Sardinian.
**Religion**: Roman Catholic.
**Time zone**: Greenwich Mean Time plus 1 hour. Daylight Savings Time from the end of March to the beginning of October.
**Currency**: euro.
**Weights and measures**: metric.
**Electricity**: 220 volts.
**International dialling code**: 39 (Italy) +070 (Cagliari).

Sardinia is the second largest island in the Mediterranean Sea. It belongs to Italy, even if there are some native Sardinians who would rather not be reminded of this fact. The distance between Sardinia and mainland Italy is almost the same as that between Sardinia and the continent of Africa (Tunisia) – 180 km (112 miles).

In the capital city of Cagliari there are about 250,000 inhabitants, in Sassari 120,000, in Alghero 38,000, in Nuoro 37,000, and in Oristano and Olbia 31,000 apiece. The island is divided into four provinces which are named after their respective capitals: Cagliari (CA), Sassari (SS), Oristano (OR) and Nuoro (NU).

Recurrent economic difficulties keep the island busy. Almost all the previously-planned industrialisation projects have not come to pass because production costs are about one-third more expensive on the island than on the mainland. The average income, however, is about 25 percent lower than in other areas in Italy. So it is still the approximately 60,000 shepherds herding about 3 million sheep – from which the world-famous pecorino cheese is produced – that lend character to the island today.

Sardinia, referred to as "Africa's Europe" due to its distance from the European continent, was discovered in the 1960s as a holiday paradise. A decisive factor in this development was the transformation of the Costa Smeralda (Emerald Coast) into a luxurious holiday resort.

*Residencias* – holiday housing developments – have been built with little regard for the environment. They are situated right on the coast, and, with the exception of a few weeks in the summer, remain empty for most of the year.

Even today Sardinia cannot totally rid itself of its "bandit island" reputation, despite the fact that many other areas in Italy – for instance, Calabria – could easily claim this title. In the meantime, however, the "Bandits of Orgosolo" have learned that easier money can be made in the form of "legalised rip-offs": the sale of tacky T-shirts to tourists.

## Climate

Summer lasts for seven months in Sardinia, thanks to its southern location and the fact that it is an island. Average temperatures on the coast are 19°C (66°F) in autumn, 10°C (50°F) in winter, 12°C (54°F) in spring, and 22°C (72°F) in summer. Sea temperatures reach 26°C (79°F) in July and August. Do remember that these are average temperatures and that in reality temperatures during the day are much higher and that during the night they often drop even in the summer. You will be surprised to find that after a very hot day you may need a pullover in the evening if you are sitting outside.

A constant presence in Sardinia is wind, notably the *maestrale*, a strong wind from the northwest. During the summer two hot winds blow: from the southwest the moist *libeccio* and from the southeast the *scirocco*. There is no best time of year to visit Sardinia – it depends what kind of holiday you are looking for – but in certain respects the best month is September because the weather is still warm and there are relatively few tourists.

## Geography

The island is made up of rock massifs dating back to the Palaeozoic Age and the predominant rock is granite, modelled by the erosion of the elements into very peculiar forms. The dominant mountain range is the Gennargento, with the three highest peaks: Punta La Marmora (1,834 m/6,017 ft), Monte Bruncu Spina (1,829 m/6,000 ft) and Monte Spada (1,595 m/5,232 ft). The island is mostly mountainous with high hills and plateaux, and a single extensive lowland, the Piana del Campidano, sloping down from Oristano to Cagliari.

The chief characteristic of Sardinia is the variety of landscapes and seascapes enlightened by very bright sunshine. There are hundreds of caves, rivers, lakes, wetlands and natural parks worth visiting.

## Government

Sardinia is an Autonomous Region of Italy with a special constitution. It has its own independent legislative body (the Regional Council of Sardinia). The Government Body is represented by a President and members of the Regional Council (Councillors). Only slightly more than 40 percent of the population is employed (19 percent of population is unemployed). The most productive sector of the economy is the service industry, where tourism plays a key role. Manufacturing and agriculture follow a long way behind.

# Planning the Trip

## Entry Regulations

Citizens from the European Union, USA and Canada can enter Sardinia with a valid passport or identity card. You only need a visa if staying for more than three months. Entry regulations for citizens coming from other countries apply as for the rest of Italy, and visas can be obtained through Italian Embassies. Tourists visiting Sardinia with cats or dogs must present proof at customs of their animals' inoculation against rabies. The vaccination must be given at least 20 days before arrival.

## Customs Regulations

From 1 July 1999, duty free sales within the EU were partly abolished. Goods brought in and exported within the EU incur no additional taxes, provided duty has been paid somewhere within the EU and the goods are for personal consumption.

## Getting There

A potential problem in visiting Sardinia in the summer months is transport: high demand and a limited number of ferries if you plan to arrive by sea mean it is essential to book well in advance.

### BY AIR

You also need to book your flight in advance, especially for the hectic July–August period. There are scheduled flights connecting Sardinia to London all year round, via Verona, with the Sardinian airline Meridiana and with Volare Web

direct to Cagliari. Ryanair has daily connections throughout the year from Stansted to Alghero. Easyjet has a new route from Luton airport to Cagliari and British Airways flies to Cagliari at weekends during the summer. Other European carriers connect Sardinia to the UK and to the rest of Europe during May–October.

In the last few years summer flights have increased because of greater demand. Many air companies of various countries schedule a large number of flights from/to European towns in July and August. Italian national flight carrier Alitalia offers the best connections but sometimes not the best fares, and the route is usually via Rome (40 minutes from Cagliari) or Milan.

The largest airport, Cagliari-Elmas, is 10 minutes drive away from the town centre, and there is a regular bus link *(see Getting Around: From the airport)*. The same is also true of the other two main airports on the island, Olbia and Alghero (Fertilia).

**Airport websites:**
Cagliari:
www.aeroportodicagliari.com
Alghero:
www.algheroaeroporto.it

---

### BY SEA

Advance reservation is vital for visiting Sardinia by boat in the summer, especially if you are taking a car with you. Reservations cannot be accepted by navigation lines for deck seats *(passaggio ponte)* – the most inexpensive way of travelling to Sardinia – unless all the cabin spaces have been sold.

The most important ferry companies, with connections to the rest of Italy, are:
**Moby lines**, tel: 078 927927, fax: 0789 27933, www.moby.it
**Sardinia-Corsica Ferries**, tel: 078 925200, www.corsicaferries.com
**Tirrenia**, from abroad tel: 081 3172999, from Italy tel: 0199 123 199, www.tirrenia.it
**Grandi Navi Veloci**, reservations tel: 010 20945919, www.gnv.it

**Saremar**, from abroad tel: 081 317 2999, from Italy tel: 0199 123 199, www.saremar.it
There is also a ferry to France, run by Compagnie Maritime Toulon-Sardaigne between Toulon and Porto Torres, and one to the north of Africa by Tirrenia (Cagliari–Tunis). There are daily connections between Cagliari and Civitavecchia (Rome), Porto Torres and Genoa, Olbia and Civitavecchia. Other connections include Cagliari with Naples, Palermo, Trapani and Tunis, Olbia with Genoa and Livorno (Tuscany), and Golfo Aranci with Livorno. Crossing from all ports takes about 10 hours, but new high-speed ferries connect Olbia to Civitavecchia in three hours.

## What to Bring

Bring practical, comfortable clothes, shoes or sandals. In summer, particularly at noon, the heat can be unbearable, so it is sensible to equip yourself with a sunhat.

## Maps

Road maps may be obtained free of charge from the Sardinian Tourist Office (ESIT: *see page 294*). For specialised maps (archaeological routes, biking or trekking itineraries), contact the local tourist information office, called PRO LOCO, in the nearest village.

## Airline Numbers

● **Alitalia** information on national flights, tel: 0848 865641; on international flights, tel: 0848 865642, www.alitalia.ie
● **Meridiana** from UK tel: 0845 3555588, or 39 0789 52682, www.meridiana.it
● **Ryanair**, tel: 0871 246 0000, www.ryanair.com
● **Easyjet**, tel: 0905 821 0905, 0871 244 2366, www.easyjet.com
● **British Airways**, tel: 0870 850 9850, www.ba.com

## Tourism Today

More than 3 million visitors come to the island annually, thereby making tourism a significant contributor to the island's economy. It is no secret that most of the money invested in this business has come from outside sources, and that the lion's share of the profits return to these sources.

## Health

No vaccinations are required for visiting Sardinia. In the summer months, problems can arise from over exposure to the sun. Stay out of the sun during the hottest hours and at other times cover up or use plenty of sunscreen, and wear a hat. It is also very important to drink plenty of water to avoid dehydration. If you need urgent medical treatment, call the First Aid number (*Pronto Soccorso*) at one of the main hospitals, or call 113 for emergencies.

## Money

The unit of currency in Sardinia, as in the rest of Italy, is the euro (approximately 1 euro = £0.70, 1 euro = US $1.20). The use of credit cards is rapidly becoming common in Sardinia, and the major international credit cards are accepted almost everywhere. They are particularly useful for settling bills in hotels or campsites, for purchasing expensive items in the bigger shops, or buying petrol. It is, however, advisable to travel with some money already changed into euros. Eurocheques and traveller's cheques can be exchanged in any bank, and they represent the safest way of bringing money into the island, although a commission fee is usually charged by the bank. An increasing number of banks in the major cities and tourist resorts are being equipped with credit card outlets (ATMs), with instructions in several languages.

## Festivals

There's not a day in the entire year when a holiday is not being celebrated somewhere in Sardinia. The tourist information centre publishes a brochure listing 1,000 festivals. Festivities may be held in honour of a town's patron saint or may be island-wide religious celebrations.

**January:** Santa Antonio Abate: a religious festival of pre-Christian origin that ends with large bonfires begin lit. First appearance of carnival masks in Orosei, Abbasanta and Siniscola.

**February:** Carnival is a high point on the Sardinian holiday calendar. Especially worth mentioning is the *Sartiglia*, a horse-riding tournament performed in historical costume, held in Oristano. The archaic ceremonies which take place during the masked parades in Mamoiada and Ottana also present a fascinating spectacle, and the lively carnival in Bosa attracts more and more enthusiasts each year.

**April:** Easter marks another high point on the calendar and is celebrated in many places with processions and brotherhood parades. The *lunissanti* in Castelsardo and Good Friday in Alghero are especially interesting, but impressive processions also take place in Sassari, Cagliari, Nuoro and Oliena.

**May:** The event of the year in Cagliari is the *Sagra di Sant'Efisio*, dedicated to the city's patron saint. Trying to get a room on 1 May in Cagliari is impossible. People dressed in ethnic and historical costumes come from all corners of the country to participate in the procession, beginning in Cagliari and finishing in Nora.

The *cavalcata sarda* in Sassari is a parade of people in ethnic dress or other outfits held solely for the purpose and pleasure of displaying old and valuable costumes. This festivity was resurrected in 1951 by the Rotary Club. In Orosei there is a boat procession on the river Cedrino from Santa Maria 'e Mare.

**July:** On 6 and 7 July the *s'Ardia* takes place in Sedilo, a daring horse race with the finishing line in front of the pilgrimage church of San Costantino. The *s'Ardia* is just as dangerous as it looks and during the race even Sardinian blood begins to boil.

The *Rassegna di Pariglie*, in Ovodda is a traditional Sardinian equestrian sport held in July.

**August:** On the first Sunday of August on the Temo river in Bosa, there's a boat procession called the Santa Maria del Mare. August is a month full of holidays. Two more to be noted for the large number of participants wearing folk costumes are the candle festival, *i candelieri*, in Sassari (14 August) and the procession, *l'Assunta*, in Orgosolo (15 August). In Cabras the Regata de is Fassonis is featuring ancient straw canoes.

## Special Interest Holidays

**Walking holidays**
Alternative Travel, Oxford
Tel: 01865 315678
Andante Travels, Salisbury
Tel: 0172 2713000
Headwater, Northwich
Tel: 01606 720033
**Special interest**
Specialtours, London
Tel: 020 7302297
**Coach holidays**
Page & Moy, Leicester
Tel: 0870 010 6400

Titan Travel, Surrey
Tel: 01293 440 033
**Self-catering holidays**
Sardatour, London
Tel: 020 7242 2455
Voyages Ilena, London
Tel: 020 7924 4440
Magic of Italy, London
Tel: 0870 1660 363
Citalia, Croydon
Tel: 0870 9014 014
Transun Holidays, Oxford
Tel: 0870 4444 747

**September:** The best-known festival in September is the *Sagra di San Salvatore*, held in Cabras. A huge throng of young men carry the holy statue at a trot from the Church of San Salvatore into Cabras.

## Useful Information

The Italian State Tourist Board has offices in most major capitals:
**London**, 1 Princes Street, London W1R 8AY, tel: 020 7408 1254; fax: 020 7399 3567. Brochure line: 008 00 00 482 542. Email: italy@italiantouristboard.co.uk, www.enit.it, www.italiantouristboard.co.uk
**Dublin**, 47 Merrion Square, Dublin 2, tel: 1 766397.
**New York**, 630 Fifth Avenue, Suite 1565, New York, NY 10111, tel: 212 245 5618; fax: 212 586 9249.
**Montreal**, 1 Place Ville Marie, Montreal, Quebec, tel: 514 866 7557; fax: 514 392 1429.
**Rome**, Via Marghera 2/6, Rome 00185, tel: 039 0649711, fax: 039 064463379, email: sedecentrale.enit@interbusiness.it

## Business Hours

Banks are open Monday to Friday 8.30am–1.30pm and (usually) 3–4.30pm. Shops are usually open from 9am–1pm and 5–8pm, but bear in mind that opening hours change from spring to summer.

## Tipping

As a general rule tipping is not a Sardinian custom, although tips are, of course, readily accepted. Most restaurants add a service charge to the bill (usually 10–15 percent), so choosing to leave a tip (*la mancia*) depends on your personal judgement. Your final bill will also include a small cover charge per person, irrespective of consumption. Taxi drivers do not expect a tip, but taxis are expensive. Tariffs are fixed and metered, so there is no haggling.

# Practical Tips

## Media

### NEWSPAPERS

It is possible to find foreign newspapers all year round in Cagliari and Sassari – usually a day late. In summer you can find daily international newspapers and other publications in the tourist centres. The London-based *Guardian* publishes a special European edition which can be bought by noon every day from June to September. There are two daily Sardinian newspapers; the best-selling is *L'Unione Sarda*, based in Cagliari, with a circulation of nearly 100,000 copies; *La Nuova Sardegna*, which mainly serves the northern part of Sardinia, is the regional version of the national *La Repubblica*. Both newspapers are useful, if you know a little Italian, because they run listings sections and also publish transport timetables. All the national Italian newspapers are available in Sardinia and the major ones are printed daily in Cagliari and Sassari.

### TELEVISION

In addition to the three national radio and television broadcasting channels run by RAI (Italian Radio and Television), there are numerous others. There are news bulletins almost every hour of the day, although the most popular are between 1 and 2pm and from 7 to 8.30pm. Cable television and Euro-Channels are also available, as well as Satellite TV. TMC broadcasts the English channel *EuroNews* in the morning (7am) and CNN from 2–7am.

## RADIO

Numerous private radio stations operate, as well as the three national public stations (RAI UNO, DUE, TRE). Most are broadcast on stereo FM. In the northeast of the island, there are also English-language stations serving the NATO bases. There are hourly traffic and weather bulletins on the RAI channels, in co-operation with ACI (Italian Automobile Association). In the summer bulletins are broadcast in English, German and French.

## Public Holidays

- **January** New Year's Day (1st), Epiphany (6th)
- **March/April** Easter Sunday and Monday
- **April** Liberation Day (25th)
- **May** Labour Day (1st)
- **August** Assumption Day (15th)
- **November** All Saints' Day (1st)
- **December** Immaculate Conception (8th), Christmas Day (25th), Santo Stefano (26th)

## Postal Services

Post offices are open Monday to Saturday 8am–1pm. Some main post offices are also open in the afternoon, 3–6pm.
Stamps are available from tobacconists and newsagents displaying a black-and-white T-sign which reads *Valori Bollati*.

## Telecommunications

The local telephone code must be used in front of every dialled number.
Public phone booths, and phones in public places, are no longer common because of the spread of mobile phones. When available, they are bright orange and are operated by TELECOM (the national phone company). Most are operated with a *carta telefonica* (phone card) sold most commonly in units of 5 and 10 euros. The cards can be bought at *edicole* (newsagents), bars, tobacconists, and, of course,

Telecom centres, from which lengthy long-distance calls may also be made.

Telegrams can be sent by phone, by calling 186, or from post offices.

## Tourist Information

The three main bodies in charge of tourism in Sardinia are ESIT (Ente Sardo Industrie Turismo), EPT (Ente Provinciale Turismo), and AAST (Aziende Autonome di Soggiorno e Turismo). Information is given in English, German, French and Spanish on request.

**ESIT**
Via Mameli 97, **Cagliari** 09124, tel: 070 664195; toll free from Italy: 8000013153; www.esit.net; e-mail: enturismoca@tiscalinet.it
There are also information offices at the airport, station and the port:
**Cagliari Airport** tel: 070 240200.
**Stazione Marittima** tel: 070 668352; email: enturismoca@tiscali.it
**Cagliari Port**: 070 668352.

**EPT**
Piazza Deffenu 9, **Cagliari** 09125, tel: 070 604241; fax: 070 663207; toll free number from Italy: 800203541.
Piazza Italia 19, **Nuoro** 08100, tel: 0784 30083/32307; fax: 0784 33432; e-mail: info@enteturismo.nuoro.it
Piazza Eleonora D'Arborea 19, **Oristano** 09170, tel: 0783 36831; fax: 0783 3683206; email: enturismo.oristano@tiscali.it
Viale Caprera 36, **Sassari** 07100, tel: 079 299544/299546/299579; fax: 079 299415.
Ufficio informazione Aeroporto **Alghero Fertilia**, tel: 079 935124

**AAST**
The website for all AAST offices is: www.regione.sardegna.it
Piazza Portaterra 9, **Alghero** 07041, tel: 079 979054; fax: 079 974881/974881; email: inotourism@infoalghero.it.
Via Lungomare Andrea Doria,

**Cannigione** 07020, tel: 0789 892019; fax: 0789 88149; e-mail aast.arzachena@regione.sardegna.it
Via Mameli 97, **Cagliari** 09124, tel: 070 664195/664196.
Piazza Matteotti 9, **Cagliari**, tel: 070 669255; fax: 070 664923; e-mail: aastca@tiscalinet.it; www.tiscalinet.it.aast-ca
Loc. Cala Gavetta, **La Maddalena** 07024, tel: 0789 736321.
Via Nazionale 94, **Palau** 07020, tel: 0789 709570; fax: 0789 709570; e-mail: aast.lmdpalau@tiscalinet.it
Via Machiavelli 3, **Muravera** 09043, tel: 070 990121; e-mail: aast.muravera@regione.sardegna.it
Piazza Italia 12, **Costa Rei** (summer only), tel: 070 991350.
Via Catello Piro 1, **Olbia** 07026, tel: 0789 21453, fax: 0789 22221.
Golfo Aranci, tel: 0789 21672.
**Olbia-Costa Smeralda Airport**, tel: 0789 21453.
Piazza V. Emanuele 24, **Santa Teresa di Gallura** 07028, tel: 0789 754127; fax: 0789 754185; e-mail: aaststg@tiscalinet.it
Via Brigata Sassari 19, **Sassari** 07100, tel: 079 233534/231331; fax: 079 237585; e-mail: aastss@tiscalinet.it

## Medical Treatment

### Insurance
EU residents are entitled to free or reduced healthcare that becomes necessary during your visit but from January 2006 your E111 will cease to be valid and you will need a European Health Insurance Card (EHIC). Apply for a card online at www.ehic.org.uk (delivery in 7 days); or by calling 0845 606 2030 (delivery in 10 days); or pick up an application pack from the Post Office (delivery in 21 days). The EHIC does not cover you for repatriation in case of illness, so you should consider taking out ordinary travel insurance.

### Illness
Vaccinations are not required, although cholera and typhoid jabs are a wise precaution if you intend to

travel on to North Africa. The worst that's likely to happen to you health-wise is suffering from the extreme heat in summer – wear a hat and drink plenty of fluid – or getting an upset stomach – shellfish is usually to blame. Tap water is safe to drink, unless there is a sign saying "acqua non potabile".

### Pharmacies
Italian pharmacists are well qualified to give you advice on minor ailments. There's usually one open all night in the bigger towns. They work on a rota system, and to find the one staying open, check the listings posted on pharmacy doors, or in the local paper.

### Dental Treatment
This is not covered by the health service (*mutua*), and is very expensive.

## Environmental Organisations

**Lega Ambiente**, Via Manno 22, Cagliari, 09124, tel: 070 671003/070 494437.
**World Wildlife Fund**, Via Sonnino 205, Cagliari, 09100, tel: 070 670308.
**Amici della Terra**, Via Cocco Ortu 32, Cagliari, tel/fax: 070 490904.

## Embassies and Consulates

**Great Britain**, Viale Colombo 160, Quartu S. Elena, tel: 070 828 628. Other nationals should contact their embassies or consulates in Rome (phone numbers available at tourist offices).

## Security and Crime

There are no special problems in Sardinia as far as personal security and safety are concerned, and no specific areas where tourists are targeted. The main problem for tourists is petty crime: pickpocketing, bag snatching, and theft from cars. As when travelling anywhere, common

- **Police**, tel: 112
- **Ambulance**
tel: 118
- **Traffic Police**
tel: 113
- **Fire Brigade** (Vigili de Fuoco),
tel: 115
- **ACI** (Automobile Club of Italy),
tel: 803116
- **Corpo Forestale** (environment),
tel: 1515
- **Coastguard** (Soccorso in
mare), tel: 1530
- **Shipping forecast** (Ballentino
Nautico), tel: 899 111202
- **Road conditions**, tel: 1518
- **Weather forecast**, tel: 412
- **Minor first-aid** (e.g. sunburn)
can be obtained free from the
Pronto Soccorso (Medical
Standby/First Aid) in all hospitals
or Guardie Mediche.

sense should prevail: bags,
cameras and other valuables
should never be left unattended in
cars, on beaches, or anywhere
else. Leave money and valuables,
including airline tickets, in the
hotel safe. Hitchhiking and walking
are as safe as anywhere, if not
safer.

## Italian Embassies Abroad

**Australia**: Level 45, Macquarie
Place, Sydney 2000 NSW, tel: 02
9392 7900.
**Britain**: No. 14, Three Kings' Yard,
London W1Y 2EH, GB, tel: 0207
312 2000.
**Canada**: 275 Slater St, Ottawa,
Ontario K1P 5H9, tel: 613 232 2401.
**USA**: 3000 Whitehaven Street, NW
Washington DC, tel: 02612 4400.

## Smoking

Smoking is not allowed in places
that can be defined as "public" or
in restaurants and bars unless they
have a separate air-conditioned
area for smokers. Smoking in
prohibited areas risks a fine of
between 25 and 250 euros.

# Getting Around

## From the Airport

**From Alghero International**
There is a FDS bus connection from
the airport to the city. Journey time
is about 25 minutes and the fare is
€0.57. A taxi costs €25 and takes
15 minutes.
**From Cagliari International**
A shuttle bus connects the airport
to the city centre. The journey time
is about 10–15 minutes and the
fare is €0.75. A taxi costs about
€15 and takes about 10 minutes.

## Public Transport

### BY TRAIN

Trains are run by **FS** (Ferrovie dello
Stato, tel: 892021), **FDS** (Ferrovie
della Sardegna, tel: 070 342341),
**FCA** (Ferrovie Complementari) and
**FMS** (Ferrovie Meridionali della
Sardegna, tel: 8000 44553).
The main train station is in Cagliari;
the main line is Cagliari–Oristano–
Porto Torres. Travelling by train in
Sardinia is sometimes slow but
worthwhile for the spectacular
landscapes. A small **"green"** train
runs from Cagliari to Sorgono or
Arbatax for more than 100 km (60
miles) through beautiful valleys and
mountains (the locomotive is the
same one that D.H. Lawrence took
in 1921). Contact: FDS, tel: 800
460220; website:
www.treninoverde.com, e-mail:
treninov@tin.it

### BY BUS

There is an extensive and efficient
network of buses and coaches with
services run by both public and
private companies. The most
reliable companies in the area are:
**ARST** (Azienda Regionale Sarda
Trasporti, tel: 800 865042, from
Sardinia, tel: 070 4998324),
**Autolinee Pani** (a private company,
tel: 079 236983),
**Turmo Travel** (a private company,
tel: 0789 21487).
It takes three hours to travel non-
stop from one end of the island to
the other (Cagliari–Sassar–Olbia).

## TAXIS

**Cagliari**, Radio Taxi: 070 400101.
**Sassari**, Radio Taxi: 079 260060.
**Oristano**: 0783 74328/70280.
**Nuoro**: 0784 31411.

## Private Transport

### BY CAR

When entering Sardinia in a car,
you'll need an international
insurance card – *Carta Verde* (Green
Card) – which should be obtained
from your own insurance company
before leaving home. The biggest
danger to unwary visiting drivers in
not poor roads but the bad driving
habits of the locals. Be warned also
that petrol in Italy and Sardinia is
quite expensive.

### *Driver's Licences*
Members of the EU who have a
national driver's licence may drive
and hire cars; non-EU drivers should
hold an International Driving Licence.

### *Car Hire*
If you want to hire a car, there are
a number of rental companies,
both international and national,
and their offices are located not
only at the airports and ports but

## Validating Tickets

It is important to remember to
validate your bus or rail ticket
before you travel. There are
machines for date-stamping your
rail ticket on station platforms
and similar machines on buses.

## Driving Information

- Seat bealts are compulsory
- The use of headlights is compulsory outside urban centres
- Children should travel in the backseat
- Maximum speed in built up areas is 50 km/h (30 mph), in other areas it is 90 km/h (55 mph). The Carlo Felice may seem like a motorway but it is not; speed limits vary along it (maximum speed is 90 km/h).
- *Senso Unico* means One Way

in towns and seaside resorts. It is advisable, once again, to book well in advance to ensure you get the vehicle you prefer (especially in August). Expect slightly higher prices than those in GB and Northern Europe in general, but good deals can be obtained through travel agencies and flight carriers when purchasing package holidays. The following is a selection of the main car hire outlets, but there are many more.

**Cagliari**
Avis, Railway Station, tel: 070-668128, Elmas Airport, tel: 070-240081.
Budget Rent-a-Car, Elmas Airport, tel: 070-240310, fax: 070-240310.
Hertz Rent a Car, Elmas Airport, tel: 070-240037.
Maggiore Rent-a-Car, Viale Monastir 116, tel: 070-273692, Elmas Airport, tel: 070-240069.
Matta Autonoleggio, Elmas Airport, tel: 070-240050
**Alghero**
Avis, Fertilia Airport, tel: 079-935064.
Budget Rent-a-Car, Fertilia Airport, tel: 079-935060.
Maggiore Rent-a-Car, Fertilia Airport, tel: 079-935045.
**Olbia**
Avis, Costa Smeralda Airport, tel: 0789-69540, Via Genova 67, tel: 0789-22420.
Budget Rent-a-Car, Costa Smeralda Airport, tel: 0789-69605; fax: 0789-66003.
Maggiore Rent-a-Car, Via G. Mameli

2, tel: 0789-22131, Costa Smeralda Airport, tel: 0789-69457.
**Oristano**
ACI Rent-a-Car/Eurorent, Via Cagliari 39, tel: 0783-212458.
Avis, Via Liguria 17/19, tel: 0783-310638.
Sardinya Rent-a-Car, Via Cagliari, tel: 0783-73389/74084.
**Sassari**
Avis, Predda Niedda, Sassari, tel: 079-260648/079-260122; fax: 079-260751.
Maggiore Rent-a-Car, Viale Italia 3, tel: 079-233507.

### Main Roads
The main road connecting the south of Sardinia with the north is the SS 131 (Carlo Felice), built in four lanes. It starts in Cagliari and reaches Porto Torres, passing by Oristano; near Abbasanta the road divides and a new branch now reaches Olbia: the SS 131 dir. The other main road is the SS 125 going from Cagliari to Arzachena, following the coast; it is a slow road which usually takes longer than anticipated, often because of lorries or campers (during the summer) which don't allow overtaking.

### Parking
Large towns like Cagliari have adopted "blue stripes" parking places: each parking place is marked with a blue line indicating that you must pay. Look for an official with a blue badge (0.50 euros for 1 hour). Always lock your car when parked; never leave anything valuable in the car and leave belongings in the boot.

## Boat Excursions

**La Maddalena** (SS): to reach the islands of the archipelago (La Maddalena and Caprera) you have to take a ferry from Palau. The crossing takes only 20 minutes and ferries run every 15 minutes during the day. The **Consorzio degli Operatori Turistici dell'Arcipelago della Maddalena**: tel: 0789 727373

organises daily excursions to the other islands of the archipelago (10am–5pm).
**Isola dei Cávoli** (CA): from Villasimius port, take the Tour Express, tel: 0339 7181193, (10am–1pm).
**Matilda,** sailing boat, (10am–5pm), tel: 0330 638234.
**Fiore di Maggio** (10am–5pm), tel: 0348 7393723.
**Donna Rosa,** tel: 0789 615130
**Golfo di Orosei:**
**Nuovo Consorzio Trasporti Marittimi Cala Gonone**, tel. 0784 93305 (9am–6.30pm).
**Isola S. Pietro:**
**Tabarka,** Carloforte, tel: 0781 855055 (10.30am–1pm).
**Cartur,** Carloforte, tel: 0781 854331 (10.30am–1pm).
**Alghero: Traghetti Navisarda,** tel: 079 950603.

## Regional Parks

- **Parco del Limbara** (Sassari province)
- **Parco del Monte Arci** (Oristano province)
- **Parco della Giava** (between the three provinces of Cagliari, Oristano and Nuoro)
- **Parco del Linas-Marganai** (Cagliari province), famous for wild deer and royal eagles
- **Parco dei Sette Fratelli** around Cagliari; takes its name from the seven peaks dominating the area
- **Parco del Sulcis** (Cagliari province); the largest, and home to more than 300 wild deer
- **Parco del Molentargius,** located within the Sardinian capital, Cagliari. More than 1,000 pink flamingos are been bred here each year.

There are two national parks: **Parco Nazionale dell'Arcipelago di La Maddalena**, in the north east of the island and the **Parco Nazionale dell'Asinara** in the north west. Also two Sea National Parks have been designated: **Parco Marino Nazionale del Golfo di Orosei** on the eastern coast, and the **Parco Marino Nazionale di Tavolara.**

# Where to Stay

## Accommodation

There is a wide range of accommodation available: hotels, tourist villages, holiday homes/flats for rental, campsites, youth hostels, and the rapidly expanding field of Agriturismo (farm holidays) and B&B. It's best to decide what kind of holiday you want and, if possible, make reservations – especially during the high season.

It is impossible to list all the agencies and useful addresses here, but further information may be found by calling the local PRO LOCO (Town Hall Information Service), or getting the free booklet (published every year by each EPT – *see page 294*) listing all the hotels and campsites in Sardinia (Annuario hotels & camping). Each province publishes only it's own. 'Loc.' stands for *località* (locality).

## Hotels

### CAGLIARI PROVINCE

#### *Cagliari*
**Calamosca Sul Mare**
Viale Calamosca 50
Tel: 070 371628
Fax: 070 370346
www.hotelcalamosca.it
On the cliffs about 3 km (1½ miles) outside the city, with beautiful views, a large garden and a private beach. You'll need a car if you choose to stay here. **$$**
**Mediterraneo**
Viale Colombo 56
Tel: 070 342361
Fax: 070 301274
www.hotelmediterraneo.net
Luxurious accommodation, with renowned bar and patisserie; faces the Basilica Bonaria on one

side, the sea on the other. **$$$**
**Regina Margherita**
V. Le Regina Margherita 44
Tel: 070 670342
Fax: 070 668325
www.hotelreginamargherita.com
Elegant central location; fully air conditioned. **$$$**
**Italia**
Via Sardegna 31
Tel: 070 660410
Fax: 070 650240
e-mail: hotelitalia@tiscalinet.it
Located in the heart of La Marina, near to all restaurants and port. **$$**
**Jolly hotel**
Circonvallazione Nuova Pirri
Tel: 070 529060
Fax: 070 502222
www.jollyhotel.it
Located on the main roundabout at the entrance of town. **$$$**
**Ulivi e Palme**
Via Membo 25
Tel: 070 485861
Fax: 070 486970
www.uliviepalme.it
Small apartments with cooking facilities; private pool, garden, gymnasium, tennis courts. **$$**
**Quattro Mori**
Via G.M. Angioy 27
Tel: 070 668535
Fax: 070 666087
www.hotel4mori.it
Comfortable hotel in the heart of the city; private taxi service to anywhere in town. **$$**
**Miramare**
Via Roma 59
Tel: 070 664021
Situated near the harbour. **$**

#### **East of Cagliari**
#### *Quartu Sant'Elena*
**Califfo**
Via Leonardo da Vinci 118
Tel: 070 890131
Fax: 070 890134
www.hotelcaliffo.com
Important conference centre; pool and tennis courts; 20 km (12 miles) from Cagliari. **$$**
**Best Western Italia**
Via Panzini
Tel: 070 827070
Fax: 070 827071
e-mail: hitalia.quartu@tiscalinet.it
A mile from the Poetto beach. **$$$**

### Price Guide

Approximate prices for a double room per night. Some hotels include breakfast in the price: check when booking.
● Luxury = **$$$$** (over 200 euro)
● Expensive = **$$$** (95–200 euro)
● Moderate = **$$** (60–95 euro)
● Inexpensive = **$** (under 60 euro)

**Il Monastero**
Geremeas
Tel/fax: 070 802200
Built on the ruins of an old monastery, this hotel has a lot of character; excellent pizzas. **$$$**
**Sighientu**
Via Serchio
Tel: 070 870072
Fax: 070 870075
www.altamarea.it
Elegant, newly built hotel. **$$$**

#### *Villasimius*
**Cala Caterina**
Via Lago Maggiore
Tel: 070 797410
Fax: 070 797473
www.mobygest.it
By a small bay; swimming pool; attractive and very relaxing. **$$$$**
**Fiore di Maggio**
Campulongu
Tel: 070 797382
Fax: 070 797382
Specialised for all diving activities, including a special swimming pool for learners. **$**
**Stella Maris**
Campulongu
Tel: 070 797100
Fax: 070 797367
www.stella-maris.com
About 2 km (1 mile) out of Villasimius, in a pine wood by the beach. **$$$**
**Tanka Village**
Tanca Elmas
Tel: 070 7951
Fax: 070 797008
www.tankavillage.com
A tourist village 45 km (28 miles) from Cagliari, positioned along a white sandy beach, it offers a large number of facilities, including specialised courses in windsurfing and sailing. **$$$**

### Castiadas
**Sant'Elmo Beach**
Sant'Elmo
Tel: 070 995161
Fax: 070 995140
www.santelmo.it
Attractively built of local stone; private beach; water sports and horse riding available. **$$$**

### Muravera
**Alba Ruja**
Via Colombo
Tel: 070 991557
Fax: 070 991459
www.albaruja.it
New and stylish residential complex; private pool, tennis courts; good pizza. **$$$**
**Free Beach Club**
Via Ichnusa 25
Costa Rei
Tel: 070 991041
Fax: 070 991054
www.gestitur.it
Situated in the renowned Costa Rei, this is one of the more popular resorts of the province of Cagliari. It offers excellent facilities, including swimming pools, private gardens, several bars and restaurants and a private beach. The hotel organises trekking, horse riding, free climbing and parasailing, as well as watersports. **$$$**

### West of Cagliari
### Assemini
**Il Grillo**
Via Carmine 132
Tel: 070 946350
Fax: 070 946826
www.hotelgrillo.it
Best known disco in the area; cocktail bar; private pool in beautiful garden; 30 km (18 miles) from Cagliari. **$$$**

### Calasetta (Isola di Sant'Antioco)
**Hotel Cala di Seta**
Via R. Margherita 61
Tel: 0781 88304
Fax: 0781 88204
www.hotelcaladiseta.it
Central; good restaurant serving local specialities; horse riding and sailing excursions can be arranged. **$$$**

**Luci del Faro**
Mangiabarche
Tel: 0781 810089
Fax: 0781 810091
www.hotellucidelfaro.com
Out in the countryside with a good view of the coast. **$$$**

### Carloforte (Isola di San Pietro)
**Hieracon**
Corso Cavour 63
Tel: 0781 854028
Fax: 0781 854893
www.hotelhieracon.cjb.net
Elegant and central; excellent fish dishes in the restaurant; fully air conditioned; lovely garden. **$$**

### Iglesias
**Hotel Artu**
Piazza Quintino Sella 15
Tel: 0781 22492
Fax: 0781 32448
www.hotelartuiglesias.it
Located in an elegant square; comfortable accommodation and a good restaurant. **$$**

### Domus de Maria-Chia
**Le Meridien Chia Laguna**
Chia
Tel: 070 92391
Fax: 070 9230141
www.lemeridien-chialaguna.com
Situated in the renowned dune area of Chia beach; excellent cuisine; pool; attractive garden; water sports and riding organised. **$$$$**

### Narcao
**Rosas**
Terrubia
Tel: 0781 959401
Fax: 0781 959402
Set in a private park, not far from the sea; swimming pool and organised excursions to nearby archaeological sites. **$$$**

### Pula
**Forte Village**
Santa Margherita
Tel: 070 92171
Fax: 070 921246
www.fortevillageresort.com
The best known hotel in the province of Cagliari, 40 km (25 miles) from the capital on the

southwest side of the island; private beach, several swimming pools, Sardinian and international restaurants; famous for its thalassotherapy centre and as a conference venue; a favourite of the stars. **$$$$**
**Is Molas Golf Hotel**
Is Molas
Tel: 070 9241006
Fax: 070 9241002
www.ismolas.it
Thirty kilometres (18 miles) from Cagliari; has the second best golf course in Sardinia; lying on gentle hills, it is known as golfers' paradise; the hotel's good too. **$$$**
**Baia di Nora**
Loc. Su Guventeddu
Tel: 070 9245551
Fax: 070 9245600
www.hotelbaiadinora.com
Very elegant; nice swimming pool; on the beach at Nora. **$$$$**

### Sant'Antìoco
**L'Eden**
Piazza Parrocchia 15/17
Tel: 0781 840768
Fax: 0781 840769
www.albergoleden.com
Large neoclassical building in the main square; comfortable rooms; renowned restaurant; air conditioning; private parking. **$$**
**Moderno**
Via Nazionale 82
Tel: 0781 83105
Fax: 0781 840252
www.tiscali.it/albergomoderno
On the main street; good service; restaurant serves local specialities. **$$**

### North of Cagliari
### Barumini
**Sa Iolla**
Via Cavour 49
Tel: 070 9368419
Fax: 070 9361107
e-mail: salollarist@libero.it
A few hundred metres away from the important archaeological site of Su Nuraxi, this is part of a restored Sardinian home; good restaurant. **$**

### Sardara
**Hotel Terme di Sardara**
Loc. Santa Maria

Tel: 070 9387200
Fax: 070 9387582
www.termedisardara.it
In the heart of the island, built on
the site of a Roman thermal bath;
offers spa facilities plus pool,
tennis and gymnasium. Good
location for island excursions. **$$**
**Eucalipti terme**
Loc.Santa Maria
Tel: 070 9385044
Fax: 070 9385345
www.termesardegna.it
New hotel with spa facilities. **$$**

*Arbus Piscinas*
**Le Dune**
Via Bau 1
Tel: 070 977130
Fax: 070 977230
www.leduneingurtosu.it
Completely isolated at the end of a
long dirt road, on the beach
between high dunes; a unique
setting for nature lovers. **$$$**

*Villanovaforru*
**Le Colline**
Loc. Funtana Jannus
Tel: 070 9300123
Fax: 070 9300134
Small hotel with good restaurant. **$**

---

## NUORO PROVINCE

*Nuoro Fratelli Sacchi*
**Grazia Deledda**
Via Lamarmora
Tel: 0784 31257
Fax: 0784 31258
In the heart of the city; comfortable
hotel with a well regarded
restaurant serving local
specialities. **$$$**
**Paradiso**
Via Aosta
Tel: 0784 35585
Fax: 0784 32286
Centrally located, private parking;
great restaurant; popular disco. **$$**

*Aritzo*
**Castello**
Corso Umberto
Tel/Fax: 0784 629266
Located in the centre of town;
large and comfortable with private
parking and a wonderful garden. **$$**

**Sa Muvara**
Via Funtana Rubia
Tel: 0784 629336
Fax: 0784 629433
Just outside town, this large elegant
complex has a pool and disco;
known for Sardinian specialities in
the excellent restaurant. **$$$**

## Price Guide

Approximate prices for a double
room per night. Some hotels
include breakfast in the price:
check when booking.
● Luxury = **$$$$** (over 200 euro)
● Expensive = **$$$** (95–200 euro)
● Moderate = **$$** (60–95 euro)
● Inexpensive = **$** (under 60 euro)

*Baunei*
**Santa Maria**
Via Plammas
Tel: 0782 615315
Fax: 0782 615396
Comfortable hotel. **$/$$**

*Belvì*
**L'Edera**
Via Roma
Tel: 0784 629898
Fax: 0784 629519
Family run; organises excursions;
horse riding. **$**

*Bitti*
**Su Lithu**
Loc. Sa Pineta
Tel: 0784 413012
Fax: 0784 413205
Many excursions nearby in the high
plateau. **$$$**

*Bosa*
**Mannu Hotel**
Via Alghero
Tel: 0785 375306
Fax: 0785 375308
Central and comfortable; private
parking and taxi service; good
restaurant. **$$**
**Perry Clan**
Via Alghero
Tel: 0785 373074
Fax: 0785 375263
Small, central and comfortable;
interesting building; pleasant
restaurant. **$**

**Al Gabbiano**
Viale Mediterraneo
Tel/Fax: 0785 374123
Facing the sea in Bosa Marina; air
conditioning; good seafood. **$$**
**Costa Corallo**
Via Colombo 11/13
Tel: 0785 375162
Fax: 0785 375528
On the coral coast, as its name
implies; beautiful sea views;
comfortable rooms; good
restaurant. **$$**
**Miramare**
Via Colombo
Tel: 0785 373400
Near the sea, hence its name. **$**

*Budoni-Agrustos*
**Li Cucutti**
Fraz. Agrustos
Tel: 0784 846001
Fax: 0784 846072
A wonderful residential village,
circled by pine woods, not far from
the Costa Smeralda, offering the
optimal combination of sea and
countryside; swimming pools and
discos; facilities ideal for group
activities. **$$$**

*Desulo*
**Gennargentu**
Via Kennedy
Tel/Fax: 0784 619270
Mountain setting; lovely views; good
cuisine; large playground. **$**
**La Nuova**
Via Lamarmora
Tel: 0784 619251
Family-run hotel on the main
road, with a good restaurant;
convenient base for mountain
excursions. **$**

*Dorgali*
**Il Querceto**
Via Lamarmora
Tel: 0784 96509
Fax: 0784 95254
Small, seasonal hotel; conveniently
located and comfortable;
garden; tennis courts; private
parking. **$$$**
**Monteviore**
Loc. Monteviore
Tel: 0784 96293
Fax: 0784 96293
Small hotel in the countryside. **$$**

### Dorgali – Cala Gonone
**Costa Dorada**
Via Lungomare
Tel: 0784 93332
Fax: 0784 93445
Seafront location, overlooking the bay of Cala Gonone; ideal starting point for private or organised boat trips along the coastline. The famous Grotto del Bue Marino (Seals' Caves) are less than 30 minutes away. **$$$**
**Palamasera**
Viale Bue Marino
Tel: 0784 93191
Fax: 0784 93072
Also an ideal location for visiting the caves and the Cala Luna beach; organised excursions can be taken to both places; comfortable rooms; good local specialities in the restaurant; garden with pool and tennis courts. **$$$**
**Cala Luna**
Via Lungomare
Tel: 0784 93133
Fax: 0784 93162
Pleasant hotel; well situated for visiting the Bue Marino caves. **$$**
**Piccolo Hotel**
Via C. Colombo
Tel: 0784 93232
Small pleasant hotel;
July–September only. **$**

### Fonni
**Cualbu**
Viale del Lavoro
Tel: 0784 57054
Fax: 0784 58403
Large comfortable hotel in village centre; great views; private parking; horse riding excursions. **$$**
**Sporting Club**
Monte Spada
Tel: 0784 57285
Fax: 0784 57220
Ten kilometres (6 miles) from the Monte Spada ski-lifts; excellent swimming pool; horse-riding excursions arranged; good place to try wild boar. **$$**

### Lanusei
**Villa Selene**
Coroddis
Tel: 0782 42471
Fax: 0782 41214
Surrounded by woods in the centre of the island; fresh water from an underground spring; garden with pool; splendid place to relax and enjoy local specialities. **$$**

### Oliena
**Su Gologone**
Su Gologone
Tel: 0784 287512
Fax: 0784 287668
Swimming pool, tennis, riding; surrounded by the Supramonte Mountains, where pure fresh water rises from an underground spring; famous for its restaurant, one of the top 10 in Sardinia; specialities include roast suckling pig, ravioli filled with ricotta or *pecorino* cheese, and delicious pastries. **$$$**
**Monte Maccione**
Monte Maccione
Tel: 0784 288363
Fax: 0784 288473
In a very panoramic location on the side of the mountain, a simple and relaxing hotel with few rooms. **$**
**Ci Kappa**
Via M.L. King
Tel: 0784 288733
Centre of village, only 6 rooms; friendly, breakfast included. **$**

### Orosei
**Lawrence**
Via del Mare
Tel: 0784 98009
Fax: 0784 997034
Named in honour of D.H. Lawrence who described his visit to the town; located half way between the beach and the centre. Minimum seven day stay. **$$$**
**Orosei Cala Liberotto**
**Cala Ginepro**
Loc. Cala Ginepro
Tel: 0784 91047
Fax: 0784 91222
Ideal for families and activities. Cabaret in the evening; excursions. **$$$**
**Club Hotel Torre Moresca**
Cala Liberotto
Tel: 0784 91230
Fax: 0784 91222
Beautiful beach, Sardinian-style; organises boat excursions. **$$$**

### Posada
**Fior di Sardegna**
S. Giovanni
Tel: 0784 810389
Fax: 0784 810659
Comfortable accommodation. **$$**

### Seui
**Moderno**
Via Roma
Tel: 0782 54621
Family run, simple,central hotel, with a good restaurant. **$**

### San Teodoro
**Due Lune**
Loc. Punta Aldia
Tel: 0784 864075
Fax: 0784 864017
Close to beautiful beaches. **$$$$**

### Tonara
**Belvedere**
Via del Belvedere
Tel: 0784 610054
Fax: 0784 63756
Small comfortable hotel. **$$**

### Tortoli' – Arbatax
**Villaggio Telis**
Porto Frailis
Tel: 0782 667790
Fax: 0782 667795
Located on the red rocks of Arbatax; good night life in summer; excellent gymnasium, several pools, tennis courts, watersports, horse riding; private beach. **$$$**

### Urzulei
**Silana**
SS 125 Orientale Sarda
Tel: 0784 95120
Family-run; panoramic views; local cuisine. Good for excursions. **$**

## ORISTANO PROVINCE

### Arborea
**Ala Birdi**
Strada No. 24
Tel: 0783 805083
Fax: 0783 801086
A few kilometres from Oristano on the coast; one of the most important equestrian centres in Italy; excellent hotel facilities including swimming pools, private beach, tennis courts; dancing; two good restaurants; summer only. **$$$**

## Oristano

**Hotel I.S.A.**
Piazza Marianao 50
Tel/Fax: 0783 360101
In the town's main square;
air conditioning; very
comfortable; offers facilities for
disabled people. **$$**

**Hotel Mistral**
Via XX Settembre
Tel: 0783 210389
Fax: 0783 211000
Excellent hotel, centrally located;
pool; two restaurants offering local
and international cuisine. **$$**

**Piccolo Hotel**
Via Martignano 19
Tel: 0783 71500
A small comfortable hotel which
makes an excellent base for visiting
the area. **$**

## Cabras San Salvatore di Sinis

**Sinis Vacanze Sa Pedrera**
7½km (4 miles) along the road to
San Giovanni
Tel: 0783 370018
Fax: 0783 370040
Isolated between lagoons; good
base for different beaches. **$$**

---

## SASSARI PROVINCE

## Sassari

**Frank Hotel**
Via A. Diaz 20
Tel/Fax: 079 276456
On a main street near the centre;
comfortable rooms; private parking.
**$$**

**Grazia Deledda**
Viale Dante 47
Tel: 079 271235
Fax: 079 280884
www.hotelgraziadeledda.it
Centrally located, recently
refurbished; excellent restaurant. **$$**

**Leonardo da Vinci**
Via Roma 79
Tel: 079 280744
Fax: 079 276456
Close to the central piazza; large
neoclassical building; good service;
private parking. **$$**

**Marini Due**
Via Pietro Nenni 2
Tel: 079 277282
Fax: 079 280300

e-mail: hotelmarini2@hotmail.com
Near the centre; large and
comfortable; restaurant, bar,
garden; private parking. **$$**

## Alghero

**La Playa**
Via Pantelleria 14
Tel: 079 950369
Fax: 079 985713
On the seafront south of town;
swimming pool in a beautiful
garden; local fish specialities in the
restaurant. **$$**

## Price Guide

Approximate prices for a
double room per night. Some
hotels include breakfast in the
price: check when booking.
● Luxury = **$$$$** (over 200 euro)
● Expensive = **$$$** (95–200 euro)
● Moderate = **$$** (60–95 euro)
● Inexpensive = **$** (under 60 euro)

**Oasis**
Viale 1 Maggio
Tel: 079 950526
Fax: 079 953432
www.hoteloasis.it
Large modern hotel just outside
town; garden, pool, tennis court;
popular disco. **$$$**

**Normandie**
Via E. Mattei
Tel: 079 975302
Fax: 079 975302
e-mail: hotelnormandie@excite.it
Family-run hotel with pleasant
service; close to the historic centre
of town. **$**

**Hotel Catalunya**
Via Catalogna 24
Tel: 079 953172
Fax: 079 953177
www.hotelcatalunya.it
Beautifully located facing the port
and backing on to public gardens.
**$$$**

**Villa Las Tronas**
Lungomare Valencia 1
Tel: 079 981818
Fax: 079 981044
www.hvlt.com
A former royal palace of the Catalan
kings. A favourite with British
tourists. **$$$$**

## Alghero – Fertilia

**Bellavista**
Lungomare Rovigno 13
Tel: 079 930190
Fax: 079 930124
e-mail: bellavistafertilia@tiscali.it
Large hotel with beautiful views,
as the name suggests; good
service; pleasant garden. **$$**

**Dei Pini**
Le Bombarde
Tel: 079 930157
Fax: 079 930259
www.hoteldeipini.it
Overlooking the spectacular Le
Bombarde beach; pool, tennis court,
gymnasium, garden; sailing and
riding excursions organised. **$$$**

## Alghero – Porto Conte

**Baia di Conte**
Tel: 079 949000
Fax: 079 949021
www.valtur.it
Set in a wonderful bay; high
standard of service and comfort;
private beach; pool, sauna,
gymnasium; excellent food; summer
only. **$$**

**Capo Caccia**
Loc Tramariglio
Tel: 079 946666
Fax: 079 946535
www.hotelcapocaccia.it
Located on the cliff above the
Neptune Caves; spectacular views;
highly recommended restaurant;
private beach; pool; boat excursions
organised; summer only. **$$$**

**El Faro**
Porto Conte
Tel: 079 942010
Fax: 079 942030
www.hotelelfaro.it
Top quality hotel situated on a
private beach; summer only. **$$$$**

**Porto Conte**
Tel: 079 942035
Fax: 079 942045
www.hotelportoconte.com
Located in a small gulf just north of
Alghero; private harbour; boat
excursions available; comfortable
rooms; restaurant in a splendid
garden; summer only. **$$$**

## Arzachena

**Hotel Delfino**
Viale Costa Smeralda

Tel: 0789 83420
Fax: 0789 83542
www.delfinohotel.it
Very comfortable; private parking;
air conditioning; 6 km (4 miles)
from Cannigione, 15 km (9 miles)
from Porto Rotondo. Although it
falls into the expensive category, it
is very reasonable by the standards
of the area. **$$$**

**Citti**
Viale Costa Smeralda 197
Tel: 0789 82662
Fax: 0789 81920
www.wel.it/hotelcitti
Medium-sized hotel on village main
street; good service; pool. **$$**

### Palau

**Cala di Lepre Park Hotel**
Capo d'Orso
Tel: 0789 702142
Fax: 0789 770281
www.delphina.it
Located by the famous Bear Rock,
this large and luxurious hotel offers
every comfort, plus pool, tennis
courts, gymnasium; bar and
restaurant in a beautiful garden. **$$$**

**Capo d'Orso**
Loc.Capo d'orso
Tel: 0789 702000
Fax: 0789 702009
www.delphina.it
On the Cala di Capra beach, with
one of the best views over to the
islands; excursions are organised.
Good restaurant; every luxury you
could want in this excellent hotel.
**$$$$**

**Excelsior Vanna**
Via Capo d'Orso 100
Tel/fax: 0789 709589
For location, comfort and views,
this hotel is hard to beat; garden
restaurant and private parking; very
reasonable considering its location.
**$$**

**Hotel Palau**
Via Baragge
Tel: 0789 708468
Fax: 0789 709817
www.palauhotel.it
Beautiful view over the Archipelago,
but could offer more. **$$$**

**Le Dune**
Porto Pollo
Tel: 0789 704013
Fax: 0789 704113

www.hotelledune.it
A good alternative to Porto Cervo
hotels: much more reasonable and
an equally beautiful setting; good
restaurant; garden; private parking.
**$$$**

## Price Guide

Approximate prices for a double
room per night. Some hotels
include breakfast in the price:
check when booking.
● Luxury = **$$$$** (over 200 euro)
● Expensive = **$$$** (95–200 euro)
● Moderate = **$$** (60–95 euro)
● Inexpensive = **$** (under 60 euro)

**Residence Hotel Portu Mannu**
Capo d'Orso
Tel: 0789 702063
Fax: 0789 702001
www.portomannu.it
Large complex, apartments and
rooms; special rates for long-stay;
pool; garden; good restaurant and
pizzeria. **$$$**

**Piccada**
Via degli Asfodeli 6
Tel/Fax: 0789 709344
www.hotelpiccada.com
Small hotel in the town; private
parking and garden; very
reasonable. **$$$**

**Serra**
Via Nazionale 17
Tel: 0789 709519
A small, family-run hotel on the
main street; comfortable; excellent
base for visiting the area. **$$**

### Arzachena – Baja Sardinia

**Cormorano**
Strada dei Pini
Tel: 0789 99020
Fax: 0789 99290
www.hotelcormorano.it
Large complex offering high-class
accommodation; beautiful garden;
pool; good restaurant. **$$$**

**La Bisaccia**
Tel: 0789 99002
Fax: 0789 99162
www.bajahotels.it
Set on a wonderful stretch of coast
near Cannigione; every comfort;
private beach; pool; summer only.
**$$$**

**Grand Hotel Smeraldo Beach**
Tel: 0789 99046
Fax: 0789 99500
www.itihotels.it
Beautiful view of the Archipelago;
private beach, piano bar. **$$$$**

**La Rocca**
Loc.Pulicinu
Tel: 0789 933131
Fax: 0789 933059
Recently built, away from village,
this hotel offers every comfort, plus
pool, garden, private parking;
summer only. **$$$**

### Arazachena – Cannigione

**Cala di Falco**
Tel: 0789 899200
Fax: 0789 899202
www.delphina.it
Comfortable small apartments. **$$$**

**Stelle Marine**
Loc.Mannena
Tel: 0789 86305
Fax: 0789 86332
www.hotelstellemarine.com
Beautifull views. **$$$**

**Club Hotel Li Capanni**
Loc. Li Capanni
Tel/Fax: 0789 86041
Right on the beach; large apartment
complex with restaurant and
garden; summer only. **$$$**

**Hotel del Porto**
Lungomare Andrea Doria
Tel: 0789 88011
Fax: 0789 88064
Nice view over the port;
comfortable; pleasant service;
sailing excursions can be arranged;
summer only. **$$**

### Arzachena – Costa Smeralda

**Cala di Volpe**
Loc. Cala di Volpe
Tel: 0789 976111
Fax: 0789 976617
www.luxurycollection.com
/caladivolpe
This hotel's distinctive
architecture was inspired by
ancient villages, a feature of the
magical landscape surrounding
the bay of Cala di Volpe;
magnificent sea-water pool, private
moorings; tennis courts; water-ski
school; reputedly the most
expensive hotel on the coast.
**$$$$**

**Capriccioli**
Capriccioli
Tel: 0789 96004
Fax: 0789 96422
www.hotelcapriccioli.it
Small hotel on a white sandy beach; good service; reputable restaurant; pool, garden, tennis courts. Very reasonable by Costa Smeralda standards; summer only. **$$$**

**Golf Hotel**
Cala di Volpe
Tel: 0789 96632
Fax: 0789 96663
www.bluhotel.it
Every imaginable comfort; sauna, pool, garden; top-class restaurant; plus one of Europe's finest golf courses; summer only. **$$$$**

**Cervo**
Porto Cervo
Tel: 0789 931111
Fax: 0789 931613
In the heart of Porto Cervo, two steps from the Piazzetta and the top-name shops; a beautiful swimming-pool, and boat to whisk you away to an unspoilt beach. **$$$$**

**Nibaru**
Cala Volpe
Tel: 0789 96038
Fax: 0789 96474
www.hotelnibaru.it
Located in the gorgeous Cala di Volpe and built entirely of pink bricks, with a swimming pool poised above the sea, and a good bar and restaurant, this hotel offers excellent value for the area; summer only. **$$$**

**Piccolo Pevero**
Golfo Pevero
Tel: 0789 94551
Fax: 0789 92683
www.piccolopevero.it
A large red-brick complex very close to the sea; rooms and apartments; bar set in a beautiful garden; reasonable prices for the area; summer only. **$$$**

**Pitrizza**
Liscia di Vacca
Tel: 0789 930111
Fax: 0789 930611
www.luxurycollection.com
/hotelpitrizza
At the end of Liscia di Vacca bay, a hotel as exceptional as the surrounding scenery, with villas nestled among rocks and flowers; splendid beach and sea-water swimming-pool carved out of the rocks overlooking the bay. **$$$$**

**Romazzino**
Loc. Romazzino
Tel: 0789 977111
Fax: 0789 96258
www.luxurycollection.com
/romazzino
A beautiful building overlooking the sea; magnificent, fragrant-flowering garden slopes gently down to the winding beach; offers watersports, tennis, and golf at the Pevero course; vies with Cala di Volpe for top-price hotel. **$$$$**

**Villa Sopravento**
Porto Cervo
Tel: 0789 94717
Fax: 0789 907380
All comforts and excellent service; top-class pool open all night; hang-out of celebrities; summer only. **$$$**

*Benetutti*
**Aurora Terme**
Loc. Sa Mandra Noa
Tel/fax: 079 796871
www.termeaurora.it
Open only during the summer; spa. **$**

**S'Astore**
Viale La Pira 9
Tel: 079 796620
Just outside the village; quiet, few rooms. **$**

*Castelsardo*
**Riviera**
Lungomare Anglona 1
Tel: 079 470143
Fax: 079 471312
www.hotelriviera.net
Beautifully located by the sea; restaurant renowned for seafood and fresh fish. **$$$**

*La Maddalena Isola*
**Giuseppe Garibaldi**
Via Lamarmora
Tel: 0789 737314
Fax: 0789 737326
www.genie.it/utenti/hotelgaribaldi
Comfortable rooms and attractive garden set on the island of La Maddalena; a good base for visiting other islands, especially Caprera, where Garibaldi is buried. **$$$**

**Nido D'Aquila**
Via Nido D'Aquila
Tel: 0789 722130
Fax: 0789 722159
Nice position on the sea, just outside the village. **$$$**

*Caprera*
**Club Mediterranée Caprera**
Isola di Caprera
Tel: 0789 727078
Extraordinary position; bungalows. **$$$**

*Olbia*
**Minerva**
Via Mazzini 7
Tel/Fax: 0789 21190
Comfortable and pleasant. **$**

**Cavour**
Via Cavour 22
Tel: 0789 204033
Fax: 0789 201096
wwwcavourhotel.it
Large clean rooms, parking places. **$$**

*Olbia Marinella*
**Palumbalza Sporting Hotel**
Tel: 0789 32005
Fax: 0789 32009
www.domina.it
e-mail: dosport@tin.it
South of Costa Smeralda; beautiful position on the sea. **$$$$**

*Olbia – Porto Rotondo*
**Green Park Hotel**
Porto Rotondo
Tel: 0789 380100
Fax: 0789 380043
e-mail: greenhtl@tin.it
Lovely hotel with bar/restaurant set in a garden by the sea; pool, tennis courts; daily sailing excursions organised; just a short distance from the Costa Smeralda; summer only. **$$$**

**Stella di Gallura**
La Caletta
Tel: 0789 35468
Fax: 0789 35467
In a picturesque valley, mini apartments with all the comforts of the nearby Costa Smeralda at a reasonable price; garden, pool, tennis courts. **$$$$**

## Price Guide

Approximate prices for a double room per night. Some hotels include breakfast in the price: check when booking.

- Luxury = $$$$ (over 200 euro)
- Expensive = $$$ (95–200 euro)
- Moderate = $$ (60–95 euro)
- Inexpensive = $ (under 60 euro)

### Olbia–San Pantaleo
**Rocce Sarde**
Tel: 0789 65265
Fax: 0789 65268
www.roccesarde.it
Set in a valley with dramatic rocks and built of local stone, this comfortable hotel has an extremely good restaurant, plus garden, pool, tennis courts, etc; summer only. $$$

### Ozieri
**Mastino**
Via Vittorio Veneto 13
Tel: 079 787041
Fax: 079 787059
www.giroscopio.com
Small comfortable village hotel, with restaurant serving excellent local specialities; good base for visiting the area. $

### Porto Torres
**Elisa**
Via Mare 2
Tel: 079 513260
Fax: 079 513768
A small, convenient hotel near the port; good view over Asinara; good food. $$
**Libyssonis**
Loc. Serra dei Pozzi
Tel: 079 501613
Fax: 079 501600
Large modern hotel just outside town; comfortable; pool by the sea, tennis court; garden with restaurant; summer only. $$

### S.Teresa di Gallura
**Grand Hotel Corallaro**
Loc. Rena Bianca
Tel: 0789 755475
Fax: 0789 755431
e-mail: info@hotelcorallaro.it
On the beach, and near centre. $$$

**Canne al Vento**
Via Nazionale 23
Tel: 0789 754219
Fax: 0789 754948
Small traditional hotel in the village. $
**La Coluccia**
Loc.Porto Pozzo
Tel: 0789 758004
Fax: 0789 752020
Interesting modern architecture. $$$

### Tempio
**Pausania Inn**
SS 133 Tempio Pausania
Tel: 079 634037
Fax: 079 634072
www.hotelpausaniainn.com
A new family-run hotel on the outskirts of Tempio, with a beautiful view of the Monti di Aggius; good restaurant; swimming pool. $$

## Bed & Breakfast

This is a new form of hospitality that is quickly spreading on the island, with a network of families renting rooms in their own homes; it provides a great opportunity to be in close contact with locals and everyday island life.

A list of recognised establishments can be found at the end of each EPT booklet (*see page 294 for contact details*). Prices usually range from 28–52 euros for a single room and from 40–70 euros for a double room per night. Booking can also be done through the following organisations:

**Associazione Sarda B&B "La Mia Casa"**
Tel: 0783 73954
www.lamiacasa.sardegna.it
**Sardegna Ospitale**
Tel: 079 214666
e-mail: info@bbsardegna.com
www.bbsardegna.com
**Centro di Turismo Culturale Leader II**
Piazza Regina Elena 11, Lunamatrona
Tel: 070 939999
Fax: 070 939991
www.sacoronarrubia.it

**Associazione Sarda Operatori Bed & Breakfast**
Tel: 3492973461
www.sardegnabedandbreakfast.it
**Domus Mediterranea**
Tel: 070 7265007
www.domusmediterranea.it

## Agriturismo

An increasing number of farms are converting to *agriturismo*, whereby visitors are offered lodging and meals in farmhouses; the advantages are a taste of excellent Sardinian food, genuine Sardinian hospitality and year-round availability. The following websites will give you an idea of what is on offer: www.agriturismo.net, www.agriturist.it, www.turismoverde.it and www.italytourist.it.

The majority need booking far in advance: you can either phone the farm directly or get in touch with the central Agriturismo offices:
**Agriturist**, Via Bottego 7, Cagliari, tel: 070 303486, fax: 070 303485.
**Consorzio Agriturismo Sardegna**, Oristano, tel: 0783 73954, fax: 0783 73924.
**Consorzio Vacanze e Natura**, Cagliari, tel: 070 668397; fax: 070 67954301.
**Coop. Allevatrici Sarde**, S. Giusta, Oristano, tel.0783 359995.
**Ekoturist Sardigna,** (organic farms), tel:070 229047; fax: 07022125, www.eurorganic.it/ekoturist.
**Terranostra**, Viale Trieste 124, Cagliari, tel: 070 280537, www.terranostra.it.
**Turismo Verde**, Via Libeccio 31, Cagliari, tel: 070 373733; fax: 070 372028, e-mail: ciasardegna@tiscali.it

## Farmhouses

The following is a selection offering accommodation: for further information contact the addresses above or the Assessorato dell' Agricoltura, Via Pessagno 4 Cagliari 09126, tel: 070 6067034, fax: 070 6066276, email: agricoltura@regione.sardegna.it.

**L'Agnata**
Tempio Pausania (SS)
Tel: 079 671384
www.agnata.it
**Il Muto di Gallura**
Aggius (SS)
Tel: 079 620559
www.mutodigallura.com
Very good meals.
**Li Licci**
Calangianus (SS)
Tel: 079 665114
**Stazzo La Cerra**
Tempio (SS)
Tel: 079 670972/0347 5606462
e-mail: stazzolacerra@eurorganic.it
Organic food and surrounded by
amazing rocks.
**Testone, Benetutti** (NU)
Tel/fax: 0784 230539
e-mail: ekoturist@ti.it
In the heart of the island; beautiful
landscape.
**S'Erulaju**
Olzai (NU)
Tel: 070 229047
e-mail: serularju@eurorganic.it
**S'Argalasi**
Austis (NU)
Tel: 0784 67113
e-mail: ekoturist@tin.it
**Ca la Somara**
Arzachena (SS)
Tel: 0789 98969.
Vegetarian cuisine.
**S'Atra Sardigna**
Piscina Manna, Pula (CA)
Tel/fax: 070 229047
e-mail: rifugio@eurorganic.it
**Fighezia**
Fluminimaggiore (CA)
Tel: 0347 8403636, 0347 6954195
www.agriturismofighezia.it
Four km (2 miles), from the pristine
coast, serves organic food.
**Sa Roia Traversa**
Cabras (OR)
Tel: 0348 6945923/0783 290404
On the Sinis peninsula.
**Canales**
Loc.Canales, Dorgali
Tel: 0340 5653881
Beautifull position on the gorge of
river Cedrino.
**Vaddidulimo**
Loc.Vaddidulimo,Luogosanto
Tel: 079 652419
**I Mandorli**
S.P.Lotzorai Talana Km 4,5

Tel: 0782 646787
www.mandorli.com

## Camping

There are at least 200 campsites in
Sardinia, with amenities ranging from
basic to excellent. As well as space
for tents and camper-vans, most of
them have small furnished
bungalows for rent. A free brochure
can be obtained from ESIT offices or
travel agents. Two useful websites
are www.camping.it or
www.campeggitalia.com. Information
can also be obtained from Faita
Sardegna, www.faitasardegna.org,
tel: 079 582109, fax: 079 582191.
Here, divided by province, is a list of
some of the best ones as far as
location and facilities are concerned.

### CAGLIARI

**Limone Beach**
Cala Sinzias
Tel: 070 995006
Fax: 070 995026
**Cala d'Ostia**
Cala d'Ostia Pula
Tel/fax: 070 921470
email: cop.tur@ti.it
www.calasinzias.com
**Camping Torre Chia**
Chia Domus de Maria
Tel: 070 9230054
Fax: 070 9230555
www.campeggiotorrechia.it
**Spiaggia del Riso**
Campolungo
Villasimius
Tel: 070 791052
Fax: 070 797150
e-mail: campriso@tiscali.it
**Capo Ferrato**
Loc.Costa Rei
Tel/fax: 070 991012
e-mail: info@campingcapoferrato.it

### ORISTANO

**Camping Is Arenas**
Narbolia – Is Arenas
Tel/Fax: 0783 52284
**Is Aruttas**
Narbolia
Tel: 0783 370001

**Europa Cuglieri**
Torre del Pozzo
Tel/Fax: 0783 38058

### NUORO

**Cala Cavallo**
San Teodoro
Tel: 0784 834156
**Cala Ginepro**
Cala Ginepro, Orosei
Tel: 0784 91017
Fax: 0784 91362
**Cala Gonone**
Dorgali
Tel: 0784 93165
Fax: 0784 93256
**La Pineta**
Planargia, Barisardo
Tel: 0782 29372
**L'Ultima Spiaggia**
Barisardo
Tel/Fax: 0782 29363
**Sos Flores**
Tortolì, Arbatax
Tel/Fax: 0782 667485

### SASSARI

**Baia Blu La Tortuga**
Vignola Mare
Aglientu
Tel: 079 602060
Fax: 079 602040
www.gruppobaiasilvella.com
**Camping Cugnana**
Cugnana, Olbia
Tel: 0789 3184
Fax: 0789 33398
www.campingcugnana.it
**Torre del porticciolo**
Alghero
Tel: 079 919007
Fax: 079 919212
www.torredelporticciolo.com
**Il Sole**
Via Indipendenza
La Maddalena – Isola
Tel: 0789 727727
**La Foce**
Via Ampurias, Valledoria
Tel: 079 582109
Fax: 079 582191
**Villaggio Isuledda Camping**
Isuledda, Arzachena – Canniggione
Tel: 0789-86003
Fax: 0789 86089

## Spas

Spas in Sardinia are undergoing a surge in popularity. To find a centre to suit your needs visit the official website of the spa association: www.spas.it

**Capo d'Orso**
Le Saline, Palau
Tel: 0789 702007
Fax: 0789 702006
www.capodorso.it
**Isola dei Gabbiani**
Porto Pollo, Palau
Tel: 0789 704019
Fax: 0789 704077
www.isoladeigabbiani.it
**Arcobaleno**
Loc.Porto Pozzo
Tel: 0789 752040
Fax: 0789 752117
www.campingarcobaleno.it

## Youth Hostels

There are only a few youth hostels in Sardinia:
**Bosa Marina**
Via Sardegna 1, Bosa
Tel: 0785 375009
**Dei Giuliani**
Via Zara 1, Alghero
Fertilia
Tel: 079 930353
e-mail: ostellodeigiuliani@tiscali.it
**Hostal de l'Alguer**
Via Parenzo, Alghero
Tel: 079 932039
Fax: 079 932039
e-mail: hostalalguer@tiscali.it
**Ostello della Torre**
Loc.Torre Dei Corsari
Arbus, Cagliari
Tel/fax: 070 977155
Open: June–Sept.
**Ostello**
Via Indipendenza, Lanusei
Tel: 0782 41051
**Il Castagneto**
Via Muggianeddu, Tonara
Tel: 0784 610005

For more information contact the **Italian Youth Hostel Association (AIG)**, Via Cavour 44, Rome 00184, tel: 0648 71152; fax: 0648 80492, www.informagiovani.it.

# Where to Eat

## Bars and Snacks

It is worth noting that snacking in bars is much more part of daily life in Sardinia than in other European countries. As a consequence, there are numerous bars throughout the island which serve a variety of sandwiches and other snacks as well as drinks. Tourist centres and villages are usually quite small, so you will usually find the best bars in the main square or its surroundings. For example, in Sassari the best bars will be Piazza Castello, in Alghero, the Piazza Civica and Piazza Sulis, in Oristano the Piazza Roma and Piazza Eleonora d'Arborea, and in Porto Cervo the Piazzetta. For help with ordering, *see page 317–319.*

### Bars in Cagliari
**Antico Caffè**, Piazza Costituzione; used to be a meeting point for writers; small terrace.
**Caffè Genovese**, Piazza S. Cosimo; next to the Church of S. Saturno; tiles by Jo Ponti.
**De Candia**, Via de Candia; night bar on the Bastions of S. Remy.
**Libarium Nostrum**, Bastions of S. Croce, in the castle; 15 different types of tea; outside terrace.
**Sotto la Torre**, Piazza S. Giuseppe; close to the Elephant tower; formed by five rooms containing two Punic cisterns; good choice of wines and liqueurs.
**Caffè Svizzero**, Largo Carlo Felice, decorated with Liberty-style frescoes and outdoor gazebo.
   The bars under the portico in Via Roma by the port, offer the largest selection of sandwiches and snacks.

## Eating Out

The Food and Drink chapter (*see pages 131–136*) describes some of the peculiarities and delights of Sardinian cuisine. Given the centrality of eating out to Sardinian social life and the pride taken in the preparation of meals, the standard of even moderately-priced restaurants is very high. All restaurants offer local variations of typical Sardinian dishes, and very few visitors are dissatisfied.

### Vegetarians
Sardinians are not very familiar with the concept of vegetarianism; often, as an alternative to meat or fish courses, you will be offered salami or ham, while the tomato sauce accompanying various pasta dishes has sometimes been cooked with meat. There are usually a couple of dishes in the *antipasti* section of the menu, and restaurants are increasingly adapting more to tourists' tastes. For a fully vegetarian restaurant, try **Agape**, Via Garibaldi 105, Cagliari or in the north of the island, if you want to have a full meal in an agriturismo, try **Vaddidulimo** loc. Vaddidulimo, Luogosanto, tel: 079 652419.

## Restaurants

### CAGLIARI PROVINCE

*Cagliari*
**S'Apposentu**
Via Sant'Alenixedda
Tel: 070 4082315
Small and elegant restaurant inside the new Teatro Lirico. Reservations needed. **$$$**
**Flora**
Via Sassari 45
Tel: 070 664735
Traditional Sardinian dishes served in a pleasant garden in the city centre. Try *pasta alla bottarga*. **$$$**
**Lo Scoglio**
Capo S. Elia. Loc. Calamosca
Tel: 070 371927
Baked fish is a speciality. **$$$**
**Ottagono**
Lungomare Poetto

Tel: 070 541719
High-class restaurant on the beach, renowned for its fish dishes. **$$$**
**Ristorante St Remy**
Via Torino 16
Tel: 070 657377
Very good international cuisine, but rather expensive. **$$$**
**Ristorante Il Corsaro**
Viale Regina Margherita 28
Tel: 070 370295/070 664318
One of the finest restaurants in the province. **$$$**
**Sa Cardiga and Su Schironi**
Capoterra, 10 km (6 miles) from Cagliari.
Tel: 070 71652/070 71613.
Vies with Il Corsaro for the title of best fish restaurant. **$$$**
**Al Porto**
Via Sardegna 44
Tel: 070 663141
Pleasant family-run trattoria near the port serves well-cooked traditional dishes. **$$**
**Antica Hostaria**
Via Cavour 60
Tel: 070 665870
Reputed to serve the best *su guisau* (lamb with artichokes) in the city. Central location. **$$**
**Italia**
Via Sardegna 30
Tel: 070 657987
Typical trattoria near the port. Warm friendly atmosphere. Good seafood. Mussel soup a speciality. **$$**
**Lillicu**
Via Sardegna 78
Tel: 070 652970
Renowned for seafood and grilled fish, but will also serve meat; beautiful marble tables. **$$**
**Pappa e Citti**
Viale Trieste 66
Tel: 070 665770
Typical Campidanese cuisine.

Specialises in *pasta alle arselle* – pasta with clams. The restaurant's name means "eat up and shut up" in dialect. **$$**

**Barumini**
**Sa Lolla**
Via Cavour 49
Roasted meats, served in a typical southern Sardinian house. **$$**

**Carbonia**
**Tanit**
Sirai
Tel: 0781 673793
Typical dishes; nice terrace; half way between town and archaeological site of Monte Sirai. **$**

**Carloforte**
**Al Tonno di Corsa**
Via Marconi 47
Tel: 0781 855106
Ligurian cooking (from the region around Genoa). Especially good are the fish-filled ravioli, tuna, fish soup and the *canestrelli* cakes. Good wine list. Closed Monday. **$$**
**Da Nicolo**
Corso Cavour 32
Tel: 0781 854048
Family-run trattoria in the town centre. Renowned for lobster and other crustaceans. **$$$**

**Giba**
**La Rosella**
Via Principe di Piemonte 135
Tel: 0781 964029
Many vegetarian starters, such as ravioli with wild artichokes. **$$**

**Nuxis**
**Letizia**
Via S. Pietro 12
Tel: 0781 957021

Delicious traditional dishes served with wild herbs. Many dishes are not served elsewhere.**$$**

**Sant'Antioco**
**La Laguna**
Lungomare A. Vespucci 37
Tel: 0781 83286
Wonderful fresh tuna. **$$**

## Price Guide

Price categories are for a meal for two with a bottle of wine:
● **$$$** 60 euros and above
● **$$** 40 to 60 euros
● **$** under 40 euros

**Villanovaforru**
**Le Colline**
Traditional dishes, conveniently situated in the countryside, not far from archaeological sites. **$$**

# ORISTANO PROVINCE

**Il Faro**
Via Bellini 25
Oristano
Tel: 0783 70002
Elegant restaurant serving seafood specialities and lamb with mint sauce. Good desserts and local wines. **$$$**
**Sa Funtà**
Via Garibaldi 25
Cabras
Tel: 0783 290685
Water comes from the well (*sa funtà*) in the middle of the restaurant. Good local dishes include smoked mullet, *fregula* (local couscous in fish broth), spaghetti with limpet sauce, and sole in walnut sauce. Try the unusual herbal drinks. **$$$**

**Cuglieri**
**Meridiana**
Via Littorio 1
Tel: 0785 39400
Said to serve the best fish in the area, at very reasonable prices. **$$**
**Ristorante Desogos**
Vico Cugia 6
Tel: 0785 39660
Small family-run restaurant, which

## Places to Eat

**Bars** serve *panini* (rolls) and *tramezzini* (small sandwiches) with alcoholic and non-alcoholic drinks. Pay first and give the receipt to the barman with the order. Most people stand at the bar, a charge is made for sitting at a table.
**Paninoteca** are sandwich bars

where you can have a quick meal.
**Trattoria** are less formal than a restaurant and serve local dishes.
**Ristorante** are the most formal places to eat. Courses are served in this order: anitpasto, pasta or soup, main course with salad or vegetables, desert and coffee.

serves some of the best wild boar on the island. **$$**

---

## NUORO PROVINCE

### Nuoro
**Da Giovanni**
Via IV Novembre 9
Tel: 0784 30562
A highly recommended place to try reasonably-priced regional cuisine. **$**
**Testone**
Altopiano Sa Serra, Nuoro
Tel: 0783 73954
Located outside in the countryside, serving an excellent sheperds' lunch. Offers a taste of real Barbaricina cuisine. Reservation only. **$$**

### Aritzo
**Sa Muvara**
Funtana Rubia
Tel: 0784 629336
Grilled meat, ravioli. **$**

### Baunei
**Il Golgo**
Tel: 0337 811828
On the high plateau; try the boiled sheep. **$**

### Bosa
**Borgo S. Ignazio**
Via S. Ignazio 33
Tel: 0785 374662
Located inside a restored home in the historical centre of the village. **$$**
**Da Tattore**
Piazza Monumento
Tel: 0785 373104
A trattoria with good first courses (*antipasti*). **$**

### Oliena
**Su Gologone**
In the hotel of the same name, Su Gologone
Tel: 0784 287512
Local specialities include roast

suckling pig, and the *pecorino* and honey pastries called *seadas*. **$$$**
**Enis**
Monte maccione
Tel: 0784 288363
Panoramic terrace facing Nuoro. **$**
**Sorgono**
Nuova Mandrolisai
Tel: 0784 60068
Near the church of S. Mauro, this is a very good fish restaurant. Try the speciality, spaghetti with mussels. **$**

### Orgosolo
**Monti del Gennargentu**
Settiles
Tel: 0784 402374
Serves a typical shepherd's lunch. **$**

---

## SASSARI PROVINCE

### Alghero
**Al Tuguri**
Via Maiorca 113
Tel: 079 976772
The best paella in Alghero, and a wide selection of Catalan dishes. **$$$**
**Pavone**
Piazza Sulis 3/4
Tel: 079 979584
Traditional restaurant renowned for quality and service. **$$$**
**Da Pietro**
Via Machin 20
Tel: 079 979645
Specialities in this centrally-located restaurant are Sardinian lamb and suckling pig. **$$**
**La Lepanto**
Via Carlo Alberto
Tel: 079 979116
Catalan style meets Sardinian fish and seafood. **$$**
**Riu**
Piazza Civica 2
Tel: 079 977240
Small family-run restaurant in the historic centre. Traditional dishes include good grilled fish. **$$**
**Porto Torres**
Li Lioni
Tel: 079 502286
Situated just outside town on the road to Sassari, this restaurant specialises in good local fish dishes served in an attractive garden. **$$**

### Sassari
**Il Senato**
Via G. Mundula 2
Tel: 079 231423
Traditional Sassarese dishes in this small, central restaurant include snails, gnocchi, and local lobster. Good wine list. **$$$**
**Castello**
Piazza Castello 6
Tel: 079 232041
Pleasant restaurant in the heart of the city. **$$**
**Florian**
Via Capitano Bellieni 27
Tel: 079 236251
Highly recommended for fresh fish and local dishes. **$$**
**Tre Stelle da Antioco**
Via Porcellana 6
Tel: 079 232431
The homely atmosphere makes it feel as if you are eating in the proprietor's front room. Fish dishes and local specialities. Good value. **$**

### Castelsardo
**La Guardiola**
Piazza del Bastione
Tel: 079 470428
Strictly seafood. Antipasti include sea truffles, oysters, pineapple prawns, lobster spaghetti. Good selection of wine. Closed Monday in winter. **$$$**
**Il Cormorano**
Via Colombo 5
Tel: 079 470628
Very good spaghetti with clams and *bottarga*. Not in the best position but the food is good. **$**

### Olbia
**Bacchus**
Via d'Annuncio 2/B
Tel: 0789 21612
A good place to try the *malloredous alla Campidanese* – local pasta with a sausage-based sauce. Good service and air conditioning. **$$**
**Gallura**
Corso Umberto 145
Tel: 0789 24648
Renowned throughout the island for excellent quality. Try *burrida ai pinoli* (cat fish with pine kernels), sea truffle and date soup, lobster

salad and *mormora al cartoccio* (fish cooked in a paper bag). Good wine list. Closed Monday. **$$$**

**Il Gambero**
Via Lamarmora 6
Tel: 0789 23874
Seafood only. Good food at very reasonable prices. **$**

*Arzachena*
**Casablanca**
Loc. Baia Sardinia
Tel: 0789 99006
Open only in the evening. **$$**

*Palau*
**La Gritta**
Porto Faro
Tel: 0789 708045
Beautifully located in a garden above the sea. Innovative Sardinian cuisine, such as prawns in pastry, ravioli stuffed with aubergine, shellfish soup, and saffron fish. Summer only. **$$$**

**Da Franco**
Via Capo d'Orso
Tel: 0789 709558
The high-class chef serves the very best classic Sardinian cuisine; superb daily selection of fish and excellent wines. **$$$**

**Del Sub**
Via Capo d'Orso
Tel: 0789 709870
Classical dishes, especially grilled fish, served in an attractive garden with views over Bear Rock. Summer only. **$$**

**Robertino**
Via Nazionale 20
Tel: 0789 709610
Small trattoria in the heart of town. The fish is especially good. **$$**

*Cannigione*
**La Quercia da Zia Paolina**
Via Tempo 7
Tel: 0789 66075
The renowned "Aunty Paolina" restaurant. Small, family-run, with a great atmosphere and seafood to match. **$$**

*Sant'Antonio di Gallura*
**La Pitraia**
Tel: 079 669381
Excellent mushroom dishes in autumn. **$-$$**

# Nightlife

## General

People usually meet up quite late in the evening in bars and clubs. Up-to-date information on concerts, theatre, nightclubs and discos can be found in the *L'Unione Sarda* and the *Nuova Sardegna*. During the summer they publish sections in English. Below are a few suggested venues for a night out. Bars and clubs change hands frequently so check details at your hotel or in the press before you set out.

## Bars and Clubs

### CAGLIARI

**De Candia**
Via De Candia, Cagliari
Night bar with a terrace on the bastions of S. Croce.

**Libarium**
Bastione S. Croce, Cagliari
American bar with music, situated in a 17th-century building.

**Sa Illetta**
SS 195 S. Gilla, Cagliari
Disco set on the lagoon, with a view of the town.

**Peyote**
Su pranu, Villasimius
Late night disco.

**Guardia Mori**
Guardia Mori, Carloforte
At the highest point on the island. Summer only.
All of the **Baretti** (kiosks/bars) on the Poetto beach from late spring to the end of September are worth a visit.

### ORISTANO

**Sa Pedrera Club House**
S. Giovanni di Sinis
Music between lagoons.

### NUORO

**Paradise**
Turas, Bosa
Probably the best place to go in town, with a late night disco.

## GALLURA

**Porto Cervo**
Enjoy an aperitif in one of the bars on the Piazzetta, but be aware of high prices.

**Baja Sardinia**
For ice creams and drinks, try the Piazzetta.

**Arzachena**
The Piazza is the place for pleasant evening drinking.

**Ritual**
Monti di lu Colbu, Baia Sardinia
Disco in a granite grotto.

**Sopravento**
Disco, on the Olbia–Porto Cervo road. Door policy at the entrance.

**Sottovento**
In front of Sopravento
Door policy at the entrance.

**Smaila's**
Poltu Quatu
Disco where TV celebrities like to go.

**Mantra**
At the entrance of Porto Rotondo

**Billionaire**
Golfo Pevero, Costa Smeralda

**La Terza Luna**
Puntaldia, S. Teodoro
Disco with strict door policy.

**Musicaldia**
S. Teodoro
Live music, pizza and beer.

**Il Ruscello**
Alghero, 3 km (2 miles) on the road to Sassari Disco, with live music in the garden.

**La Siesta**
Scala Piccada, Alghero
Beautiful view.

**L'Isolotto**
Stintino
Piano bar over the port.
Festivals and food fairs take place all over Sardinia. Keep an eye on local newspapers or visit the local tourist office for details of events.

# Culture

## Music Festivals

**Time in Jazz**
Annual festival in Berchidda in August; of international importance.
**Concordia Vocis-Festival Internazionale di cori polifonici** (International festival of polyphonic choirs): takes place in Cagliari in various churches such as the Romanesque S. Saturnino or S. Domenico.
**Acquilandia, International Kite Festival**, Cagliari: each year at the end of May on the Poetto beach.
**Notte dei Poeti** (Night of Poets) Concerts and plays in the Roman theatre of Nora, Pula in July and August.
**Sciampitta**
International festival of folklore in Quartu S. Elena; takes place every year in the first fortnight of July, with international and Sardinian folk groups.
**Echi lontani**
A festival of music in historical places, Cagliari: April–June.
**Festival Rocce Rosse & Blues**
In Arbatax; every summer, usually at the end of August.
**Estate Musicale Internazionale**
cloister of S. Francesco, Alghero. Every July and August.

## Craft Fairs

**Biannual Exhibition of Sardinian Knives (Arresojas).** Sardinia is famous for its handmade pocket knives, made of bone and steel and traditionally used by shepherds. In July and August there is an exhibition of knives at Montevecchio, Guspini.
**Fiera del cestino**, Sinnai, August: a basket making fair.
**Sagra degli agrumi**, Muravera,

March: orange and lemon fair.
**Sagra delle castagne**, Aritzo, October: a chestnut fair.
**In canto con l'arte**, Tuili, May: local crafts fair.
**Mostra mercato Artigiani della Marmilla**, Villanovaforru, September: local crafts fair.

## Food Fairs

There are a large number of *Sagre* (food fairs) on the island all around the year except December.
**January–February**: the Lu bogamarì (sea urchin) festival. For a month Alghero's restaurants have a sea urchin based menu.
**Easter**: nougat fair in Tonara.
**May**: Mugil fair in Cabras.
Strawberry fair in Arborea.
Cous cous fair in Carloforte.
**June**: tuna fair in Carloforte.
The Tundimenta seulesa (sheep shearing festival) in Seulo.
Cherry fair in Belvì.
Honey fair in Montevecchio.
**July**: a Culurjones (local version of ravioli) fair is held in Tortolì.
Fish fair in Santa Teresa di Gallura.
**August**: Vermentino (wine) fair in Monti.
Wild boar fair in Domus de Maria.
**September**: Villaggio Pescatori (fish festival) in Cagliari
**November**: La montagna (mountian produce) fair in Desulo.
The Novello d'oro (wine tasting festival) takes place on the Trenino Verde, Arzana.

## Specialist Guided Tours

Most archaeological sites and some museums have a local guide and the entrance fee includes a guided tour with a non-professional guide who often does not speak English. It is possible to hire English speaking professional/licensed guides for a half or full day for particular areas of interest.
For guided excursions in north-east Sardinia contact Alison Ellis, tel: mobile 0333 6904931, fax: 079 652401, e-mail:
e.alison@tiscali.it
In Cagliari and province contact

## Local Museums

If you have time, take a look at some of the museums devoted to farming and sheep rearing, as they are so much a part of the island's history and culture. There are also a number of smaller museums dotted throughout the island, devoted to topics as varied as *menhirs* and tuna fishing.
The opening times of museums and galleries are subject to change at the last minute. It is advisable to telephone the museum beforehand to check or contact the local tourist office.
At the time of going to press a number of museums were closed, with no indication of when they will reopen. Call ESIT for further information on 800 013153.

Maggie Bridges, tel: mobile 0328 6133932.
In Chiara Garau contact Daniela Pinna, tel: mobile 0339 7782271, e-mail: danipinna@hotmail.com

# Sport

## General

Many hotels, holiday villages and campsites have their own private tennis courts, and there are courts in municipal parks. During the main tourist season you can take a windsurfing course just about anywhere along the coast. Surfboards, small sailing boats and motorboats are available for rent. Waters around the off-shore islands and the rocky segments of the coast offer snorkellers and scuba divers ideal conditions. Information about sports activities is easily obtainable locally, so consult the local tourist office (*see page 294*), or just ask around, but the following information may be useful.

## BIRDWATCHING

The best places to see birds are the coastal marshes and lagoons all along the coast. The province of Oristano has the highest concentration and largest wetlands, followed by Cagliari, which has a greater variety of species. The most important lagoons/marshes near Oristano are:
**Stagno di Sale'e**, Porcus: 350 ha (865 acres); interesting for the large number of birds stopping for the winter here, among which are flamingos, black-winged stilts and shelducks.
**Stagno di Cabras**: the largest in Sardinia.
**Stagno di Mistras**: grey herons, little terns, marsh harriers, kingfishers.
**Stagno di S. Giusta**: mallards, little grebe.
**Stagno di S'Ena Arrubia**: purple heron, bittern, purple gallinule.

### Near Cagliari
**Stagno di Molentargius**: the most important on the island, with 187 different species of birds; it's also a nesting point for flamingos. Organisations: Comitato per la salvaguardia del parco, tel: 070 671003, LIPU, tel: 070 400507.

### Cagliari province
**Stagni di Colostrai and Feraxi** (Muravera area)
**Oasi of Carloforte (Island of Carloforte)**: the most important nesting area of Eleonora's falcon. Organisation: LIPU, tel: 070 837458.

### Eastern coast
**Foce del Cedrino** (Orosei area): the last part of the Cedrino river.
**Stagno di S.Teodoro**: separated from the sea by a beautiful beach.

## CLIMBING

Your instructor should have a licence called *Abilitazione di Istruttore per Arrampicata Sportiva* and should be part of the Italian Federation of Climbers (FASI, main office in Turin, Via S. Secondo 92, tel: 011 5683154; Sardinian Delegation, tel: 070 666680). Cala Gonone is the most organised area for free climbing.

## Golf

Sardinia is home to two of the most beautiful 18-hole golf courses in the world:
**Is Molas Golf Club**
S. Margherita di Pula, Cagliari
Tel: 070 9241013
www.ismolas.it
**Pevero Golf Club**
Cala di Volpe, Costa Smeralda
Tel: 0789 958000
Other courses include:
**Puntaldia**
Punta Sabbatino, San Teodoro
Tel: 0784 864477
www.duelune.com
**Is Arenas**
Pineta Is Arenas, Narbolia (OR)
Tel: 0783 56588
www.isarenas.it

## SPORTS ASSOCIATIONS

For a guide call GAE (Guide Ambientali Escursionistiche), tel: 070 9758076, e-mail: melis@gae.it or contact one of the following organisations:
**Artrek** Daniele Bigozzi, Cagliari, tel: 070 666680.
**Is Pistillonis** Marco Busso, Via Dettori 5, Oristano.
**ASCS Oliena**, Giuseppe Garippa, Via Martin Luther King 32, Oliena.
**Associazione Arrampicata Sportiva Mutapi**, Via Tempio 78, Sassari, tel: 079 27018.

## DIVING

There are around 80 diving centres around the island, the highest concentration being on the northeast coast. Activities range from night diving to underwater photography. The marine parks make Sardinia a great natural aquarium. The parks are: Capo Carbonara-Villasimius (Cagliari Province – CA); Golfo di Orosei (Nuoro Province – NU); Tavolara-Capo Coda Cavallo (Sassari Province – SS); Arcipelago della Maddalena (National Park, Sassari Province); Isola Asinara (National Park, Sassari Province); Capo Caccia-Porto Conte (Sassari Province); Sinis-Mal di Ventre (Oristano Province – OR).

Information on dive schools can be obtained from the following websites www.anissub.com, www.fias.it, www.fipsas.it, www.uisp.it, www.padi.com, www.ssi-italy.org, or from Comitato Regionale FIPSAS c/o Palestra Montemixi, Via dello Sport, Cagliari 09125 and Federazione Italiana FIPSAS, Via Pessagno, Cagliari, tel: 070 304723. A few of the best schools are listed below:

### Palau, La Maddalena, Arzachena
**Oyster Sub**
c/o Camping Capo d'Orso
Golfo delle Saline, Palau

## Cycling

ESIT *(see page 294)* has published a map of about 25 cycling itineraries *(The Little Guidebook to Mountain Biking in Sardinia)*. A few organisations also offer local tours:
**Sardecosophy**, Porto Columbu (Sarroch), tel/fax: 070 9253183
**MTB Porto Conte**, Alghero tel: 0329 4606604, www.mtbportoconte.it
**Naturavventura**
San Vero Milis, tel: 0783 52197 or 0329 6120372.
**www.sardiniabybike.cjb.net** is a non-commercial website providing information about cycling tours on the island. Information is also available from **Federazione Ciclistica Italiana**, Via Sonnino 155, Cagliari 09127, tel: 070 663231/070 663243, www.federciclismo.it

Tel/Fax: 0789 702070; mobile 0338 6227911
**Silvestri Diving Center**
Isola dei Gabbiani
Loc.Isola dei Gabbiani, Palau
Tel/fax: 0789 704053
e-mail: silvestri@silvestri.it
www.silvestri.it
**Diving Centre Lavezzi**
Via Giulio Cesare, La Maddalena
Fax: 0789 9737289
**Proteus Diving**
Strada dei Pini
Baia Sardinia, Arzachena
Tel/Fax: 0789 99727
www.diveitalycom/proteusdiving
e-mail: info@proteusdiving.it
**Nautilus Diving Centre**
Via Roma 12
Palau
Tel/fax: 0789 709058
e-mail: spidercrab2001@yahoo.com

### *Porto Rotondo, Golfo Aranci, Olbia, San Teodoro*
**Centro Sub Tavolara**
Via Molara 4, Porto S. Paolo
Tel: 0789 40360
Fax: 0789 40186
e-mail: info@csubtavolara.com

**Atmosphere Diving Centre**
Via Sardegna 38, S. Teodoro
Tel/Fax: 0784 865130
www.paginegialle.it/atmosphere
**Dive In**
Porto Ottiolu, Budoni (NU)
Tel/Fax: 0784 8464
e-mail: portoottiolu@divein.net
www.divein.net

### *Siniscola, Cala Gonone, Arbatax*
**Argonauta Diving Club**
Via dei Lecci 10, Cala Gonone (NU)
Tel/Fax: 0784 93046
e-mail: info@argonauta.it
www.argonauta.it
**Nautica Centro Sub**
Via Monti Oili 3, S. Maria Navarrese (NU)
Tel/Fax: 0782 615522
www.portosantamaria@tiscalinet.it
**Mediterranea Centro Sub**
Via Lungomare 46, Arbatax (NU)
Tel/Fax: 0782 667880
e-mail: mediterranea@hardnet1.net

### *Muravera, Villasimius, Quartu S. Elena, Cagliari*
**Centro Immersioni Sardegna**
Via delle Agavi, Loc. Costa Rei, Muravera (CA)
Tel/Fax: 070 991399
www.sardinia.net/tirso/servizi/cis
**Air Sub Service**
Via Roma, Villasimius (CA)
Tel: 070 79033/0336 815681
e-mail: airsubsv@tin.it
**Scuba Service**
c/o Villaggio "Fiore di Maggio", Campolongu, Villasimius
Tel: 070 797382/0335 6580175

### *Chia, Isola di S. Antioco, Isola di S. Pietro*
**Centro Sub Fralomar**
Porto Turistico Cala Verde, S. Margherita di Pula (CA)
Tel: 070 9241042
Fax: 070 9241040
e-mail: fralomar@webhit.net
www.web.tin.it/FRALOMAR
**Nautica Sardinia**
Largo C. Colombo 13 Calasetta (CA)
Tel/Fax: 0781 420011
e-mail: mapusced@tin.it
**Tabarka Diving**
Corso Cavour 38, Carloforte (CA)

Tel: 0781 855526
e-mail: tabardi@tin.it
**Malu Entu Diving S'Archittu**
Lungomare, S'Archittu, Cuglieri
Tel/fax: 0785 38352
e-mail: maluentu@tin.it
**Bosa Diving Center**
Via Colombo 2, Bosa Marina
Tel: 0785 375649
Fax: 0785 375633
e-mail: vincenzo.p@tiscalinet.it

### *Alghero, Stintino*
**Adventure & Diving Centro**
**Immersioni Porto Conte**
c/o Base Nautica, Porto Conte, Alghero (SS)
Tel/Fax: 079 942205
e-mail: divingcentre@poroconte.it
**Porto dell'ancora, Stintino**
Tel/fax: 079 527000
e-mail: info@roccarujasub.com

### *Castelsardo, Santa Teresa di Gallura*
**Diving Punto Sub**
Via S. Barbara 3, Isola Rossa, Trinità d'Agultu (SS)
Fax: 079 681331, mobile: 0368 554095.

---

## HIKING

Sardinia offers an incredible variety of different landscapes, ideal for hikers. The following areas of great environmental interest are in the process of becoming regional or national parks: Sette Fratelli, north west of Cagliari; Monte Arcosu and Monte Linas west of Cagliari; Giara di Gesturi and Gennargentu in the centre of the island; and Limbara in the north east.

The Supramonte in the Barbagia region is one of the best hiking areas on the island. The tourist agency EPT *(see page 294)* has a map which describes 10 hiking routes in this area. Hikes are also arranged by trekking guides, who should belong to the GAE (Guide Ambientali Escursionistiche). GAE Sardegna/Cooperativa Turistica Sinis is a collaboration of numerous operators with knowledgeable and reliable guides. For information tel: 073 852283. The Sardinian branch of the Italian Touring Club, Alpino Italiani CAI, can also provide information: tel: Cagliari 070 667877 or Nuoro 0784 34926.

**L'Altra Sardegna,** Mariano Balbina; trekking throughout the island.
Tel: 0338 8329818
**L'Asfodelo,** Daniele Caredda; trekking all over Sardinia.
Tel: 070 827977 0336 810437
**Barbagia Insolita**
Oliena
Tel: 0784 288167
Fax: 0784 285661
**Bios,** Sinnai
Night excursions.
Tel 070 765236
e-mail: coop.bios@tiscalinet.it
**Il Caprifoglio,** Uta (CA)
Tel: 070 968714
**Centro Escursioni In Sardegna**
Dorgali
Tel: 0329 6139328
Fax: 0784 94690
**Circolo Avventura**
Tel: 0781 670528
e-mail:
circoloavventura@tiscalinet.it
**Coop. Fillirea,** Santadi
Tel: 0781 9554983
e-mail: fillirea@tiscali.olt
**Gennargentu Escursioni**
Fonni
Tel: 0348 8544850
**La Gherardesca,** Iglesias
Tel: 0781 33850
**Coop. Ghivine**
Dorgali
Tel: 0784 496721
e-mail: giampmul@tin.it
**Coop. Goloritzè**
Golgo di Baunei
Tel: 0336 541285
**Gorropu, Urzulei**
Tel: 0782 649282
e-mail: france@tiscali.it
**Ichnos,** Ozieri
Tel: 079 770065
**Keya,** Cagliari
Tel: 070 848480
Fax: 070 848067
e-mail: keyast@tin.it
**Promoserapis,** Montevecchio
Guspini
Tel: 0368 538997
**Sini Servizi,** Cabras
Tel: 0783 392376
e-mail: amavrou@tin.it

**Cooperativa Turistica Enis**
Monte Maccioni, Oliena
Tel: 0784 288363
**Tiscali Trekking**
Nuoro
Tel: 0784 202953
**Centro Servizi Turistici**
Aritzo
Tel/Fax: 0784 629442
e-mail: censertur@tiscali.it

## MINES AND ARCHAEOLOGY

Sardinia has a large number of caves and several disused mines some which are open to the public.

**Montevecchio**
Loc.Montevecchio, Guspini
Declared a UNESCO World Heritage Site. One of the largest mining complexes in Europe with frescoes and machinery dating from 1900.
Tel: 0368 538997/070 972537, www.europroject.it/montevecchio
**Funtana Raminosa**
Gadoni (NU)
Tel: 0781 491300
e-mail: segr.igea@virgilio.it
**Porto Flavia**
Loc.Masua ( Iglesias)
Tel: 0781 491300
e-mail: segr.igea@virgilio.it

## HORSE RIDING

Exploring Sardinia on horseback is a popular way to see the island. Programmes vary: you can take half-day excursions, expeditions lasting several days, or ones which traverse the entire island. Information is available at local tourist agencies, at ESIT in Cagliari, or from ANTE **Sardegna** (Riders' Association), Via Pasteur 4, Cagliari, tel: 070 305816 or at Via Carso 35a, Sassari, tel: 079 299889. The **Instituto Incremento Ippico della Sardegna,** Piazza Borghia 4, Ozieri, tel: 079 787852, www.sardegnacavalli.it and the institute of riding schools **Guide Equestri Ambientali,** Oasi de Sale Porcus,

San Vero Milis, tel: 0783 528100, www.situgea.net also provide information. Sassari's provincial tourism office has published a booklet with riding itineraries to follow and connected facilities called *Guida alle Ippovie del Nord Sardegna.* Also don't forget to see one of the Pariglie (horse riding competitions) which usually take place during the summer in central Sardinia.

Here are a few horse riding centres:
**Circolo Ippíco Is Arenas**
Via Medau Su Cramu
Tel: 070 372657
**Hotel Ala Birdi**
Strada Mare, 24, Arborea, Oristano
Tel: 0783 800268
A renowned equestrian centre which specialises in horse riding excursions.
**Centro Ippico Agrituristico**
S. Priamo, Muravera
Tel: 070 999078
**Club Ippico Parco Blu**
Dorgali (NU)
Tel: 0347 7209696

### Grottoes

**Grotta di Su Marmuri**
Ulassai (NU)
Tel: 0782 79859 open April to October.
**Grotte di Su Mannau**
Fluminimaggiore (CA)
Tel: 0781 580189/0347 5413624
e-mail: sumannau@tiscali.it
Open from April to October
**Grotta di S.Barbara**
Loc. San Giovanni, Iglesias (CA)
Tel: 0781 491300/0348 1549556
e-mail: segr.igea@virgilio.it
**Grotte Is Zuddas**
Santadi (CA)
Tel: 0782 59001
**Grotte di Nettuno**
Capo Caccia,Alghero
Tel: 079 979054 (boat ), 079 946540 (caves)
**Grotte del Bue Marino**
Cala Gonone, Dorgali
Tel: 0784 96243

**Circolo Orte & Corru Ranch**,
Marina di San Vero Milis (OR)
Tel: 0783 52200
**Centro Equitazione Golgo** (Baunei)
Tel: 0336 541285
**Centro Equitazione Arbatax**
Bellavista, Arbatax
Tel: 0782 667176
Tel/fax: 0782 610599

#### Donkey trekking
**A.R.P.A.**
Via Siotto Pintor 24, Bonarcado
Ecological rides on donkeys.
Tel/fax: 0783 56601
e-mail: arpasnc@tiscali.it
**Ca' La Somara**
Loc,Balestra, Arzachena
Tel: 0789 98969
e-mail: calasomara@tiscali.it

## PARACHUTING

**Aeroclub Oristano**
Tel: 0783 73511
Parachuting and ultra light flights.
**Artrek Flight**
Tel: 0335 8431851/0337 815744
School and in tandem.

## CANOE AND KAYAK

There are a few local organisations
which offer canoe excursions or
canoe rental to the River Cedrino,
lago del Liscia or the River Coghinas:
**New Kayak**, Valledoria ( SS),
tel/fax: 079 582900,
www.newkayaksardinia.it
**Prima Sardegna**, Lungomare
Palmasera, Cala Gonone, tel/fax:
0784 93367, e-mail:
prima.sardegna@tiscali.it
**ArcheoAssemini**, canoes and
mountain bikes, tel: 0347
0716200, e-mail:
archeoassemini@tiscali.it
**Daniela Poggi**, e-mail:
danielapoggi@virgilio.it,
www.sikayakitaly.com
You can also contact **Federazione
Italiana Canoa/Kayak**, Via Sonino
208, Cagliari, tel: 070 652748,
www.federcanoa.it or **Federazione
Italiana Canottaggio**, Via Aosta 33,
Cagliari, tel: 070 305617,
www.canottaggio.org

## SAILING

The tourist agency ESIT (*see page
294*) distributes on request a map
of Sardinia's ports free of charge
or visit the website
www.portidellasardegna.org.

#### Sailing Schools
Almost all coastal resorts have
sailing schools and equipment hire
facilities. Further information from
**Federazione Italiana Vela**, Viale
Merello 41, Cagliari, tel: 070
663005, www.federvela.it or
**Circolo Nautico della Lega Navale
Italiana**, www.leganavale.it.
Some of the most popular schools
are listed below:
**Centro Velico Caprera**
Punta Coda, Caprera
Tel: 0789 738529
The residential courses last from 1
to 2 weeks.
**Yacht Club Capo d'Orso**
Capo D'Orso, Palau
Tel: 0789 709583
**Velamare Club**
Le Saline, Palau
Tel: 0789 702002
**Yacht Club**
Marina Piccola, Cagliari
Tel: 070 373099
The oldest club in Sardinia, with a
long-term tradition of regattas.

#### Charter Companies
**Cruising Charter**
Nautical base Porto Rotondo, Cagliari
Tel: 0789 25944
e-mail: Cruising@Tin.it
**Navigare**
Nautical base Palau, Cagliari
Tel: 070 9209881
Fax: 070 9209699
**Sardinian Charter**
Mauro Sirigu, Via Roma 198, Sinnai
Tel: 0335 467848
website: www.sardegna
Short and longer term boat hire;
self-sail or with a skipper.
**Centro Velico Orion**
Nautical base Alghero
Tel: 079 977215
Fax: 079 977349
**Palau Mare/Carlotta Chiesa**
Via Fontanavecchia 76, Caprera
Tel: 0789 709260
Fax: 0789 709757

● **Maxi Yacht Rolex Cup**,
Porto Cervo (YCCS or Yacht
Club Costa Smeralda)
Tel: 0789 902200
In the first week of September;
this is where you can see the
largest and most famous
yachts.
● **Regata della Vela Latina**
(Latin Sail Regatta), Stintino
(SS); at the end of August.
● **Sardinia Cup,** Porto Cervo
(YCCS); held in September, this
is the Mediterranean alternative
to the Admiral's Cup.

For hiring on a daily basis or
longer term, with or without a
skipper.
**Dovequinto**
La Maddalena (SS)
Tel: 0789 727685/0348 3401592
www.velierodovequinto.com
Excursions in the archipelago.

## WINDSURFING

The favourite place for windsurfers
is the **Isola Dei Gabbiani**, in the
northeastern province of Sassari.
Tel: 0789 704053
**Windsurfing Club**
Via Marina Piccola, Cagliari
Tel/Fax: 070 372649
Specialised in courses and
windsurfing regattas.

## WATER SKIING

Information regarding water skiing
is available from **Federazione
Italiana Sci nautico (FISN)** Via
G.Mary, La Maddalena, tel:
0789727768, www.scinautico.com

# Shopping

## Where to Shop

Shopping areas in the island are situated on the main road of each town, leading to the main square. The exception is Cagliari, where shops are concentrated along the two pedestrian streets Via Manno and Via Garibaldi; here you will find mostly clothes and shoes.

Alghero is famous for its jewellery shops, all concentrated in the old part of town, where you will also find coral.

Castelsardo is a centre for basket-weaving; women offer their products in front of their homes.

Porto Cervo is the place to look for the best and most expensive fashions; the shops are scattered all around the Piazzetta.

## Crafts

If you are interested in local crafts, the best shops belong to an organisation known as ISOLA (Sardinian Institute of Handicraft). These shops can be a little more expensive than the single work of the local artisan, but they guarantee quality and offer a vast range of products.
**Cagliari:** Via Bacaredda 176
Tel: 070 492756
Cagliari: Via S. Croce 37
Tel: 070 651488
(open summer)
**Sassari:** Padiglione dell'artigianato, Viale Mancini
Tel: 079 230101
**Nuoro:** Via Monsignor Bua 10
Tel: 0784 31507
**Porto Cervo:** Sottopiazza
Tel: 0789 94428

Below are the main cooperatives of artisans belonging to ISOLA who offer their work locally; remember to phone in advance, because often they are not shops but workshops:
**Coop. Sa Fanuga**
Vittorio Emanuele, Atzara
Tel: 0784 65382
**Coop. Su Trobasciu**
Via Gramsci 1, Mogoro
Tel: 0783 990581
**Coop. Madonna del Rimedio**
Via Roma 12, Nule (SS)
**Coop. Lugherras**
Via della Libertà 42, Paulilatino
Tel: 0785 55244
**Coop. Sant'Antioco Marire**
Lungomare Vespucci 30, S. Antioco
Tel: 0781 82085
**Coop. Madre Teresa**
Via Roma, Zona Pip, Villamar
Tel: 070 9309115
**Coop. Artigianato di Villanova**
Via Nazionale 71, Villanova Monteleone
Tel: 079 960474
**Coop. Ceramiche Maestri d'Arte**
Via Cagliari, Oristano
**Coop. Cestinaie**
Via Roma 106, Castelsardo
**Coop. S. Eligio**
Via Cattaneo, Iglesias
Tel: 0781 259064

## Local Producers

In most of the villages along the coast there are shops specialising in local food and wine products. This is a list of producers from whom you can buy directly:
**Az. Sa Bresca Dorada**
Local liqueurs, jam and honey
Monte liuru, Muravera (CA)
Tel: 070 9949219
**Bellosi**
Honey
S. Priamo, Muravera (CA)
Tel: 070 99902
**Coop. Solorche**
Honey
Via S. Sabina Pattada (SS)
Tel: 079 755855
**Helis Erbe**
Herbal products and liqueurs
Loc. Fundu di Monti, Tempio (SS)
Tel/fax: 079 660541
e-mail: heliserbe@tiscali.it

**Annino Orecchioni**
Honey
Loc.Laretu, Aglientu (SS)
Usai
Cheese
Loc.Muntesu, Tempio (SS)
Tel: 079 633079
**Olearia Dorgalese**
Olive oil
Via Fleming 4 Dorgali (NU)
Tel: 0784 96522
**Artigiana Salumi**
Salami and sausages
Loc.Sa Raga, Pattada (NU)
Tel: 079 754150
**Maribba**
Traditional cakes, amaretti
Via Nazionale 33 Maracalagonis
**Arangino**
Traditional cakes
Viale IV Novembre 70, Belvi (NU)

### *Wine producers (Cantine)*
**Argiolas & C.**
Via Roma 56 Serdiana (CA)
Tel: 070 740606
**Cantina del vermentino**
Via San Paolo 2, Monti (SS)
Tel: 0789 44012
**Cantina Gallura**
Via Val di Cossu,Tempio (SS)
Tel: 079 631241
**Cantina Giogantinu**
Via Milano 30, Berchidda (SS)
Tel: 079 704163
**Jerzu Antichi poderi**
Via Umberto 1,Jerzu (NU)
Tel: 0782 70028
**Tenute Sella & Mosca**
Loc. I Piani, Alghero (SS)
Tel: 079997700

## Flea Markets

In Cagliari at the Bastioni di San Remy there is a market of collectables held every Sunday. Every third Sunday of the month there is also an antique and collectables market at the Piazza Matteotti in Olbia.

# Children

## Excursions

Children are welcomed in Sardinia, even in bars and restaurants. Many of the coastal hotels are ideal for family holidays, and lay on a variety of entertainment and activities for kids and parents.

Below are some ideas for child-oriented excursions.

**Museo Naturalistico di Sa Corona Arrubia**
Villanovaforru, Cagliari Province
Temporary exhibitions for children; dinosaur exhibits.
Tel: 070 9341009,
www.sacoronaspa.com

**Il Trenino Turistico di Cagliari**
(The Little Train of Cagliari)
The station is in Piazza Yenne.

**Catalan small train**, Alghero
Station in the port.
Tel: 0336 691836

**Parco Sardegna in miniatura**
(Sardinia in miniature), Via Michelangelo 6, Tuili.
Tel: 070 9361004
www.sardegnainminiatura.it

**Aquadream** (water park)
Baja Sardinia, Sassari
Tel: 0789 99511
The biggest park of its kind on the island. All kinds of fun water activities and mini golf.

**Small train, Porto Cervo**
Station in bus parking lot

**Fantasilandia** (Fantasyland water park)
Monastero, Loc. Geremeas (Quartu S.Elena)
Tel: 070 802200

# Language

## Basic Communication

**Yes**  *Sì*
**No**  *No*
**Thank you**  *Grazie*
**Many thanks**  *Mille grazie/tante grazie/molte grazie*
**You're welcome**  *Prego*
**Alright/Okay/That's fine**  *Va bene*
**Please**  *Per favore or per cortesia.*
**Excuse me**  (to get attention) *Scusi* (singular), *Scusate* (plural)
**Excuse me**  (to get through a crowd) *Permesso*
**Excuse me**  (to attract attention, e.g. of a waiter) *Senta!*
**Excuse me**  (sorry) *Mi scusi* (singular), *Scusatemi* (plural)
**Wait a minute!**  (informal) *Aspetta!* (formal) *Aspetti!*
**Could you help me?**  (formal) *Potrebbe aiutarmi?*
**Certainly**  *Ma certo*
**Can I help you?**  (formal) *Posso aiutarLa?*
**Can you show me ...?**  (formal) *Può indicarmi ...?*
**Can you help me?**  (formal) *Può aiutarmi, per cortesia?*
**I need ...**  *Ho bisogno di ...*
**I'm lost**  *Mi sono perso*
**I'm sorry**  *Mi dispiace*
**I don't know**  *Non lo so*
**I don't understand**  *Non capisco*
**Do you speak English/French/German?**  *Parla inglese/francese/tedesco?*
**Could you speak more slowly, please?**  *Può parlare piú lentamente, per favore?*
**Could you repeat that please?**  (formal) *Può ripetere, per piacere?*
**here/there**  *qui/lá*
**What?**  *Cosa?*
**When/why/where?**  *Quando/perchè/dov'è?*
**Where is the lavatory?**  *Dov'è il bagno?*

## Emergencies

**Help!**  *Aiuto!*
**Stop!**  *Fermate!*
**I've had an accident**  *Ho avuto un incidente*
**Watch out!**  *Attenzione!*
**Call a doctor**  *Per favore, chiami un medico*
**Call an ambulance**  *Chiami un'ambulanza*
**Call the police**  *Chiami la Polizia/i Carabinieri*
**Call the fire brigade**  *Chiami i pompieri*
**Where is the telephone?**  *Dov'è il telefono?*
**Where is the nearest hospital?**  *Dov'è l'ospedale più vicino?*
**I would like to report a theft**  *Voglio denunciare un furto*

## Greetings

**Hello (Good day)**  *Buon giorno*
**Good afternoon/evening**  *Buona sera*
**Good night**  *Buona notte*
**Goodbye**  *Arrivederci*
**Hello/Hi/Goodbye**  (familiar) *Ciao*
**Mr/Mrs/Miss**  *Signor/Signora/Signorina*
**Pleased to meet you (formal)**  *Piacere di conoscerLa*
**I am English/American**  *Sono inglese/americano*
**Irish/Scottish/Welsh**  *irlandese/scozzese/gallese*
**Canadian/Australian**  *canadese/australiano*
**Do you speak English? (formal)**  *Parla inglese?*
**I'm here on holiday**  *Sono qui in vacanza*
**Do you like it here? (formal)**  *Si trova bene qui?*
**How are you (formal/informal)?**  *Come sta/come stai?*
**Fine thanks**  *Bene, grazie*
**See you later**  *A più tardi*
**See you soon**  *A presto*
**Take care (formal)**  *Stia bene,* **(informal)** *Stammi bene*

## Telephone calls

**the area code**  *il prefisso telefonico*

**I'd like to make a reverse charges call** *Vorrei fare una telefonata a carico del destinatario*

**May I use your telephone, please?** *Posso usare il telefono?*

**Hello (on the telephone)** *Pronto*

**My name's** *Mi chiamo/Sono*

**Could I speak to ...?** *Posso parlare con ...?*

**Sorry, he/she isn't in** *Mi dispiace, è fuori*

**Can he call you back?** *Può richiamarLa?*

**I'll try again later** *Riproverò più tardi*

**Can I leave a message?** *Posso lasciare un messaggio?*

**Please tell him I called** *Gli dica, per favore, che ho telefonato*

**Hold on** *Un attimo, per favore*

**A local call** *una telefonata locale*

**Can you speak up please? (formal)** *Può parlare più forte, per favore?*

## In the Hotel

**Do you have any vacant rooms?** *Avete camere libere?*

**I have a reservation** *Ho fatto una prenotazione*

**I'd like...** *Vorrei...*

**a single/double room (with a double bed)** *una camera singola/doppia (con letto matrimoniale)*

**a room with twin beds** *una camera a due letti*

**a room with a bath/shower** *una camera con bagno/doccia*

**for one night** *per una notte*

**for two nights** *per due notti*

**We have one with a double bed** *Ne abbiamo una matrimoniale.*

**Could you show me another room please?** *Potrebbe mostrarmi un'altra camera?*

**How much is it?** *Quanto costa?*

**on the first floor** *al primo piano*

**Is breakfast included?** *É compresa la prima colazione?*

**Is everything included?** *É tutto compreso?*

**half/full board** *mezza pensione/pensione completa*

**It's expensive** *É caro*

**Do you have a room with a balcony/view of the sea?** *C'è una camera con balcone/con vista sul mare?*

**a room overlooking the park/the street/the back** *una camera con vista sul parco/che dà sulla strada/sul retro*

**Is it a quiet room?** *É una stanza tranquilla?*

**The room is too hot/cold/noisy/small** *La camera è troppo calda/fredda/rumorosa/piccola*

**Can I see the room?** *Posso vedere la camera?*

**What time does the hotel close?** *A che ora chiude l'albergo?*

**I'll take it** *La prendo*

**big/small** *grande/piccola*

**What time is breakfast?** *A che ora è la prima colazione?*

**Please give me a call at...** *Mi può chiamare alle...*

**Come in!** *Avanti!*

**Can I have the bill, please?** *Posso avere il conto, per favore.*

**Can you call me a taxi please?** *Può chiamarmi un taxi, per favore?*

**dining room** *la sala da pranzo*

**key** *la chiave*

**lift** *l'ascensore*

**towel** *l'asciugamano*

**toilet paper** *la carta igienica*

**pull/push** *tirare/spingere*

## Eating Out

### Bar snacks and drinks

**I'd like...** *Vorrei...*

**coffee** *un caffè* (espresso: small, strong and black)

*un cappuccino* (with hot, frothy milk)

*un caffelatte* (like *café au lait* in France)

*un caffè lungo* (weak)

*un corretto* (laced with alcohol – usually brandy or grappa. You should specify)

**tea** *un tè*

**lemon tea** *un tè al limone*

**herbal tea** *una tisana*

**hot chocolate** *una cioccolata calda*

**orange/lemon juice (bottled)** *un succo d'arancia/di limone*

**fresh orange/lemon juice** *una spremuta di arancia/di limone*

**orangeade** *un'aranciata*

**water (mineral)** *acqua* (minerale)

**fizzy/still mineral water** *acqua minerale gasata/naturale*

**a glass of mineral water** *un bicchiere di minerale*

**with/without ice** *con/senza ghiaccio*

**red/white wine** *vino rosso/bianco*

## Pronunciation and Grammar Tips

Italian speakers claim that pronunciation is straight-forward: you pronounce it as it is written. This is approximately true but there are a couple of important rules for English speakers to bear in mind: *c* before *e* or *i* is pronounced "ch", e.g. *ciao, mi dispiace, la coincidenza. Ch* before *i* or *e* is pronounced as "k", e.g. *la chiesa.* Likewise, *sci* or *sce* are pronounced as in "sheep" or "shed" respectively. *Gn* in Italian is rather like the sound in "onion", while *gl* is

softened to resemble the sound in "bullion".

Nouns are either masculine (*il,* plural *i*) or feminine (*la,* plural *le*). Plurals of nouns are most often formed by changing an *o* to an *i* and an *a* to an *e,* e.g. *il panino, i panini; la chiesa, le chiese.*

Words are stressed on the penultimate syllable unless an accent indicates otherwise.

Like many languages, Italian has formal and informal words for "You". In the singular, *Tu* is informal while

*Lei* is more polite. Confusingly, in some parts of Italy or in some circumstances, you will also hear *Voi* used as a singular polite form. (In general, *Voi* is reserved for "You" plural, however.) For visitors, it is simplest and most respectful to use the formal form unless invited to do otherwise.

There is, of course, rather more to the language than that, but you can get a surprisingly long way towards making friends with a mastery of a few basic phrases.

beer (draught) *una birra (alla spina)*
a gin and tonic *un gin tonic*
a bitter (Vermouth, etc.) *un amaro*
milk *latte*
a (half) litre *un (mezzo) litro*
bottle *una bottiglia*
ice cream *un gelato*
cone *un cono*
pastry *una pasta*
sandwich *un tramezzino*
roll *un panino*
Anything else? *Desidera qualcos'altro?*
Cheers *Salute*
Let me pay *Offro io*
That's very kind of you *Grazie, molto gentile*

### In a restaurant

I'd like to book a table *Vorrei riservare un tavolo*
Have you got a table for... *Avete un tavolo per...*
I have a reservation *Ho fatto una prenotazione*
lunch/supper *il pranzo/la cena*
We do not want a full meal *Non desideriamo un pasto completo*
Could we have another table? *Potremmo spostarci?*
I'm a vegetarian *Sono vegetariano/a*
Is there a vegetarian dish? *C'è un piatto vegetariano?*
May we have the menu? *Ci dà il menu, per favore?*
wine list *la lista dei vini*
What would you like? *Che cosa prende?*
What would you recommend? *Che cosa ci raccomanda?*
home-made *fatto in casa*
What would you like as a main course/dessert? *Che cosa prende di secondo/di dolce?*
What would you like to drink? *Che cosa desidera da bere?*

### Bar Notices

*Prezzo in terrazza.*
Terrace price, often double what you pay standing at the bar.
*Si prende lo scontrino alla cassa.*
Pay at the cash desk, then take the receipt to the bar to be served.

a carafe of red/white wine *una caraffa di vino rosso/bianco*
fixed price menu *il menu a prezzo fisso*
the dish of the day *il piatto del giorno*
VAT (sales tax) *IVA*
cover charge *il coperto/pane e coperto*
That's enough; no more, thanks *Basta (così)*
The bill, please *Il conto per favore*
Is service included? *Il servizio è incluso?*
Where is the lavatory? *Dovè il bagno?*
Keep the change *Va bene così*
I've enjoyed the meal *Mi è piaciuto molto*

### Menu Decoder

### Antipasti (hors d'oeuvres)

*antipasto misto* **mixed hors d'oeuvres** (including cold cuts, possibly cheeses and roast vegetables – ask, however)
*buffet freddo* **cold buffet** (often excellent)
*caponata* **mixed aubergine, olives and tomatoes**
*insalata caprese* **tomato and mozzarella salad**
*insalata di mare* **seafood salad**
*insalata mista/verde* **mixed/green salad**
*melanzane alla parmigiana* **fried or baked aubergine** (with parmesan cheese and tomato)
*mortadella/salame* **salami**
*pancetta* **bacon**
*peperonata* **vegetable stew** (made with peppers, onions, tomatoes and sometimes aubergines)

### Primi (first courses)

Typical first courses include soup, *risotto, gnocchi* or numerous varieties of pasta in a wide range of sauces. *Risotto* and *gnocchi* are more common in the North of Italy.

*il brodetto* **fish soup**
*il brodo* **consommé**
*i crespolini* **savoury pancakes**
*gli gnocchi* **potato dumplings**
*la minestra* **soup**

### Pasta dishes

**Common Pasta Shapes**
*cannelloni* (large stuffed tubes of pasta); *farfalle* (bow- or butterfly-shaped pasta); *tagliatelle* (flat noodles, similar to *fettuccine*); *tortellini* and *ravioli* (different types of stuffed pasta packets); *penne* (quill-shaped tubes, smaller than *rigatoni*).

**Typical Pasta Sauces**
*pomodoro* (tomato); *pesto* (with basil and pine nuts); *matriciana* (bacon and tomato); *arrabbiata* (spicy tomato); *panna* (cream); *ragù* (meat sauce); *aglio e olio* (garlic and olive oil); *burro e salvia* (butter and sage).

*il minestrone* **thick vegetable soup**
*pasta e fagioli* **pasta and bean soup**
*il prosciutto (cotto/crudo)* **ham** (cooked/cured)
*i supplí* **rice croquettes**
*i tartufi* **truffles**
*la zuppa* **soup**

### Secondi (main courses)

Typical main courses are fish-, seafood- or meat-based, with accompaniments *(contorni)* that vary greatly from region to region.

### La carne (meat)

*allo spiedo* **on the spit**
*arrosto* **roast meat**
*i ferri* **grilled**
*al forno* **baked**
*al girarrosto* **spit-roasted**
*alla griglia* **grilled**
*involtini* **skewered veal, ham, etc.**
*stagionato* **hung, well-aged**
*stufato* **braised, stewed**
*ben cotto* **well-done** (steak, etc.)
*al puntino* **medium** (steak, etc.)
*al sangue* **rare** (steak, etc.)
*l'agnello* **lamb**
*a bresaola* **dried salted beef**
*la bistecca* **steak**
*il capriolo/cervo* **venison**
*il carpaccio* **lean beef fillet**

*il cinghiale* **wild boar**
*il coniglio* **rabbit**
*il controfiletto* **sirloin steak**
*le cotolette* **cutlets**
*il fagiano* **pheasant**
*il fegato* **liver**
*il filetto* **fillet**
*la lepre* **hare**
*il maiale* **pork**
*il manzo* **beef**
*l'ossobuco* **shin of veal**
*la porchetta* **roast suckling pig**
*il pollo* **chicken**
*le polpette* **meatballs**
*il polpettone* **meat loaf**
*la salsiccia* **sausage**
*saltimbocca (alla romana)* **veal escalopes with ham**
*le scaloppine* **escalopes**
*lo stufato* **stew**
*il sugo* **sauce**
*il tacchino* **turkey**
*la trippa* **tripe**
*il vitello* **veal**

### Frutti di mare (seafood)

Beware the word "*surgelati*", meaning frozen rather than fresh.
*affumicato* **smoked**
*alle brace* **charcoal grilled/barbecued**
*alla griglia* **grilled**
*fritto* **fried**
*ripieno* **stuffed**
*al vapore* **steamed**
*le acciughe* **anchovies**
*l'anguilla* **eel**
*l'aragosta* **lobster**
*il baccalà* **dried salted cod**
*i bianchetti* **whitebait**
*il branzino* **sea bass**
*i calamari* **squid**
*i calamaretti* **baby squid**
*la carpa* **carp**
*i crostacei* **shellfish**
*le cozze* **mussels**
*il fritto misto* **mixed fried fish**
*i gamberi* **prawns**
*i gamberetti* **shrimps**
*il granchio* **crab**
*il merluzzo* **cod**
*le moleche* **soft-shelled crabs**
*le ostriche* **oysters**
*il pesce* **fish**
*il pesce spada* **swordfish**
*il polipo* **octopus**
*il risotto di mare* **seafood risotto**
*le sarde* **sardines**
*la sogliola* **sole**

*le seppie* **cuttlefish**
*la triglia* **red mullet**
*la trota* **trout**
*il tonno* **tuna**
*le vongole* **clams**

### I legumi/la verdura (vegetables)

*a scelta* **of your choice**
*i contorni* **accompaniments**
*ripieno* **stuffed**
*gli asparagi* **asparagus**
*la bietola* **similar to spinach**
*il carciofo* **artichoke**
*le carote* **carrots**
*i carciofini* **artichoke hearts**
*il cavolo* **cabbage**
*la cicoria* **chicory**
*la cipolla* **onion**
*i funghi* **mushrooms**
*i fagioli* **beans**
*i fagiolini* **French (green) beans**
*le fave* **broad beans**
*il finocchio* **fennel**
*l'indivia* **endive/chicory**
*l'insalata mista* **mixed salad**
*l'insalata verde* **green salad**
*la melanzana* **aubergine**
*le patate* **potatoes**
*le patatine fritte* **chips/French fries**
*i peperoni* **peppers**
*i piselli* **peas**
*i pomodori* **tomatoes**
*le primizie* **spring vegetables**
*il radicchio* **red, slightly bitter lettuce**
*la rughetta* **rocket**
*i ravanelli* **radishes**
*gli spinaci* **spinach**
*la verdura* **green vegetables**
*la zucca* **pumpkin/squash**
*gli zucchini* **courgettes**

### I dolci (desserts)

*al carrello* **(desserts) from the trolley**
*un semifreddo* **semi-frozen dessert (many types)**
*la bavarese* **mousse**
*la cassata* **Sicilian ice cream with candied peel**
*le frittelle* **fritters**
*un gelato (di lampone/limone)* **(raspberry/lemon) ice cream**
*una granita* **water ice**
*una macedonia di frutta* **fruit salad**
*il tartufo (nero)* **(chocolate) ice cream dessert**

*il tiramisù* **cold, creamy cheese and coffee dessert**
*la torta* **cake/tart**
*lo zabaglione* **sweet dessert made with eggs and Marsala wine**
*lo zuccotto* **ice cream liqueur**
*la zuppa inglese* **trifle**

### La frutta (fruit)

*le albicocche* **apricots**
*le arance* **oranges**
*le banane* **bananas**
*il cocomero* **watermelon**
*le ciliegie* **cherries**
*i fichi* **figs**
*le fragole* **strawberries**
*i frutti di bosco* **fruits of the forest**
*i lamponi* **raspberries**
*la mela* **apple**
*il melone* **melon**
*la pesca* **peach**
*la pera* **pear**

## Coffee Italian-Style

**Espresso:** small black and strong
**Cappuccino:** with hot, frothy milk
**Caffè lungo:** espresso watered down
**Caffè macchiato:** espresso with a drop of milk
**Caffè corretto:** espresso with a shot of alcohol
**Caffè latte:** half milk half coffee in large cup or glass

*il pompelmo* **grapefruit**
*l'uva* **grapes**
### Basic foods
*l'aceto* **vinegar**
*l'aglio* **garlic**
*il burro* **butter**
*il formaggio* **cheese**
*la focaccia* **oven-baked snack**
*la frittata* **omelette**
*il grana* **hard grating cheese, similar to parmesan**
*i grissini* **bread sticks**
*l'olio* **oil**
*la marmellata* **jam**
*il pane* **bread**
*il pane integrale* **wholemeal bread**
*il parmigiano* **parmesan cheese**
*il pepe* **pepper**
*il riso* **rice**

il sale **salt**
la senape **mustard**
le uova **eggs**
lo yogurt **yoghurt**
lo zucchero **sugar**

## Sightseeing

Si può visitare? **Can one visit?**
il custode **custodian**
il sacrestano **sacristan**
Suonare il campanello **ring the bell**
aperto/a **open**
chiuso/a **closed**
chiuso per la festa **closed for the festival**
chiuso per ferie **closed for the holidays**
chiuso per restauro **closed for restoration**
**Is it possible to see the church?**
É possibile visitare la chiesa?
Entrata/uscita **Entrance/exit**
**Where can I find the custodian/sacristan/key?**
Dove posso trovare il custode/il sacrestano/la chiave?
**We have come a long way just to see...** Siamo venuti da lontano proprio per visitare...
**It is really a pity it is closed**
É veramente peccato che sia chiuso
(The last two should be tried in desperation – pleas for sympathy can sometimes open a few doors.)

## At the Shops

**What time do you open/close?**
A che ora apre/chiude?
**Closed for the holidays** (typical sign) Chiuso per ferie

**Pull/push** (sign on doors)
Tirare/spingere
**Entrance/exit** Entrata/uscita
**Can I help you?** (formal) Posso aiutarLa?
**What would you like?** Che cosa desidera?
**I'm just looking** Sto soltanto guardando
**How much does it cost?** Quant'è, per favore?
**How much is this?** Quanto viene?
**Do you take credit cards?**
Accettate carte di credito?
**I'd like...** Vorrei...
**this one/that one** questo/quello
**I'd like that one, please** Vorrei quello lì, per cortesia
**Have you got ...?** Avete ...?
**We haven't got (any)** ... Non (ne) abbiamo...
**Can I try it on?** Posso provare?
**the size (for clothes)** la taglia
**What size do you take?** Qual'é a sua taglia?
**the size (for shoes)** il numero
**Is there/do you have ...?** C'è ...?
**Yes, of course** Sì, certo
**No, we don't (there isn't)**
No, non c'è
**That's too expensive** É troppo caro
**Please write it down for me**
Me lo scriva, per favore
**cheap** economico
**Don't you have anything cheaper?**
Ha niente che costa di meno?
**It's too small/big** É troppo piccolo/grande
**brown/blue/black**
marrone/blu/nero
**green/red/white/yellow**
verde/rosso/bianco/giallo

**pink/grey/gold/silver**
rosa/grigio/oro/argento
**No thank you, I don't like it**
Grazie, ma non è di mio gusto
**I (don't) like it** (Non) mi piace
**I'll take it/I'll leave it**
Lo prendo/Lo lascio
**It's a rip-off (impolite)** Una ruberia
**This is faulty. Can I have a replacement/refund?** C'è un difetto. Me lo potrebbe cambiare/rimborsare?
**Anything else?** Altro?
**The cash desk is over there**
Si accomodi alla cassa
**Give me some of those** Mi dia alcuni di quelli lì
**a (half) kilo** un (mezzo) chilo
**100 grams** un etto
**200 grams** due etti
**more/less** più/meno
**with/without** con/senza
**a little** un pochino
**That's enough/No more**
Basta così

### Types of shops

**antique dealer** l'antiquario
**bakery/cake shop**
la panetteria/pasticceria
**bank** la banca
**bookshop** la libreria
**boutique/clothes shop** il negozio di moda
**bureau de change** il cambio
**butcher's** la macelleria
**chemist's** la farmacia
**delicatessen** la salumeria
**department store** il grande magazzino
**dry cleaner's** la tintoria
**fishmonger's** la pescheria
**food shop** l'alimentari

## Numbers

| | | | | | |
|---|---|---|---|---|---|
| **1** | Uno | **13** | Tredici | **70** | Settanta |
| **2** | Due | **14** | Quattordici | **80** | Ottanta |
| **3** | Tre | **15** | Quindici | **90** | Novanta |
| **4** | Quattro | **16** | Sedici | **100** | Cento |
| **5** | Cinque | **17** | Diciassette | **200** | Duecento |
| **6** | Sei | **18** | Diciotto | **500** | Cinquecento |
| **7** | Sette | **19** | Diciannove | **1,000** | Mille |
| **8** | Otto | **20** | Venti | **2,000** | Duemila |
| **9** | Nove | **30** | Trenta | **5,000** | Cinquemila |
| **10** | Dieci | **40** | Quaranta | **50,000** | Cinquantamila |
| **11** | Undici | **50** | Cinquanta | **1 Million** | Un milione |
| **12** | Dodici | **60** | Sessanta | | |

## Conversion Charts

**Metric–Imperial:**
1 centimetre = 0.4 inch
1 metre = 3 ft 3 ins
1 kilometre = 0.62 mile
1 gram = 0.04 ounce
1 kilogram = 2.2 pounds
1 litre = 1.76 UK pints

**Imperial–Metric:**
1 inch = 2.54 centimetres
1 foot = 30 centimetres
1 ounce = 28 grams
1 pound = 0.45 kilogram
1 pint = 0.57 litre
1 UK gallon = 4.55 litres
1 US gallon = 3.78 litres

**florist** *il fioraio*
**grocer's** *l'alimentari*
**greengrocer's** *il fruttivendolo*
**hairdresser's (women)**
*il parrucchiere*
**ice cream parlour** *la gelateria*
**jeweller's** *il gioielliere*
**leather shop** *la pelletteria*
**market** *il mercato*
**news-stand** *l'edicola*
**post office** *l'ufficio postale*
**shoe shop** *il negozio di scarpe*
**stationer's** *la cartoleria*
**supermarket** *il supermercato*
**tobacconist** *il tabaccaio* (also
usually sells travel tickets, stamps,
phone cards)
**travel agency** *l'agenzia di viaggi*
(also usually books train tickets for
domestic and international
journeys).

## Travelling

### Transport
**airport** *l'aeroporto*
**arrivals/departures** *arrivi/partenze*
**boat** *la barca*
**bus** *l'autobus/il pullman*
**bus station** *l'autostazione*
**car** *la macchina*
**connection** *la coincidenza*
**ferry** *il traghetto*
**ferry terminal** *la stazione marittima*
**first/second class**
*la prima/seconda classe*
**flight** *il volo*
**left luggage office**
*il deposito bagagli*

**motorway** *l'autostrada*
**no smoking** *vietato fumare*
**platform** *il binario*
**porter** *il facchino*
**railway station** *la stazione*
*(ferroviaria)*
**return ticket** *un biglietto di andata*
*e ritorno*
**single ticket** *un biglietto di andata*
*sola*
**sleeping car** *la carrozza letti/il*
*vagone letto*
**smokers/non-smokers**
*fumatori/non-fumatori*
**stop** *la fermata*
**taxi** *il taxì*
**ticket office** *la biglietteria*
**train** *il treno*
**WC** *la toilette*

### Road Signs
*Accendere le luci in galleria*
**Lights on in tunnel**
*Alt* **Stop**
*Autostrada* **Motorway**
*Attenzione* **Caution**
*Avanti* **Go/walk**
*Caduta massi* **Danger of**
**falling rocks**
*Casello* **Toll gate**
*Dare la precedenza* **Give way**
*Deviazione* **Diversion**
*Divieto di campeggio* **No camping**
**allowed**
*Divieto di sosta/Sosta vietata* **No**
**parking**
*Divieto di passaggio/Senso*
*vietato* **No entry**
*Dogana* **Customs**
*Entrata* **Entrance**
*Galleria* **Tunnel**
*Guasto* **Out of order** (e.g. phone
box)
*Incrocio* **Crossroads**
*Limite di velocità* **Speed limit**
*Non toccare* **Don't touch**
*Passaggio a livello* **Railway**
**crossing**
*Parcheggio* **Parking**
*Pedaggio* **Toll road**
*Pericolo* **Danger**
*Pronto Soccorso* **First aid**
*Rallentare* **Slow down**
*Rimozione forzata* **Parked cars**
**will be towed away**
*Semaforo* **Traffic lights**
*Senso unico* **One way street**
*Sentiero* **Footpath**
*Solo uscita* **No entry**

*Strada interrotta* **Road blocked**
*Strada chiusa* **Road closed**
*Strada senza uscita/Vicolo cieco*
**Dead end**
*Tangenziale* **Ring road/bypass**
*Traffico di transito* **Through**
**traffic**
*Uscita* **Exit**
*Uscita (autocarri)* **Exit for lorries**
*Vietato il sorpasso* **No overtaking**
*Vietato il transito* **No**
**thoroughfare**

### At the airport
**I'd like to book a flight to Venice**
*Vorrei prenotare un volo per*
*Venezia*
**When is the next flight to ...?**
*Quando parte il prossimo*
*aereo per ...?*
**Are there any seats available?**
*Ci sono ancora posti liberi?*
**Have you got any hand luggage?**
*Ha bagagli a mano?*
**I'll take this hand luggage with me**
*Questo lo tengo come bagaglio a*
*mano*
**My suitcase has got lost** *La mia*
*valigia è andata persa*
**My suitcase has been damaged**
*La mia valigia è rovinata*
**The flight has been delayed** *Il volo*
*è rimandato*
**The flight has been cancelled**
*Il volo è stato cancellato*
**I can put you on the waiting list**
*Posso metterLa sulla lista d'attesa*

### At the station
**Can you help me please?** *Mi può*
*aiutare, per favore?*
**Where can I buy tickets?** *Dov'è*
*posso fare i biglietti?*
**at the ticket office/at the counter**
*alla biglietteria/allo sportello*
**What time does the train leave?**
*A che ora parte il treno?*
**What time does the train arrive?**
*A che ora arriva il treno?*
**Can I book a seat?** *Posso*
*prenotare un posto?*
**Are there any seats available?**
*Ci sono ancora posti liberi?*
**Is this seat free/taken?**
*É libero/occupato questo posto?*
**I'm afraid this is my seat** *É il mio*
*posto, mi dispiace*
**You'll have to pay a supplement**
*Deve pagare un supplemento*

**Do I have to change?** *Devo cambiare?*
**Where does it stop?** *Dove si ferma?*
**Which platform does the train leave from?** *Da quale binario parte il treno?*
**The train leaves from platform one** *Il treno parte dal binario uno*
**How long will it take to get there?** *Quanto tempo ci vuole per arrivare?*
**Will we arrive on time?** *Arriveremo puntuali?*
**Next stop please** *La prossima fermata per favore*
**Is this the right stop?** *É la fermata giusta?*
**The train is late** *Il treno è in ritardo*
**Can you tell me where to get off?** *Mi può dire dove devo scendere?*

### Directions
**right/left** *a destra/a sinistra*
**first left/second right** *la prima a sinistra/la seconda a destra*

## Tourist Signs

Most regions in Italy have handy signs indicating the key tourist sights in any given area:

*Abbazia (Badia)* **Abbey**
*Basilica* **Church**
*Belvedere* **Viewpoint**
*Biblioteca* **Library**
*Castello* **Castle**
*Centro storico* **Old town/ historic centre**
*Chiesa* **Church**
*Duomo/Cattedrale* **Cathedral**
*Fiume* **River**
*Giardino* **Garden**
*Lago* **Lake**
*Mercato* **Market**
*Monastero* **Monastery**
*Monumenti* **Monuments**
*Museo* **Museum**
*Parco* **Park**
*Pinacoteca* **Art gallery**
*Ponte* **Bridge**
*Ruderi* **Ruins**
*Scavi* **Excavations/ archaeological site**
*Spiaggia* **Beach**
*Tempio* **Temple**
*Torre* **Tower**
*Ufficio turistico* **Tourist office**

## Days and Dates

**morning/afternoon/evening** *la mattina, il pomeriggio, la sera*
**yesterday/today/tomorrow** *ieri/oggi/domani*
**the day after tomorrow** *dopodomani*
**now/early/late** *adesso/presto/ritardo*
**a minute** *un minuto*
**an hour** *un'ora*
**half an hour** *un mezz'ora*
**a day** *un giorno*

**a week** *una settimana*
**Monday** *lunedì*
**Tuesday** *martedì*
**Wednesday** *mercoledì*
**Thursday** *giovedì*
**Friday** *venerdì*
**Saturday** *sabato*
**Sunday** *domenica*
**first** *il primo/la prima*
**second** *il secondo/la seconda*
**third** *il terzo/la terza*

**Turn to the right/left** *Gira a destra/sinistra*
**Go straight on** *Va sempre diritto*
**Go straight on until the traffic lights** *Va sempre diritto fino al semaforo*
**Is it far away/nearby?** *É lontano/vicino?*
**It's five minutes' walk** *Cinque minuti a piedi*
**It's 10 minutes by car** *Dieci minuti con la macchina*
**You can't miss it** *Non può non vederlo*
**opposite/next to** *di fronte/ accanto a*
**up/down** *su/giù*
**traffic lights** *il semaforo*
**junction** *l'incrocio, il bivio*
**building** *il palazzo*
**Where is ...?** *Dov'è ...?*
**Where are ...?** *Dove sono ...?*
**Where is the nearest bank/ petrol station/bus stop/ hotel/garage?** *Dov'è la banca/il benzinaio/la fermata di autobus/l'albergo/l'officina più vicino/a?*
**How do I get there?** *Come si può andare?* (or: *Come faccio per arrivare a ...?*)
**How long does it take to get to ...?** *Quanto tempo ci vuole per andare a ...?*
**Can you show me where I am on the map?** *Può indicarmi sulla cartina dove mi trovo?*
**You're on the wrong road** *Lei è sulla strada sbagliata*

### On the road
**Where can I rent a car?** *Dove posso noleggiare una macchina?*

**Is comprehensive insurance included?** *É completamente assicurata?*
**Is it insured for another driver?** *É assicurata per un altro guidatore?*
**By what time must I return it?** *A che ora devo consegnarla?*
**underground car park** *il garage sotterraneo*
**driving licence** *la patente (di guida)*
**petrol** *la benzina*
**petrol station/garage** *la stazione di servizio*
**oil** *l'olio*
**Fill it up please** *Faccia il pieno, per favore*
**lead free/unleaded/diesel** *senza piombo/benzina verde/diesel*
**My car won't start** *La mia macchina non s'accende*
**My car has broken down** *La mia macchina è guasta*
**How long will it take to repair?** *Quanto tempo ci vorrà per la riparazione?*
**The engine is overheating** *Il motore si surriscalda*
**There's something wrong (with/in the) ...** *C'è un difetto (nel/nella/nei/nelle) ...*
**... accelerator** *l'acceleratore*
**... brakes** *i freni*
**... engine** *il motore*
**... exhaust** *lo scarico/ scappamento*
**... fanbelt** *la cinghia del ventilatore*
**... gearbox** *la scatola del cambio*
**... headlights** *le luci*
**... radiator** *il radiatore*
**... spark plugs** *le candele*

... **tyre(s)** *la gomma (le gomme)*
... **windscreen** *il parabrezza*

## Health

**Is there a chemist's nearby?** *C'è una farmacia qui vicino?*
**Which chemist is open at night?** *Quale farmacia fa il turno di notte?*
**I don't feel well** *Non mi sento bene*
**I feel ill** *Sto male/Mi sento male*
**Where does it hurt?** *Dove Le fa male?*
**It hurts here** *Ho dolore qui*
**I suffer from ...** *Soffro di ...*
**I have a headache** *Ho mal di testa*
**I have a sore throat** *Ho mal di gola*
**I have a stomach ache** *Ho mal di pancia*
**Have you got something for air sickness?** *Ha/Avete qualcosa contro il mal d'aria?*
**Have you got something for sea sickness?** *Ha/Avete qualcosa contro il mal di mare?*
**antiseptic cream** *la crema antisettica*
**sunburn** *scottatura da sole*
**sunburn cream** *la crema antisolare*
**sticking plaster** *il cerotto*
**tissues** *i fazzoletti di carta*
**toothpaste** *il dentifricio*
**upset stomach pills** *le pillole per mal di stomaco*
**insect repellent** *l'insettifugo*
**mosquitoes** *le zanzare*
**wasps** *le vespe*

# Further Reading

## General Reading

**Sea and Sardinia,** D.H. Lawrence, Cambridge University Press 1997. Lawrence recalls his journey to Sardinia in 1921. His observations cover the island in all its dimensions, including the people, politics and landscape.
**Studies in Sardinian Archaeology: Sardinia in the Mediterranean,** Miriam S. Balmuth (Editor), University of Michigan Press 1986. The title says it all; invaluable to those who want more than a light holiday read and want to discover more about the island.
**Sardinian Chronicles,** Bernard Lortat-Jacob (translated by Teresa L Fagan), University of Chicago Press, 1995.
Rural Sardinia is brought to life through its music, dance and family portraits. The book includes black and white photographs and a CD of Sardinian music.
**The Foods of Sicily, Sardinia and the Smaller Islands,** Giuliano Bugialli (photography by John Dominis), Rizzoli Bookstore, 1996. A broad spectrum of authentic regional recipes beautifully presented with full-colour photos.
**Sardinia, An Archaeological Guide** ABACO, edition 1996. A good archaeological guide written in Italian, French and English, giving key facts about the major sites and museums.

## Other Insight Guides

Insight Guides produce more titles than any guide book publisher in the world. There are more than 200 *Insight Guides*, as well as *Insight City Guides* and two other series: *Insight Pocket Guides* and *Insight Compact Guides*. Titles covering Italy include: Italy, Rome, South Tyrol, Tuscany, Florence, Venice, Umbria, Bay of Naples, Sicily and Southern Italy.

## Feedback

We do our best to ensure the information in our books is as accurate and up-to-date as possible. The books are updated on a regular basis, using local contacts, who painstakingly add, amend and correct as required. However, some mistakes and omissions are inevitable and we are ultimately reliant on our readers to put us in the picture.

We would welcome your feedback on any details related to your experiences using the book "on the road". Maybe we recommended a hotel that you liked (or another that you didn't), as well as interesting new attractions, or facts and figures you have found out about the country itself. The more details you can give us (particularly with regard to addresses, e-mails and telephone numbers), the better.

We will acknowledge all contributions, and we'll offer an Insight Guide to the best letters received.

Please write to us at:
**Insight Guides**
**PO Box 7910**
**London SE1 1WE**
**United Kingdom**
Or send e-mail to:
**insight@apaguide.demon.co.uk**

# ART & PHOTO CREDITS

**AKG London** 18, 54
**E. Cerretelli/Marka** 97
**Joachim Chwaszcza** front flap bottom, back cover left, back flap bottom, front flap top, back cover centre, back cover right, 8/9, 20, 23, 25, 26, 27, 28, 30, 32, 35, 37, 39, 42, 43, 50, 51, 57, 65, 74L/R, 76L/R, 81, 84, 86/87, 90, 106, 131, 140/141, 150, 152, 154, 155, 160, 167, 173, 173T, 176, 182, 189, 200, 201, 205, 205T, 210, 211, 222, 223, 224, 234, 235, 237, 240/241, 243, 244, 245, 246, 248, 250, 265, 272, 278
**Jerry Dennis** 41, 45, 62, 94, 153T, 157, 163, 165, 180T, 182T, 191, 198, 206, 214T, 215, 220, 220T, 235T, 237T, 245T, 253, 277
**Nevio Doz** 2/3, 4/5, 6/7, 10/11, 12/13, 88/89, 112, 117, 120, 132, 133, 134, 135, 136, 137, 138/139, 167T, 170, 172, 175, 175T, 178, 179, 179T, 219, 221, 228, 230T, 231, 231T, 249, 260, 261, 263T, 266T, 273, 274, 275L, 281, 282, 282T, 283, 285, 286, 287
**Jean-Léo Dugast/Panos Pictures** 5B, 160T, 275R
**Mary Evans Picture Library** 19, 58, 59
**L. Fioroni/Marka** 223T
**B. Gradnik** 232
**Iain Green/NHPA** 91

**Robert Harding Picture Library** 193
**John Heseltine** 44, 153
**Dirk Hoffman** 183, 194/195, 197, 288
**Alberto Nardi/NHPA** 181, 236
**M. Parmesani** 115
**Rainer Pauli** back cover top right, spine top, 1, 21, 22, 24, 33, 34, 40, 47, 49L, 55, 71, 72, 79, 101, 111, 144, 169, 186/187, 192, 199, 204, 207, 233, 239, 249T, 263, 264
**Andrea Pistolesi** 93, 267
**A. Quattrocchi/Marka** 4BL, 4BR, 36, 92, 95, 96, 105, 118, 123, 124, 125, 155T, 156, 158T, 176T, 177, 184, 203, 229, 229T, 247, 247T, 252, 268, 269T, 270, 270T, 279, 279T, 280T
**Andy Rouse/NHPA** back cover bottom, 267T
**Jorg Reuther** 14, 78, 80, 82, 83, 85, 103, 142/143, 151, 185, 226, 227, 238, 251, 255, 269, 276
**L. Sechi/Marka** 113
**Cathy Smith** 178T
**Franco Stephano Ruiu** 52, 53, 63, 100, 102, 104, 107, 108/109, 110, 116, 119, 121, 126, 130, 164, 171, 225, 254, 256/257, 259, 262, 266, 271, 280
**Toni Schneider** 29, 49R, 56, 114
**Joe Viesti/Viesti Associates** spine centre, 284
**Gregory Wrona** back flap top, 2B, 127, 158, 159, 161, 161T, 162,

168, 180, 188, 190, 191T, 200T, 202, 202T, 208/209, 213, 214, 215T, 230

## Picture Spreads

**Pages 98/99**
*Top row, left to right:* Hellio & Van Ingen/NHPA, A. Quattrocchi/Marka, Vincent Garcia Canseco/NHPA, Nevio Doz. *Centre row:* Jerry Dennis, Vincent Garcia Canseco/NHPA. *Bottom row:* Dr. Eckart Pott/NHPA, Cathy Smith, Jerry Dennis, John Shaw/NHPA.

**Pages 128/129**
*Top row, left to right:* B. Gradnik, Joe Viesti, Nevio Doz, Nevio Doz. *Centre row:* Jean-Léo Dugast/Panos Pictures, L. Sechi/Marka. *Bottom row:* Nevio Doz, L. Sechi/Marka, L. Sechi/Marka, B. Gradnik.

**Pages 216/217**
*Top row, left to right:* B. Gradnik, Cathy Smith, Nevio Doz, B. Gradnik, *Centre row:* Andrea Pistolesi. *Bottom row:* Clare Griffiths, A. Quattrocchi/Marka, Nevio Doz, Nevio Doz.

**Map Production** Colourmap Scanning Ltd.

© 2006 Apa Publications GmbH & Co. Verlag KG (Singapore branch)

**INSIGHT GUIDE**
**SARDINIA**

Cartographic Editor **Zoë Goodwin**
Production **Linton Donaldson**
Design Consultants
**Carlotta Junger, Graham Mitchener**
Picture Research
**Hilary Genin, Monica Allende**

# Index

*Numbers in italics refer to photographs*

# Insight Guides Website
## *www.insightguides.com*

*Don't travel the
planet alone.
Keep in step with
Insight Guides'
walking eye,
just a click away*

# INSIGHT GUIDES

## *The classic series that puts you in the picture*

Alaska
Amazon Wildlife
American Southwest
Amsterdam
Argentina
Arizona & Grand Canyon
Asia's Best Hotels & Resorts
Asia, East
Asia, Southeast
Australia
Austria
Bahamas
Bali
Baltic States
Bangkok
Barbados
Barcelona
Beijing
Belgium
Belize
Berlin
Bermuda
Boston
Brazil
Brittany
Brussels
Buenos Aires
Burgundy
Burma (Myanmar)
Cairo
California
California, Southern
Canada
Caribbean
Caribbean Cruises
Channel Islands
Chicago
Chile
China
Colorado
Continental Europe
Corsica
Costa Rica
Crete
Croatia
Cuba
Cyprus
Czech & Slovak Republic
Delhi, Jaipur & Agra
Denmark

Dominican Rep. & Haiti
Dublin
East African Wildlife
Eastern Europe
Ecuador
Edinburgh
Egypt
England
Finland
Florence
Florida
France
France, Southwest
French Riviera
Gambia & Senegal
Germany
Glasgow
Gran Canaria
Great Britain
Great Gardens of Britain
& Ireland
Great Railway Journeys
of Europe
Greece
Greek Islands
Guatemala, Belize
& Yucatán
Hawaii
Hong Kong
Hungary
Iceland
India
India, South
Indonesia
Ireland
Israel
Istanbul
Italy
Italy, Northern
Italy, Southern
Jamaica
Japan
Jerusalem
Jordan
Kenya
Korea
Laos & Cambodia
Las Vegas
Lisbon
London

Los Angeles
Madeira
Madrid
Malaysia
Mallorca & Ibiza
Malta
Mauritius Réunion
& Seychelles
Mediterranean Cruises
Melbourne
Mexico
Miami
Montreal
Morocco
Moscow
Namibia
Nepal
Netherlands
New England
New Mexico
New Orleans
New York City
New York State
New Zealand
Nile
Normandy
North American &
Alaskan Cruises
Norway
Oman & The UAE
Oxford
Pacific Northwest
Pakistan
Paris
Peru
Philadelphia
Philippines
Poland
Portugal
Prague
Provence
Puerto Rico
Rajasthan

Rio de Janeiro
Rome
Russia
St Petersburg
San Francisco
Sardinia
Scandinavia
Scotland
Seattle
Shanghai
Sicily
Singapore
South Africa
South America
Spain
Spain, Northern
Spain, Southern
Sri Lanka
Sweden
Switzerland
Sydney
Syria & Lebanon
Taiwan
Tanzania & Zanzibar
Tenerife
Texas
Thailand
Tokyo
Trinidad & Tobago
Tunisia
Turkey
Tuscany
Umbria
USA: The New South
USA: On The Road
USA: Western States
US National Parks: West
Venezuela
Venice
Vienna
Vietnam
Wales
Walt Disney World/Orlando

## INSIGHT GUIDES

### *The world's largest collection of visual travel guides & maps*